PREVIOUSLY

THE RUNAWAYS LEFT THEIR UNDERGROUND HOME A FEW MONTHS BACK WHEN A CONSTRUCTION CREW STARTED WORK IN THE CANYON OVERHEAD. THE KIDS STAYED WITH LOS ANGELES' OWN DOC JUSTICE, WHO SOON RECRUITED ALMOST EVERYONE INTO HIS SUPER HERO GROUP, THE J-TEAM. HE EVEN TOOK YOUNG ELDER GOD GIB, WHO WAS DYING WITHOUT THE SUSTENANCE OF A SACRIFICED SOUL. DOC LEFT GERT BEHIND, THOUGH. THAT SHOULD HAVE RAISED SOME FLAGS, BUT EVEN VICTOR WAS TOO TAKEN WITH BEING "KID JUSTICE" TO BE SUSPICIOUS. LUCKILY, GERT DISCOVERED DOC'S PLAN TO HAVE KAROLINA KILLED ON A MISSION FOR PUBLICITY, AND STOPPED HIM JUST IN TIME. OLD LACE DEALT THE KILLING BLOW, AND OFFERED DOC'S SOUL TO GIB.

RUNAWAYS

Come Away With Me

WRITER **RAINBOW ROWELL**

ARTISTS **NATACHA BUSTOS** (#32)
& ANDRÈS GENOLET (#33-38)
WITH **ADRIAN ALPHONA** (#38) & **KRIS ANKA** (#38)

COLOR ARTISTS
DEE CUNNIFFE WITH **MATTHEW WILSON** (#38)
LETTERER **VC's JOE CARAMAGNA**
COVER ART **KRIS ANKA**

ASSISTANT EDITOR **SHANNON ANDREWS BALLESTEROS**
ASSOCIATE EDITOR **KATHLEEN WISNESKI**
EDITOR **NICK LOWE**

RUNAWAYS CREATED BY **BRIAN K. VAUGHAN & ADRIAN ALPHONA**

COLLECTION EDITOR JENNIFER GRÜNWALD | ASSISTANT EDITOR DANIEL KIRCHHOFFER | ASSISTANT MANAGING EDITOR MAIA LOY
ASSISTANT MANAGING EDITOR LISA MONTALBANO | VP PRODUCTION & SPECIAL PROJECTS JEFF YOUNGQUIST
BOOK DESIGNER JAY BOWEN | SVP PRINT, SALES & MARKETING DAVID GABRIEL | EDITOR IN CHIEF C.B. CEBULSKI

RUNAWAYS BY RAINBOW ROWELL VOL. 6: COME AWAY WITH ME. Contains material originally published in magazine form as RUNAWAYS (2017) #32-38. First printing 2021. ISBN 978-1-302-92556-7. Published by MARVEL WORLDWIDE, INC., a subsidiary of MARVEL ENTERTAINMENT, LLC. OFFICE OF PUBLICATION: 1290 Avenue of the Americas, New York, NY 10104. © 2021 MARVEL No similarity between any of the names, characters, persons, and/or institutions in this magazine with those of any living or dead person or institution is intended, and any such similarity which may exist is purely coincidental. Printed in Canada. KEVIN FEIGE, Chief Creative Officer; DAN BUCKLEY, President, Marvel Entertainment; JOE QUESADA, EVP & Creative Director; DAVID BOGART, Associate Publisher & SVP of Talent Affairs; TOM BREVOORT, VP, Executive Editor; NICK LOWE, Executive Editor, VP of Content, Digital Publishing; DAVID GABRIEL, VP of Print & Digital Publishing; JEFF YOUNGQUIST, VP of Production & Special Projects; ALEX MORALES, Director of Publishing Operations; DAN EDINGTON, Managing Editor; RICKEY PURDIN, Director of Talent Relations; JENNIFER GRÜNWALD, Senior Editor, Special Projects; SUSAN CRESPI, Production Manager; STAN LEE, Chairman Emeritus. For information regarding advertising in Marvel Comics or on Marvel.com, please contact Vit DeBellis, Custom Solutions & Integrated Advertising Manager, at vdebellis@marvel.com. For Marvel subscription inquiries, please call 888-511-5480. Manufactured between 7/23/2021 and 8/24/2021 by SOLISCO PRINTERS, SCOTT, QC, CANADA.

10 9 8 7 6 5 4 3 2 1

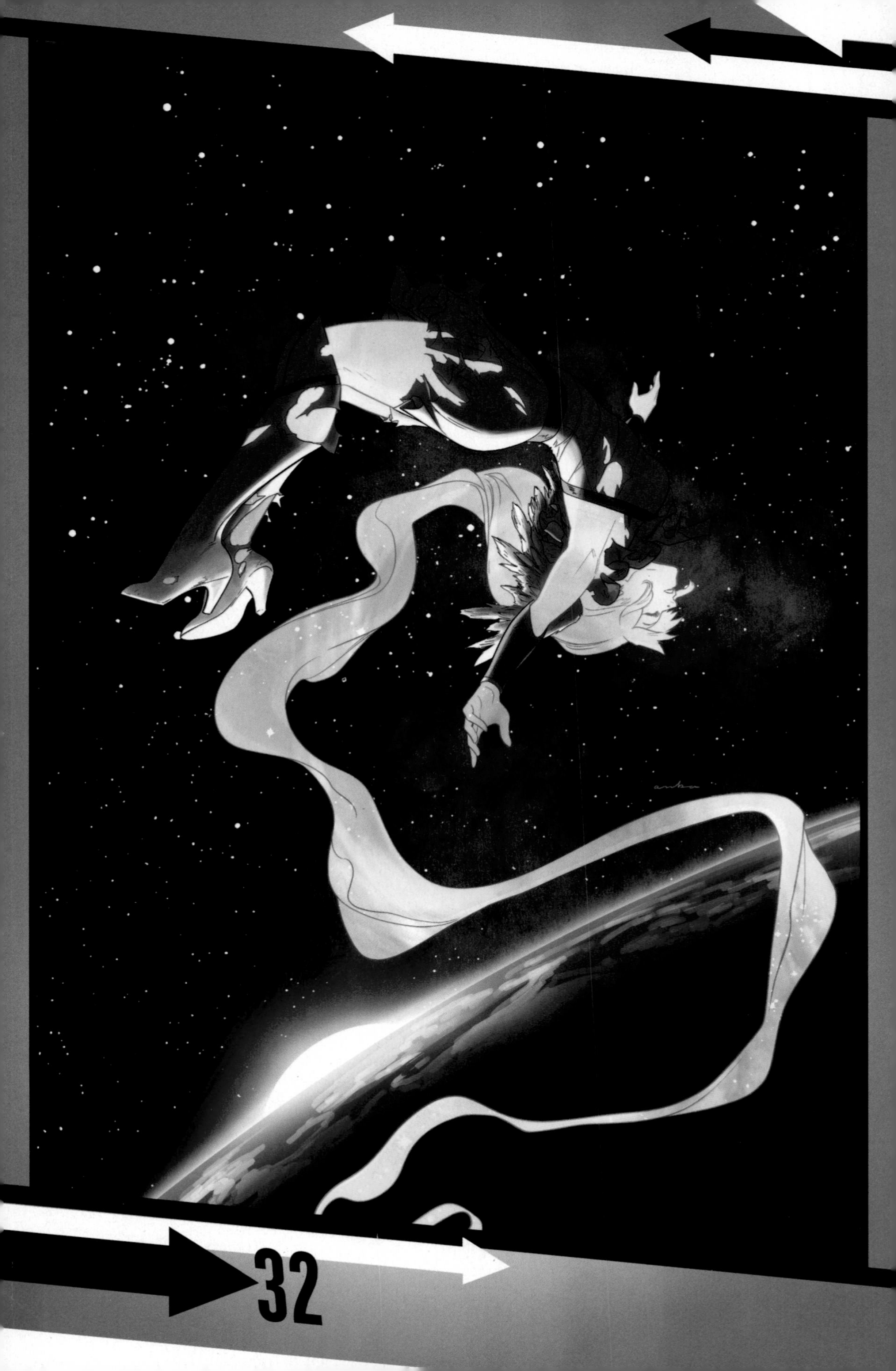

32

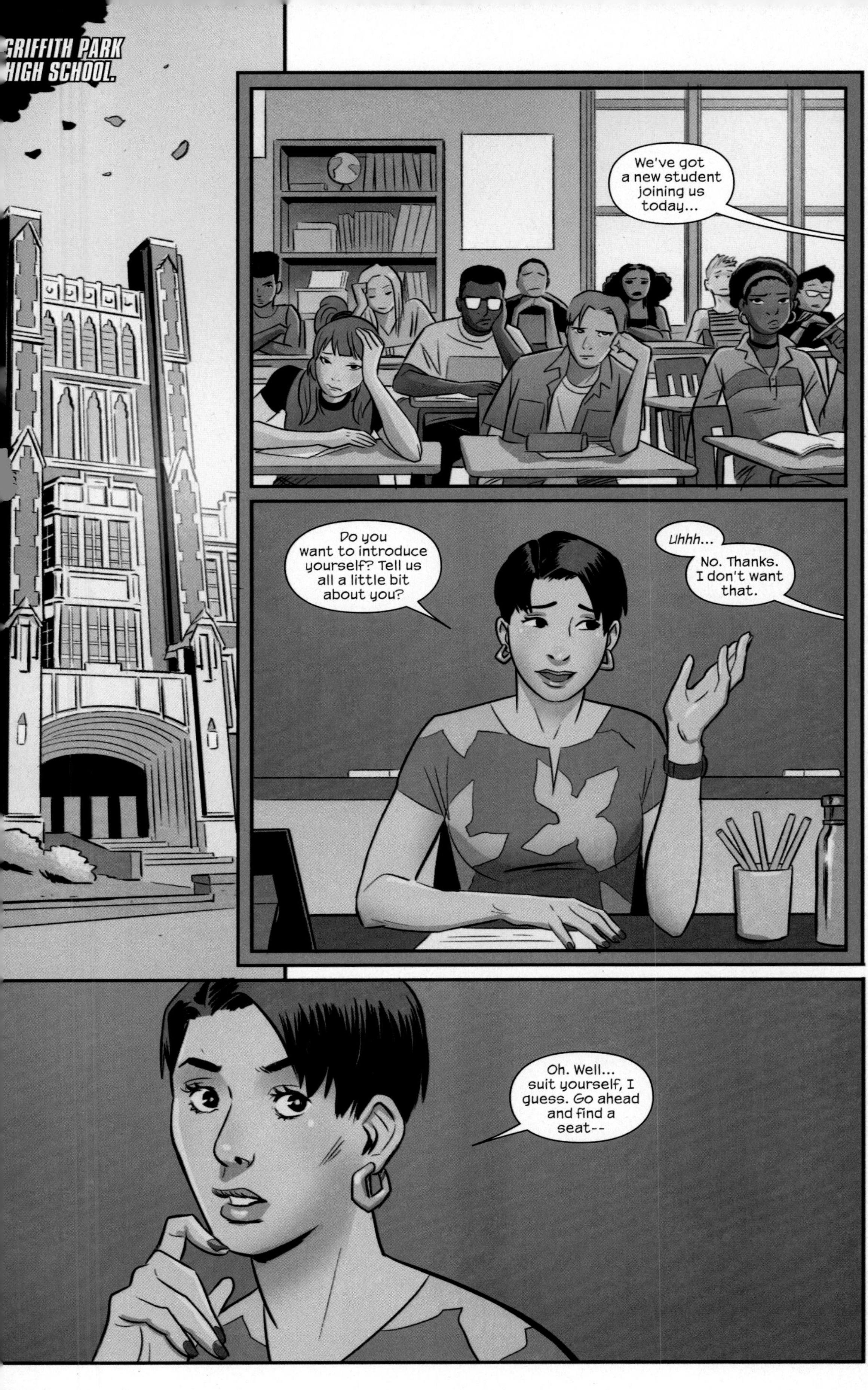

GRIFFITH PARK HIGH SCHOOL.
We've got a new student joining us today...
Do you want to introduce yourself? Tell us all a little bit about you?
Uhhh...
No. Thanks. I don't want that.
Oh. Well... suit yourself, I guess. Go ahead and find a seat--

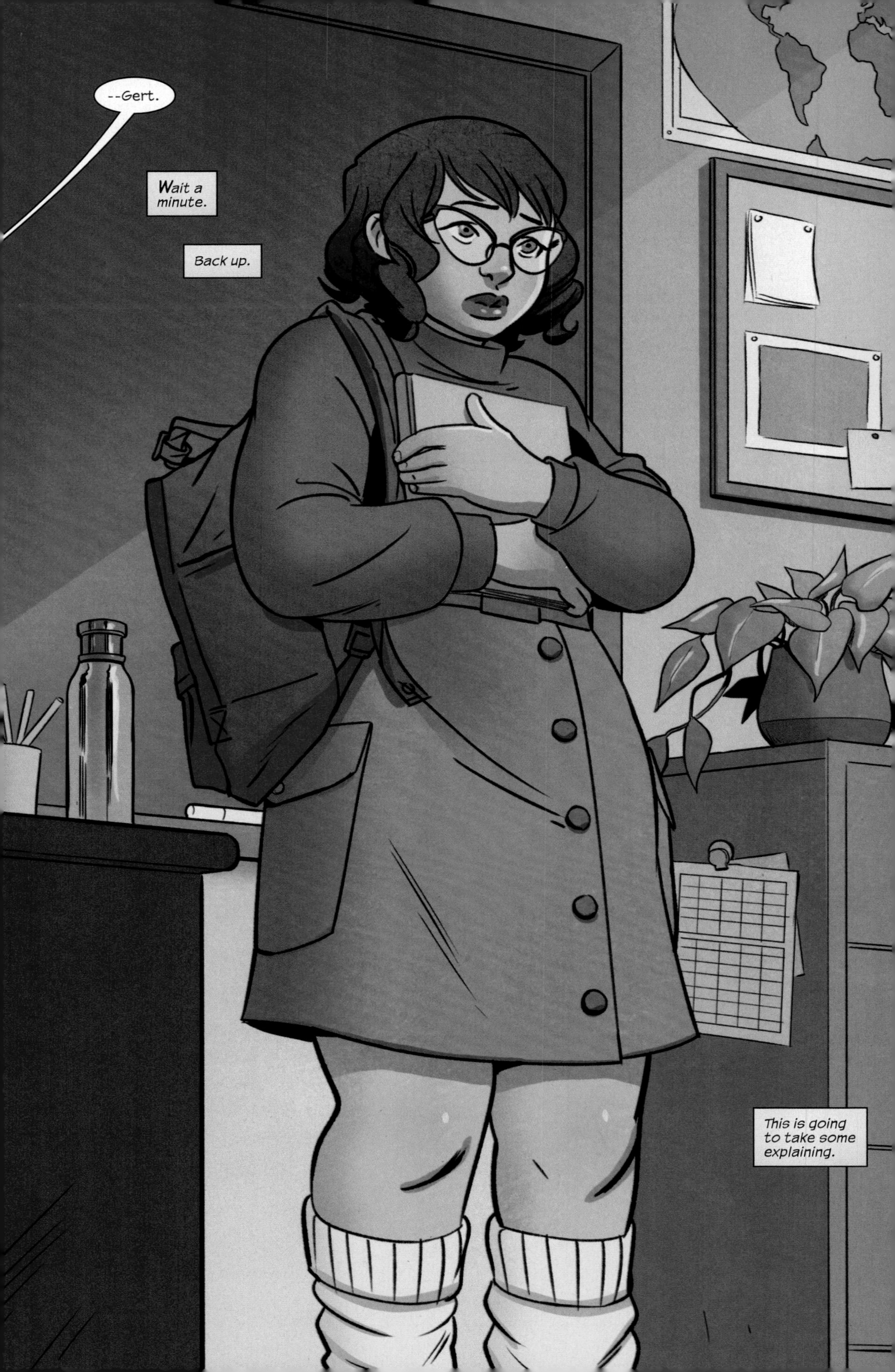

--Gert.
Wait a minute.
Back up.
This is going to take some explaining.

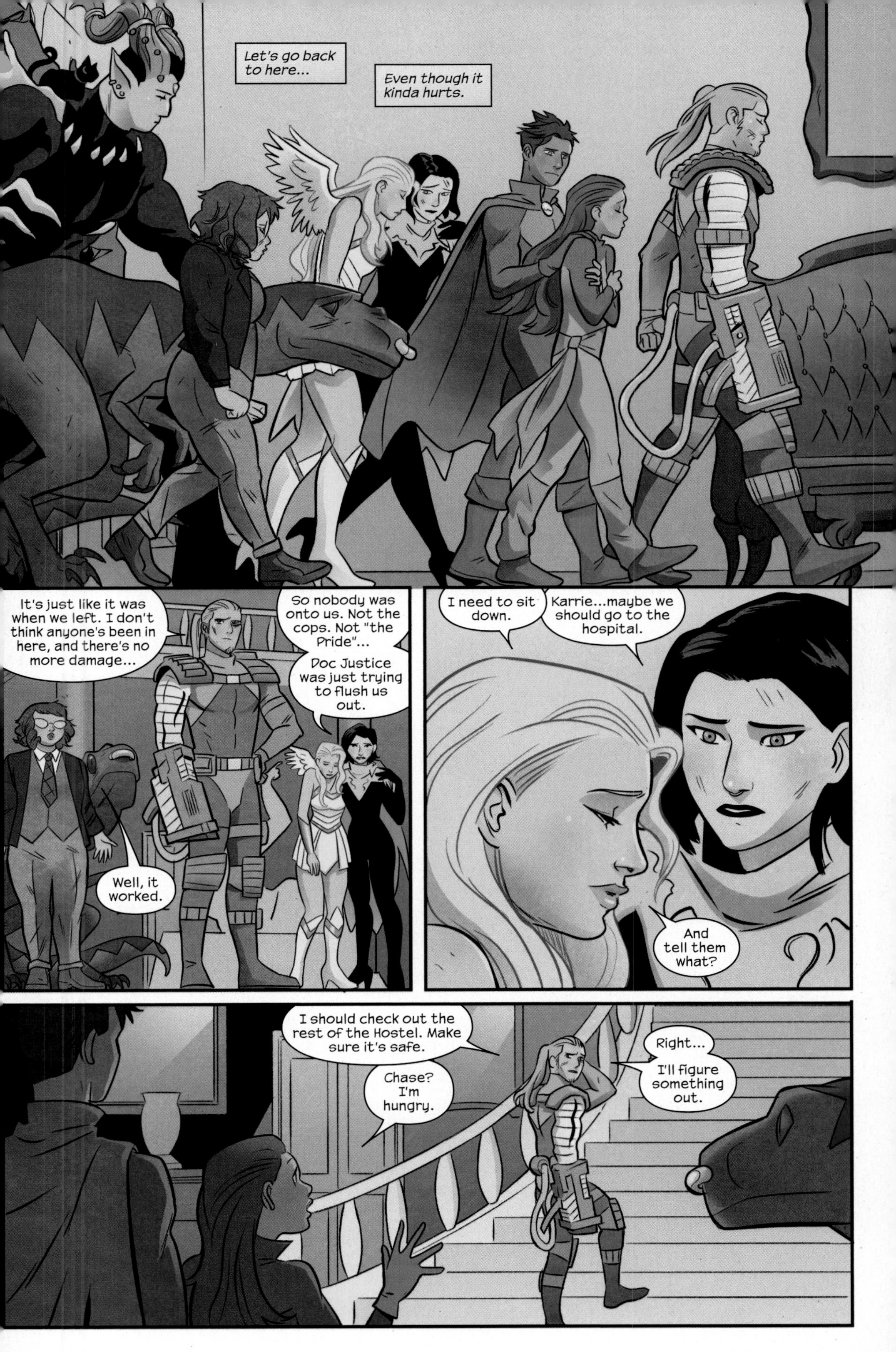
Let's go back to here...
Even though it kinda hurts.
It's just like it was when we left. I don't think anyone's been in here, and there's no more damage...
So nobody was onto us. Not the cops. Not "the Pride"...
Doc Justice was just trying to flush us out.
Well, it worked.
I need to sit down.
Karrie...maybe we should go to the hospital.
And tell them what?
I should check out the rest of the Hostel. Make sure it's safe.
Chase? I'm hungry.
Right...
I'll figure something out.

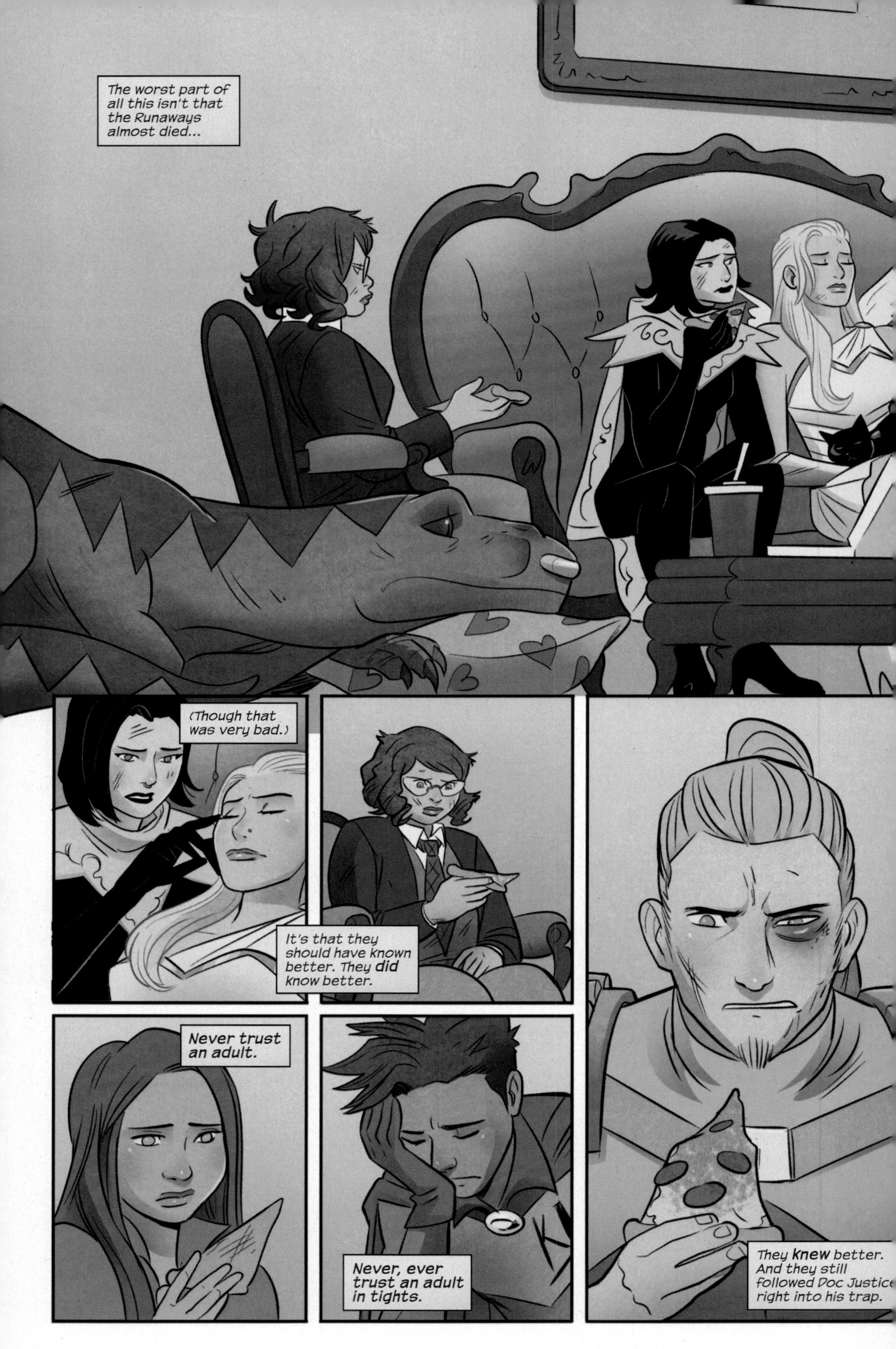
The worst part of all this isn't that the Runaways almost died...
(Though that was very bad.)
It's that they should have known better. They did know better.
Never trust an adult.
Never, ever trust an adult in tights.
They knew better. And they still followed Doc Justice right into his trap.

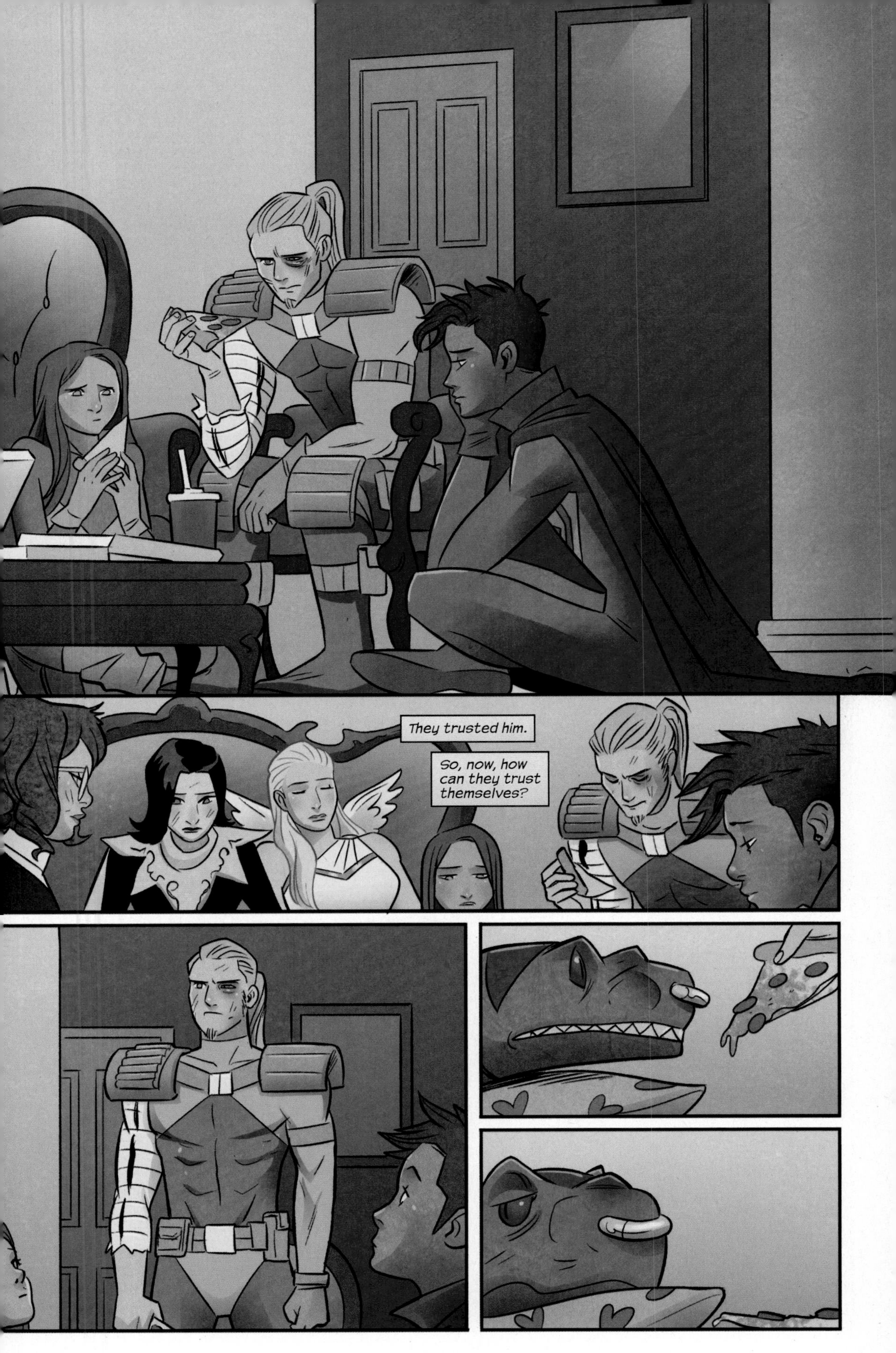
They trusted him.
So, now, how can they trust themselves?

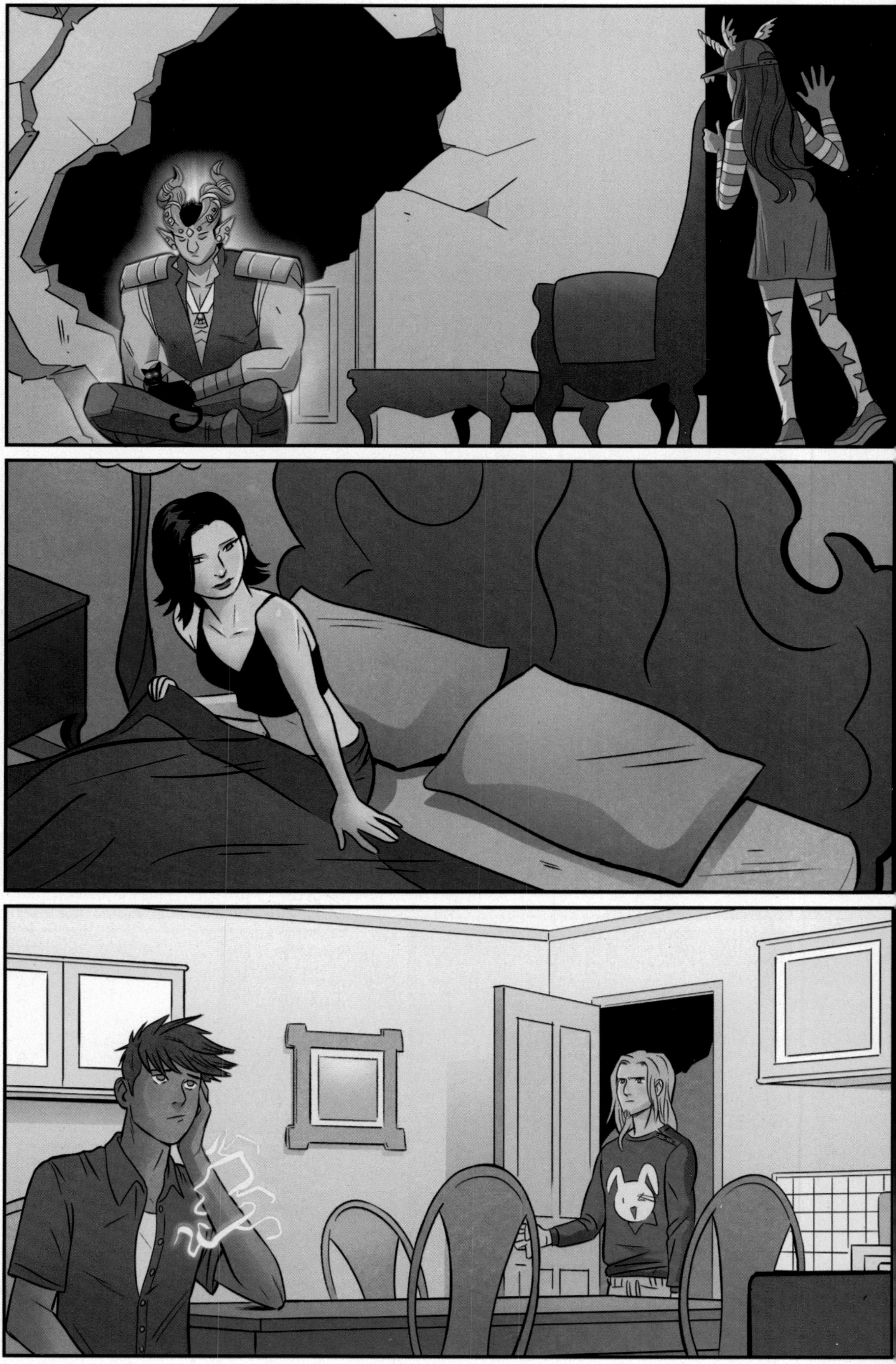

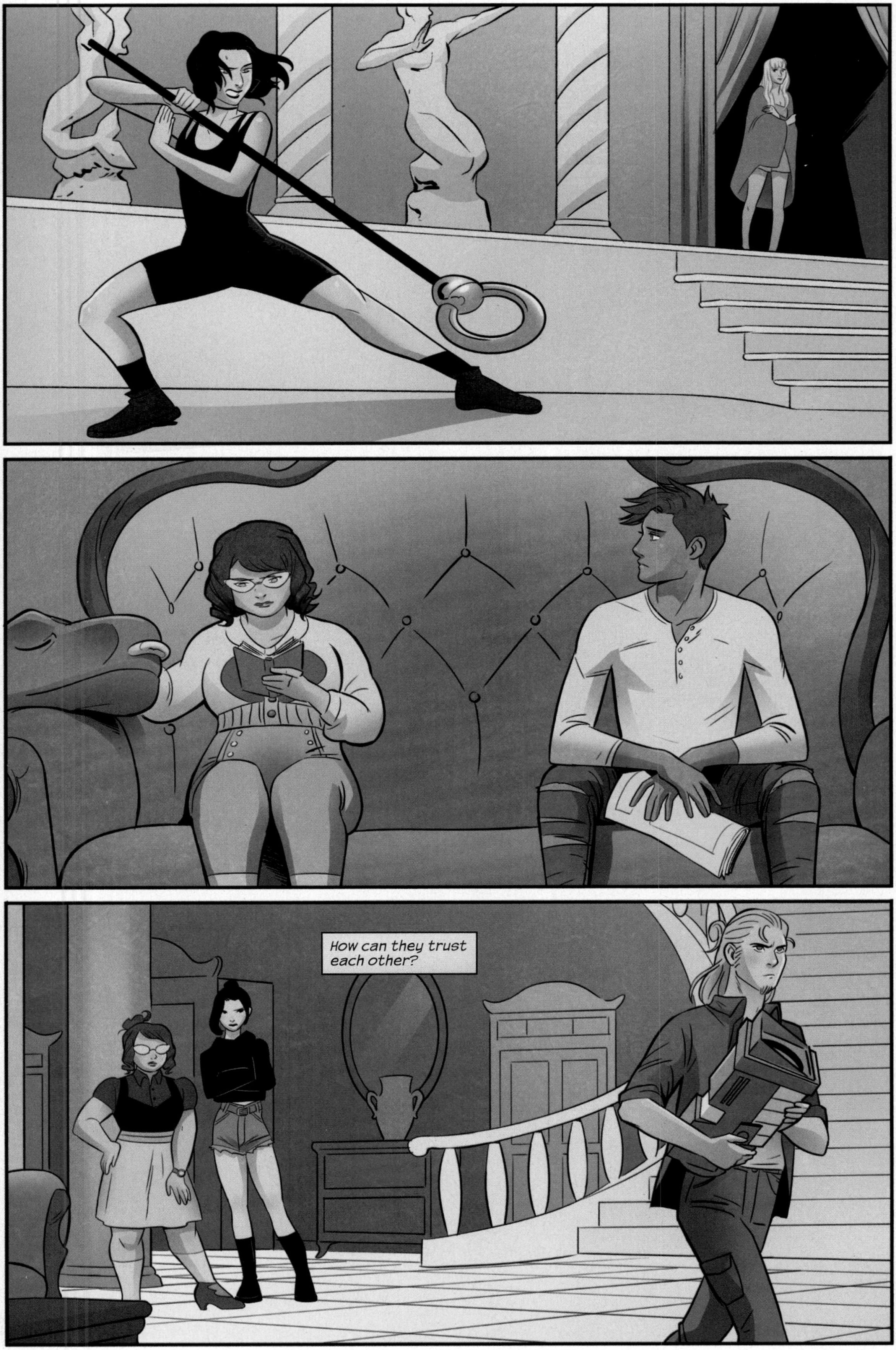
How can they trust each other?

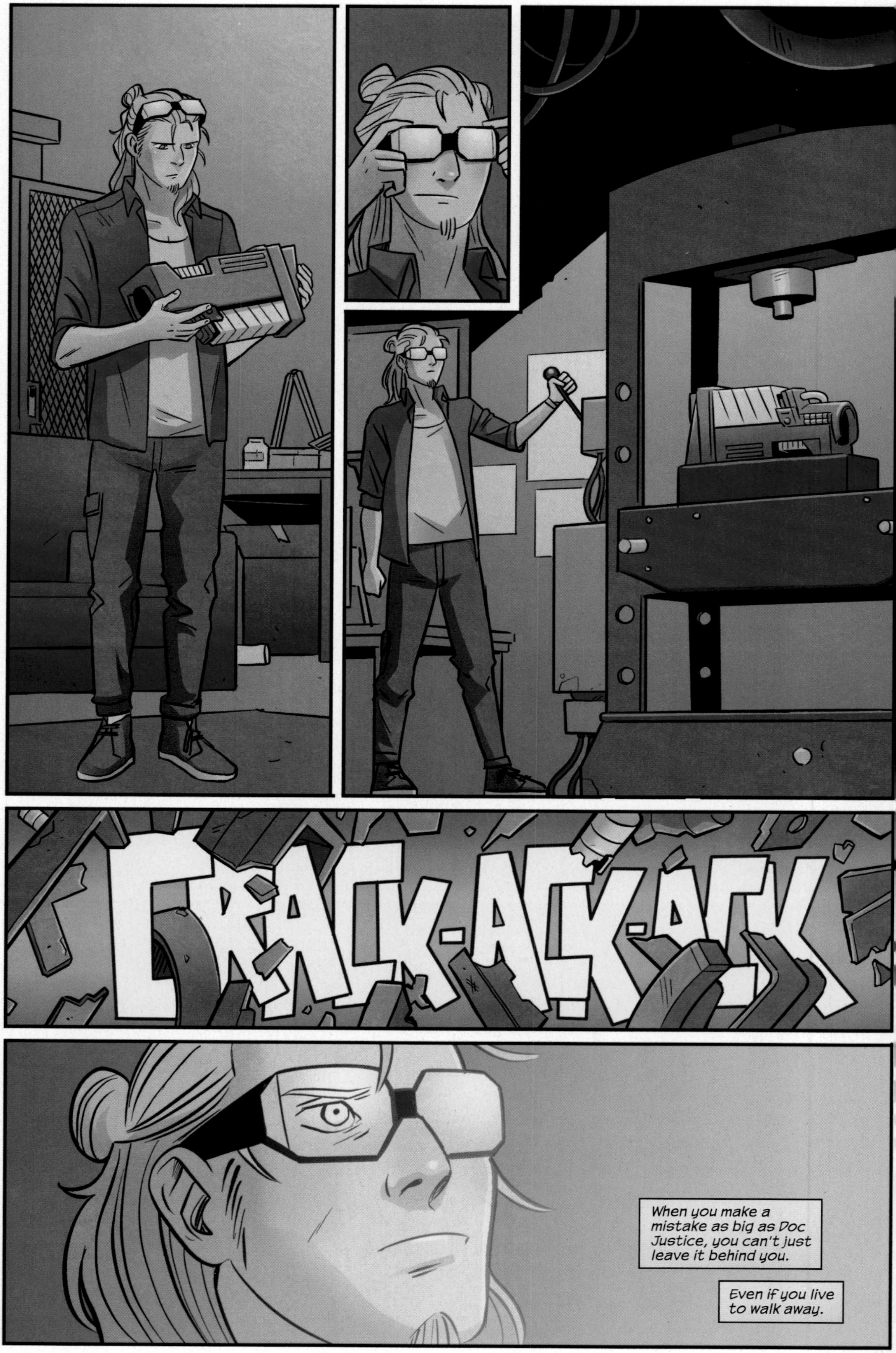
CRACK-ACK-ACK
When you make a mistake as big as Doc Justice, you can't just leave it behind you.
Even if you live to walk away.

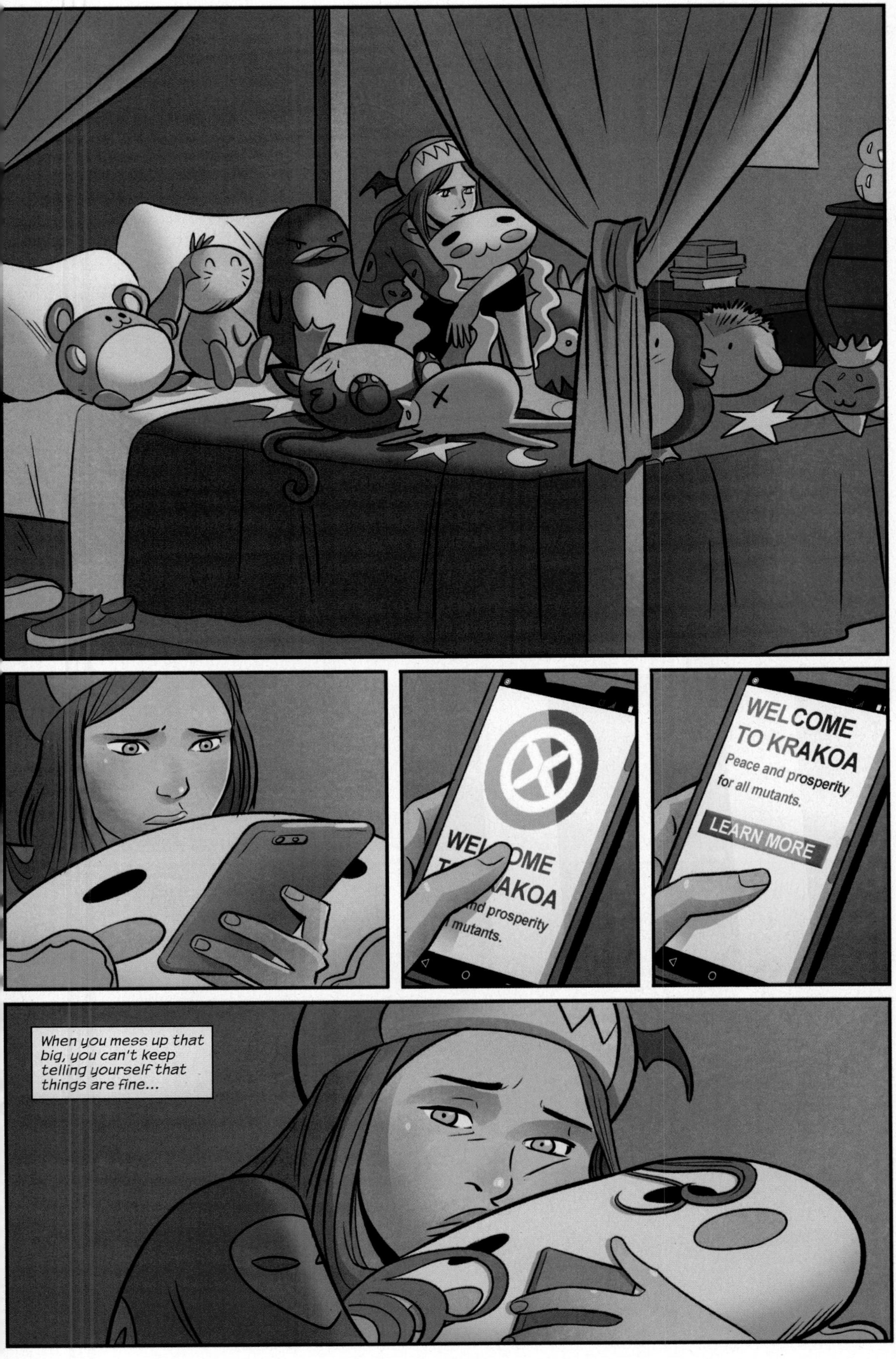
WELCOME
TO KRAKOA
Peace and prosperity
for all mutants.
LEARN MORE
When you mess up that big, you can't keep telling yourself that things are fine...

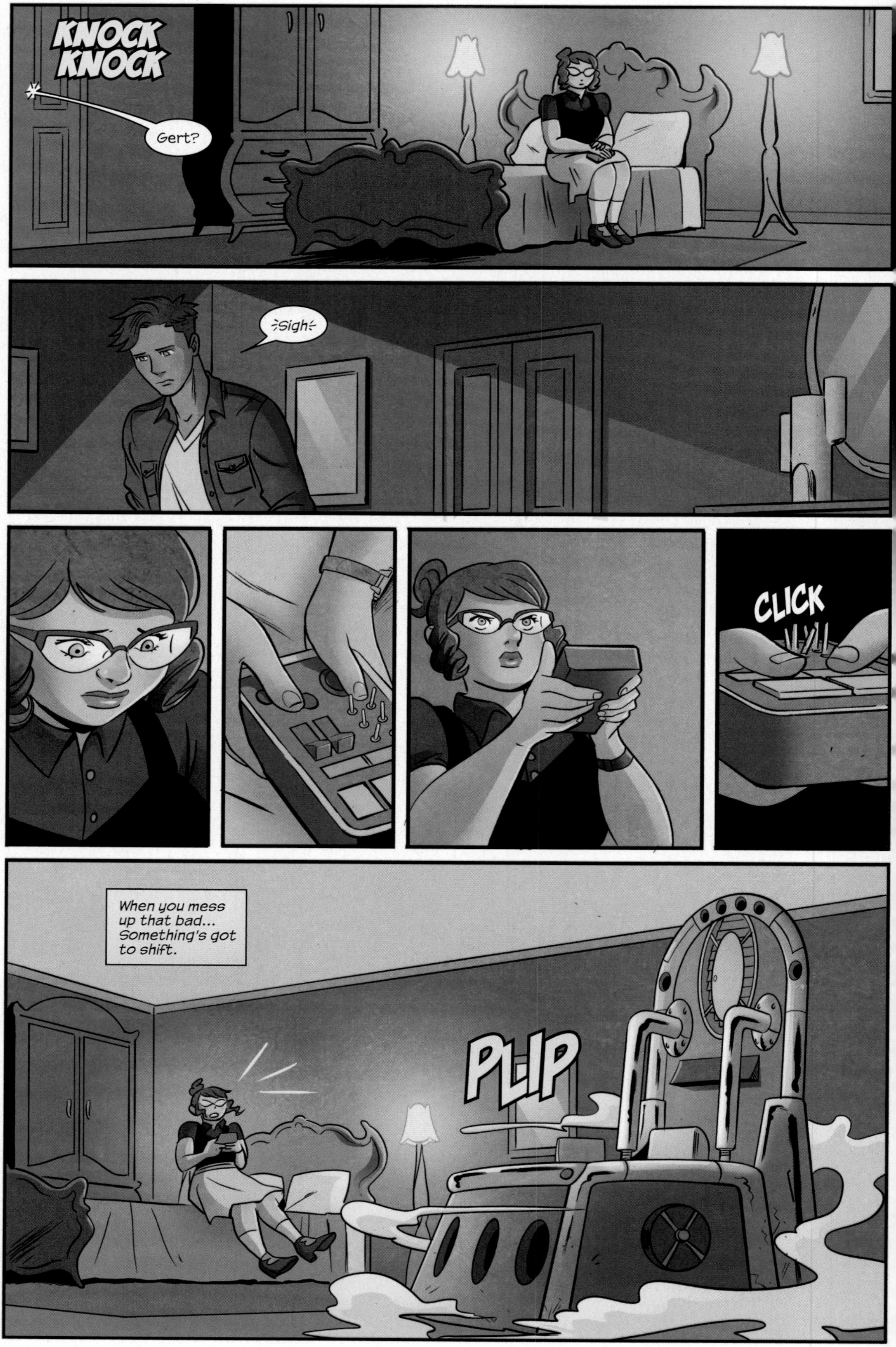
KNOCK KNOCK
Gert?
Sigh
CLICK
When you mess up that bad... Something's got to shift.
PLIP

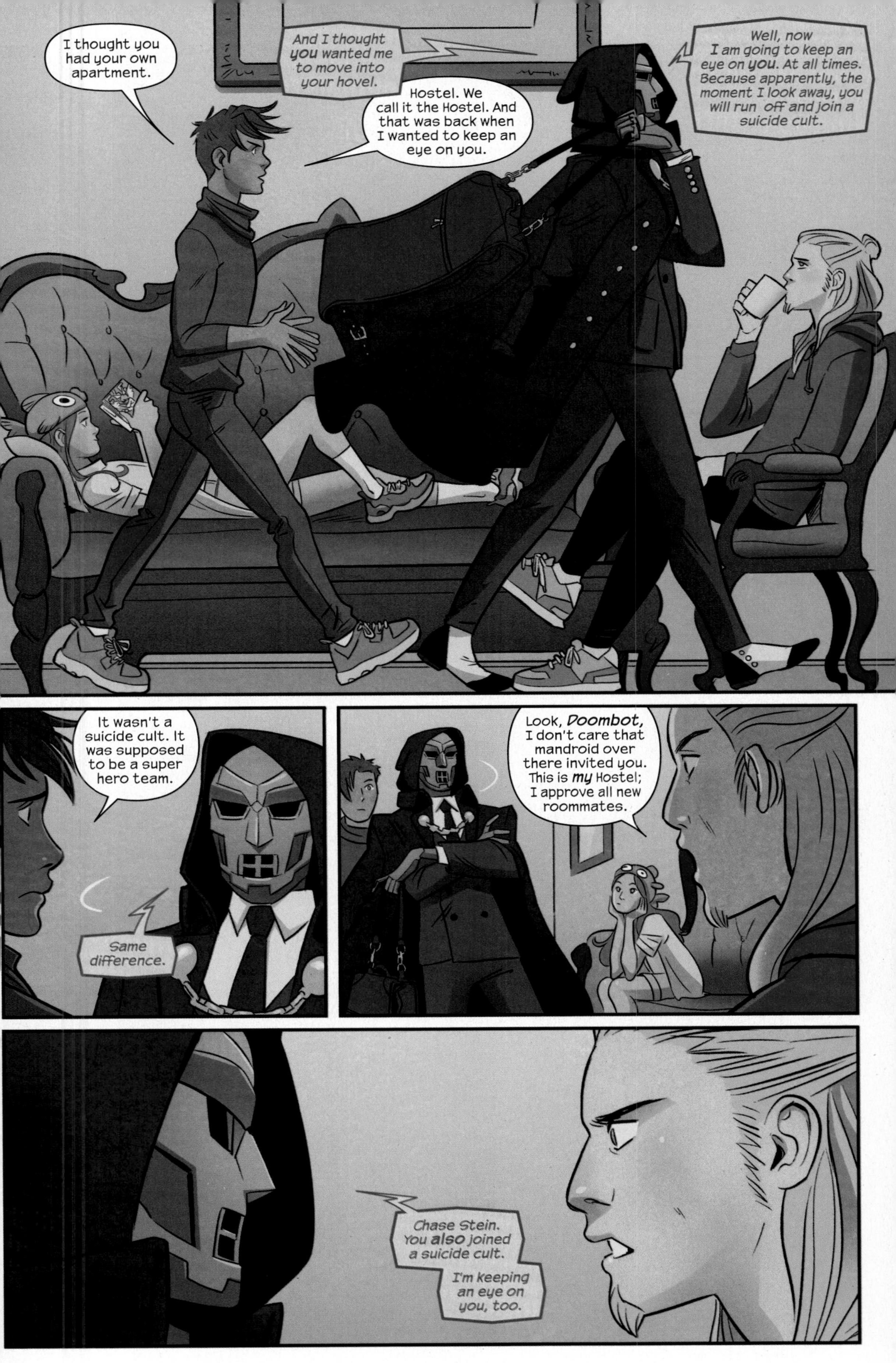
I thought you had your own apartment.
And I thought you wanted me to move into your hovel.
Hostel. We call it the Hostel. And that was back when I wanted to keep an eye on you.
Well, now I am going to keep an eye on you. At all times. Because apparently, the moment I look away, you will run off and join a suicide cult.
It wasn't a suicide cult. It was supposed to be a super hero team.
Same difference.
Look, Doombot, I don't care that mandroid over there invited you. This is my Hostel; I approve all new roommates.
Chase Stein. You also joined a suicide cult.
I'm keeping an eye on you, too.

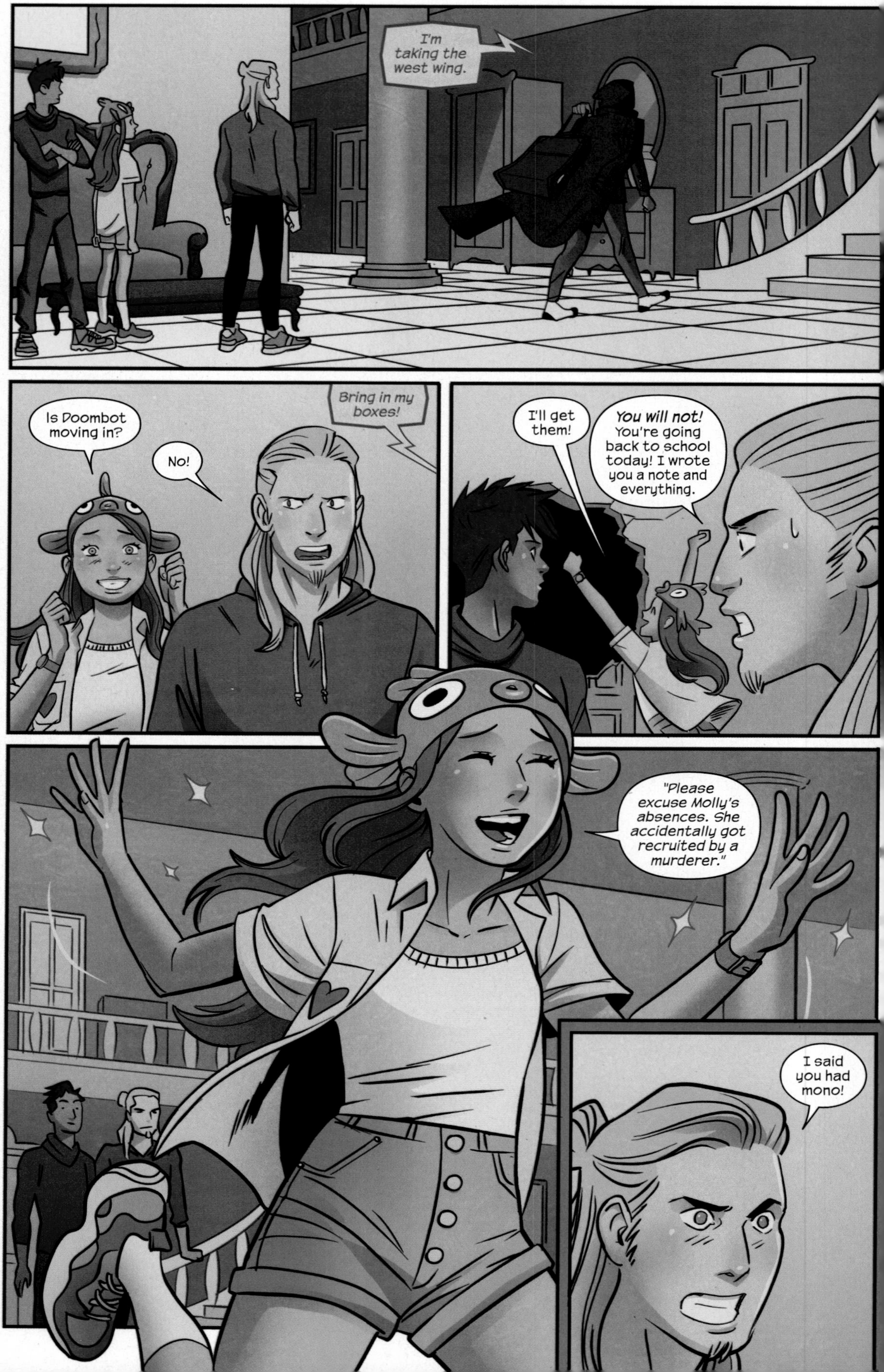
I'm taking the west wing.
Is Doombot moving in?
No!
Bring in my boxes!
I'll get them!
You will not! You're going back to school today! I wrote you a note and everything.
"Please excuse Molly's absences. She accidentally got recruited by a murderer."
I said you had mono!

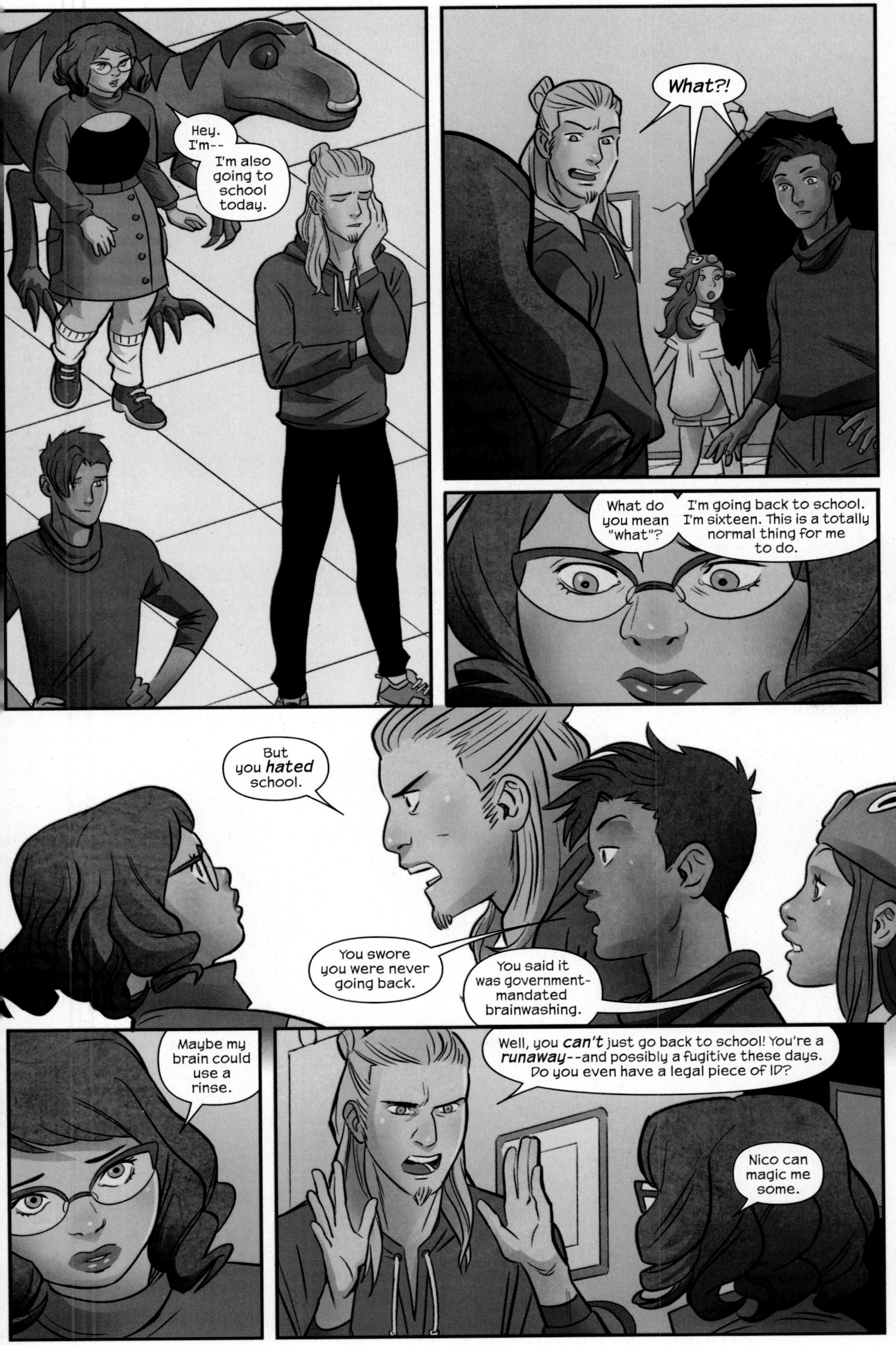
Hey. I'm--
I'm also going to school today.
What?!
What do you mean "what"?
I'm going back to school. I'm sixteen. This is a totally normal thing for me to do.
But you *hated* school.
You swore you were never going back.
You said it was government-mandated brainwashing.
Maybe my brain could use a rinse.
Well, you *can't* just go back to school! You're a *runaway*--and possibly a fugitive these days. Do you even have a legal piece of ID?
Nico can magic me some.

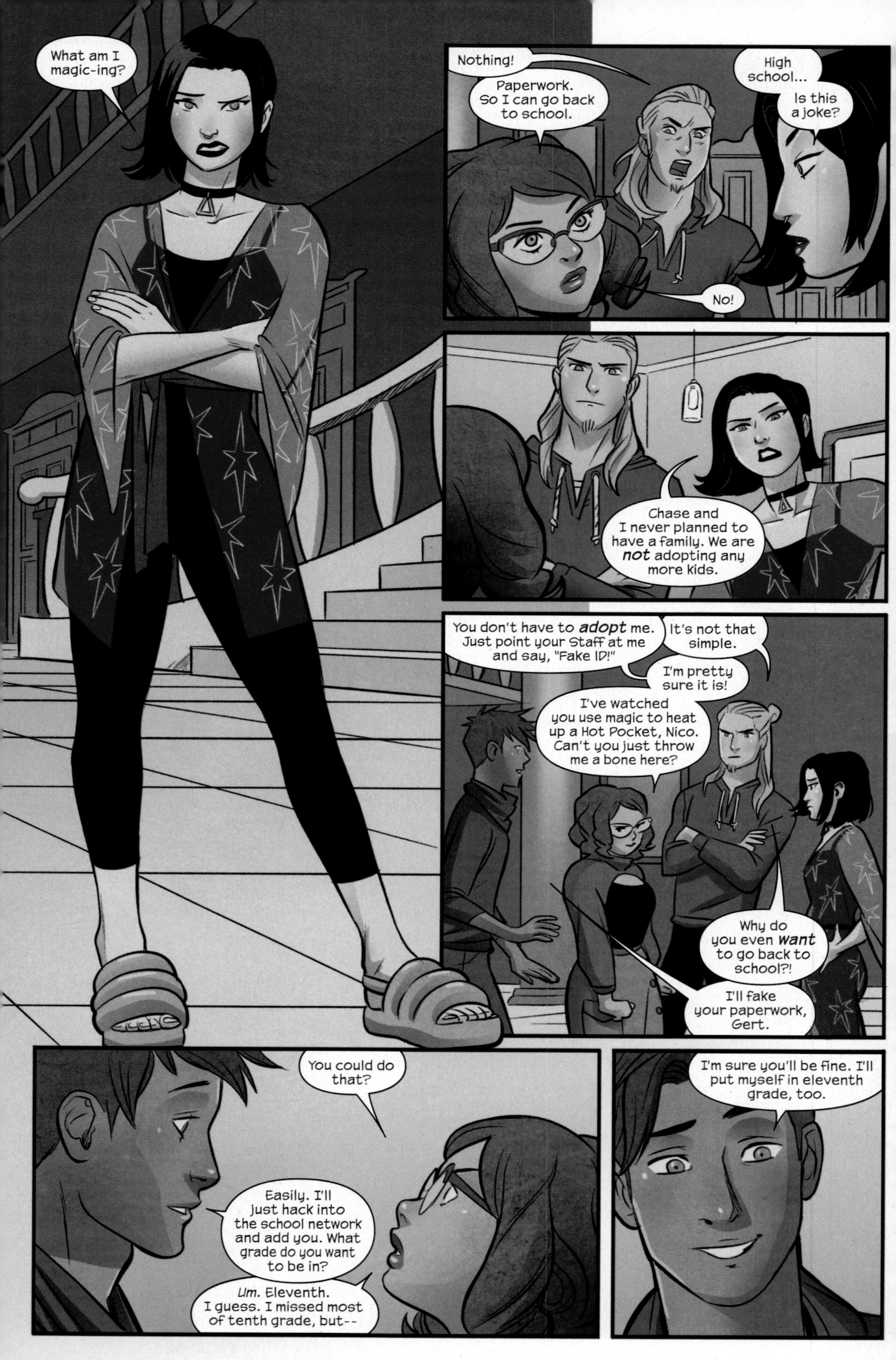
What am I magic-ing?
Nothing!
Paperwork. So I can go back to school.
High school...
Is this a joke?
No!
Chase and I never planned to have a family. We are *not* adopting any more kids.
You don't have to *adopt* me. Just point your Staff at me and say, "Fake ID!"
It's not that simple.
I'm pretty sure it is!
I've watched you use magic to heat up a Hot Pocket, Nico. Can't you just throw me a bone here?
Why do you even *want* to go back to school?!
I'll fake your paperwork, Gert.
You could do that?
Easily. I'll just hack into the school network and add you. What grade do you want to be in?
Um. Eleventh. I guess. I missed most of tenth grade, but--
I'm sure you'll be fine. I'll put myself in eleventh grade, too.

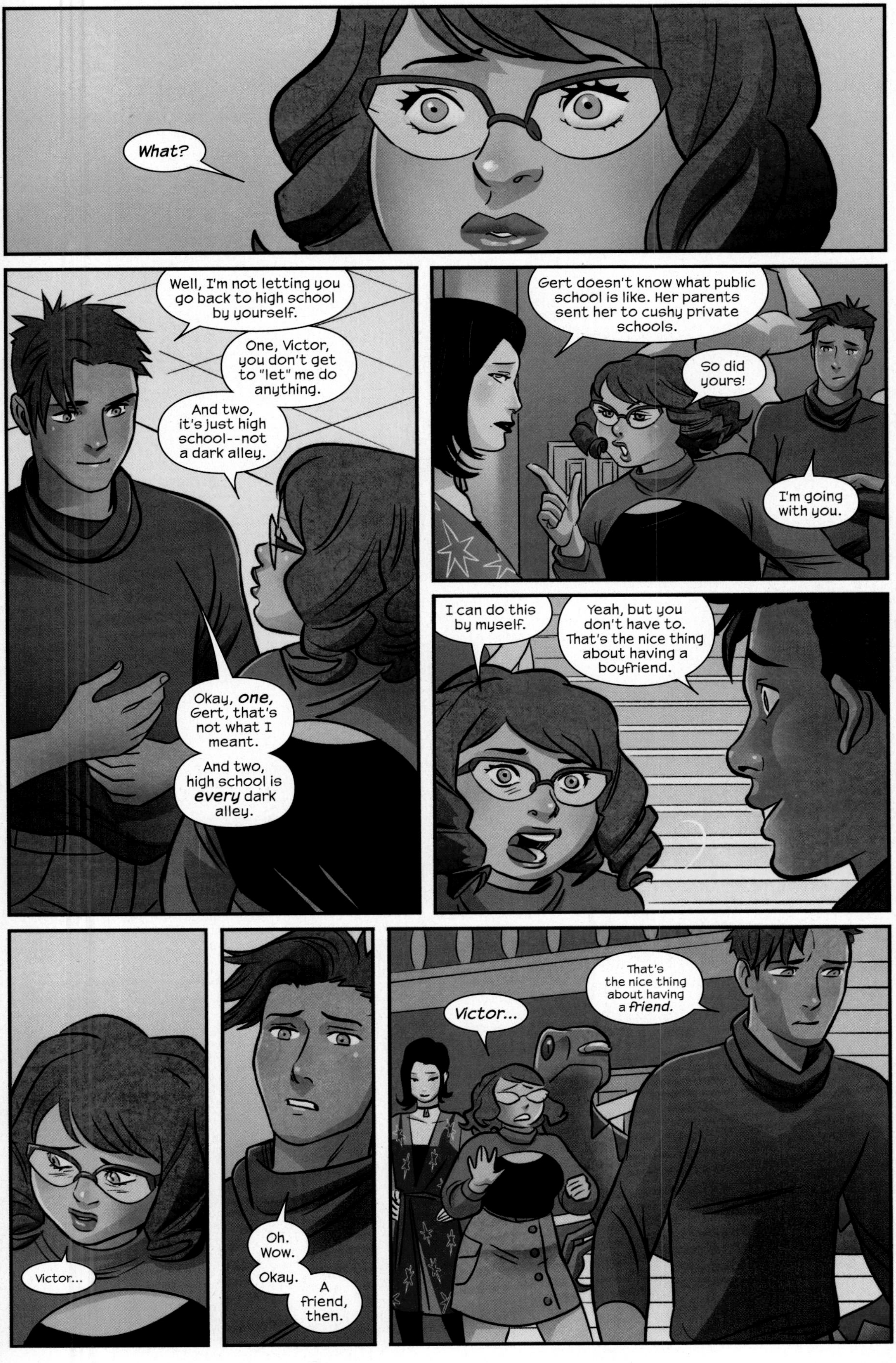
What?
Well, I'm not letting you go back to high school by yourself.
One, Victor, you don't get to "let" me do anything.
And two, it's just high school--not a dark alley.
Okay, *one,* Gert, that's not what I meant.
And two, high school is *every* dark alley.
Gert doesn't know what public school is like. Her parents sent her to cushy private schools.
So did yours!
I'm going with you.
I can do this by myself.
Yeah, but you don't have to. That's the nice thing about having a boyfriend.
Victor...
Oh. Wow.
Okay.
A friend, then.
Victor...
That's the nice thing about having a *friend.*

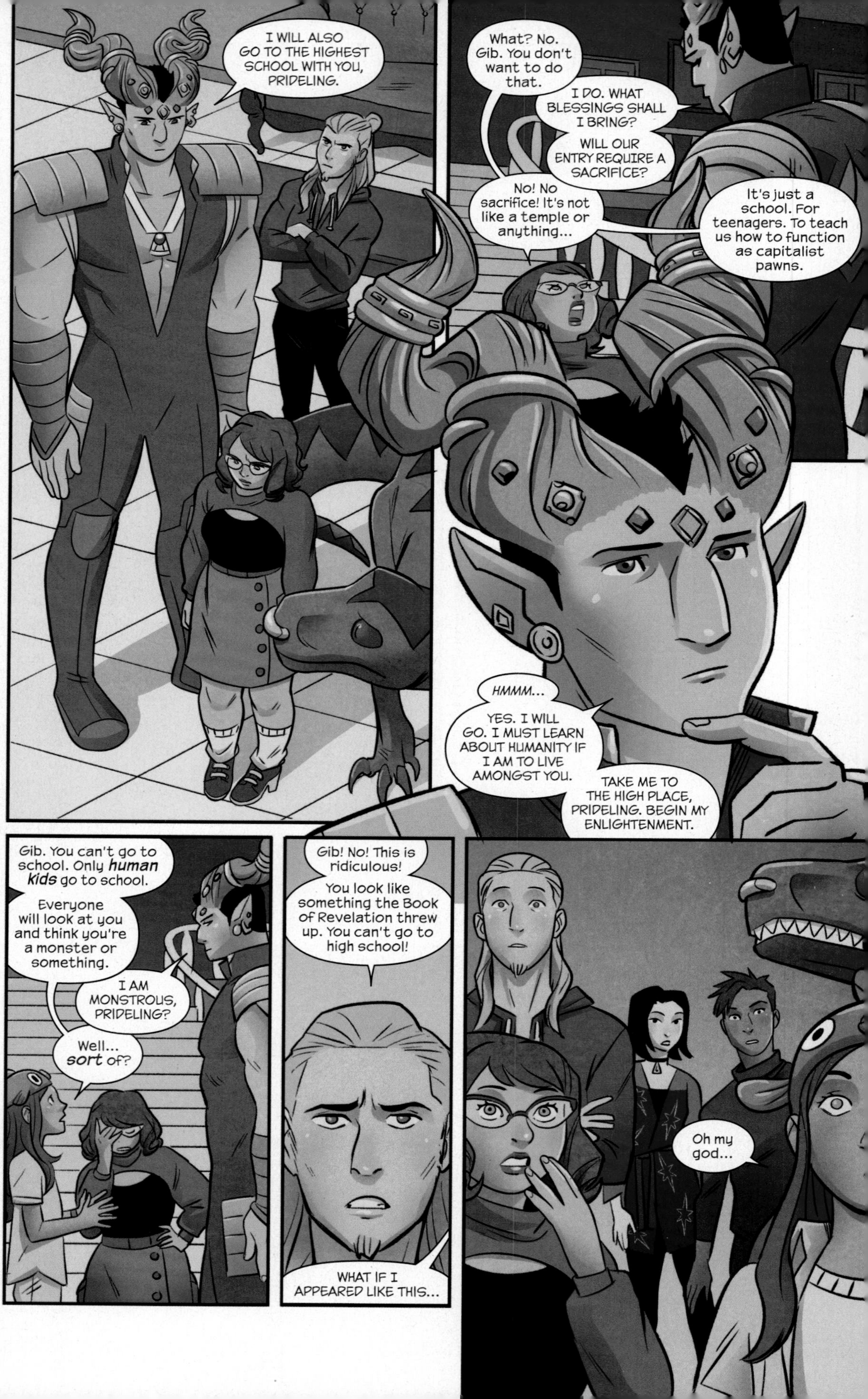
I WILL ALSO GO TO THE HIGHEST SCHOOL WITH YOU, PRIDELING.
What? No. Gib. You don't want to do that.
I DO. WHAT BLESSINGS SHALL I BRING?
WILL OUR ENTRY REQUIRE A SACRIFICE?
No! No sacrifice! It's not like a temple or anything...
It's just a school. For teenagers. To teach us how to function as capitalist pawns.
HMMM...
YES. I WILL GO. I MUST LEARN ABOUT HUMANITY IF I AM TO LIVE AMONGST YOU.
TAKE ME TO THE HIGH PLACE, PRIDELING. BEGIN MY ENLIGHTENMENT.
Gib. You can't go to school. Only human kids go to school.
Everyone will look at you and think you're a monster or something.
I AM MONSTROUS, PRIDELING?
Well... sort of?
Gib! No! This is ridiculous!
You look like something the Book of Revelation threw up. You can't go to high school!
WHAT IF I APPEARED LIKE THIS...
Oh my god...

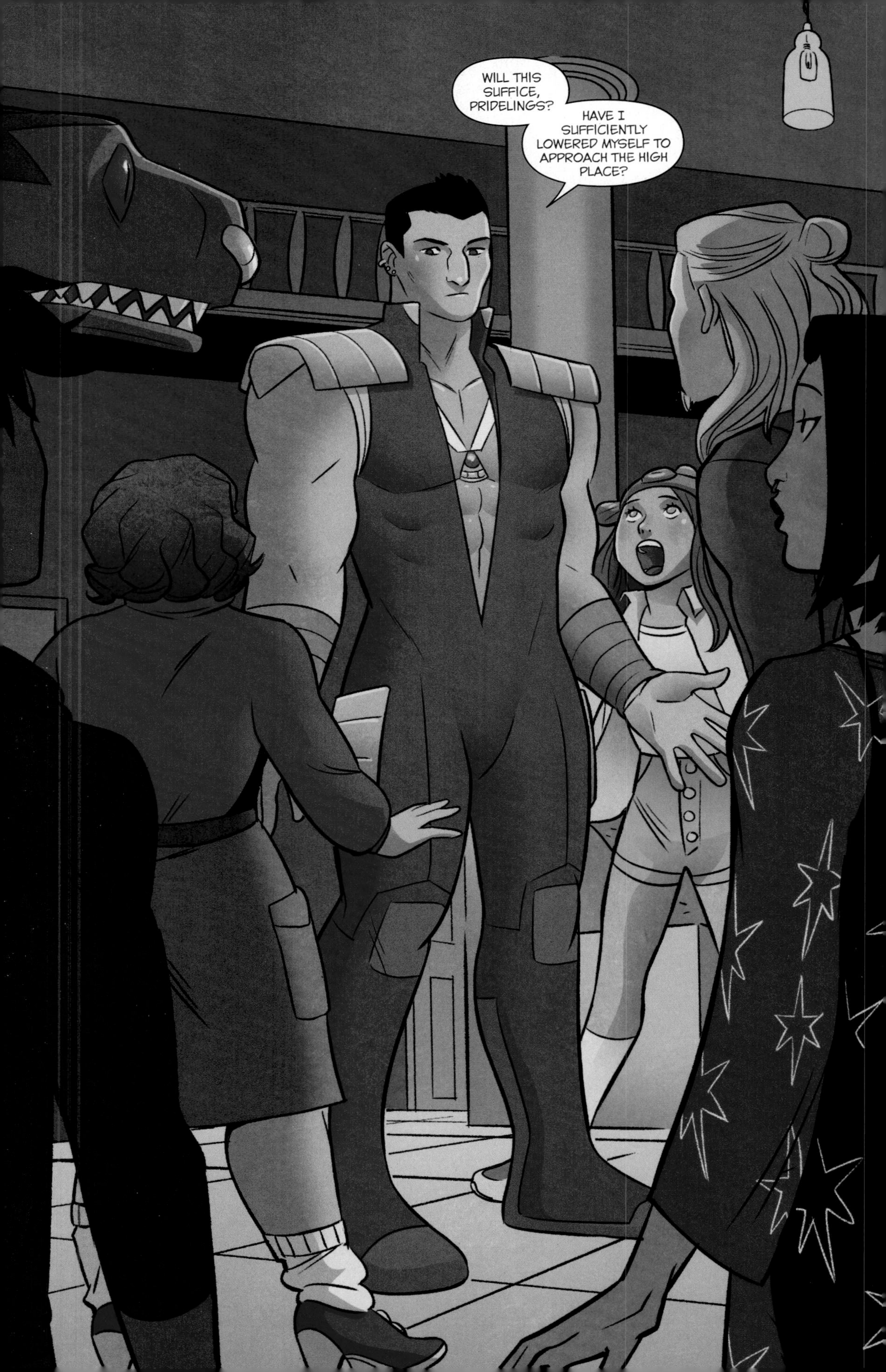
WILL THIS SUFFICE, PRIDELINGS?
HAVE I SUFFICIENTLY LOWERED MYSELF TO APPROACH THE HIGH PLACE?

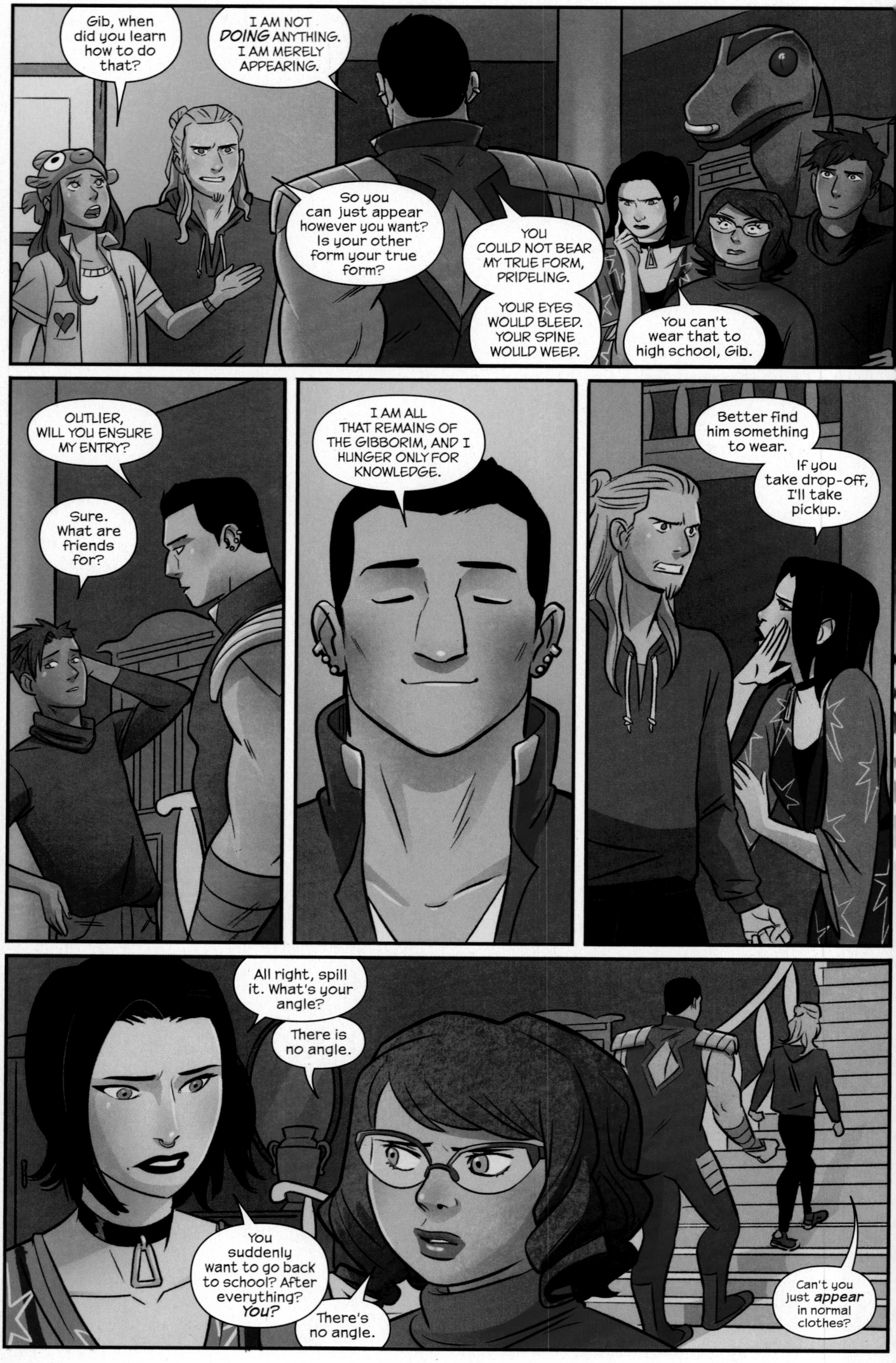

Gib, when did you learn how to do that?
I AM NOT *DOING* ANYTHING. I AM MERELY APPEARING.
So you can just appear however you want? Is your other form your true form?
YOU COULD NOT BEAR MY TRUE FORM, PRIDELING.
YOUR EYES WOULD BLEED. YOUR SPINE WOULD WEEP.
You can't wear that to high school, Gib.
OUTLIER, WILL YOU ENSURE MY ENTRY?
Sure. What are friends for?
I AM ALL THAT REMAINS OF THE GIBBORIM, AND I HUNGER ONLY FOR KNOWLEDGE.
Better find him something to wear.
If you take drop-off, I'll take pickup.
All right, spill it. What's your angle?
There is no angle.
You suddenly want to go back to school? After everything? *YOU?*
There's no angle.
Can't you just *appear* in normal clothes?

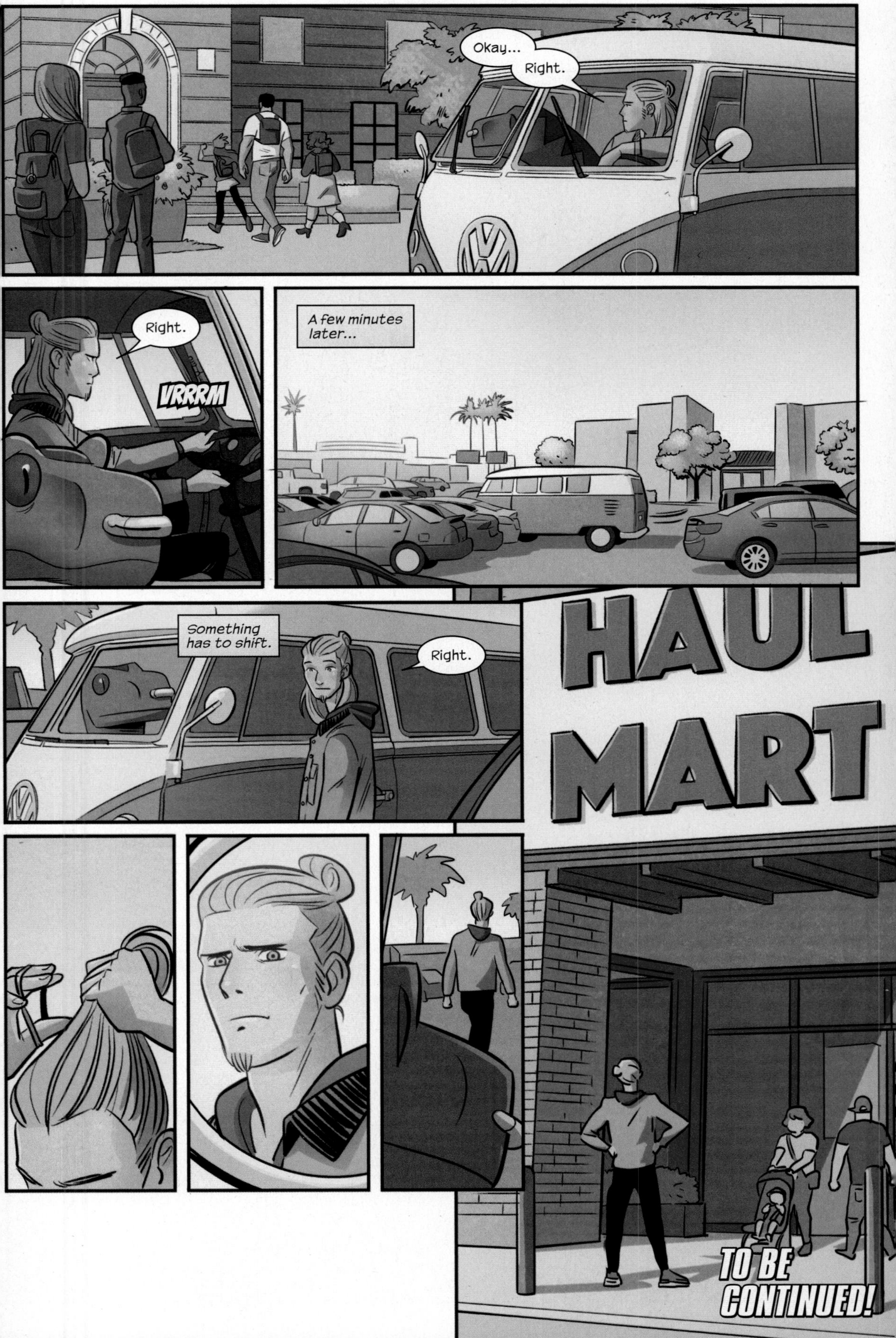
Okay...
Right.
Right.
VRRRM
A few minutes later...
Something has to shift.
Right.
HAUL MART
TO BE CONTINUED!

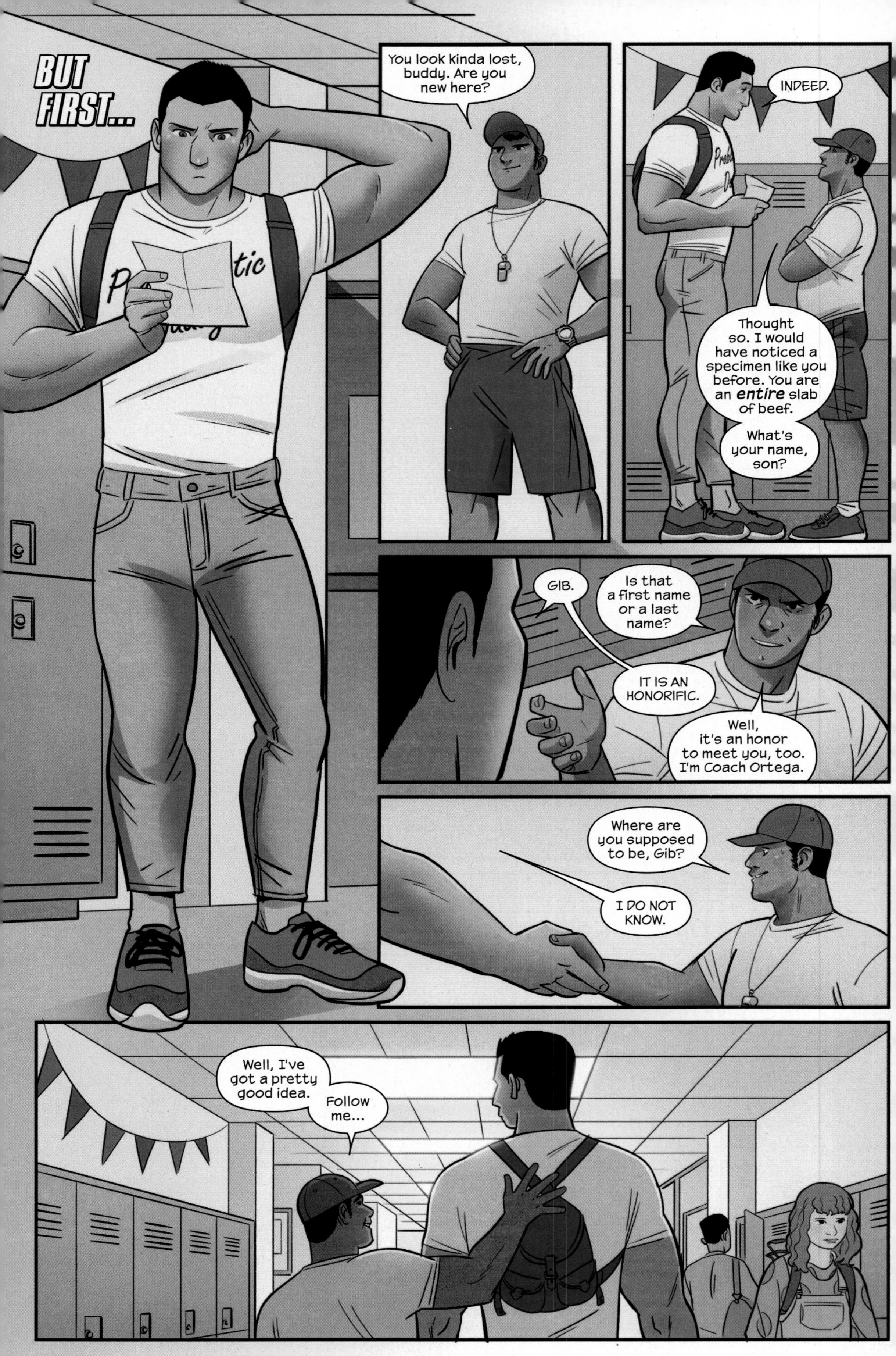
BUT FIRST...
You look kinda lost, buddy. Are you new here?
INDEED.
Thought so. I would have noticed a specimen like you before. You are an *entire* slab of beef.
What's your name, son?
GIB.
Is that a first name or a last name?
IT IS AN HONORIFIC.
Well, it's an honor to meet you, too. I'm Coach Ortega.
Where are you supposed to be, Gib?
I DO NOT KNOW.
Well, I've got a pretty good idea.
Follow me...

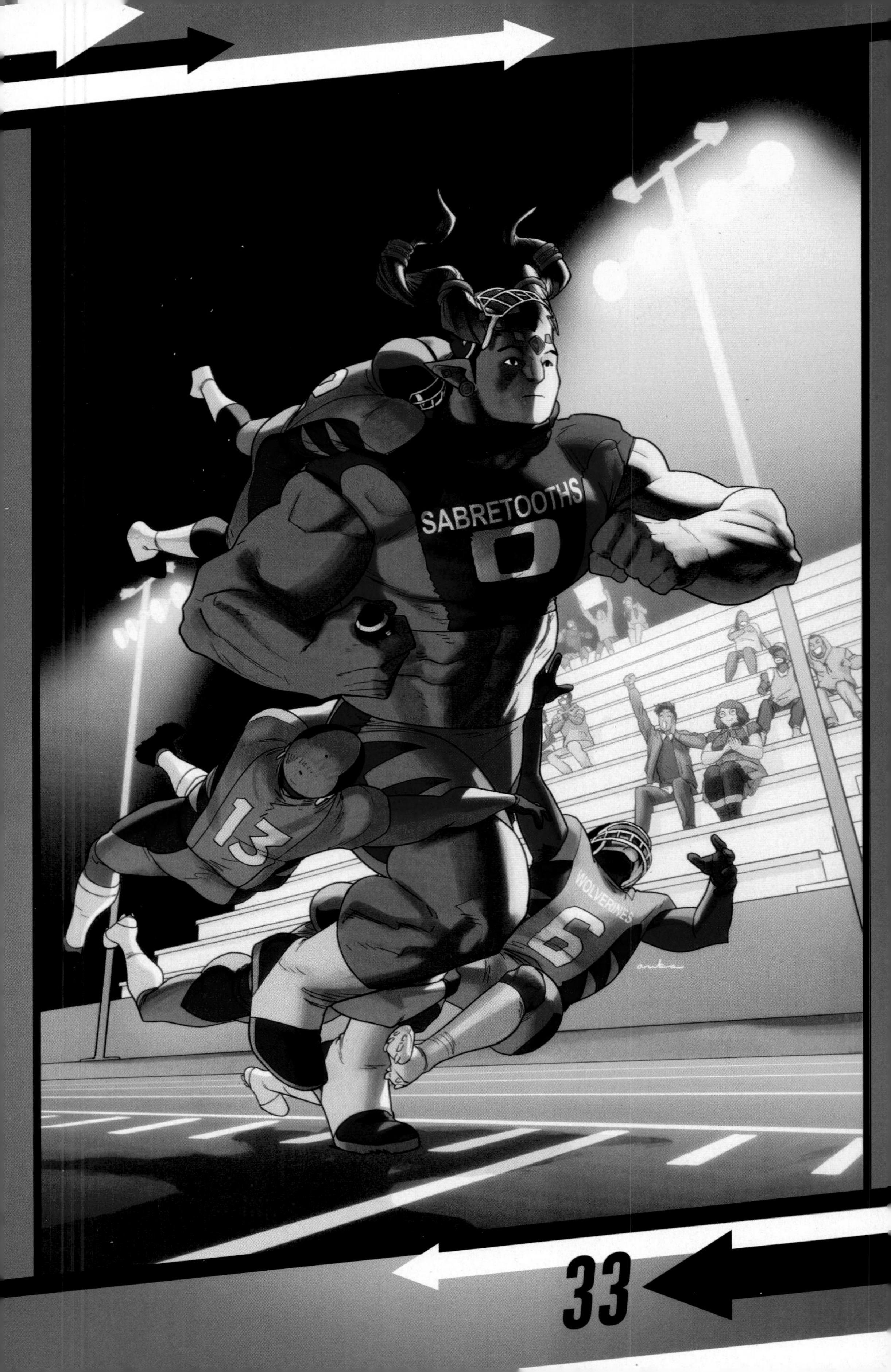
SABRETOOTHS
13
WOLVERINES
6
33

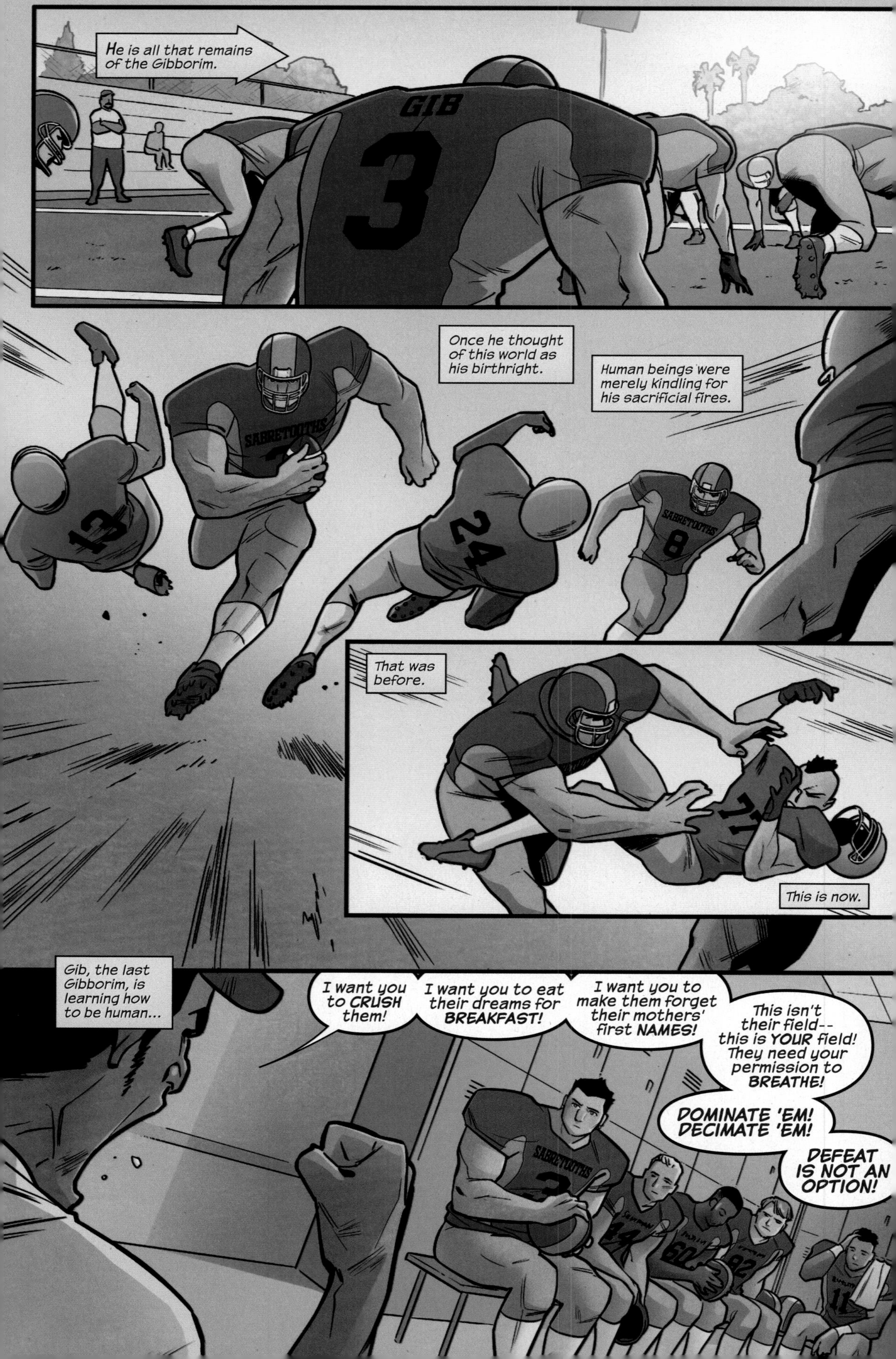

He is all that remains of the Gibborim.
GIB 3
Once he thought of this world as his birthright.
Human beings were merely kindling for his sacrificial fires.
SABRETOOTHS
That was before.
This is now.
Gib, the last Gibborim, is learning how to be human...
I want you to CRUSH them!
I want you to eat their dreams for BREAKFAST!
I want you to make them forget their mothers' first NAMES!
This isn't their field-- this is YOUR field! They need your permission to BREATHE!
DOMINATE 'EM! DECIMATE 'EM!
DEFEAT IS NOT AN OPTION!

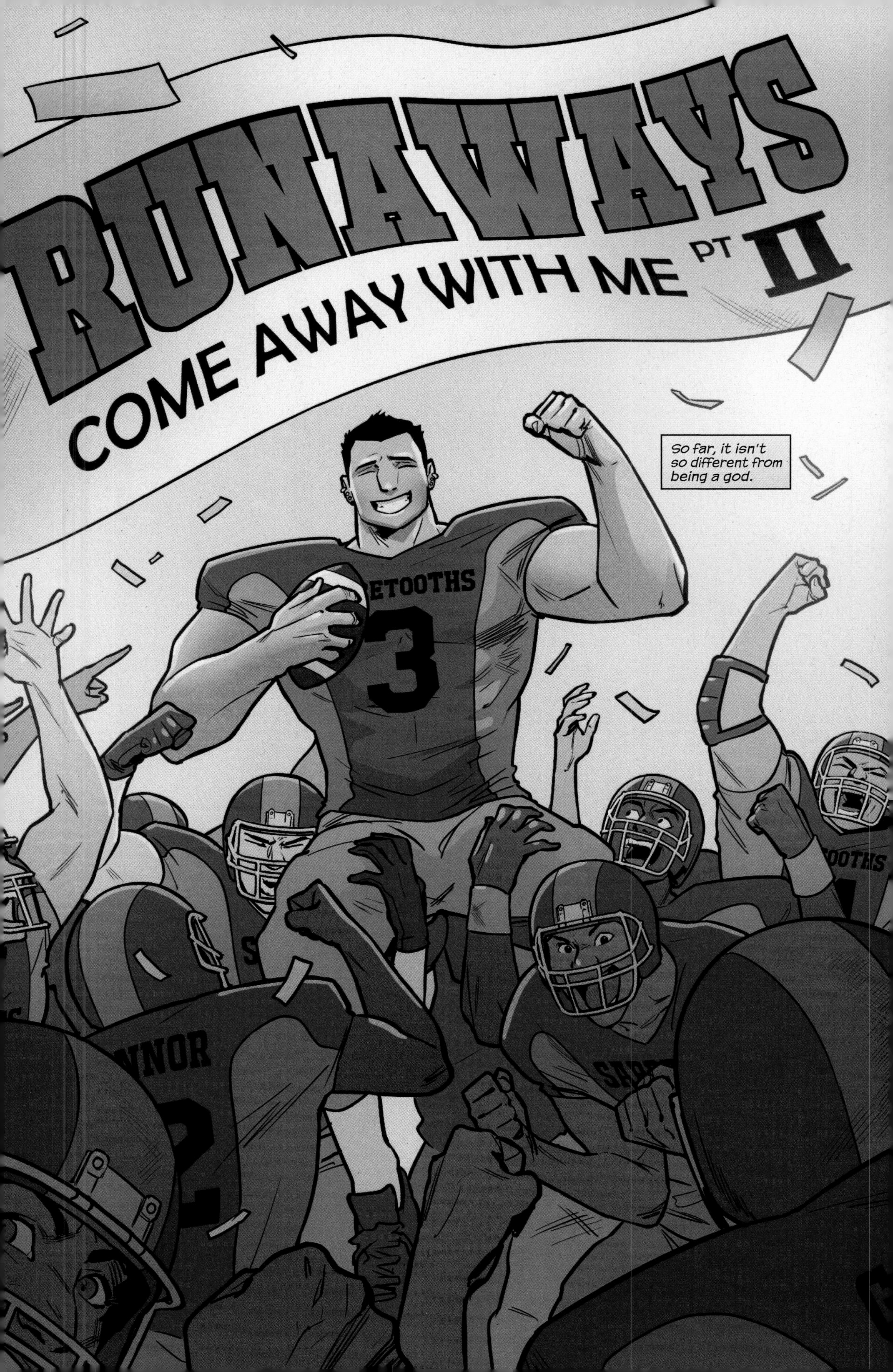
RUNAWAYS
COME AWAY WITH ME PT II
So far, it isn't so different from being a god.

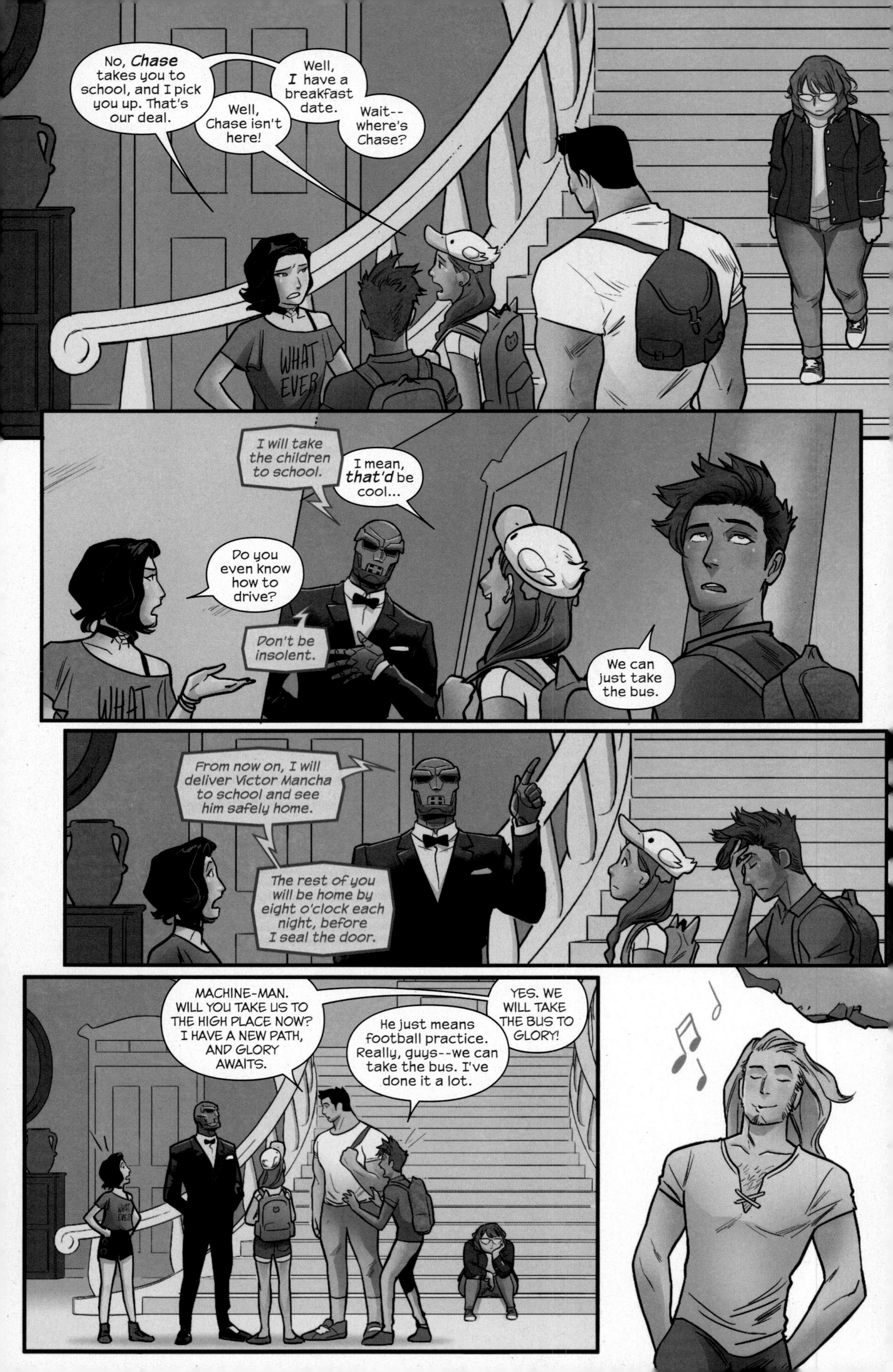
No, *Chase* takes you to school, and I pick you up. That's our deal.
Well, *I* have a breakfast date.
Well, Chase isn't here!
Wait--where's Chase?
I will take the children to school.
I mean, *that'd* be cool...
Do you even know how to drive?
Don't be insolent.
We can just take the bus.
From now on, I will deliver Victor Mancha to school and see him safely home.
The rest of you will be home by eight o'clock each night, before I seal the door.
MACHINE-MAN. WILL YOU TAKE US TO THE HIGH PLACE NOW? I HAVE A NEW PATH, AND GLORY AWAITS.
YES. WE WILL TAKE THE BUS TO GLORY!
He just means football practice. Really, guys--we can take the bus. I've done it a lot.

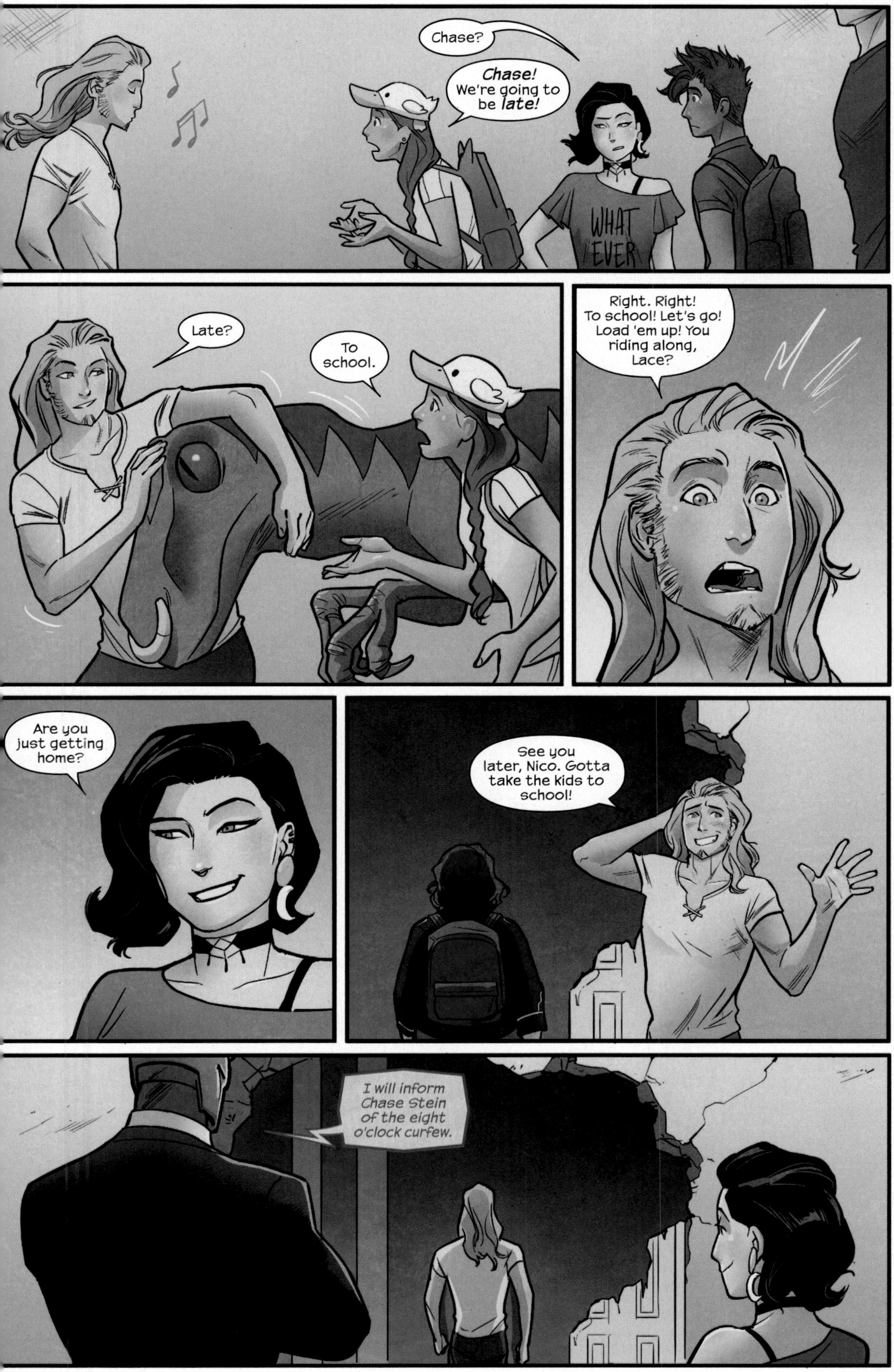
Chase?
Chase! We're going to be late!
Late?
To school.
Right. Right! To school! Let's go! Load 'em up! You riding along, Lace?
Are you just getting home?
See you later, Nico. Gotta take the kids to school!
I will inform Chase Stein of the eight o'clock curfew.

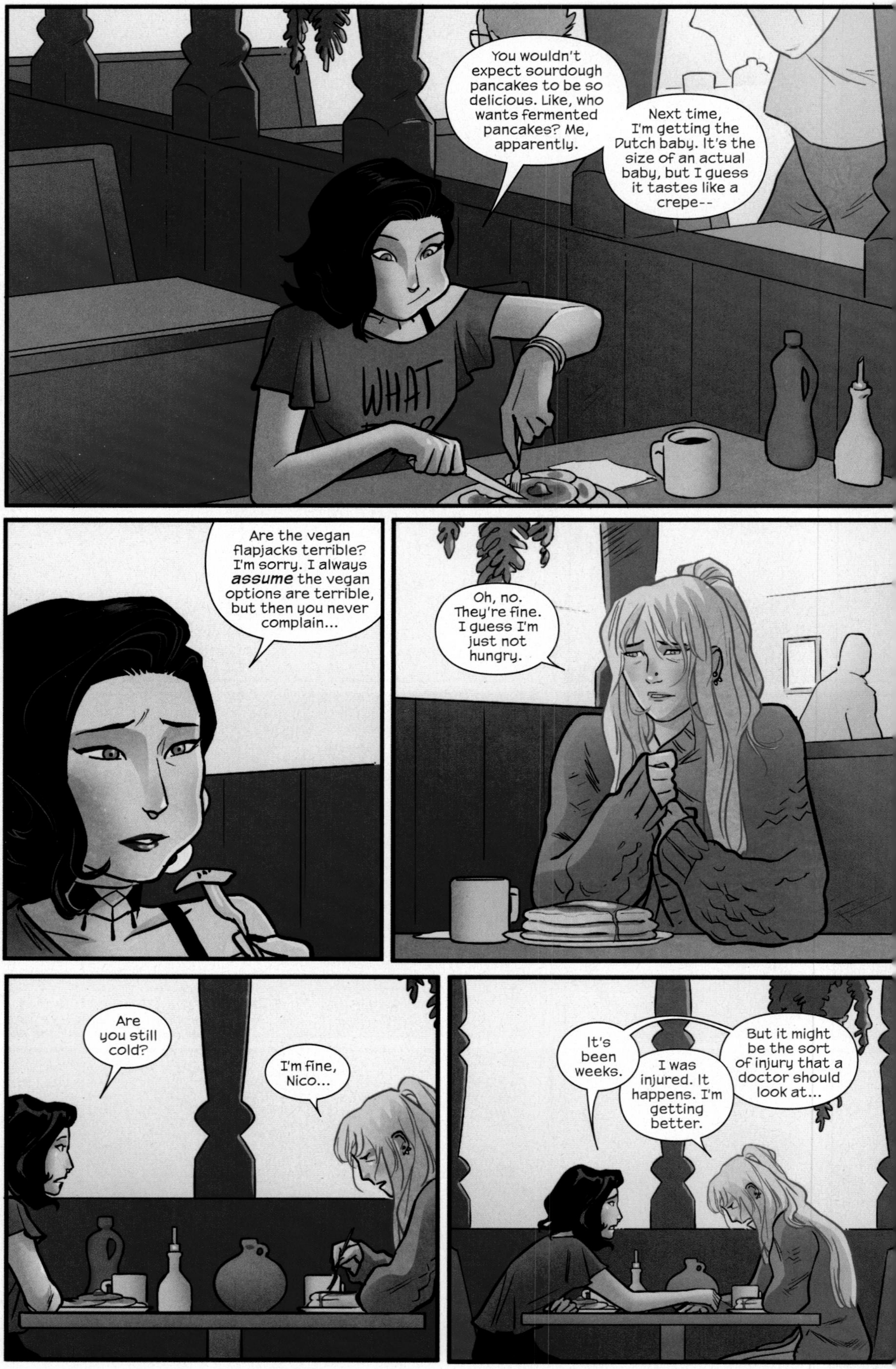
You wouldn't expect sourdough pancakes to be so delicious. Like, who wants fermented pancakes? Me, apparently.
Next time, I'm getting the Dutch baby. It's the size of an actual baby, but I guess it tastes like a crepe--
WHAT
Are the vegan flapjacks terrible? I'm sorry. I always *assume* the vegan options are terrible, but then you never complain...
Oh, no. They're fine. I guess I'm just not hungry.
Are you still cold?
I'm fine, Nico...
It's been weeks.
I was injured. It happens. I'm getting better.
But it might be the sort of injury that a doctor should look at...

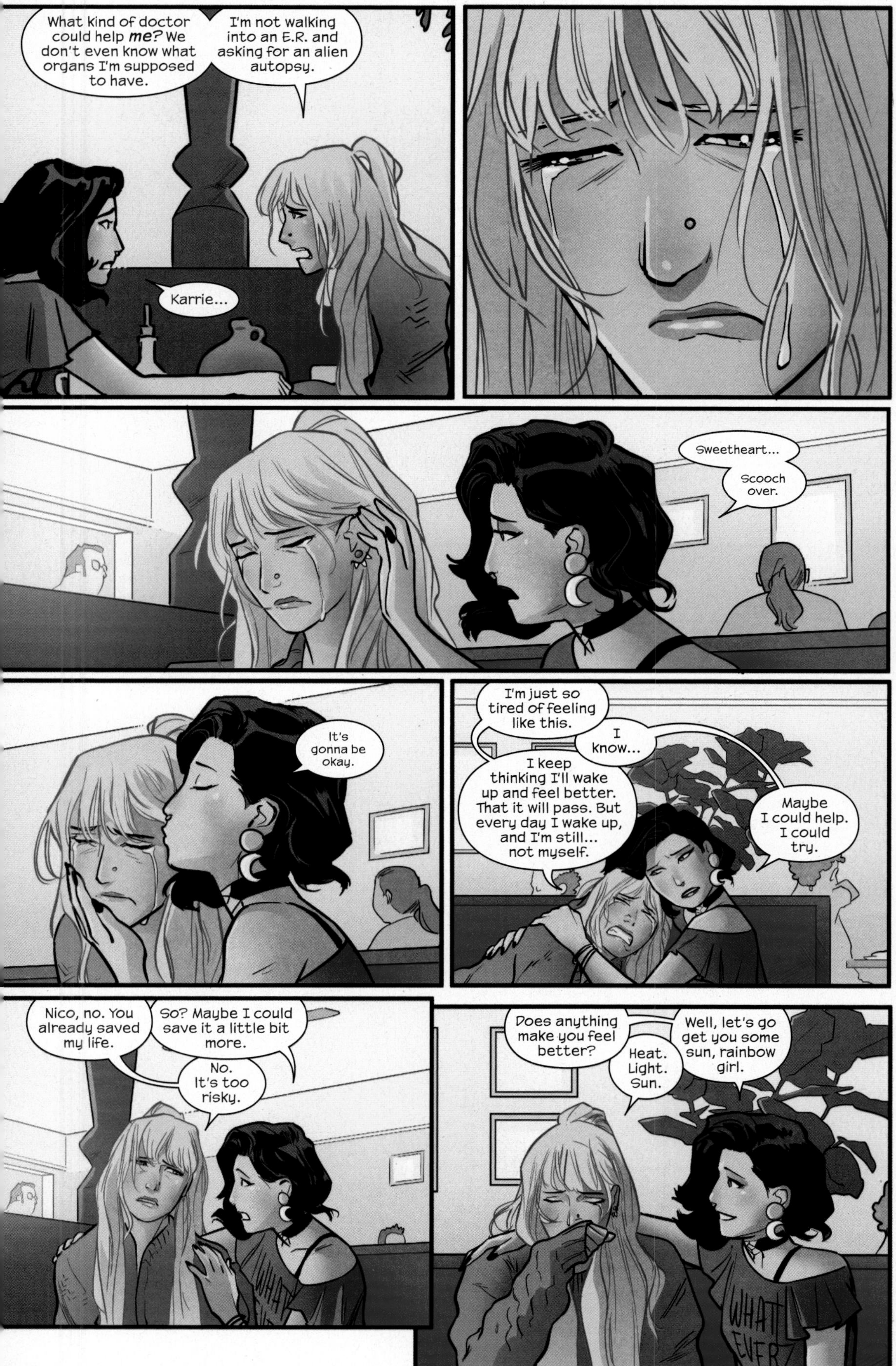
What kind of doctor could help *me?* We don't even know what organs I'm supposed to have.
I'm not walking into an E.R. and asking for an alien autopsy.
Karrie...
Sweetheart...
Scooch over.
It's gonna be okay.
I'm just so tired of feeling like this.
I know...
I keep thinking I'll wake up and feel better. That it will pass. But every day I wake up, and I'm still... not myself.
Maybe I could help. I could try.
Nico, no. You already saved my life.
So? Maybe I could save it a little bit more.
No. It's too risky.
Does anything make you feel better?
Heat. Light. Sun.
Well, let's go get you some sun, rainbow girl.

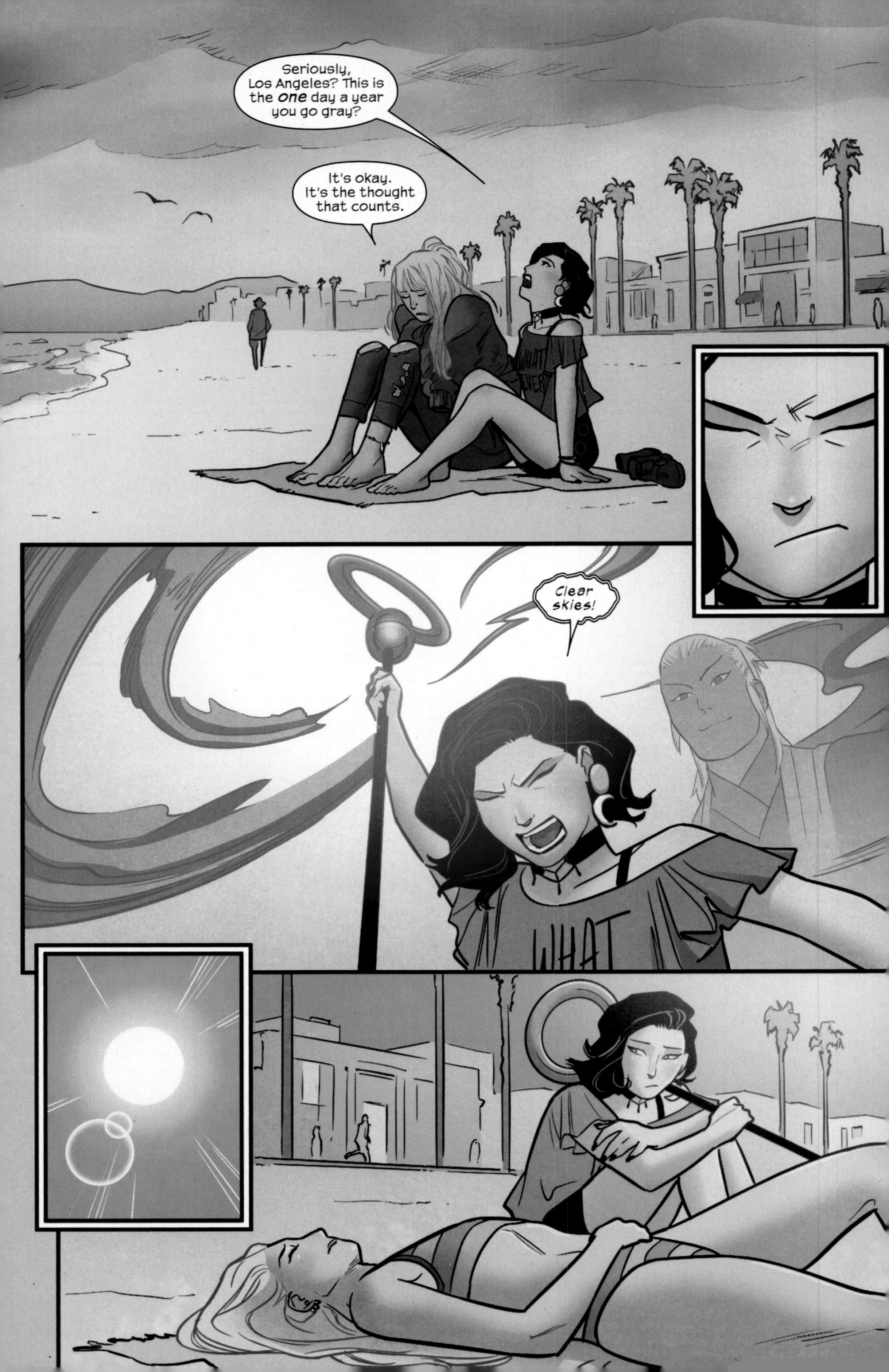
Seriously, Los Angeles? This is the *one* day a year you go gray?
It's okay. It's the thought that counts.
Clear skies!

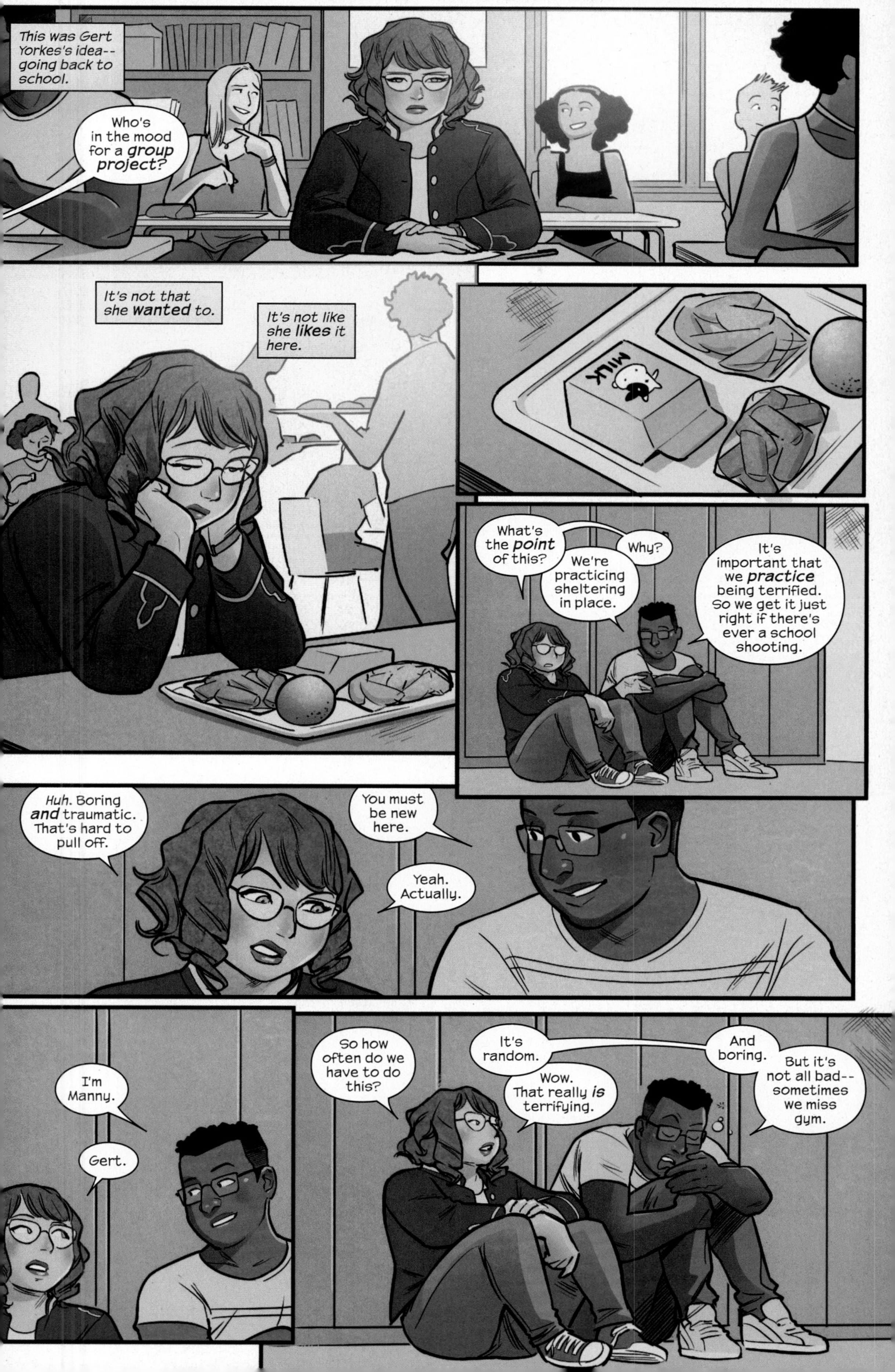
This was Gert Yorkes's idea--going back to school.
Who's in the mood for a group project?
It's not that she wanted to.
It's not like she likes it here.
MILK
What's the point of this?
Why?
We're practicing sheltering in place.
It's important that we practice being terrified. So we get it just right if there's ever a school shooting.
Huh. Boring and traumatic. That's hard to pull off.
You must be new here.
Yeah. Actually.
I'm Manny.
Gert.
So how often do we have to do this?
It's random.
And boring.
Wow. That really is terrifying.
But it's not all bad--sometimes we miss gym.

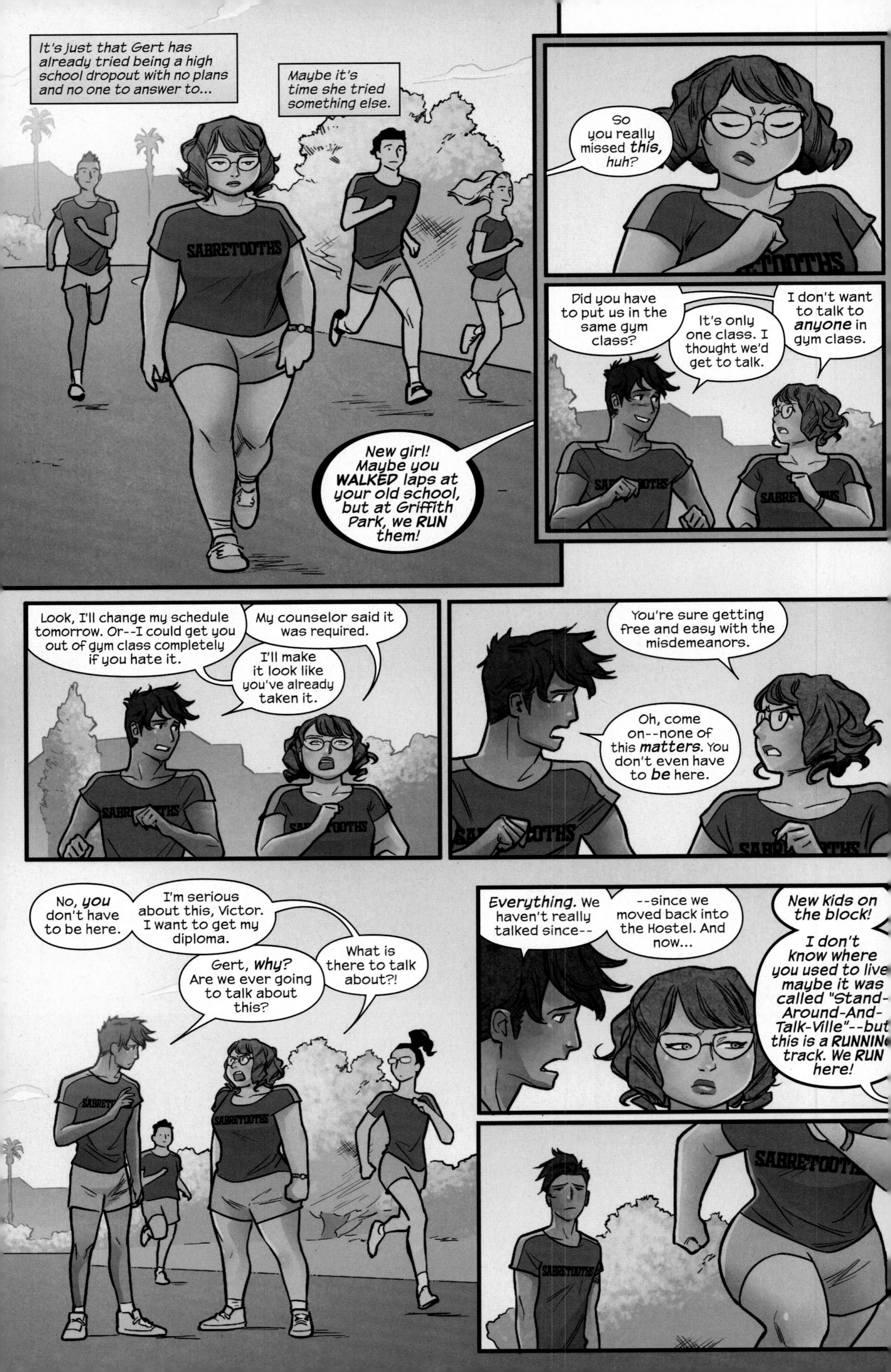

It's just that Gert has already tried being a high school dropout with no plans and no one to answer to...
Maybe it's time she tried something else.
SABRETOOTHS
New girl! Maybe you WALKED laps at your old school, but at Griffith Park, we RUN them!
So you really missed this, huh?
Did you have to put us in the same gym class?
It's only one class. I thought we'd get to talk.
I don't want to talk to anyone in gym class.
Look, I'll change my schedule tomorrow. Or--I could get you out of gym class completely if you hate it.
My counselor said it was required.
I'll make it look like you've already taken it.
You're sure getting free and easy with the misdemeanors.
Oh, come on--none of this matters. You don't even have to be here.
No, you don't have to be here.
I'm serious about this, Victor. I want to get my diploma.
Gert, why? Are we ever going to talk about this?
What is there to talk about?!
Everything. We haven't really talked since--
--since we moved back into the Hostel. And now...
New kids on the block!
I don't know where you used to live maybe it was called "Stand-Around-And-Talk-Ville"--but this is a RUNNING track. We RUN here!

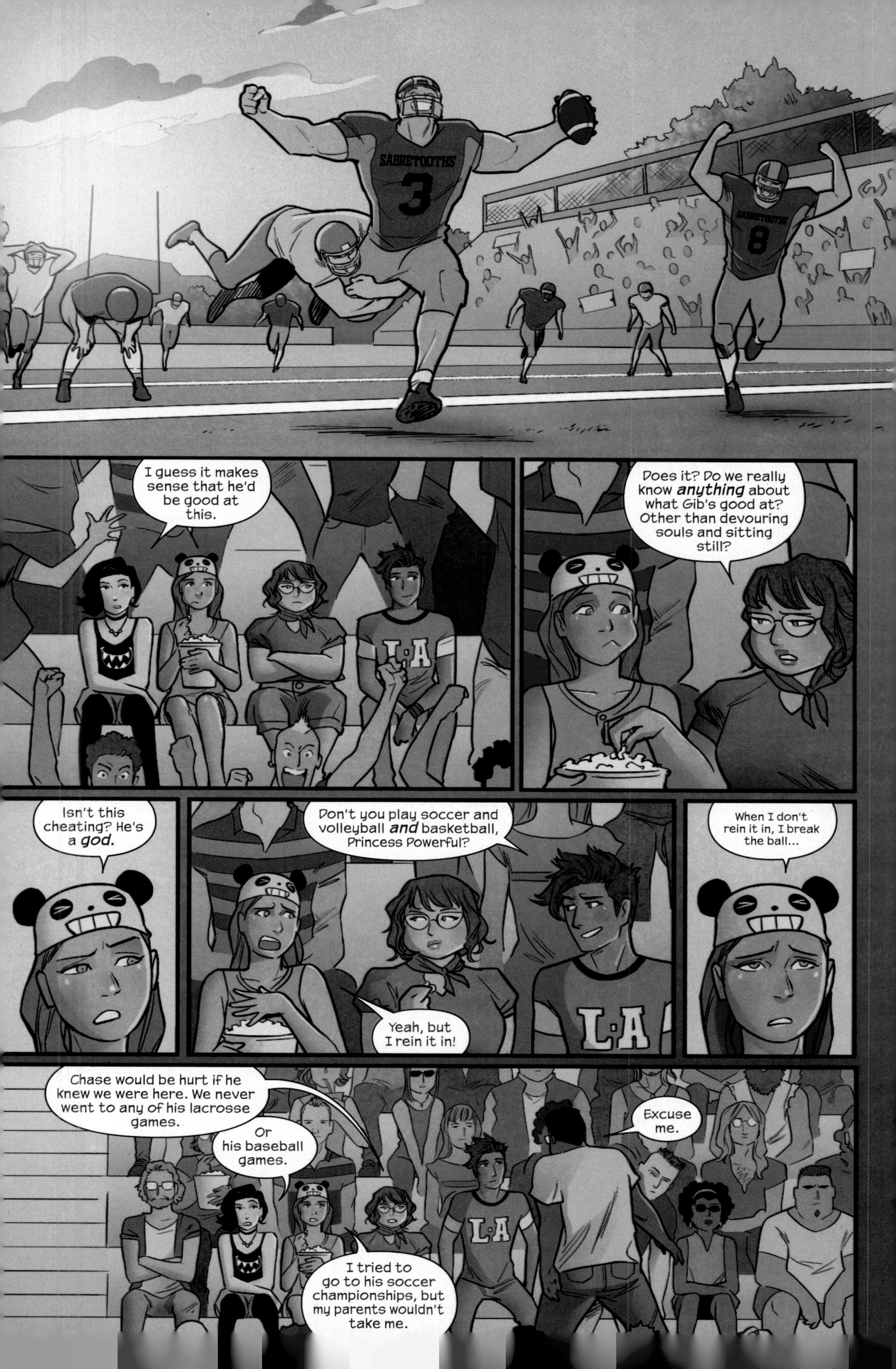

SABRETOOTHS 3
SABRETOOTHS 8
I guess it makes sense that he'd be good at this.
Does it? Do we really know *anything* about what Gib's good at? Other than devouring souls and sitting still?
Isn't this cheating? He's a *god.*
Don't you play soccer and volleyball *and* basketball, Princess Powerful?
Yeah, but I rein it in!
When I don't rein it in, I break the ball...
Chase would be hurt if he knew we were here. We never went to any of his lacrosse games.
Or his baseball games.
Excuse me.
I tried to go to his soccer championships, but my parents wouldn't take me.

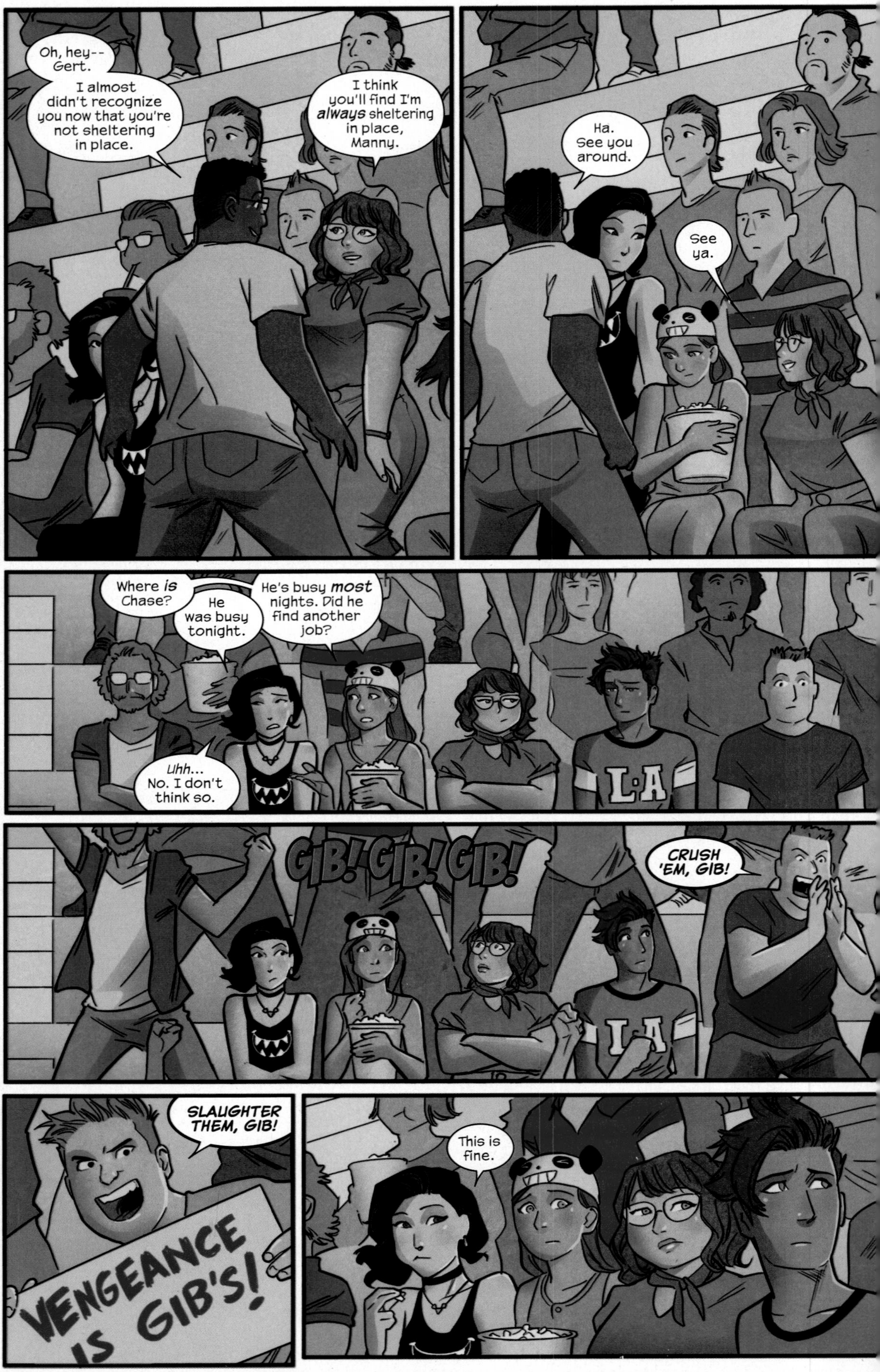

Oh, hey-- Gert.
I almost didn't recognize you now that you're not sheltering in place.
I think you'll find I'm *always* sheltering in place, Manny.
Ha. See you around.
See ya.
Where *is* Chase?
He was busy tonight.
He's busy *most* nights. Did he find another job?
Uhh... No. I don't think so.
GIB! GIB! GIB!
CRUSH 'EM, GIB!
SLAUGHTER THEM, GIB!
VENGEANCE IS GIB'S!
This is fine.

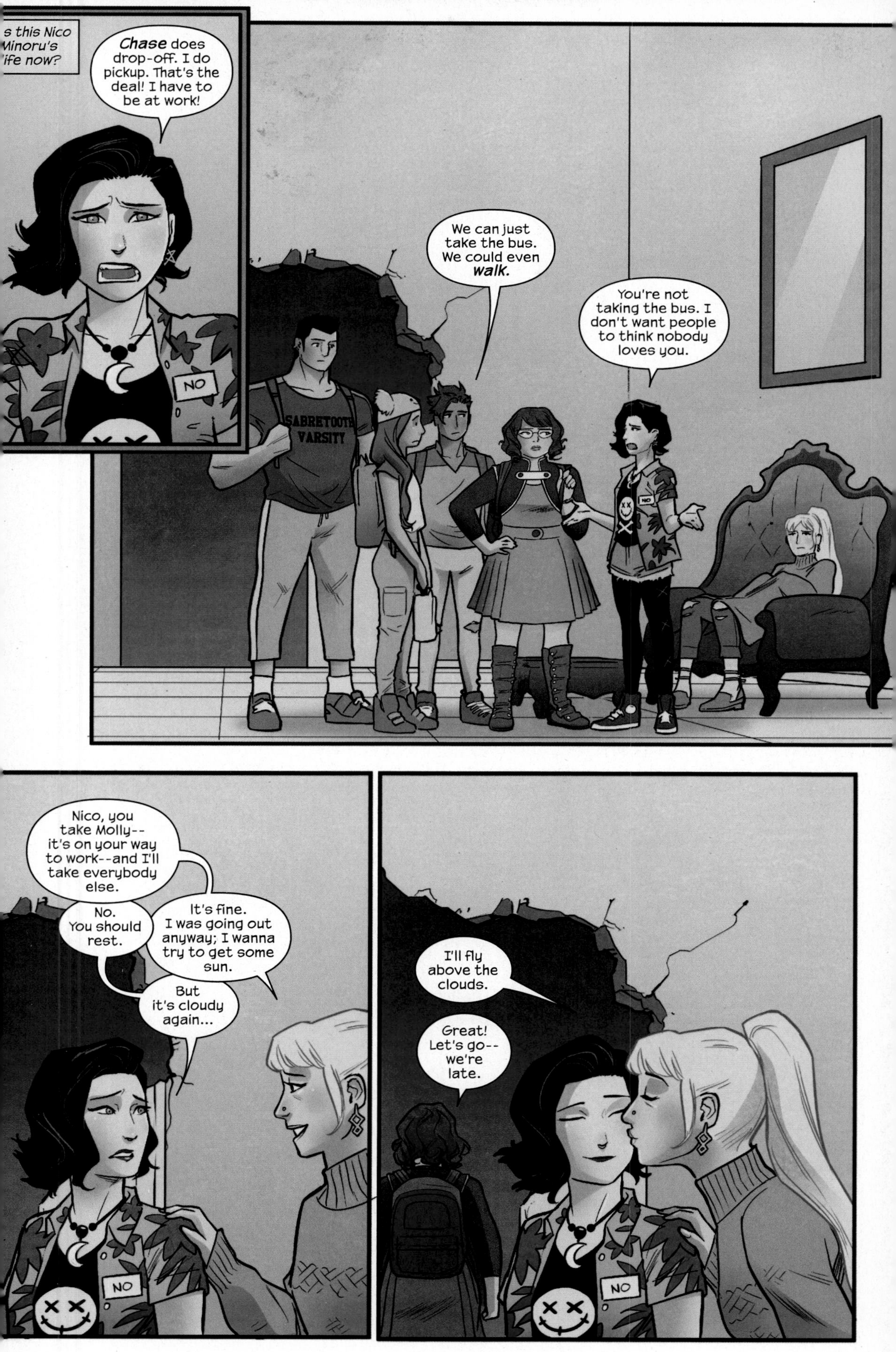

s this Nico Minoru's ife now?
Chase does drop-off. I do pickup. That's the deal! I have to be at work!
NO
SABRETOOTH VARSITY
We can just take the bus. We could even walk.
You're not taking the bus. I don't want people to think nobody loves you.
Nico, you take Molly-- it's on your way to work--and I'll take everybody else.
No. You should rest.
It's fine. I was going out anyway; I wanna try to get some sun.
But it's cloudy again...
NO
I'll fly above the clouds.
Great! Let's go-- we're late.
NO

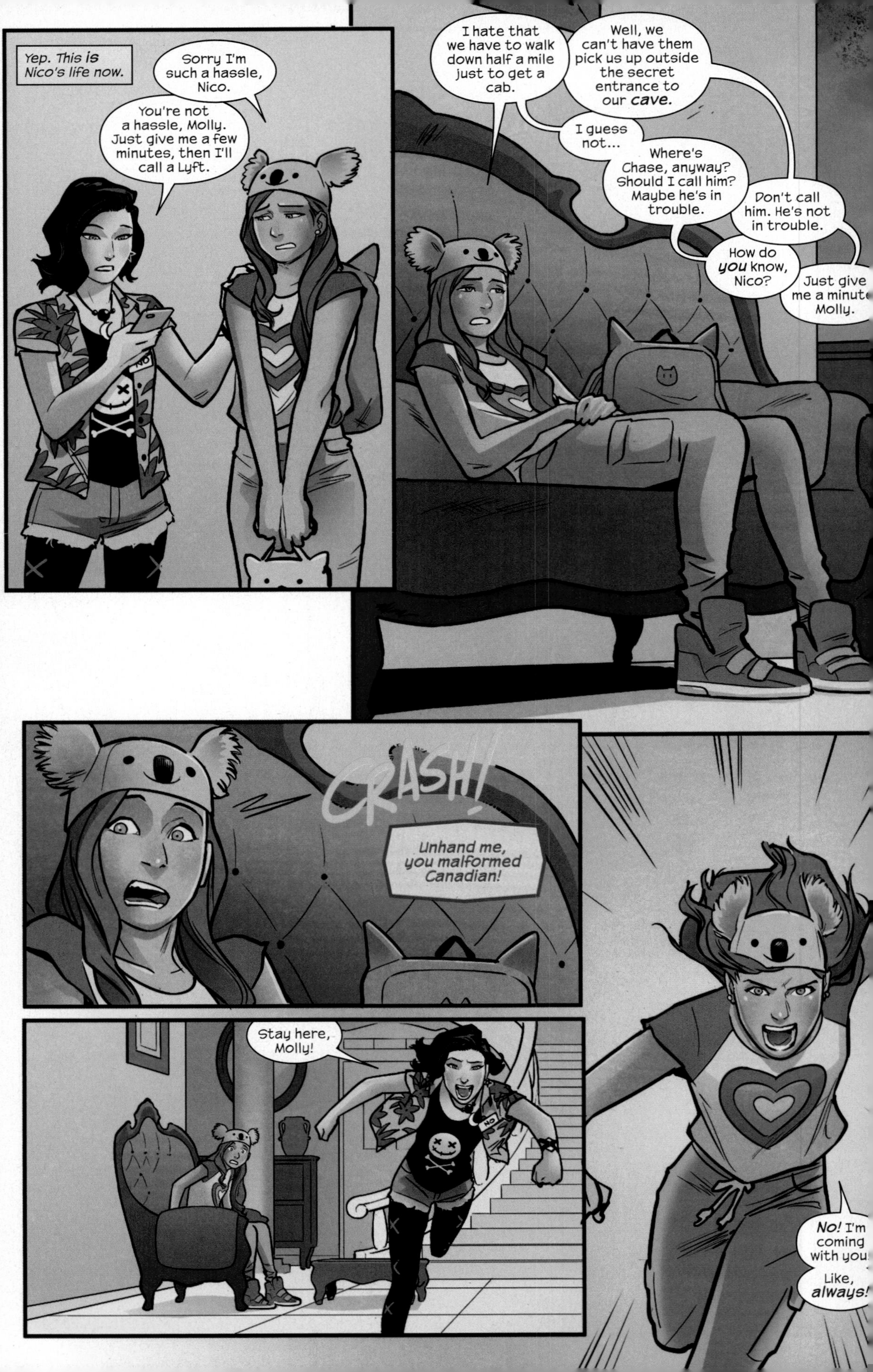
Yep. This *is* Nico's life now.
Sorry I'm such a hassle, Nico.
You're not a hassle, Molly. Just give me a few minutes, then I'll call a Lyft.
NO
I hate that we have to walk down half a mile just to get a cab.
Well, we can't have them pick us up outside the secret entrance to our *cave.*
I guess not...
Where's Chase, anyway? Should I call him? Maybe he's in trouble.
Don't call him. He's not in trouble.
How do *you* know, Nico?
Just give me a minute, Molly.
CRASH!
Unhand me, you malformed Canadian!
Stay here, Molly!
NO
No! I'm coming with you!
Like, *always!*

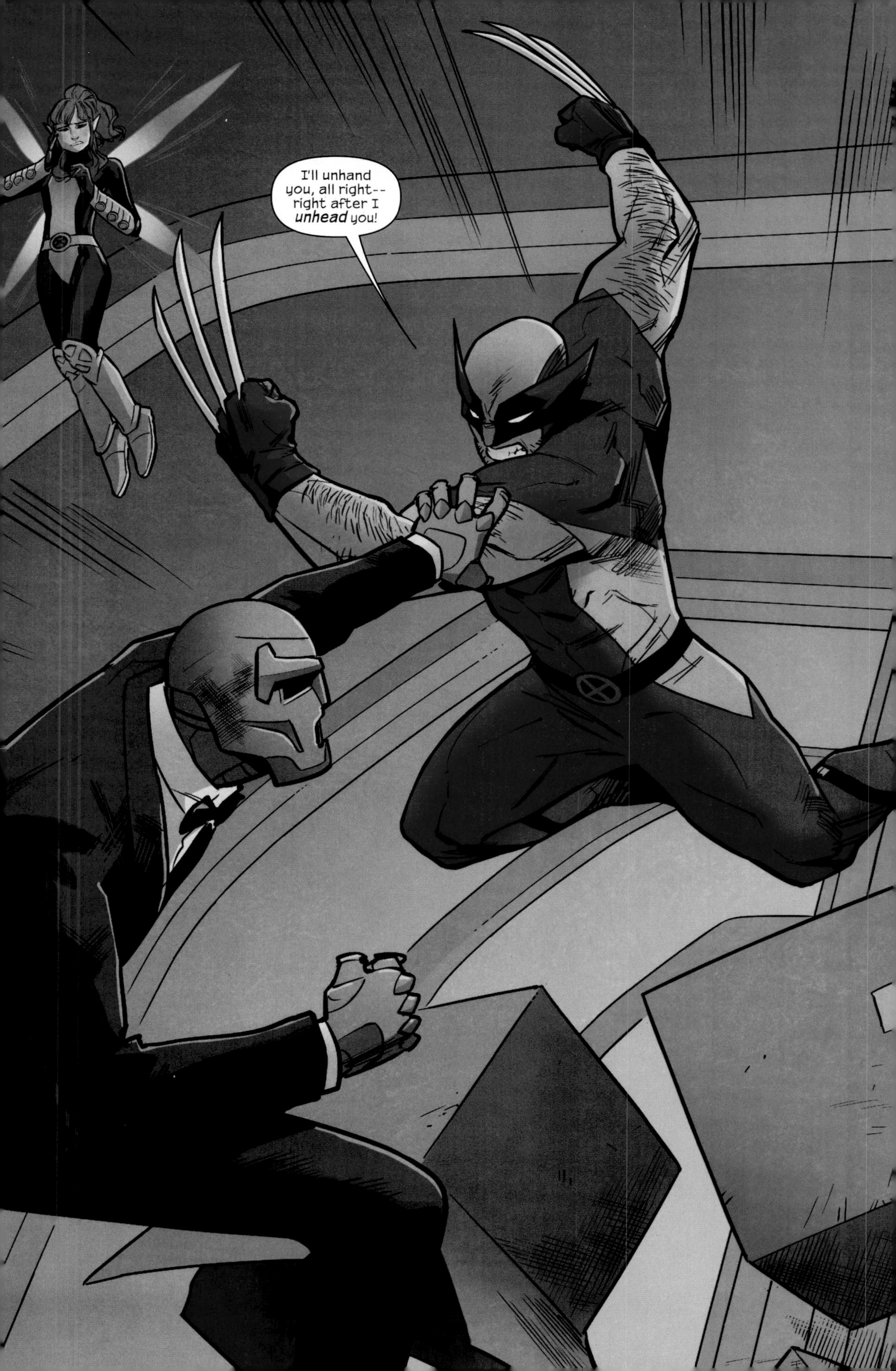
I'll unhand you, all right--right after I *unhead* you!

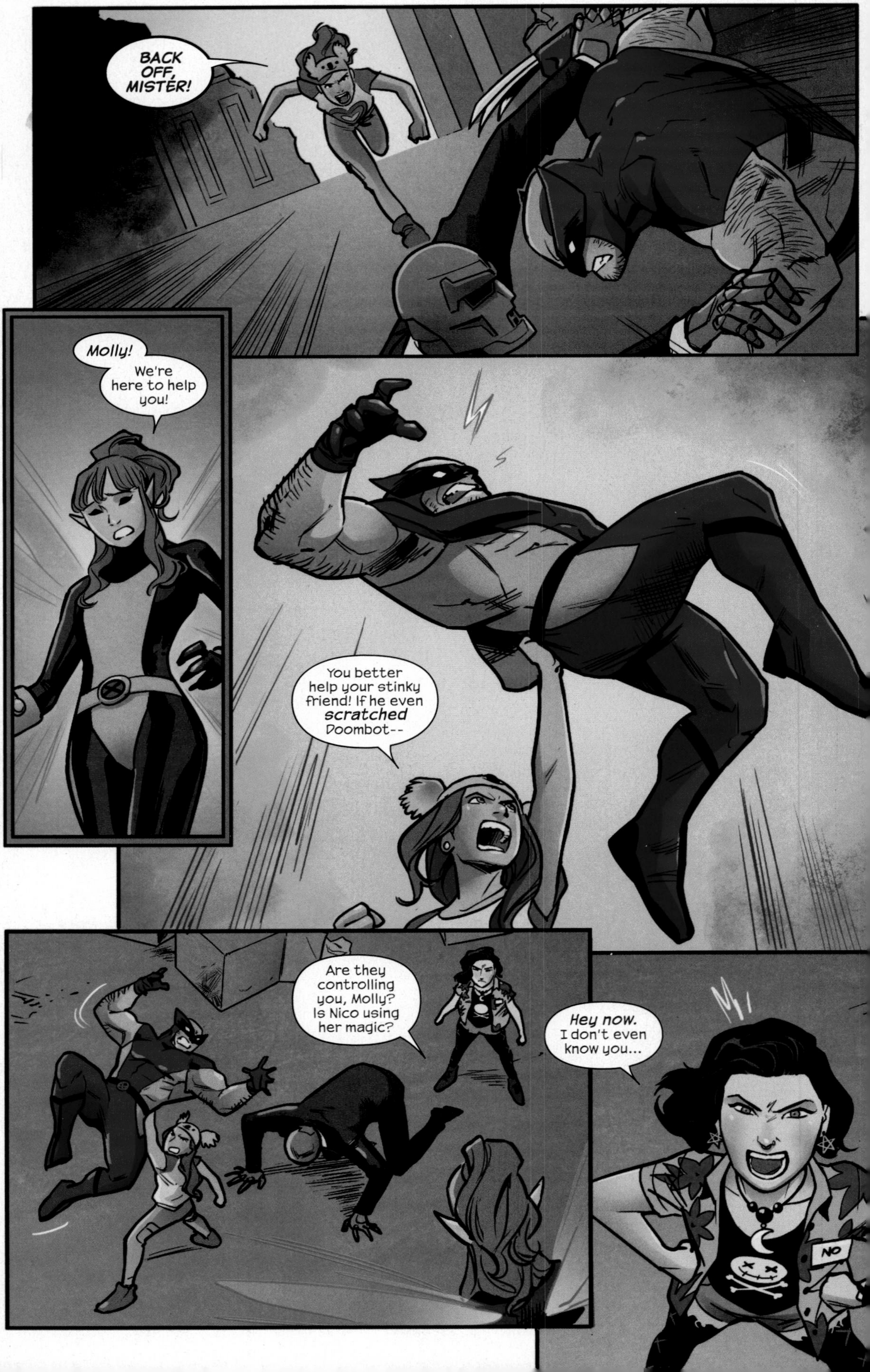
BACK OFF, MISTER!
Molly! We're here to help you!
You better help your stinky friend! If he even *scratched* Doombot--
Are they controlling you, Molly? Is Nico using her magic?
Hey now. I don't even know you...
NO

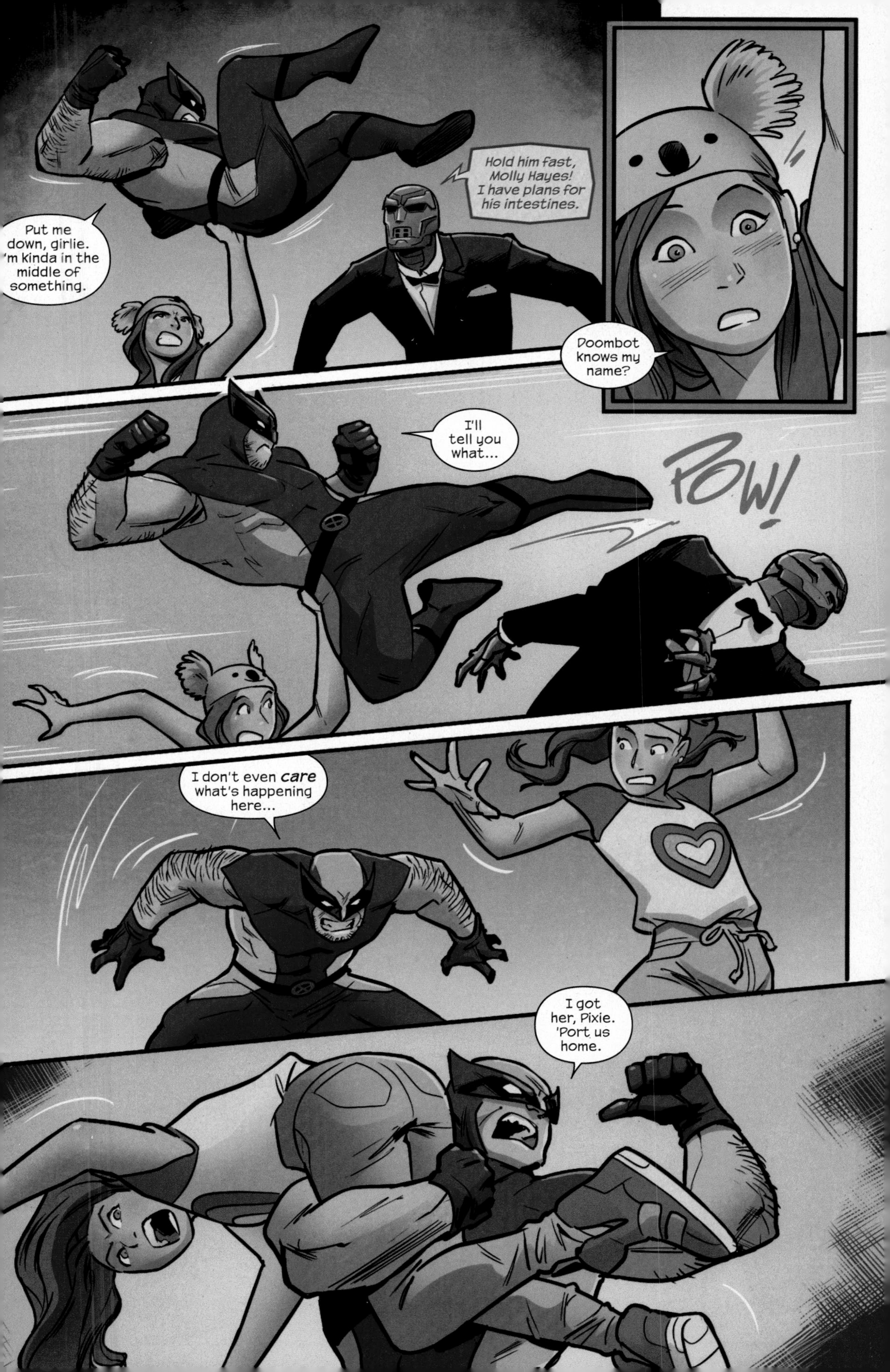

Put me down, girlie. 'm kinda in the middle of something.
Hold him fast, Molly Hayes! I have plans for his intestines.
Doombot knows my name?
I'll tell you what...
POW!
I don't even care what's happening here...
I got her, Pixie. 'Port us home.

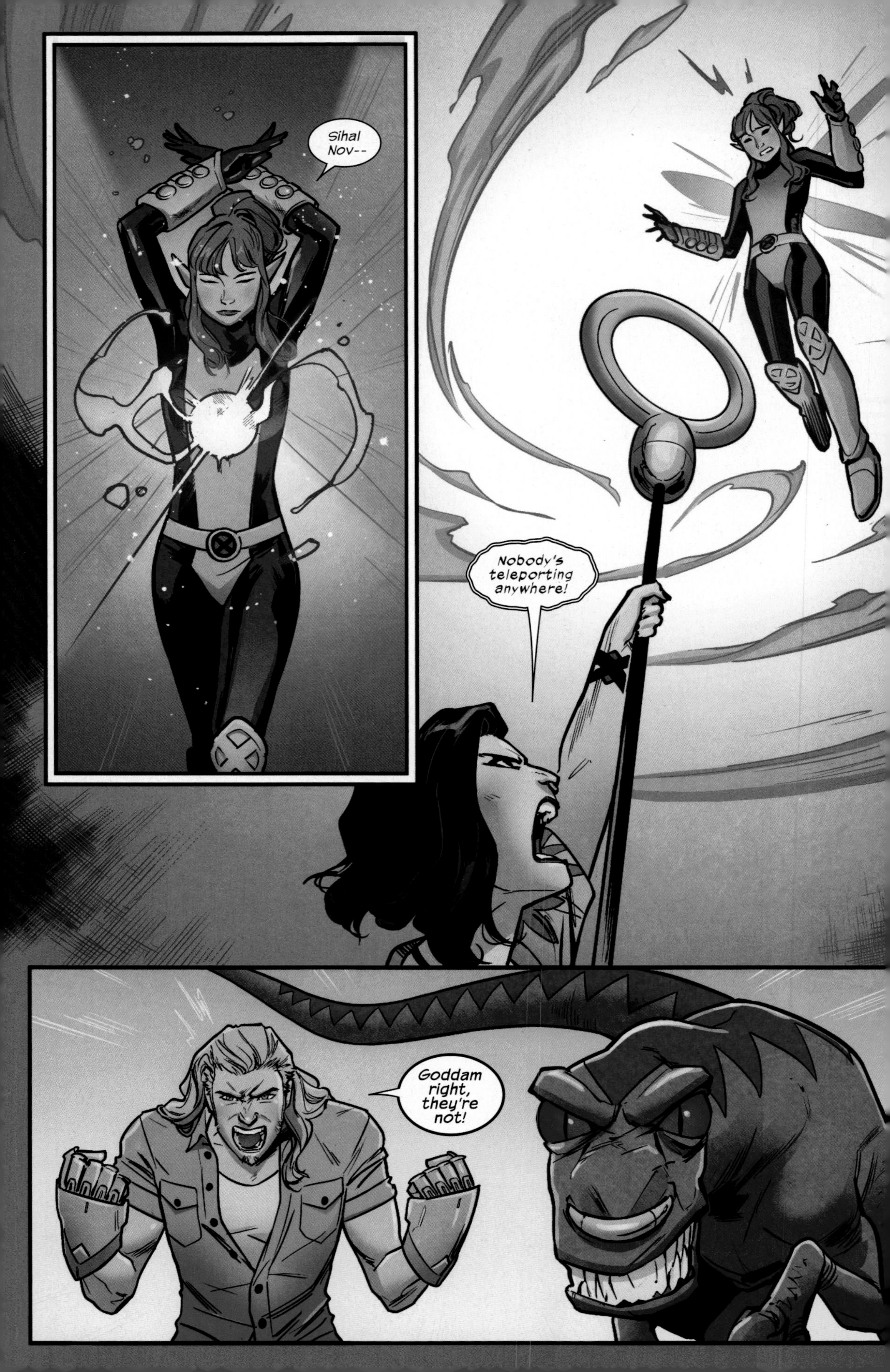
Sihal Nov--
Nobody's teleporting anywhere!
Goddam right, they're not!

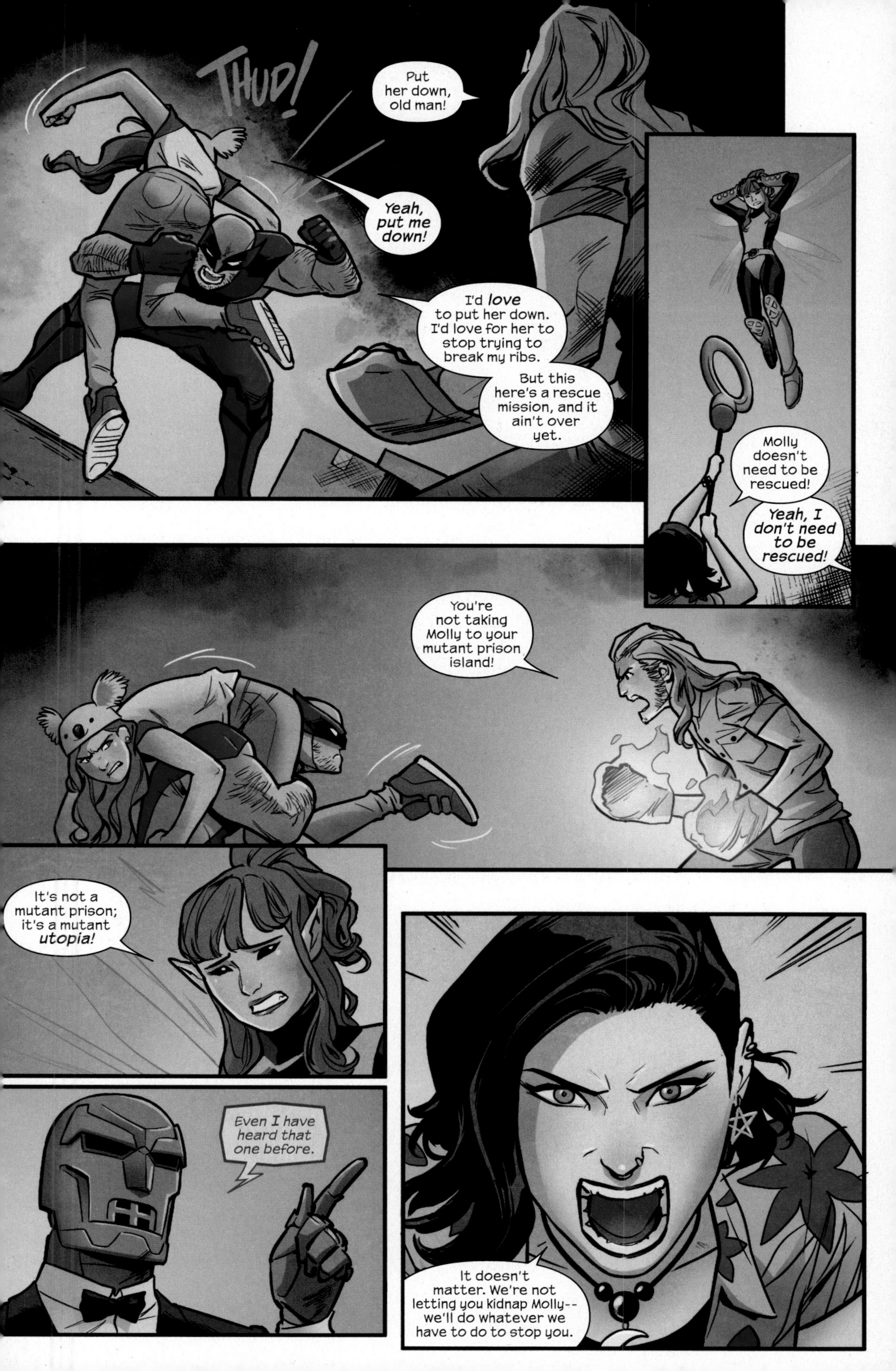
THUD!
Put her down, old man!
Yeah, put me down!
I'd *love* to put her down. I'd love for her to stop trying to break my ribs.
But this here's a rescue mission, and it ain't over yet.
Molly doesn't need to be rescued!
Yeah, I don't need to be rescued!
You're not taking Molly to your mutant prison island!
It's not a mutant prison; it's a mutant *utopia!*
Even I have heard that one before.
It doesn't matter. We're not letting you kidnap Molly-- we'll do whatever we have to do to stop you.

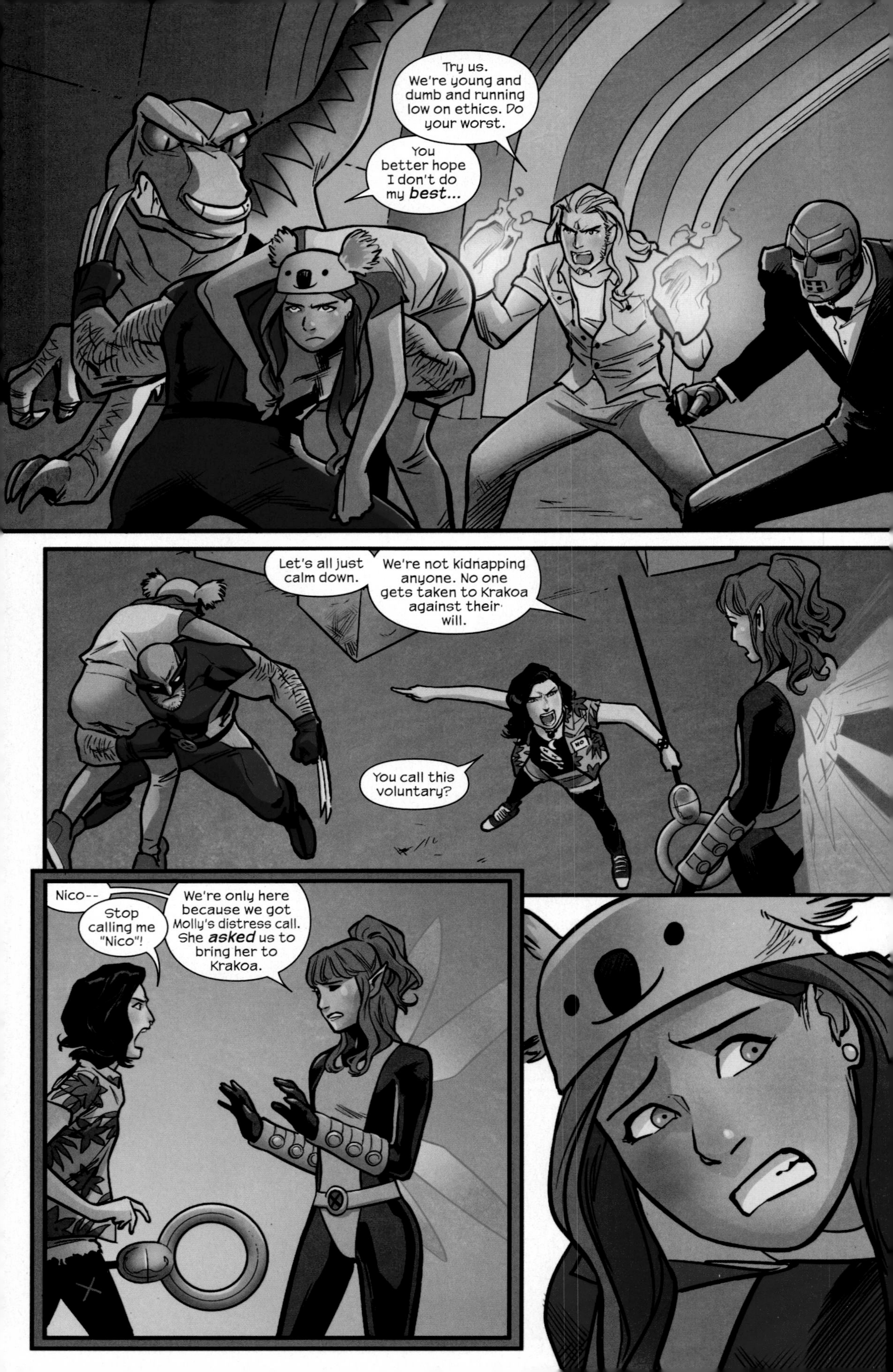

Try us. We're young and dumb and running low on ethics. Do your worst.
You better hope I don't do my **best...**
Let's all just calm down.
We're not kidnapping anyone. No one gets taken to Krakoa against their will.
You call this voluntary?
Nico--
Stop calling me "Nico"!
We're only here because we got Molly's distress call. She **asked** us to bring her to Krakoa.

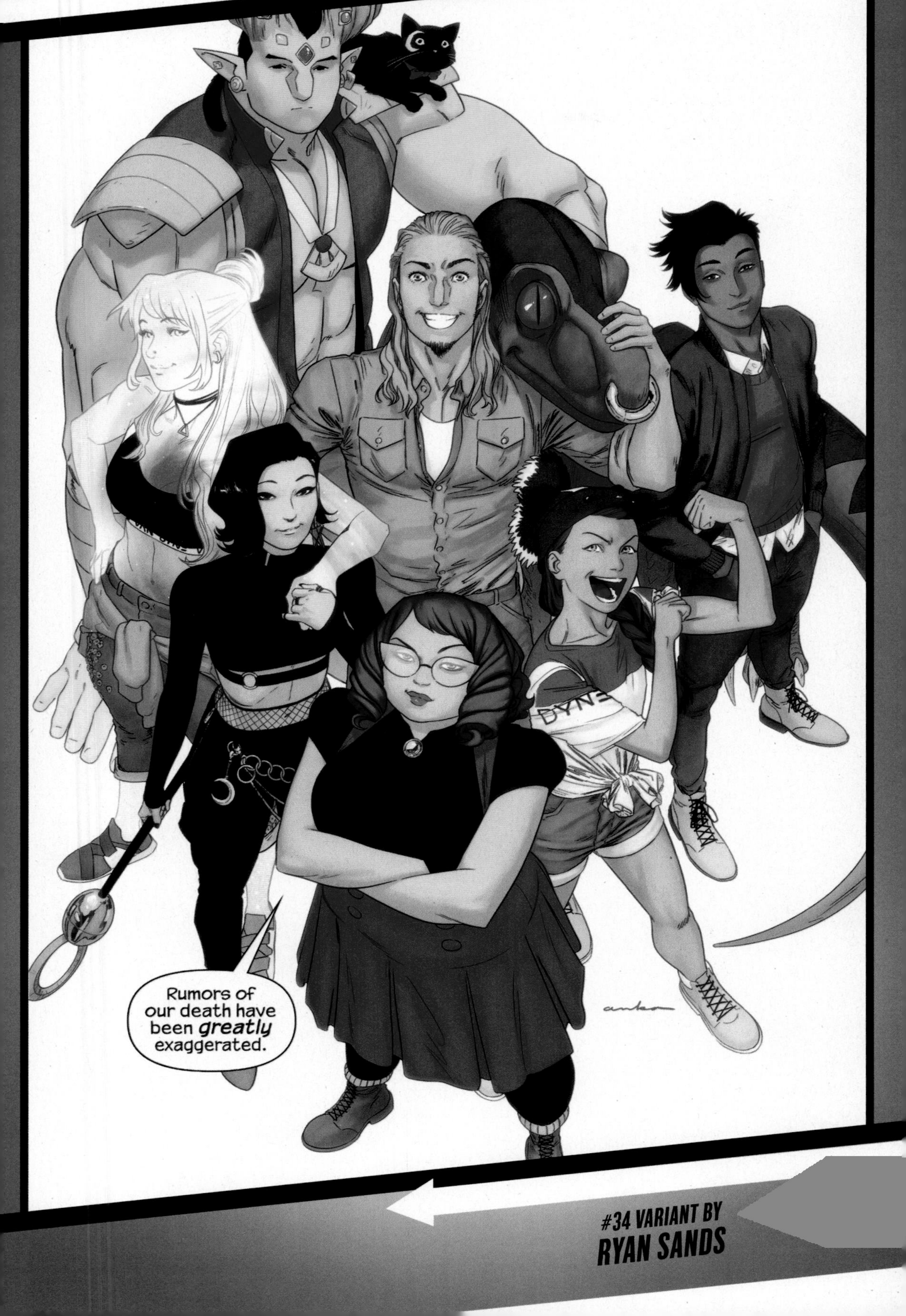
Rumors of our death have been *greatly* exaggerated.
DYNE

#34 VARIANT BY
RYAN SANDS

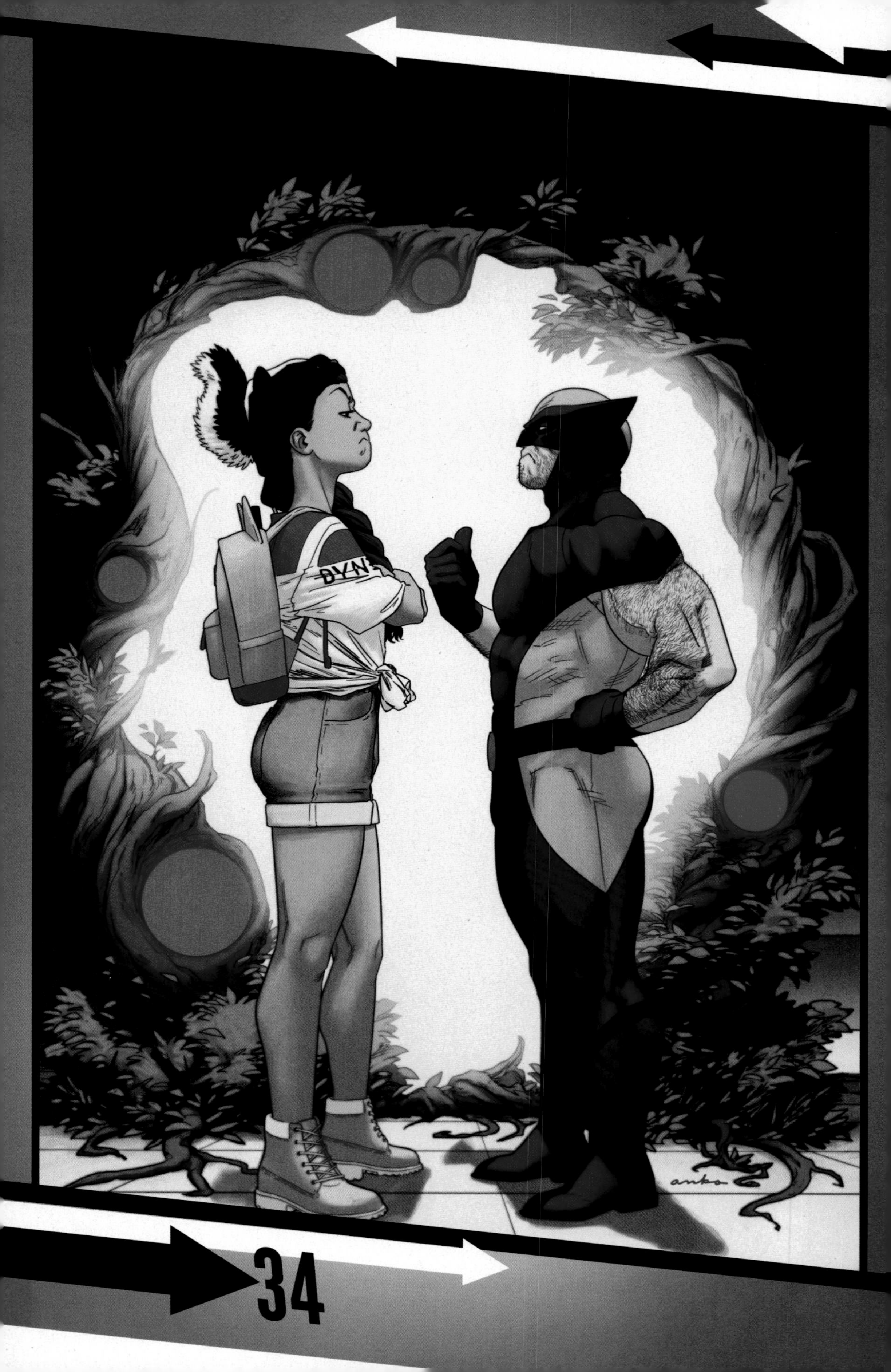
DYN
anka
34

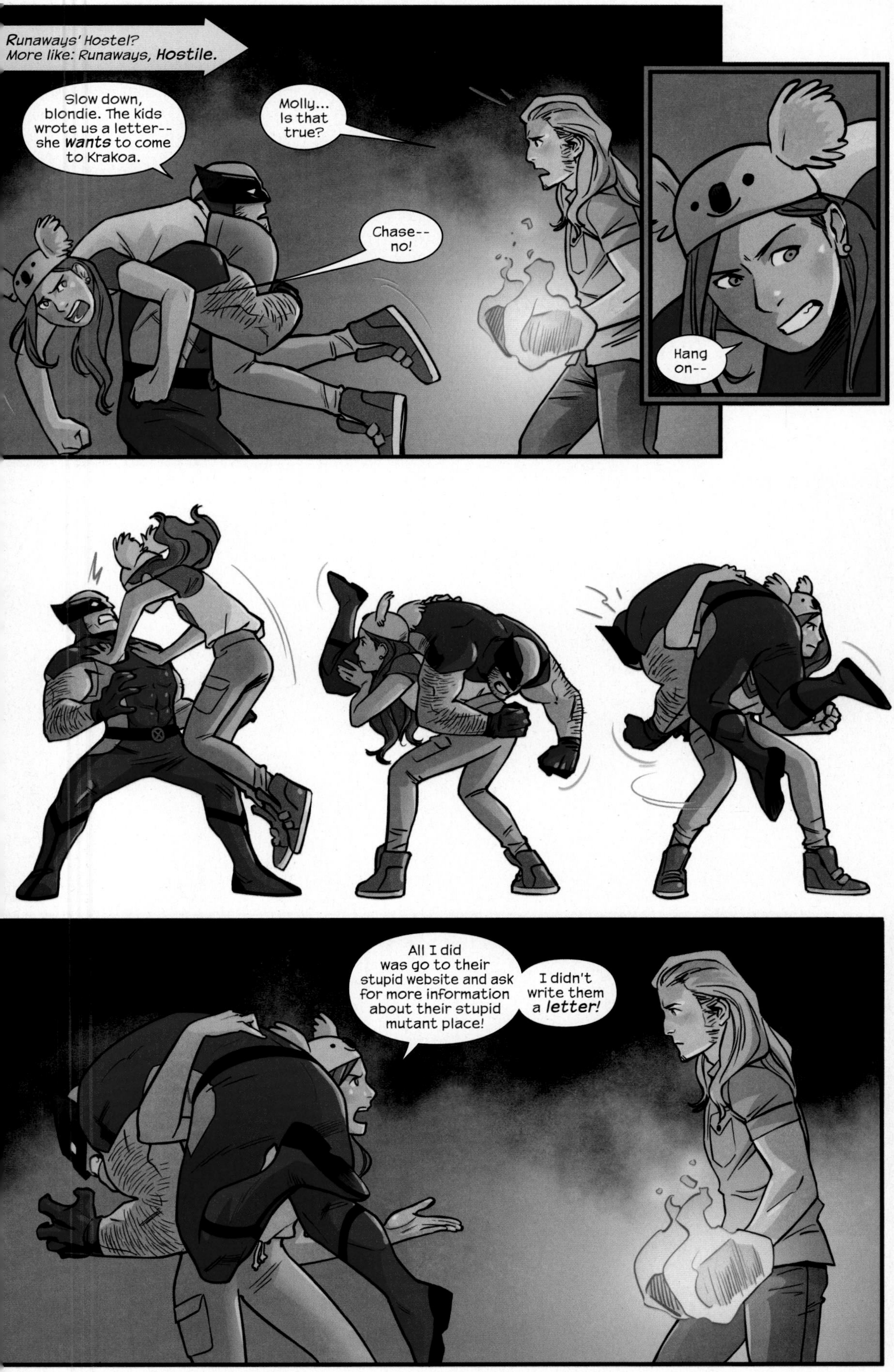
Runaways' Hostel?
More like: Runaways, Hostile.
Slow down, blondie. The kids wrote us a letter--she wants to come to Krakoa.
Molly... Is that true?
Chase--no!
Hang on--
All I did was go to their stupid website and ask for more information about their stupid mutant place!
I didn't write them a letter!

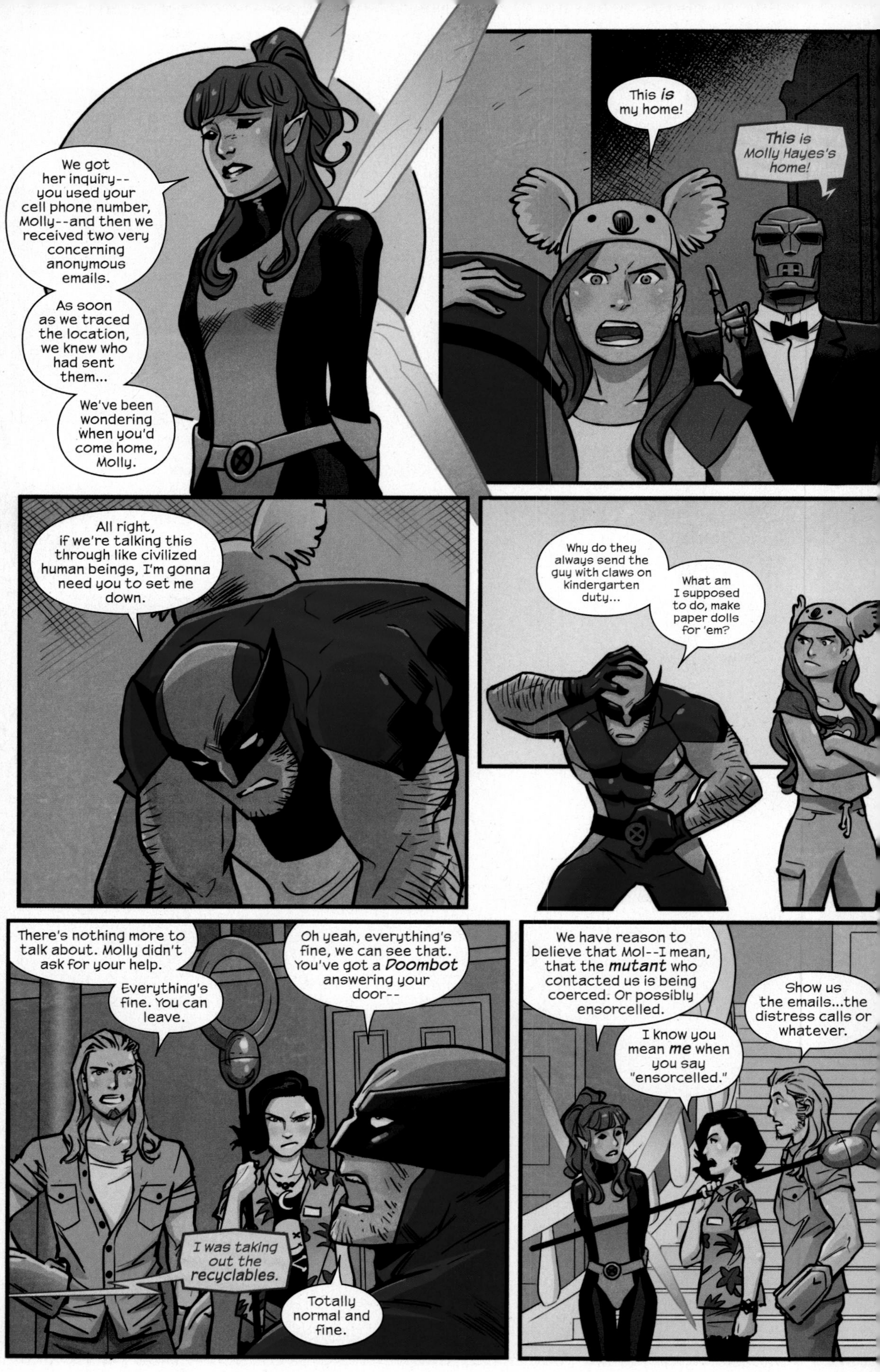
We got her inquiry--you used your cell phone number, Molly--and then we received two very concerning anonymous emails.
As soon as we traced the location, we knew who had sent them...
We've been wondering when you'd come home, Molly.
This *is* my home!
This is Molly Hayes's home!
All right, if we're talking this through like civilized human beings, I'm gonna need you to set me down.
Why do they always send the guy with claws on kindergarten duty...
What am I supposed to do, make paper dolls for 'em?
There's nothing more to talk about. Molly didn't ask for your help.
Everything's fine. You can leave.
Oh yeah, everything's fine, we can see that. You've got a ***Doombot*** answering your door--
I was taking out the recyclables.
Totally normal and fine.
We have reason to believe that Mol--I mean, that the ***mutant*** who contacted us is being coerced. Or possibly ensorcelled.
I know you mean ***me*** when you say "ensorcelled."
Show us the emails...the distress calls or whatever.

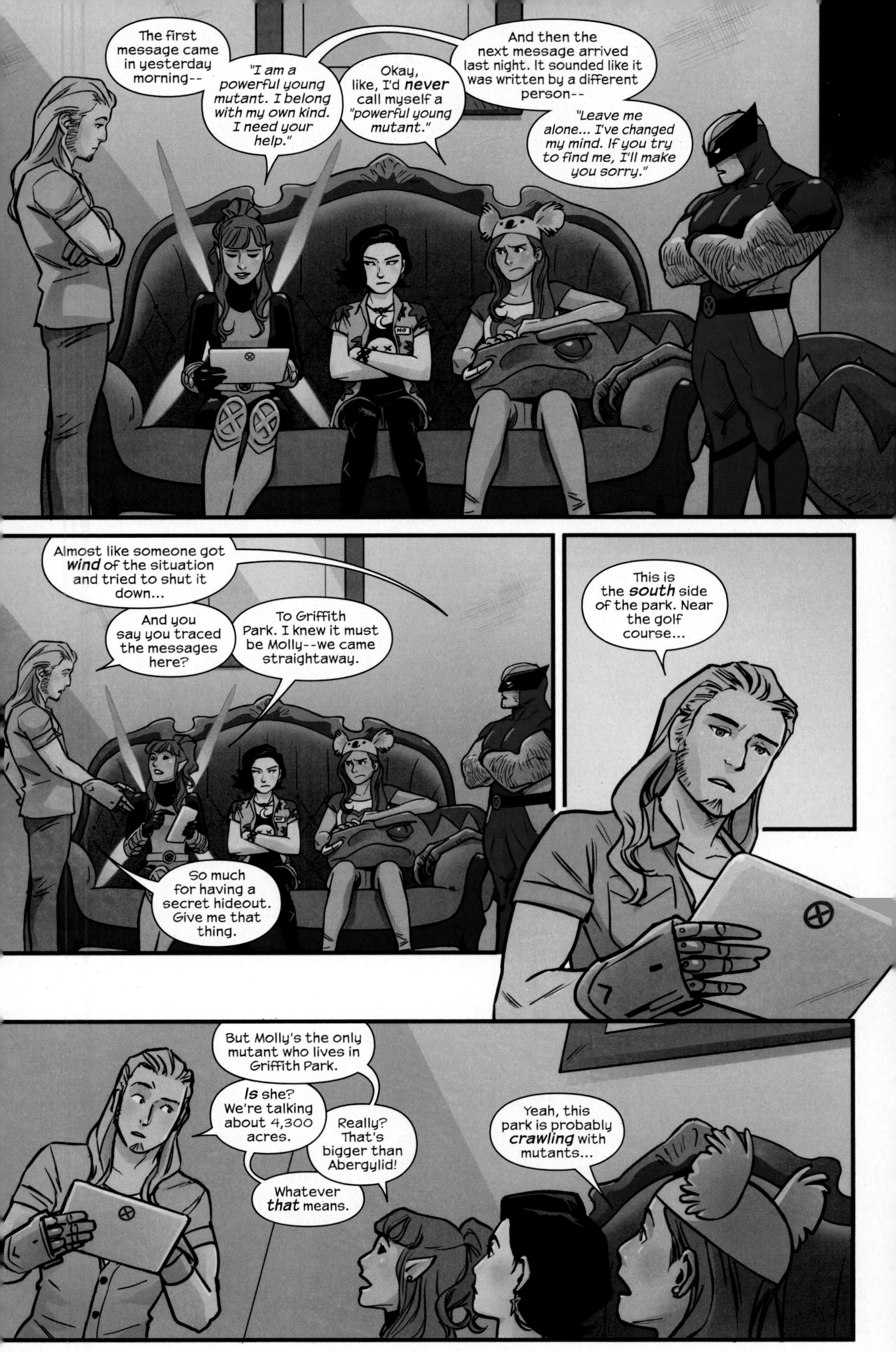
The first message came in yesterday morning--
"I am a powerful young mutant. I belong with my own kind. I need your help."
Okay, like, I'd *never* call myself a "powerful young mutant."
And then the next message arrived last night. It sounded like it was written by a different person--
"Leave me alone... I've changed my mind. If you try to find me, I'll make you sorry."
Almost like someone got *wind* of the situation and tried to shut it down...
And you say you traced the messages here?
To Griffith Park. I knew it must be Molly--we came straightaway.
So much for having a secret hideout. Give me that thing.
This is the *south* side of the park. Near the golf course...
But Molly's the only mutant who lives in Griffith Park.
Is she? We're talking about 4,300 acres.
Really? That's bigger than Abergylid!
Whatever *that* means.
Yeah, this park is probably *crawling* with mutants...

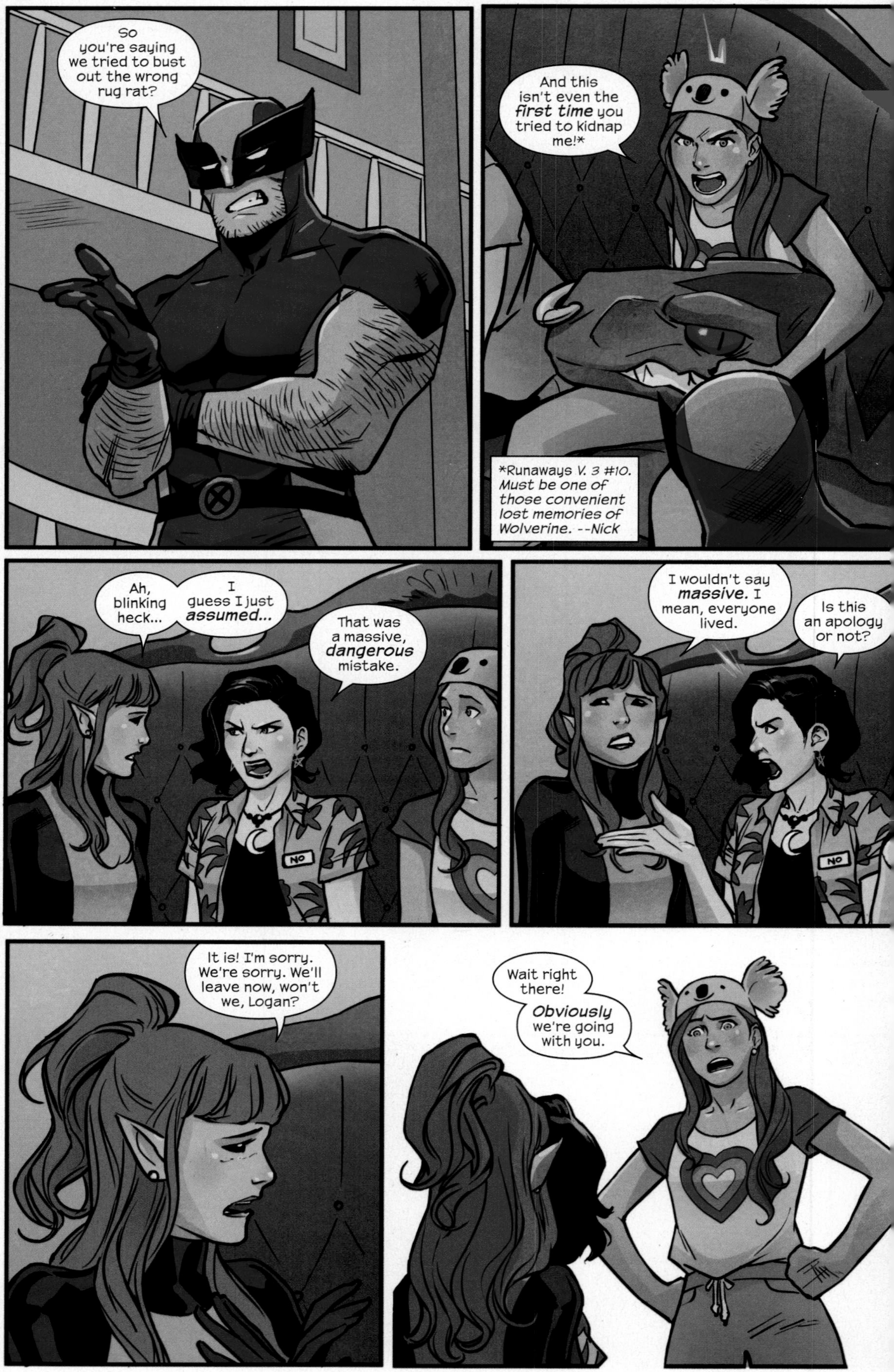

So you're saying we tried to bust out the wrong rug rat?
And this isn't even the *first time* you tried to kidnap me!*
*Runaways V. 3 #10. Must be one of those convenient lost memories of Wolverine. --Nick
Ah, blinking heck...
I guess I just *assumed...*
That was a massive, *dangerous* mistake.
NO
I wouldn't say *massive.* I mean, everyone lived.
Is this an apology or not?
NO
It is! I'm sorry. We're sorry. We'll leave now, won't we, Logan?
Wait right there! *Obviously* we're going with you.

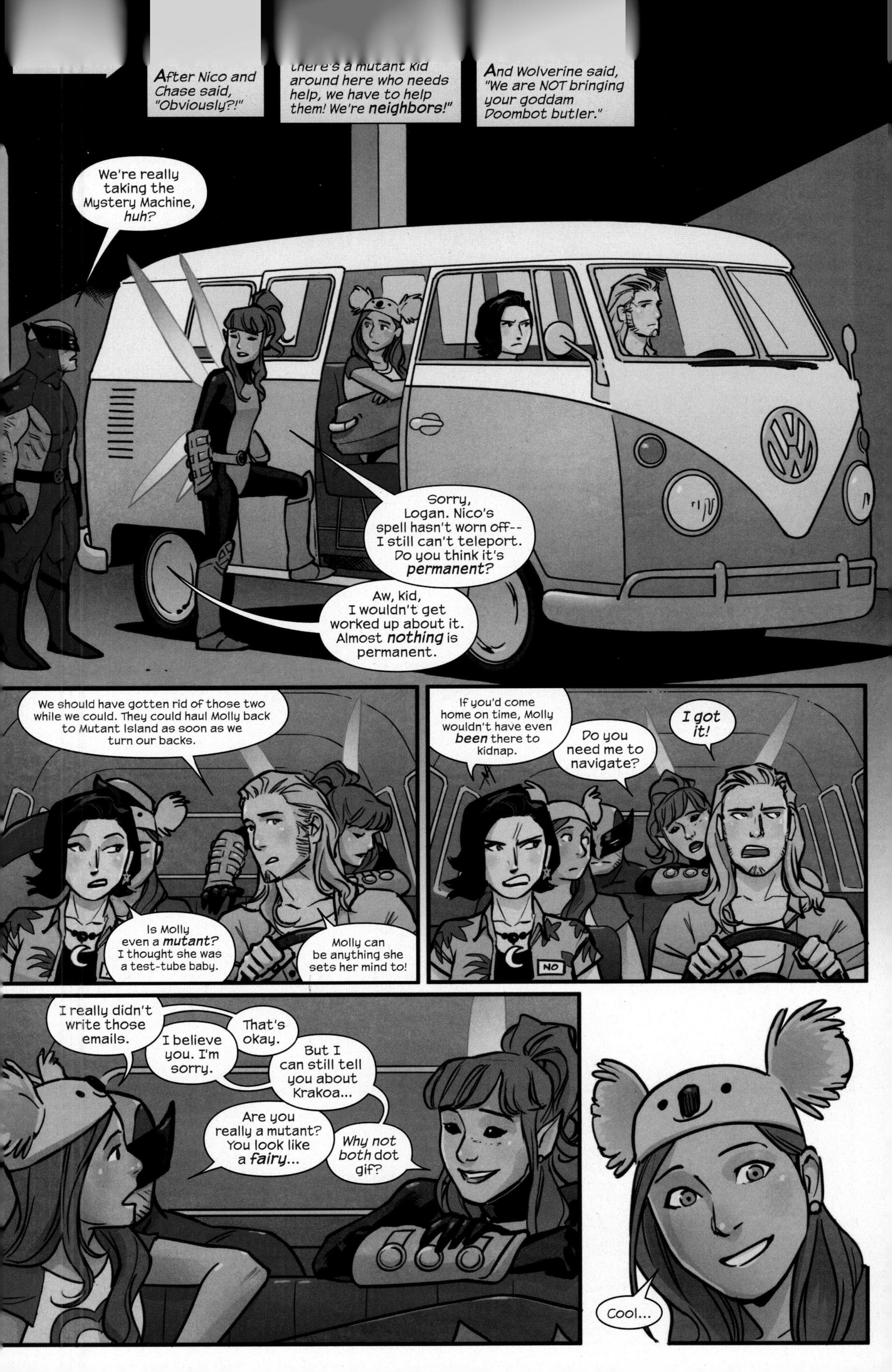
After Nico and Chase said, "Obviously?!"
there's a mutant kid around here who needs help, we have to help them! We're neighbors!"
And Wolverine said, "We are NOT bringing your goddam Doombot butler."
We're really taking the Mystery Machine, huh?
Sorry, Logan. Nico's spell hasn't worn off-- I still can't teleport. Do you think it's permanent?
Aw, kid, I wouldn't get worked up about it. Almost nothing is permanent.
We should have gotten rid of those two while we could. They could haul Molly back to Mutant Island as soon as we turn our backs.
Is Molly even a mutant? I thought she was a test-tube baby.
Molly can be anything she sets her mind to!
If you'd come home on time, Molly wouldn't have even been there to kidnap.
Do you need me to navigate?
I got it!
NO
I really didn't write those emails.
I believe you. I'm sorry.
That's okay.
But I can still tell you about Krakoa...
Are you really a mutant? You look like a fairy...
Why not both dot gif?
Cool...

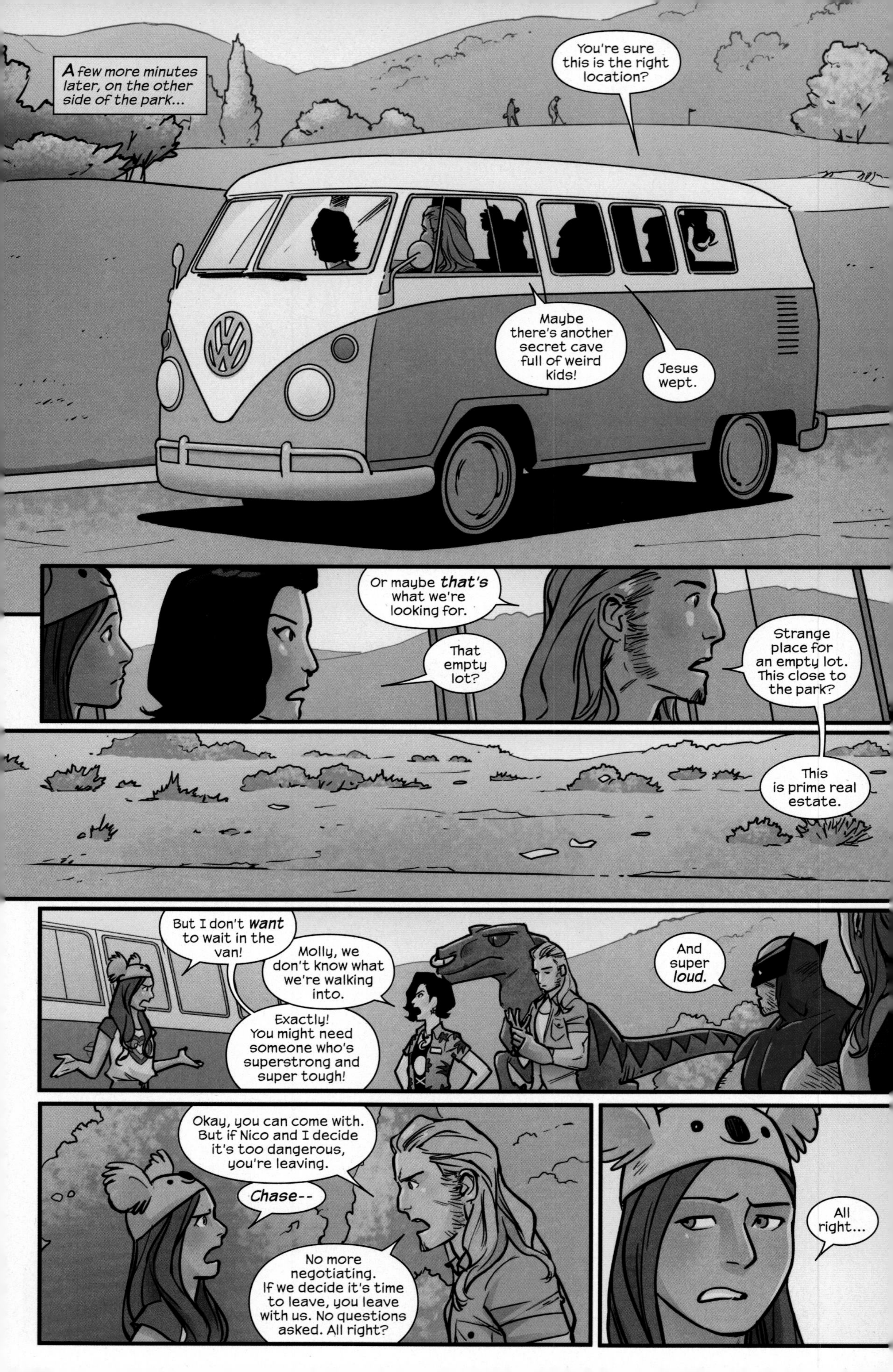
A few more minutes later, on the other side of the park...
You're sure this is the right location?
Maybe there's another secret cave full of weird kids!
Jesus wept.
Or maybe *that's* what we're looking for.
That empty lot?
Strange place for an empty lot. This close to the park?
This is prime real estate.
But I don't *want* to wait in the van!
Molly, we don't know what we're walking into.
Exactly! You might need someone who's superstrong and super tough!
And super *loud.*
Okay, you can come with. But if Nico and I decide it's too dangerous, you're leaving.
Chase--
No more negotiating. If we decide it's time to leave, you leave with us. No questions asked. All right?
All right...

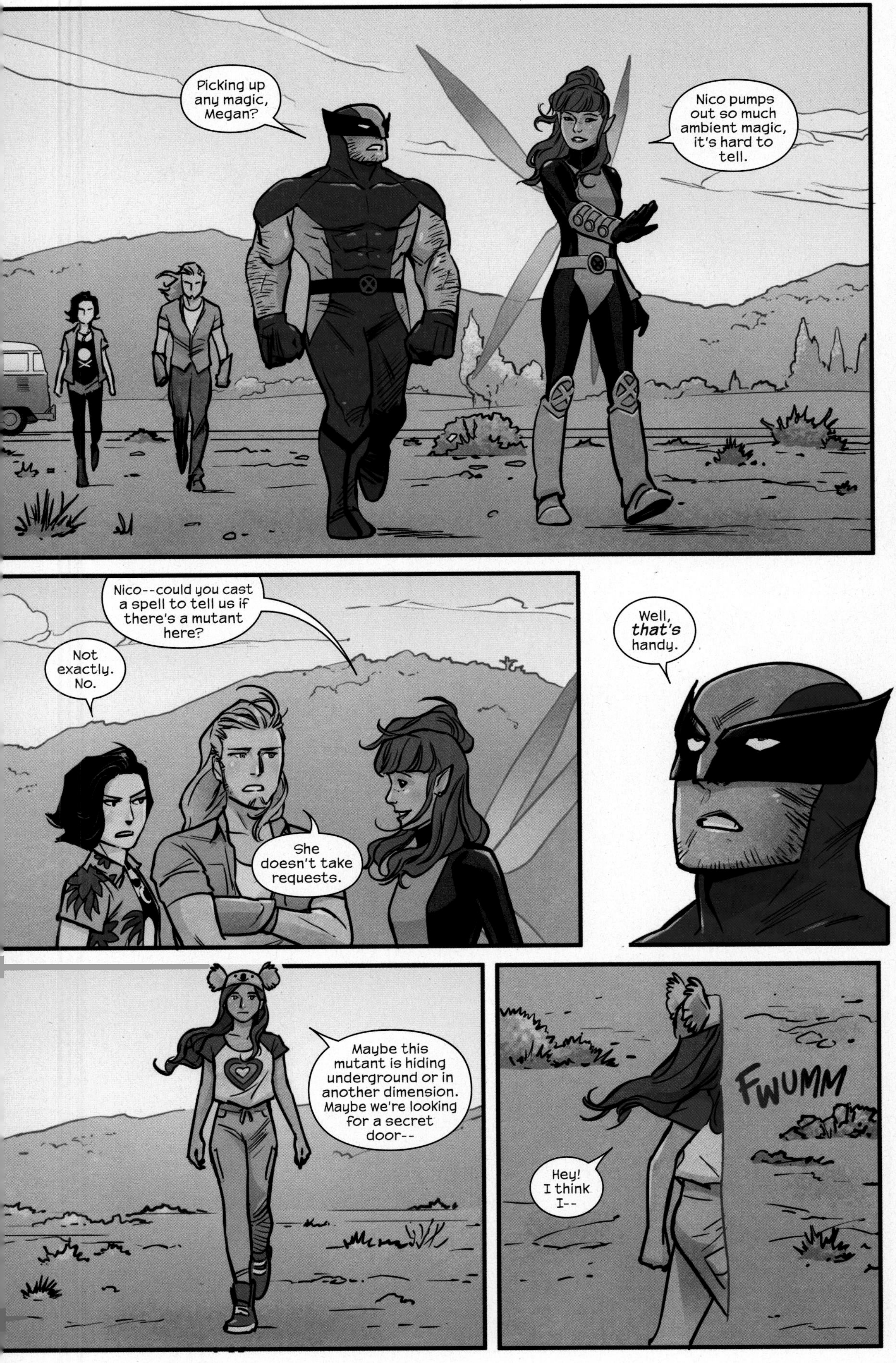
Picking up any magic, Megan?
Nico pumps out so much ambient magic, it's hard to tell.
Nico--could you cast a spell to tell us if there's a mutant here?
Not exactly. No.
She doesn't take requests.
Well, *that's* handy.
Maybe this mutant is hiding underground or in another dimension. Maybe we're looking for a secret door--
FWUMM
Hey! I think I--

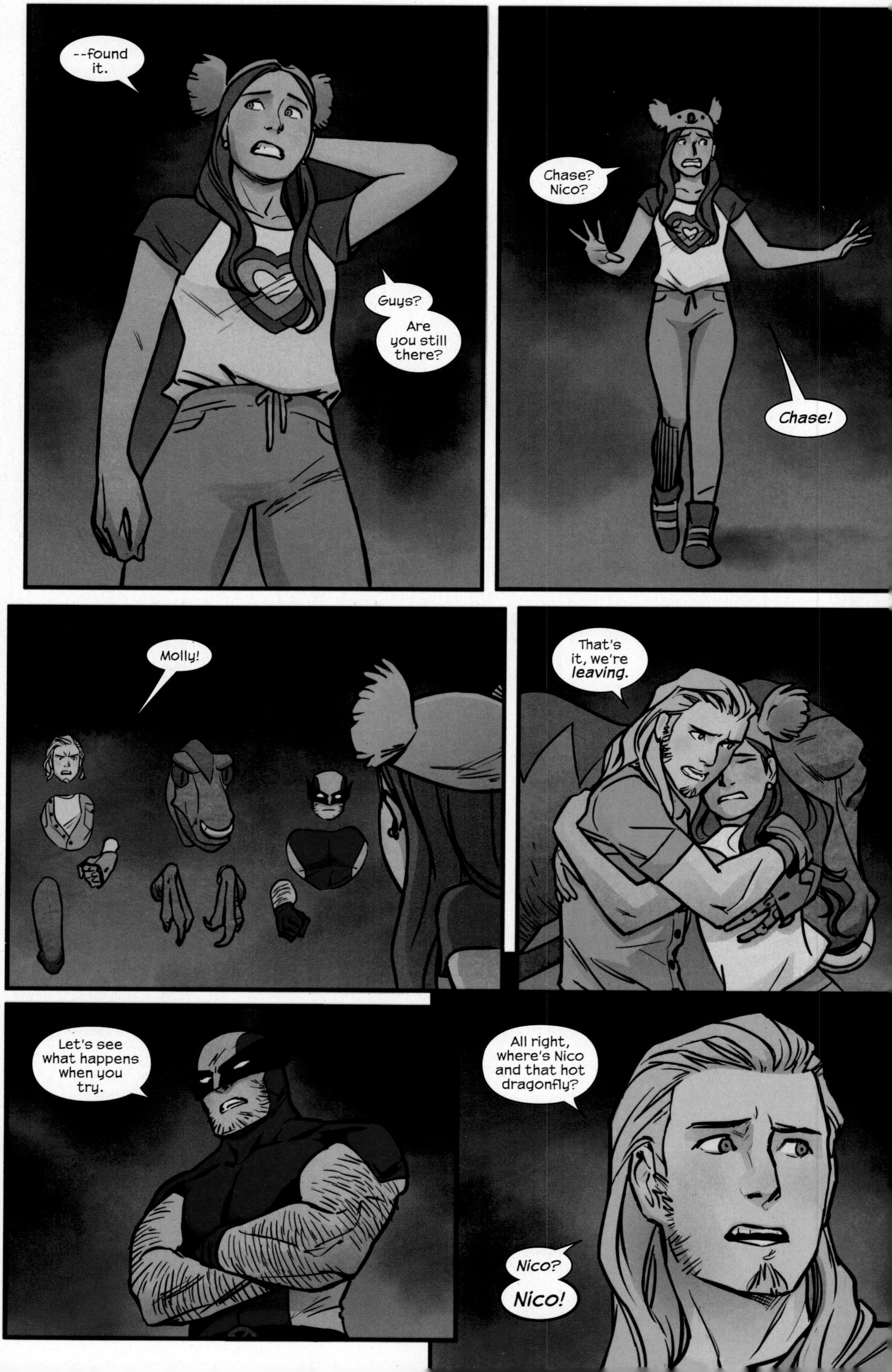
--found it.
Guys?
Are you still there?
Chase? Nico?
Chase!
Molly!
That's it, we're leaving.
Let's see what happens when you try.
All right, where's Nico and that hot dragonfly?
Nico?
Nico!

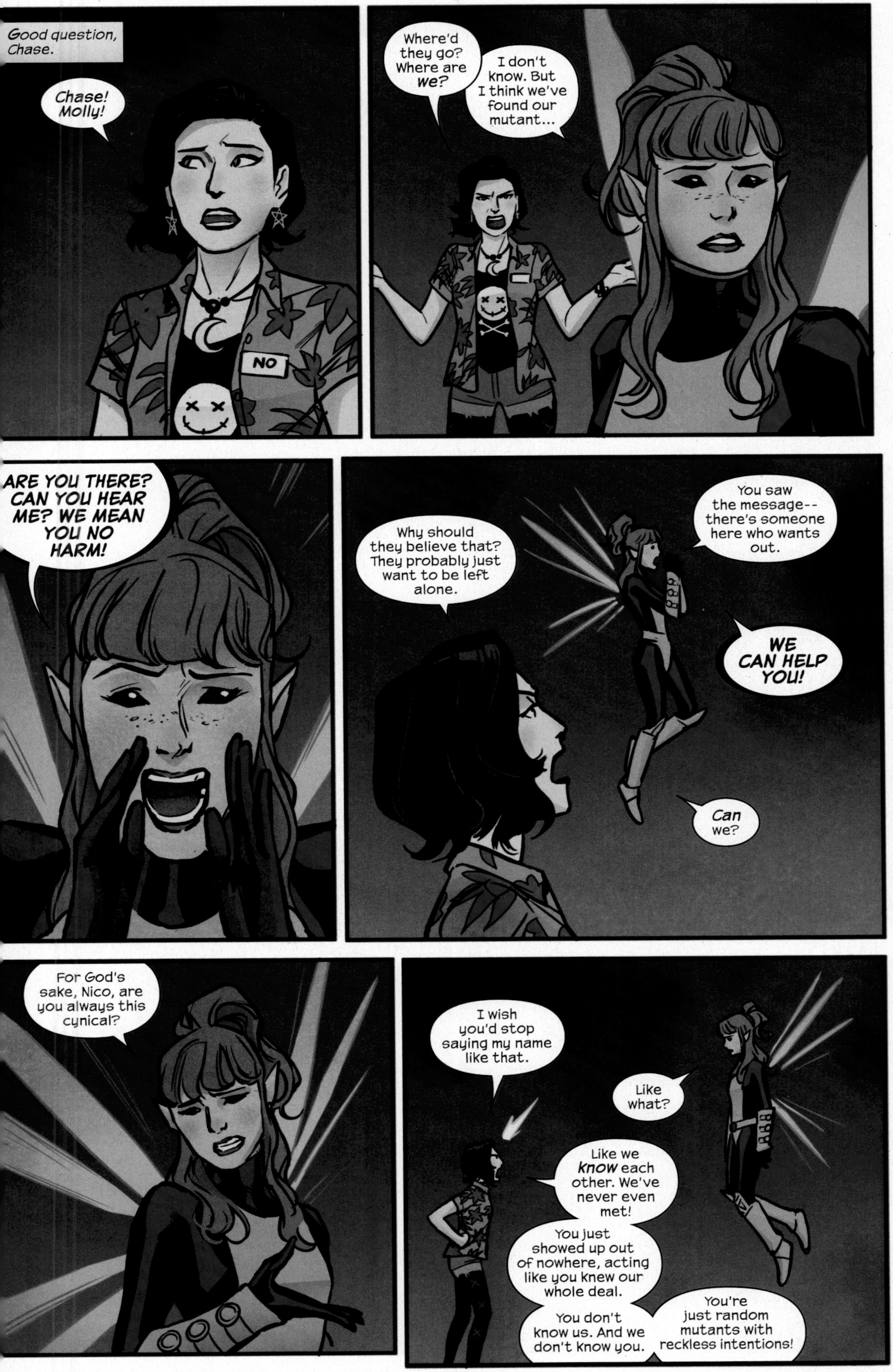
Good question, Chase.
Chase! Molly!
Where'd they go? Where are *we*?
I don't know. But I think we've found our mutant...
NO
ARE YOU THERE? CAN YOU HEAR ME? WE MEAN YOU NO HARM!
Why should they believe that? They probably just want to be left alone.
You saw the message--there's someone here who wants out.
WE CAN HELP YOU!
Can we?
For God's sake, Nico, are you always this cynical?
I wish you'd stop saying my name like that.
Like what?
Like we *know* each other. We've never even met!
You just showed up out of nowhere, acting like you knew our whole deal.
You don't know us. And we don't know you.
You're just random mutants with reckless intentions!

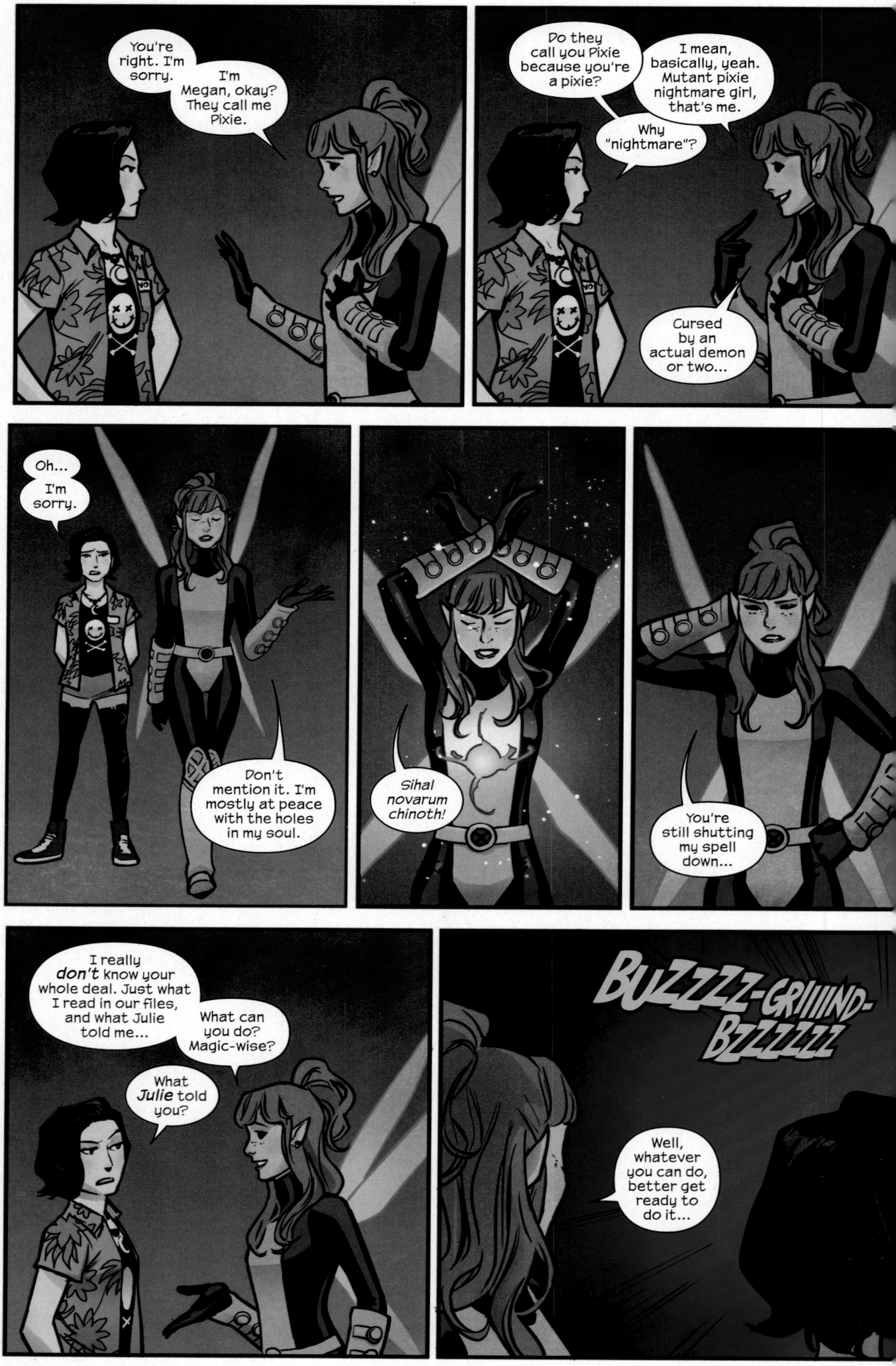

You're right. I'm sorry.
I'm Megan, okay? They call me Pixie.
Do they call you Pixie because you're a pixie?
I mean, basically, yeah. Mutant pixie nightmare girl, that's me.
Why "nightmare"?
Cursed by an actual demon or two...
Oh...
I'm sorry.
Don't mention it. I'm mostly at peace with the holes in my soul.
Sihal novarum chinoth!
You're still shutting my spell down...
I really **don't** know your whole deal. Just what I read in our files, and what Julie told me...
What can you do? Magic-wise?
What *Julie* told you?
BUZZZZ-GRIIIIND-BZZZZZZ
Well, whatever you can do, better get ready to do it...

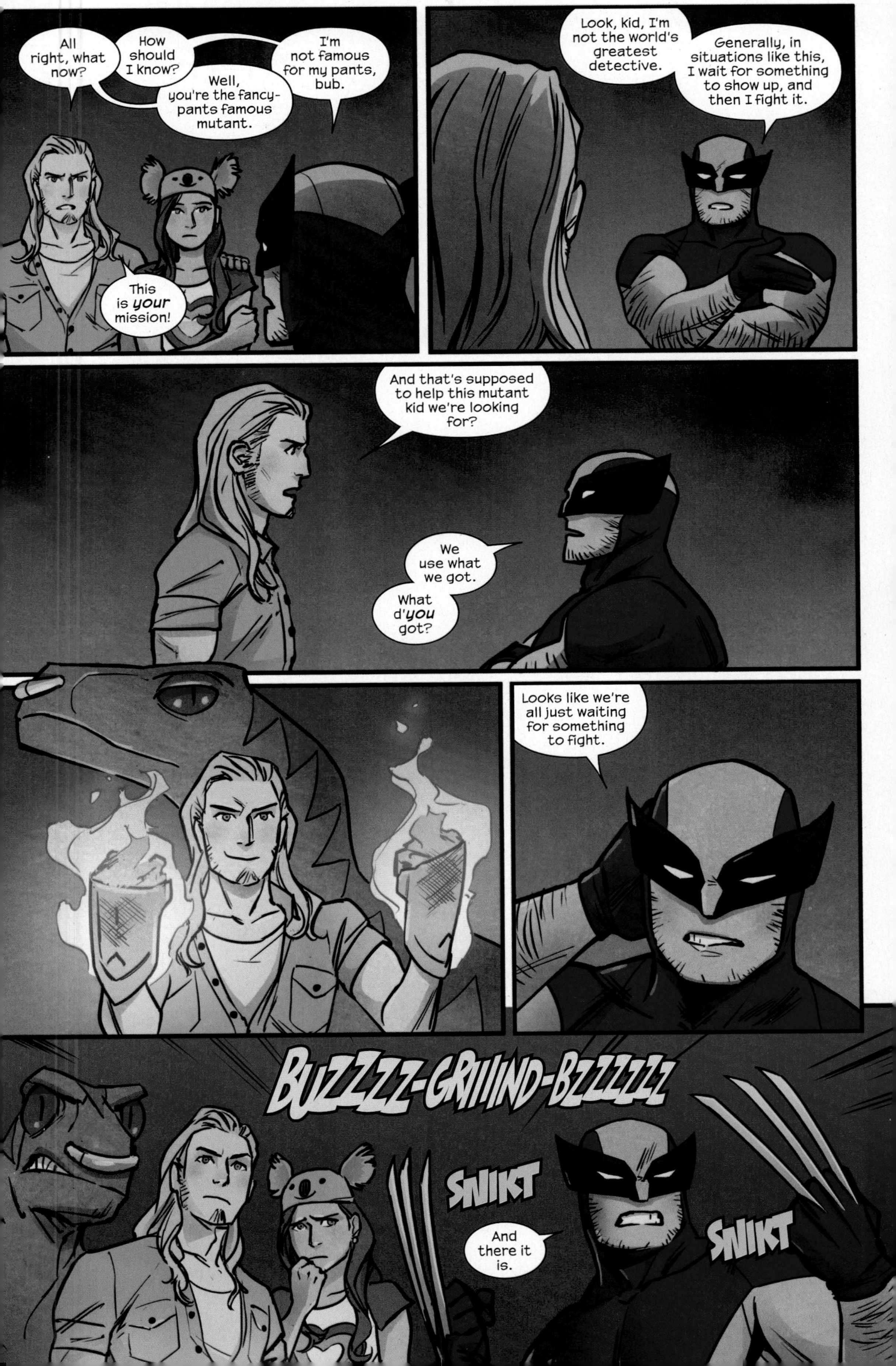
All right, what now?
How should I know?
I'm not famous for my pants, bub.
Well, you're the fancy-pants famous mutant.
This is *your* mission!
Look, kid, I'm not the world's greatest detective.
Generally, in situations like this, I wait for something to show up, and then I fight it.
And that's supposed to help this mutant kid we're looking for?
We use what we got.
What d'*you* got?
Looks like we're all just waiting for something to fight.
BUZZZZ-GRIIIND-BZZZZZZ
SNIKT
SNIKT
And there it is.

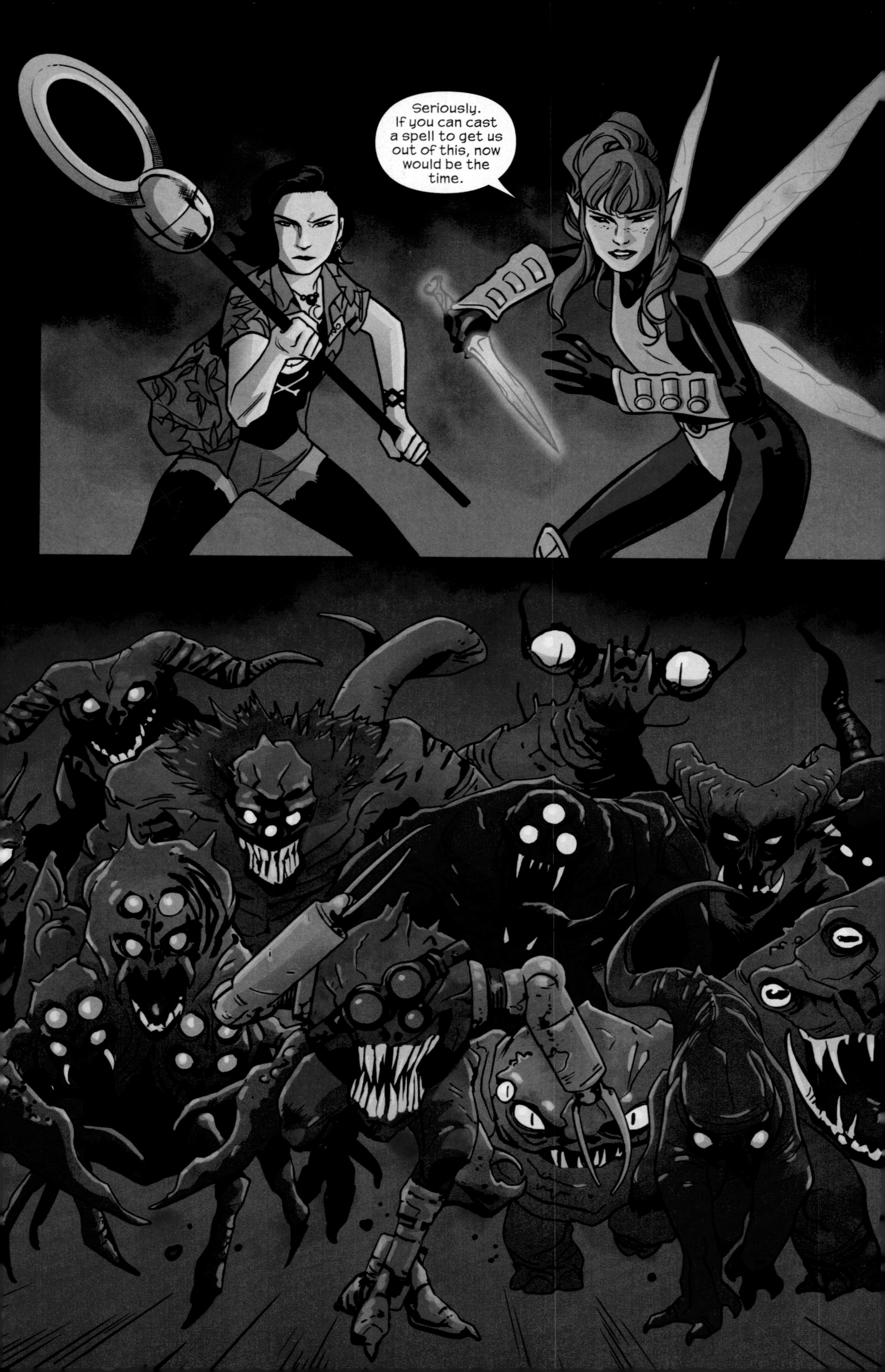
Seriously. If you can cast a spell to get us out of this, now would be the time.

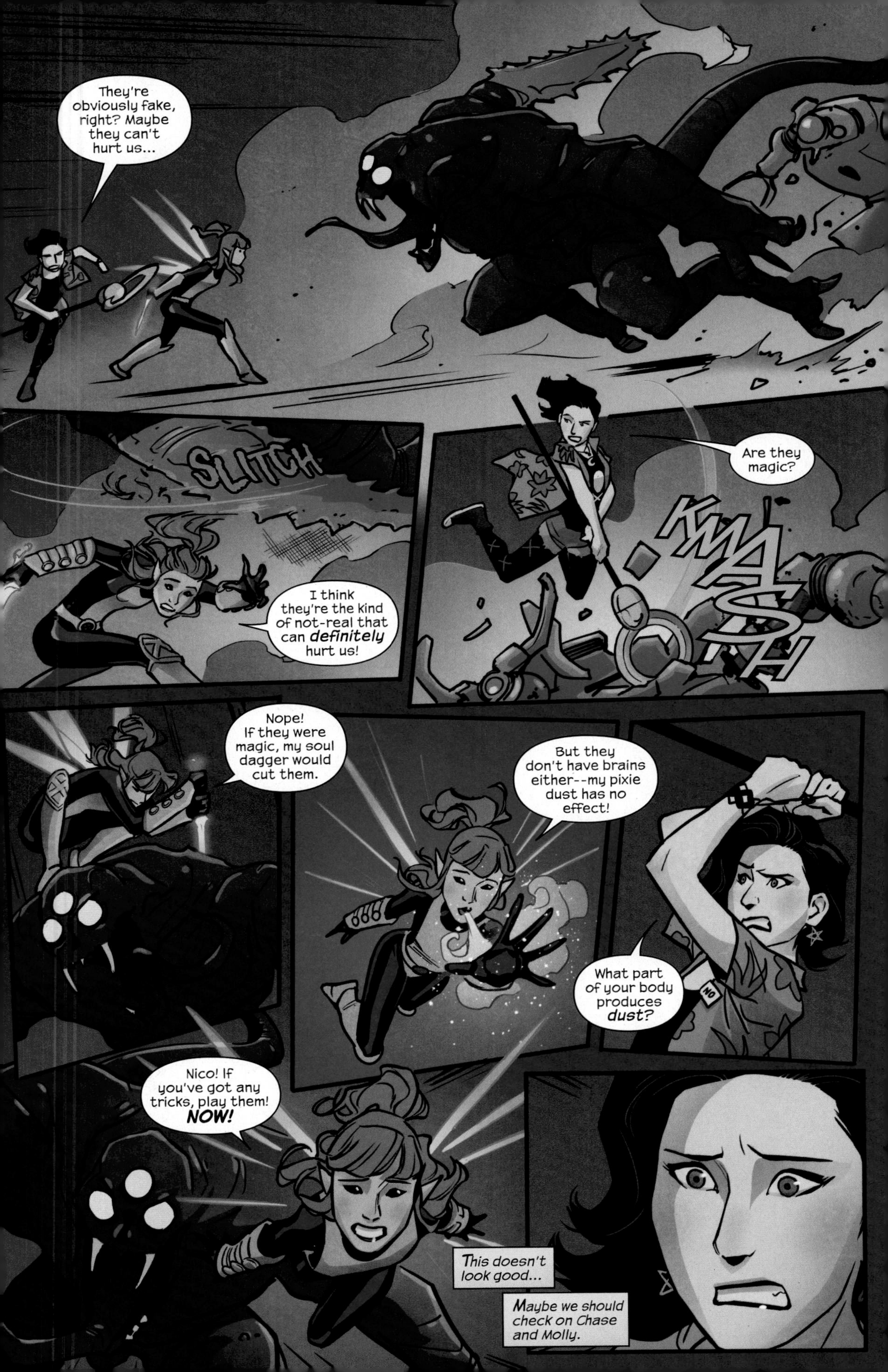

They're obviously fake, right? Maybe they can't hurt us...
SLITCH
I think they're the kind of not-real that can *definitely* hurt us!
Are they magic?
KWASH
Nope! If they were magic, my soul dagger would cut them.
But they don't have brains either--my pixie dust has no effect!
What part of your body produces *dust?*
Nico! If you've got any tricks, play them! ***NOW!***
This doesn't look good...
Maybe we should check on Chase and Molly.

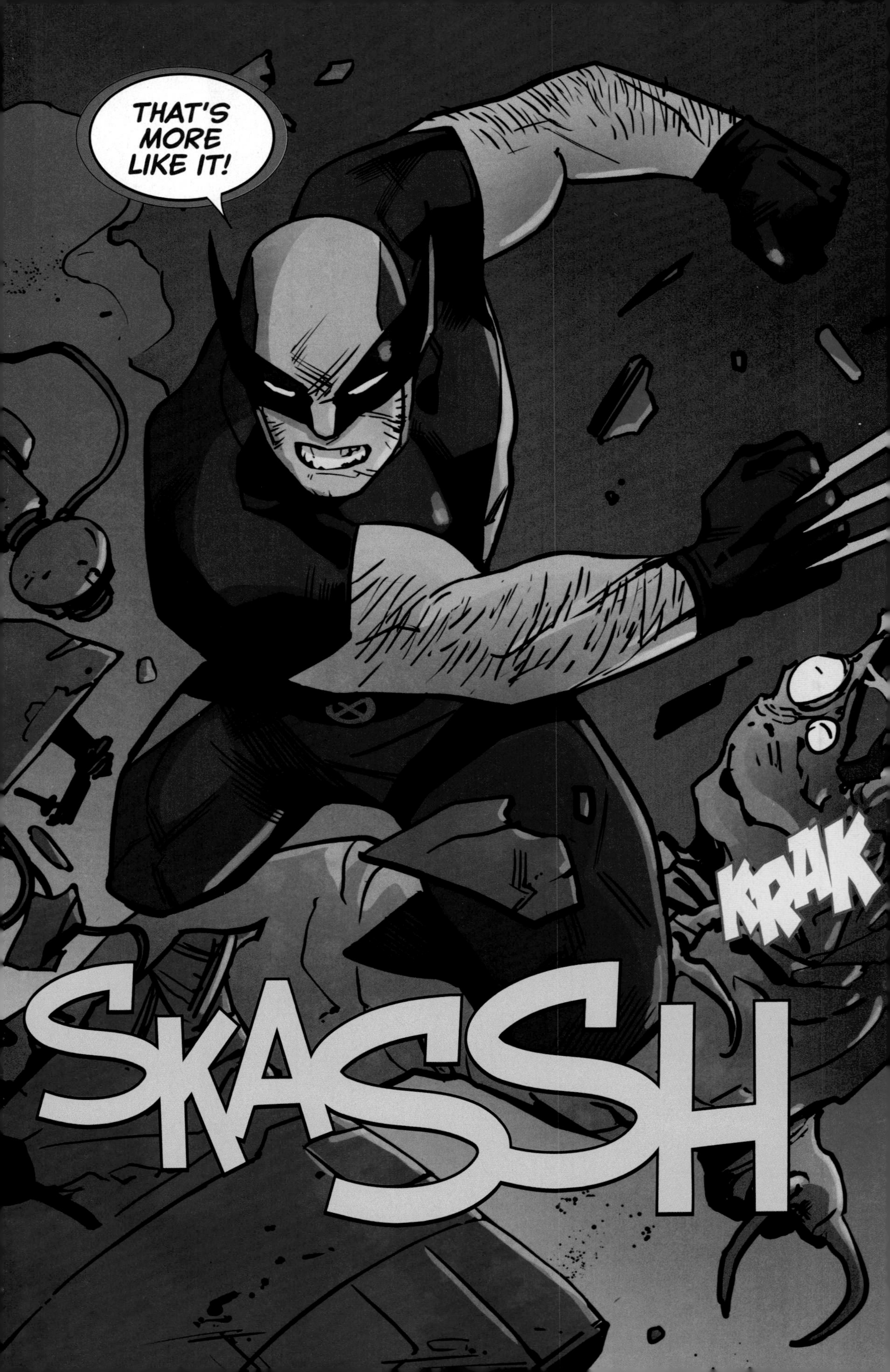
THAT'S MORE LIKE IT!
KRAK
SKASSH

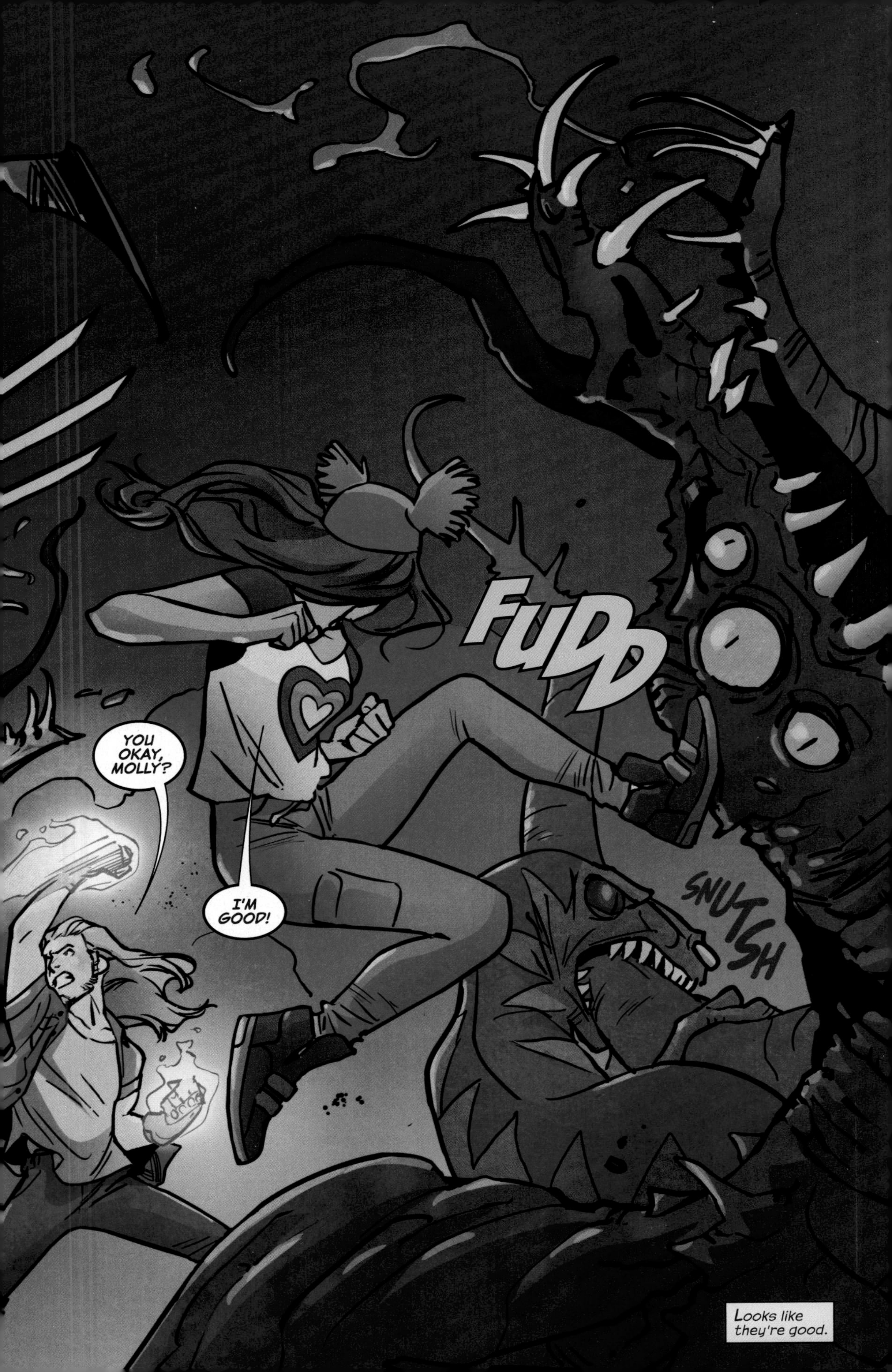
FUDD
YOU OKAY, MOLLY?
I'M GOOD!
SNUTSH
Looks like they're good.

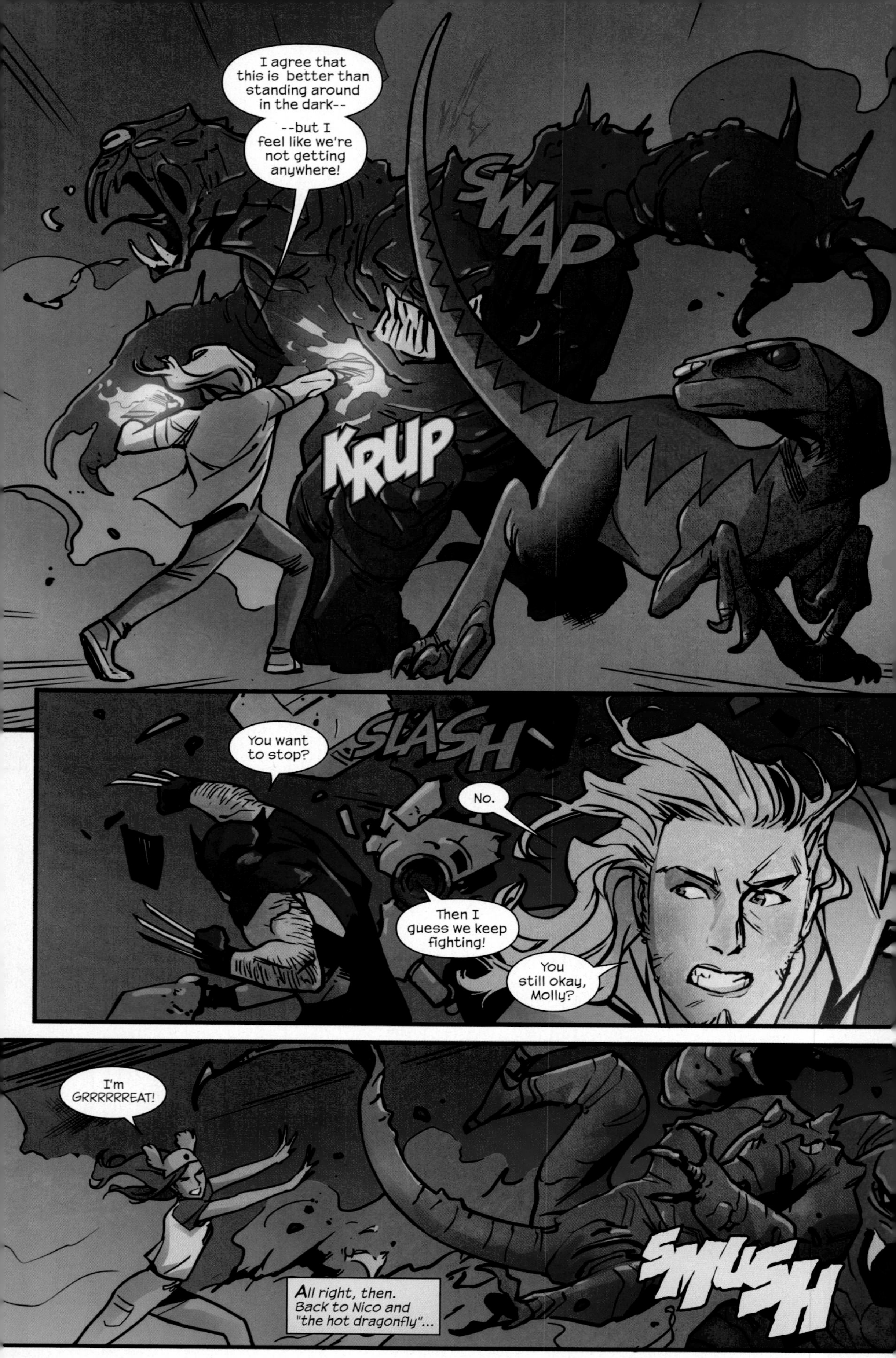
I agree that this is better than standing around in the dark--
--but I feel like we're not getting anywhere!
SWAP
KRUP
You want to stop?
SLASH
No.
Then I guess we keep fighting!
You still okay, Molly?
I'm GRRRRRREAT!
All right, then. Back to Nico and "the hot dragonfly"...
SMUSH

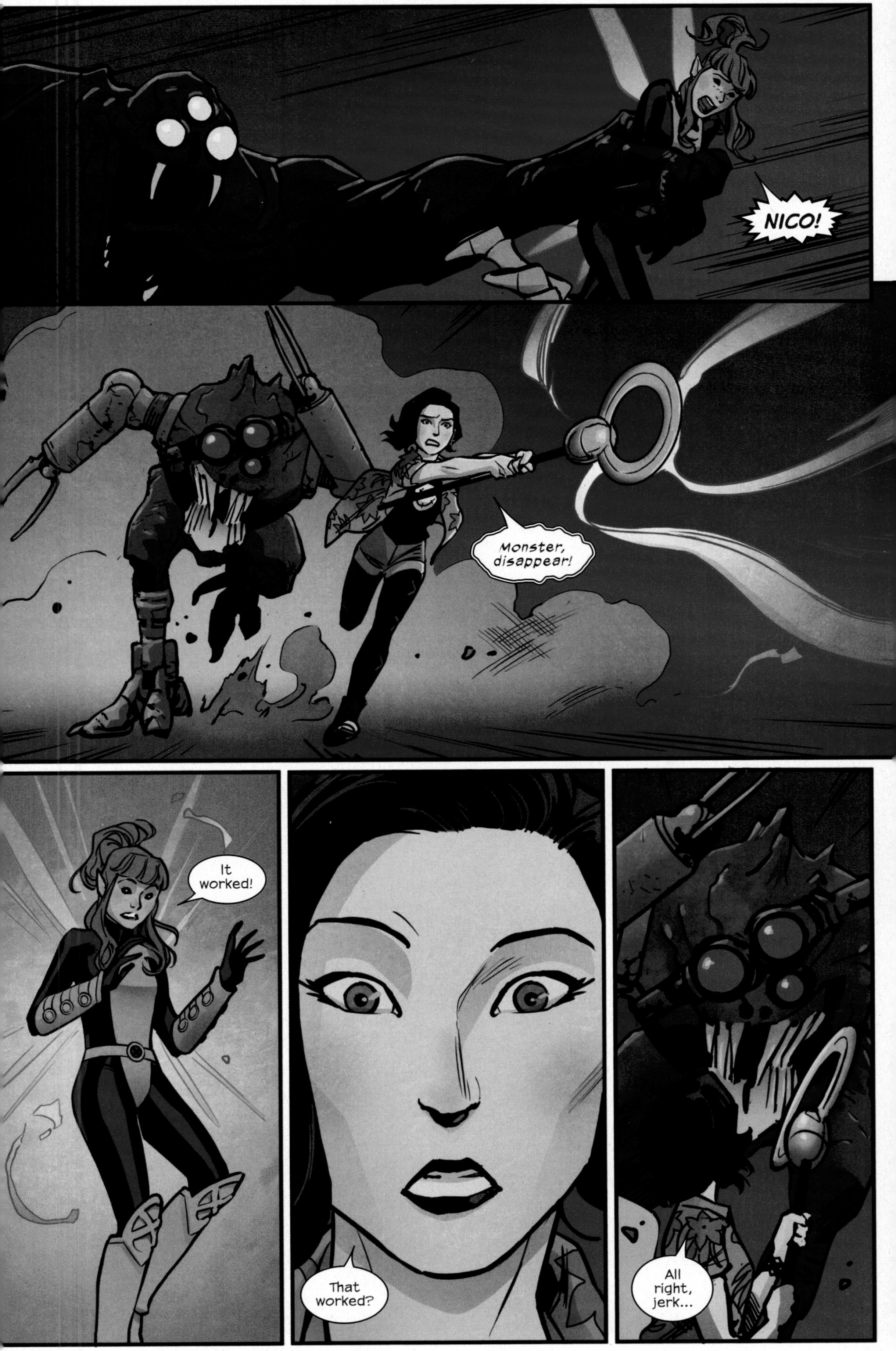
NICO!
Monster, disappear!
It worked!
That worked?
All right, jerk...

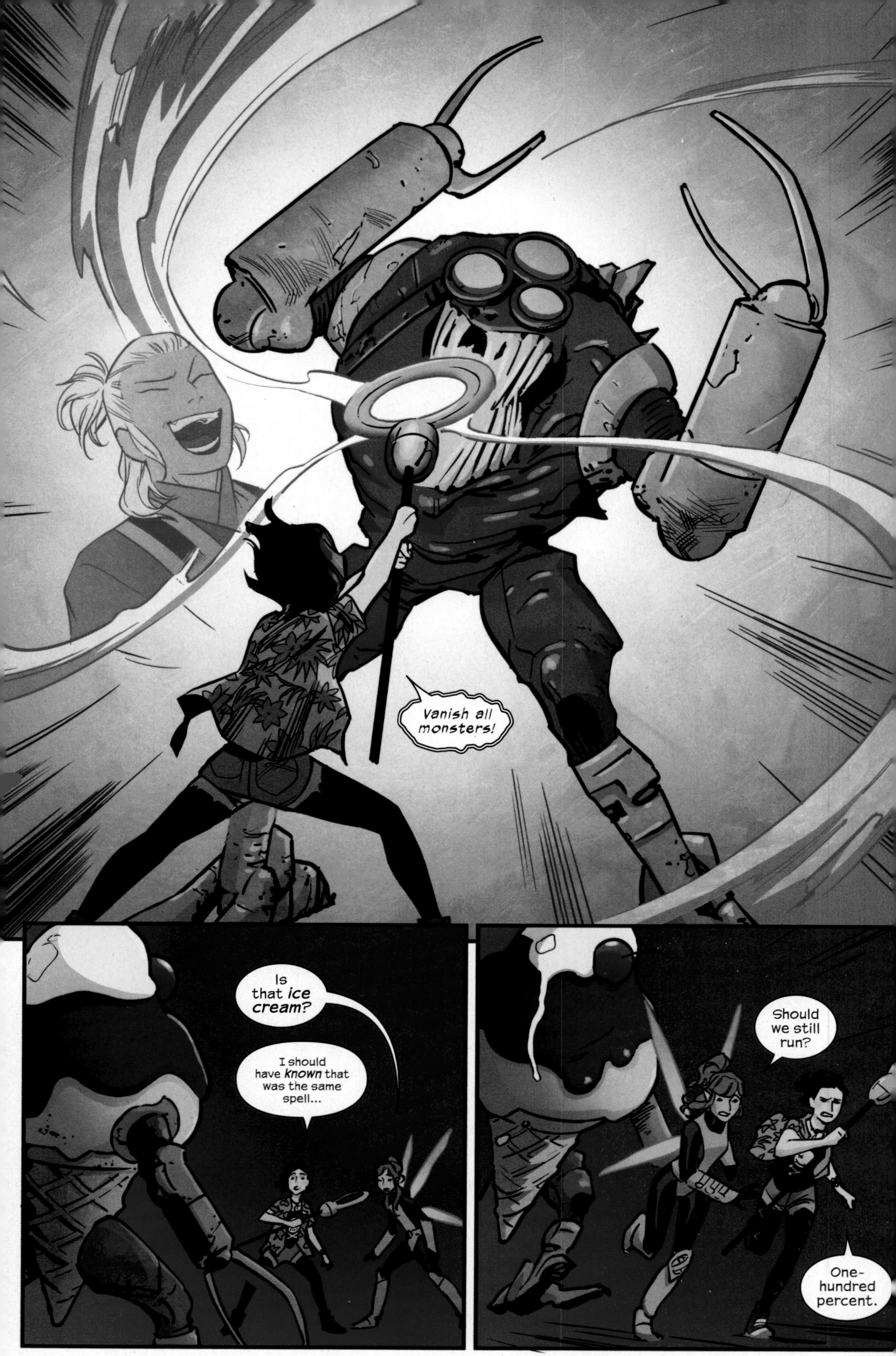
Vanish all monsters!
Is that *ice cream?*
I should have ***known*** that was the same spell...
Should we still run?
One-hundred percent.

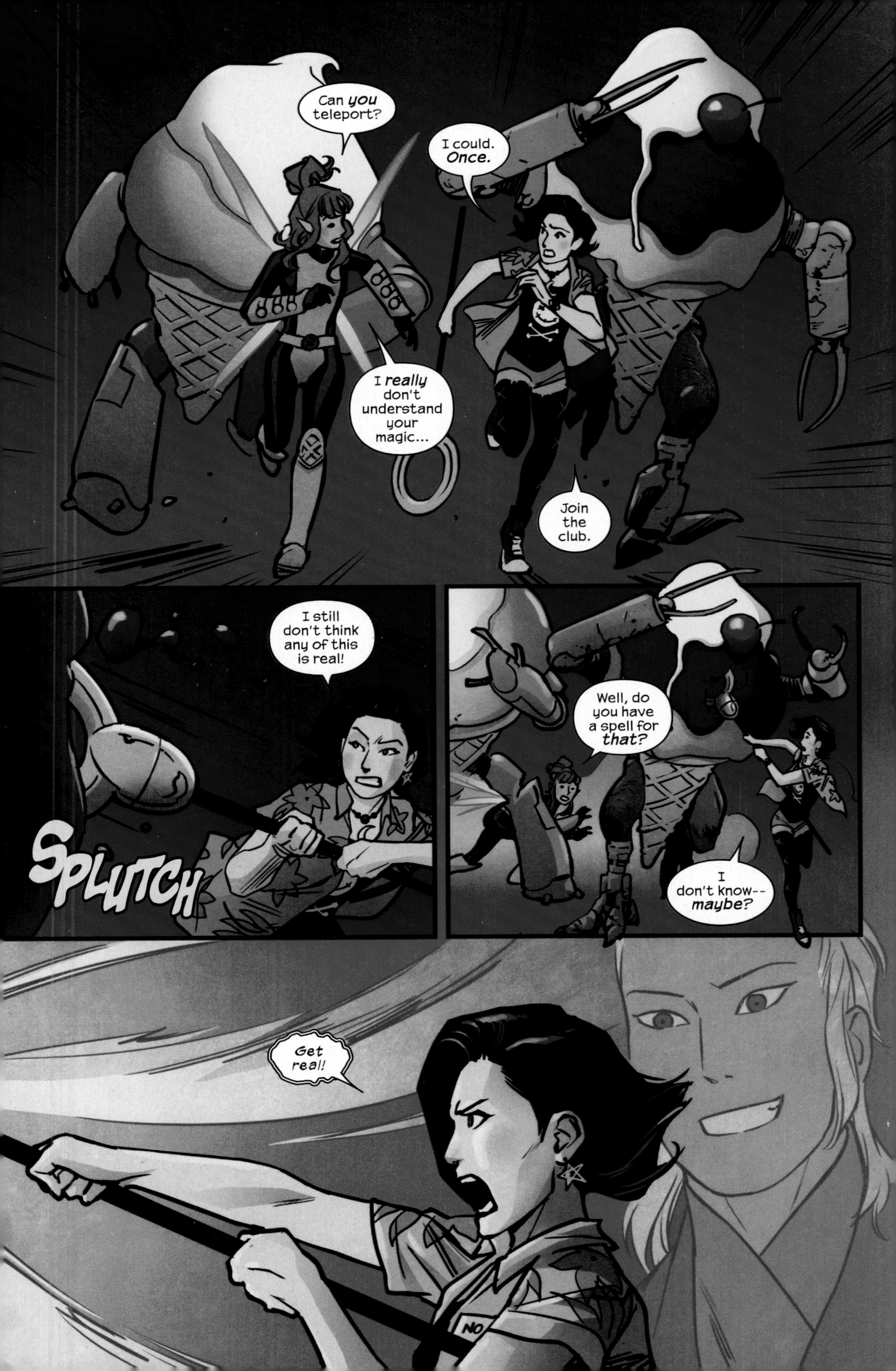
Can you teleport?
I could. Once.
I really don't understand your magic...
Join the club.
I still don't think any of this is real!
SPLUTCH
Well, do you have a spell for that?
I don't know-- maybe?
Get real!
NO

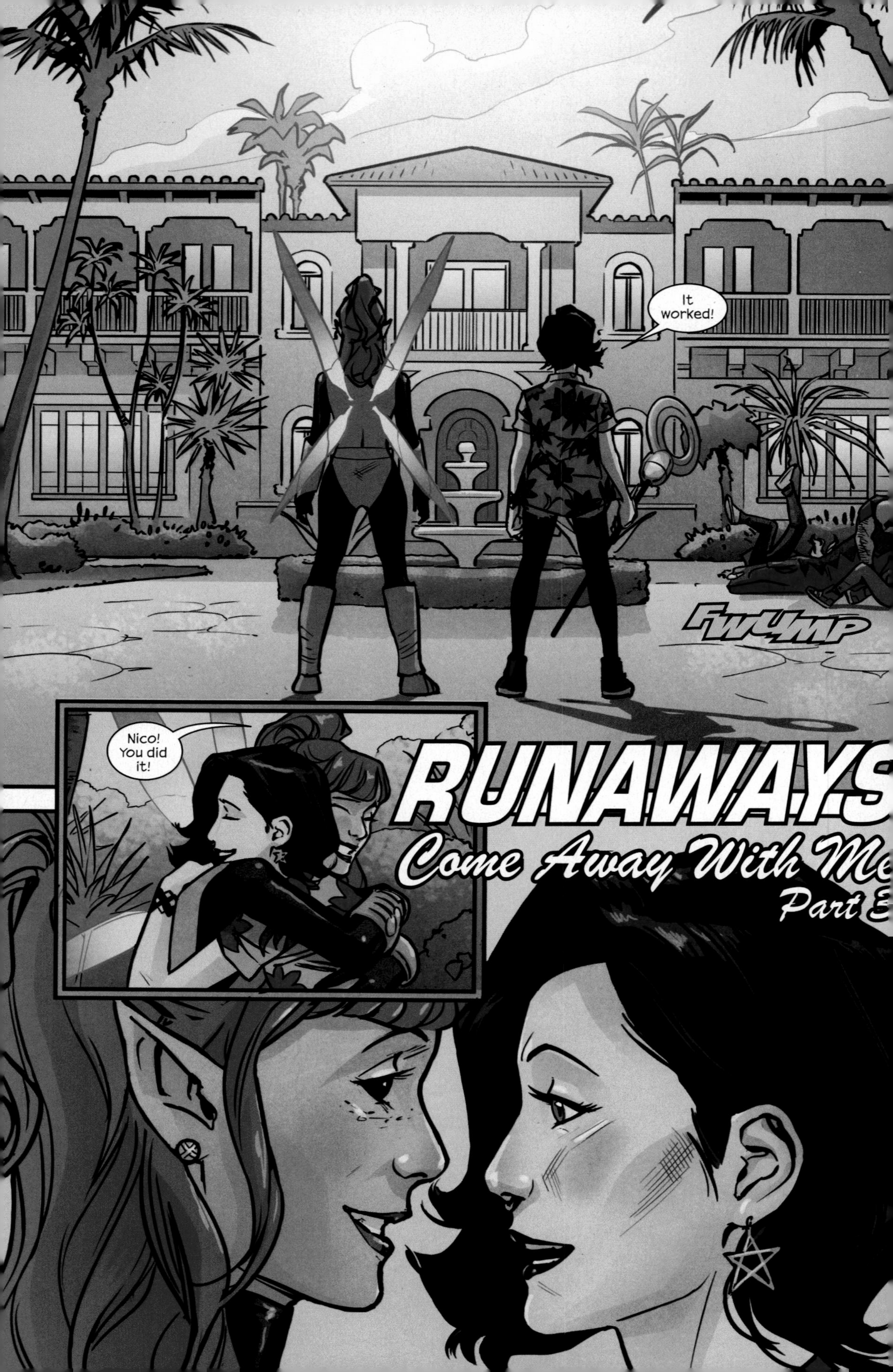
It worked!
FWUMP
Nico! You did it!
RUNAWAYS
Come Away With Me
Part

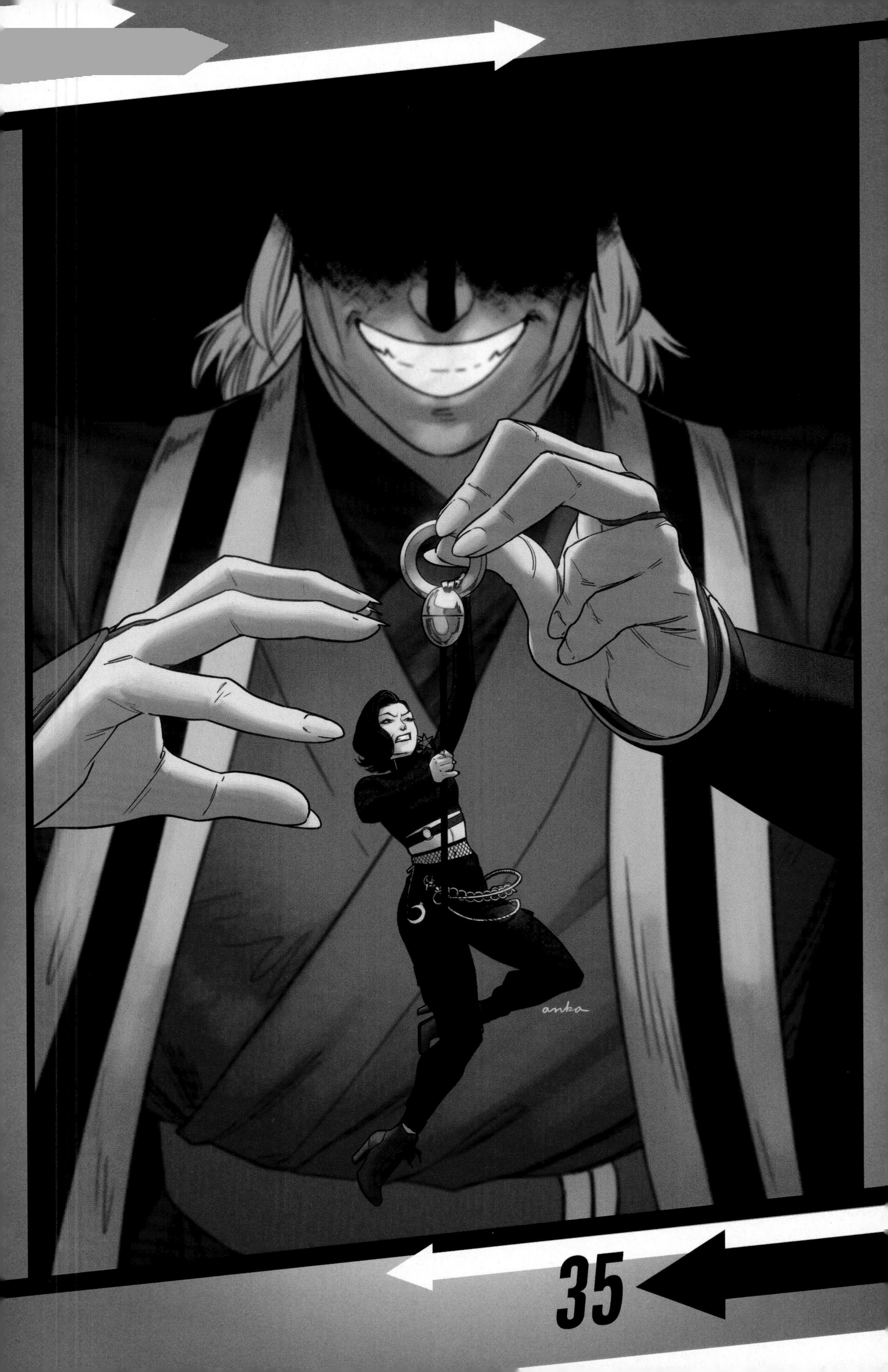
anka
35

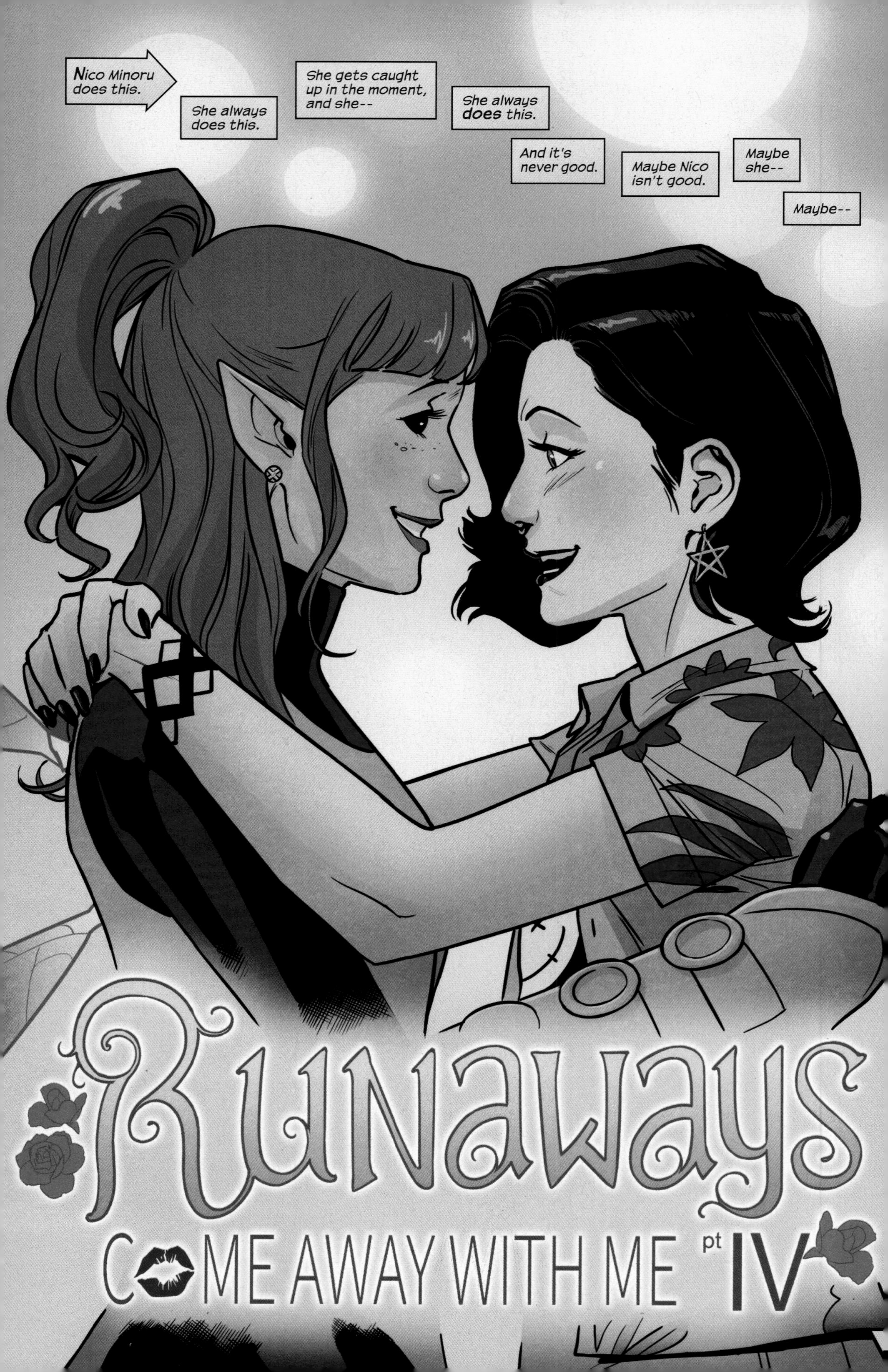
Nico Minoru does this.
She always does this.
She gets caught up in the moment, and she--
She always **does** this.
And it's never good.
Maybe Nico isn't good.
Maybe she--
Maybe--
Runaways
COME AWAY WITH ME pt IV

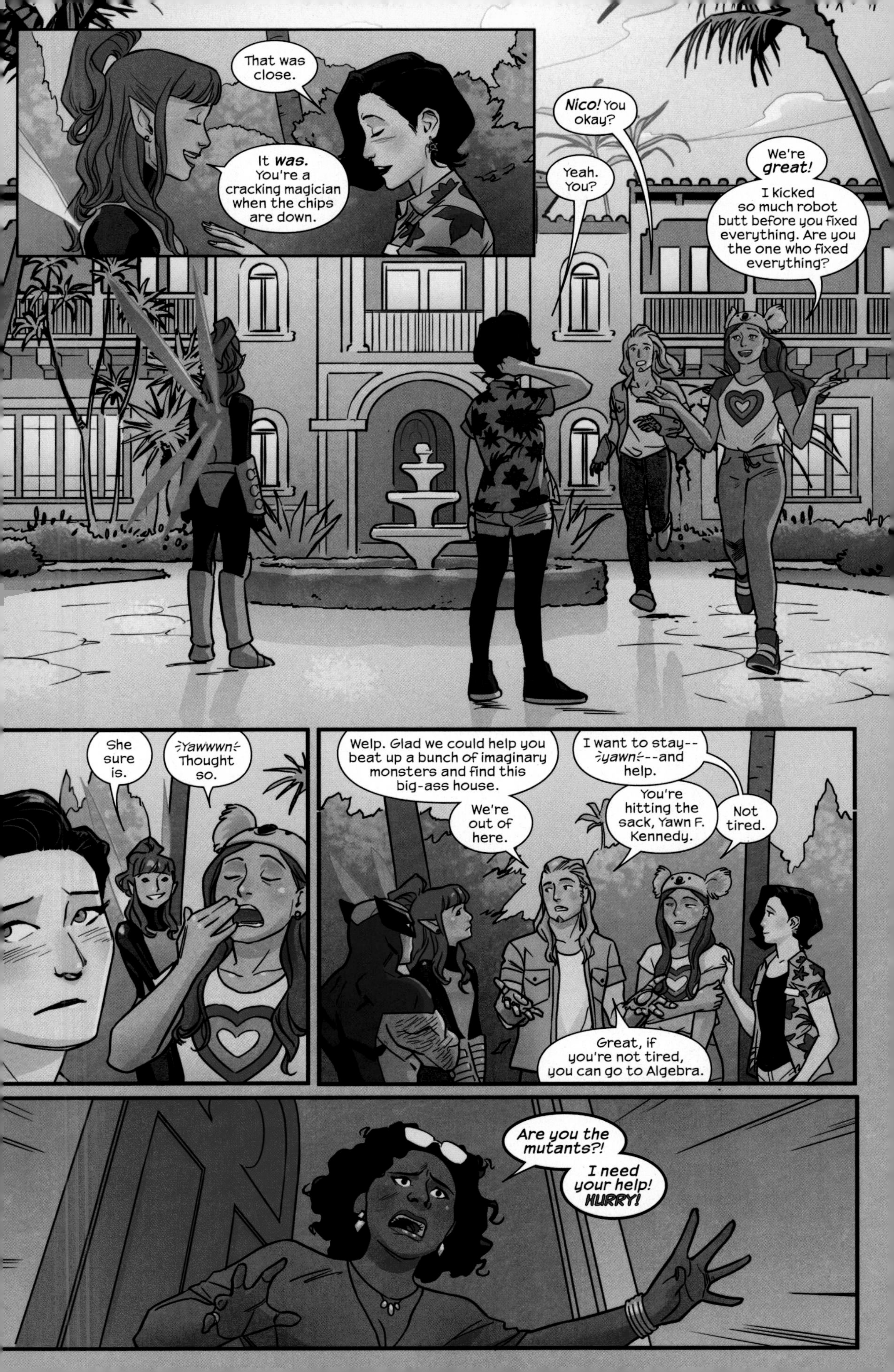
That was close.
It *was.* You're a cracking magician when the chips are down.
Nico! You okay?
Yeah. You?
We're *great!*
I kicked so much robot butt before you fixed everything. Are you the one who fixed everything?
She sure is.
Yawwwn Thought so.
Welp. Glad we could help you beat up a bunch of imaginary monsters and find this big-ass house.
We're out of here.
I want to stay-- yawn --and help.
You're hitting the sack, Yawn F. Kennedy.
Not tired.
Great, if you're not tired, you can go to Algebra.
Are you the mutants?!
I need your help! ***HURRY!***

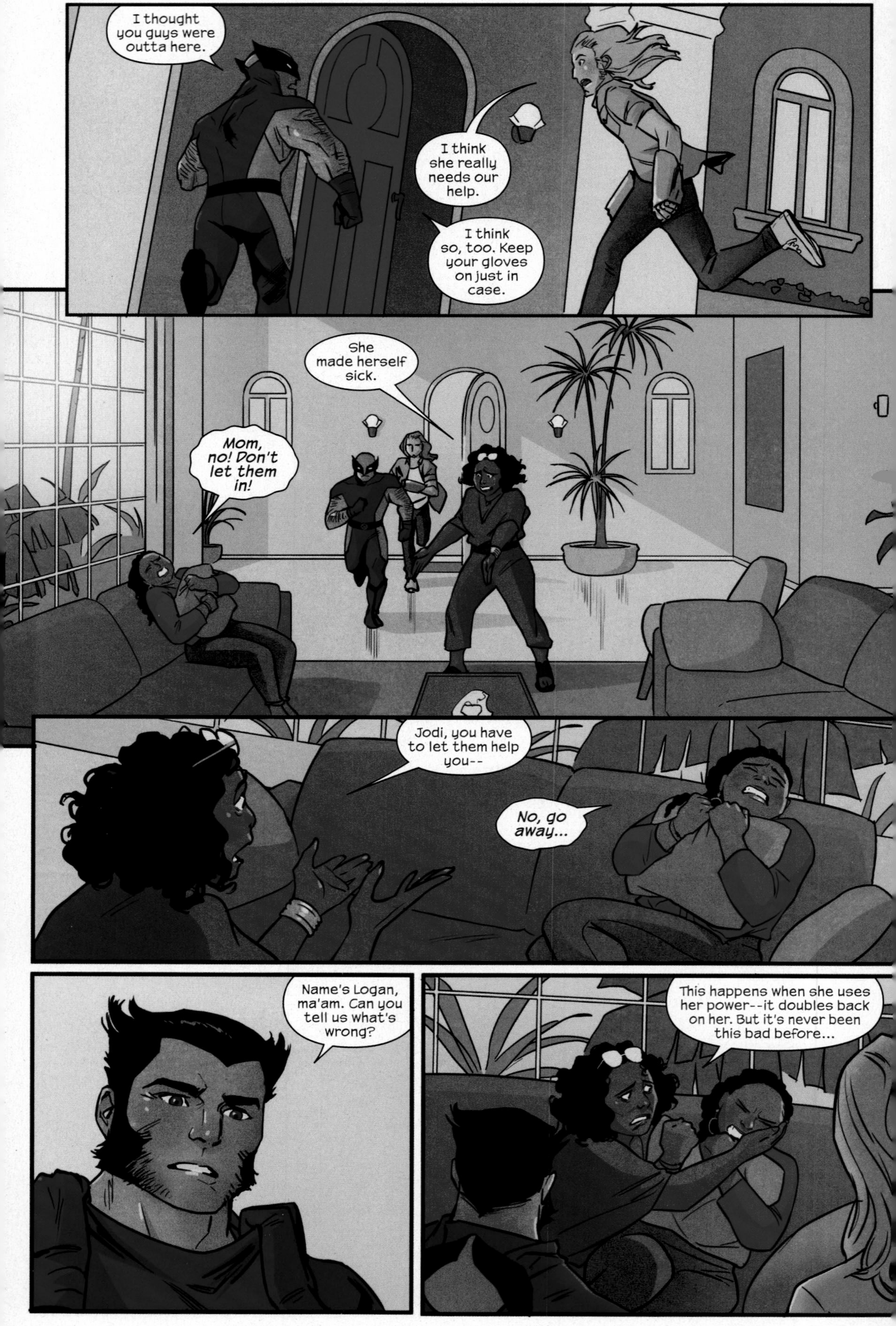
I thought you guys were outta here.
I think she really needs our help.
I think so, too. Keep your gloves on just in case.
She made herself sick.
Mom, no! Don't let them in!
Jodi, you have to let them help you--
No, go away...
Name's Logan, ma'am. Can you tell us what's wrong?
This happens when she uses her power--it doubles back on her. But it's never been this bad before...

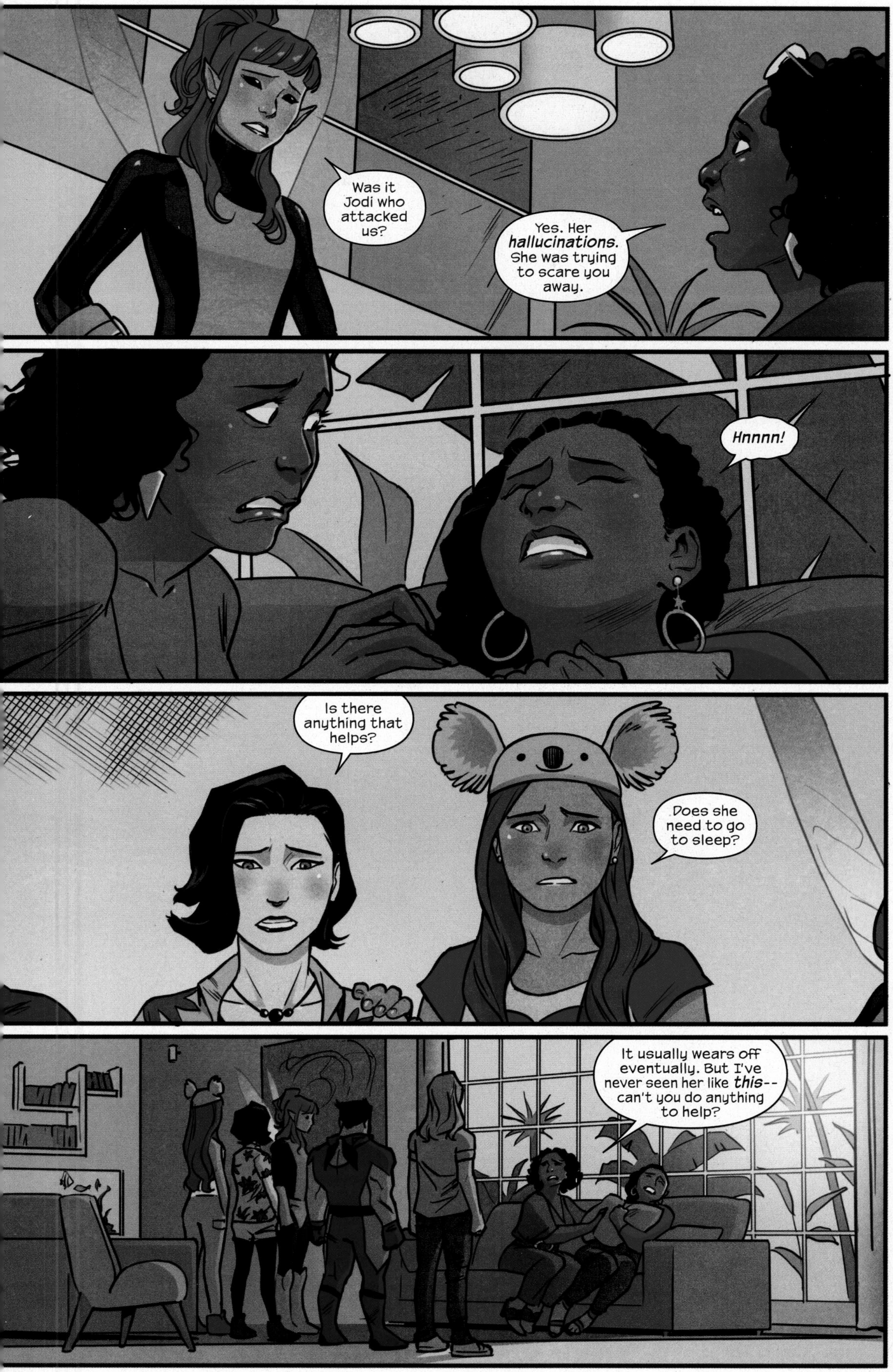
Was it Jodi who attacked us?
Yes. Her *hallucinations.* She was trying to scare you away.
Hnnnn!
Is there anything that helps?
Does she need to go to sleep?
It usually wears off eventually. But I've never seen her like *this*-- can't you do anything to help?

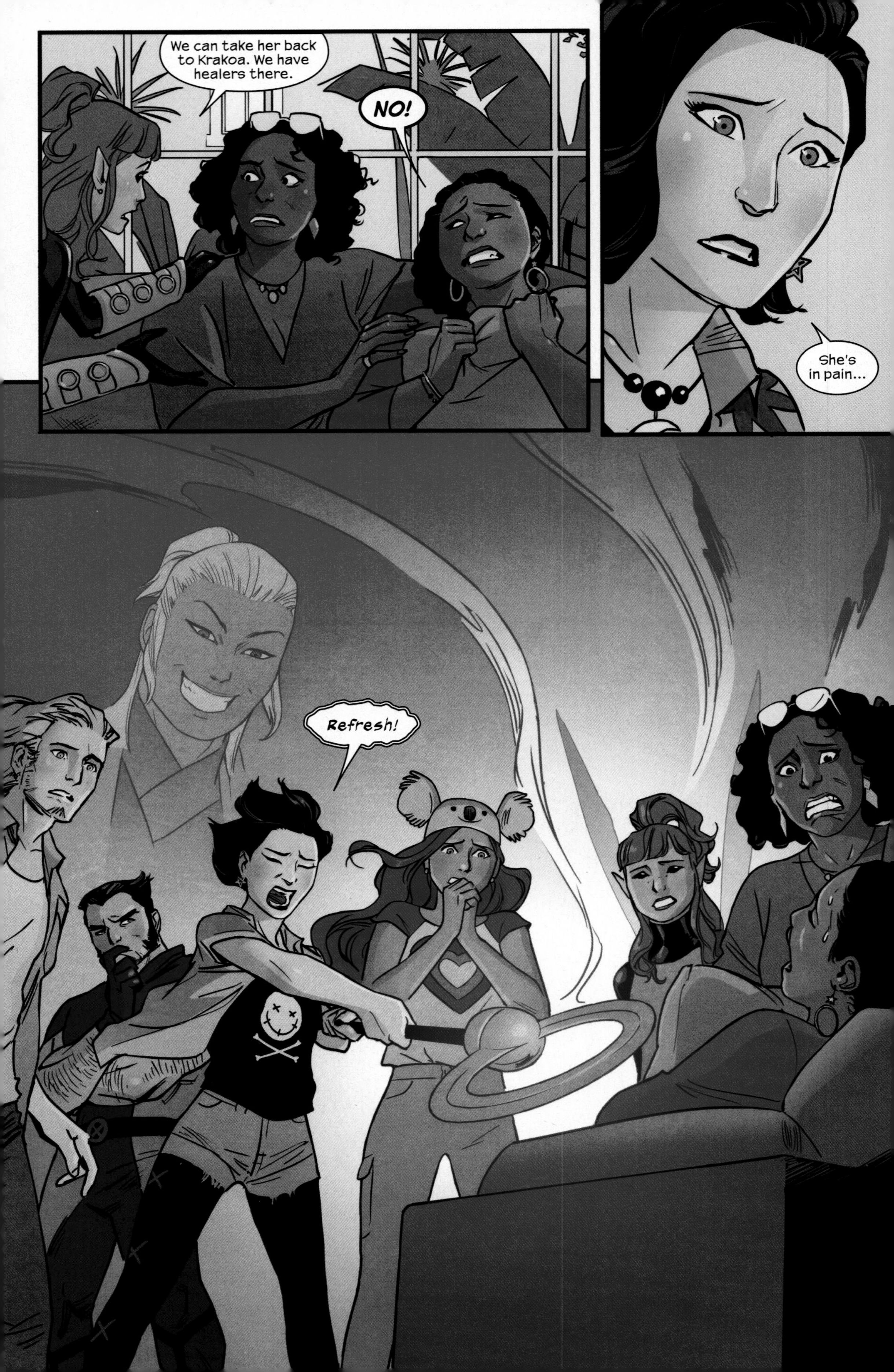
We can take her back to Krakoa. We have healers there.
NO!
She's in pain...
Refresh!

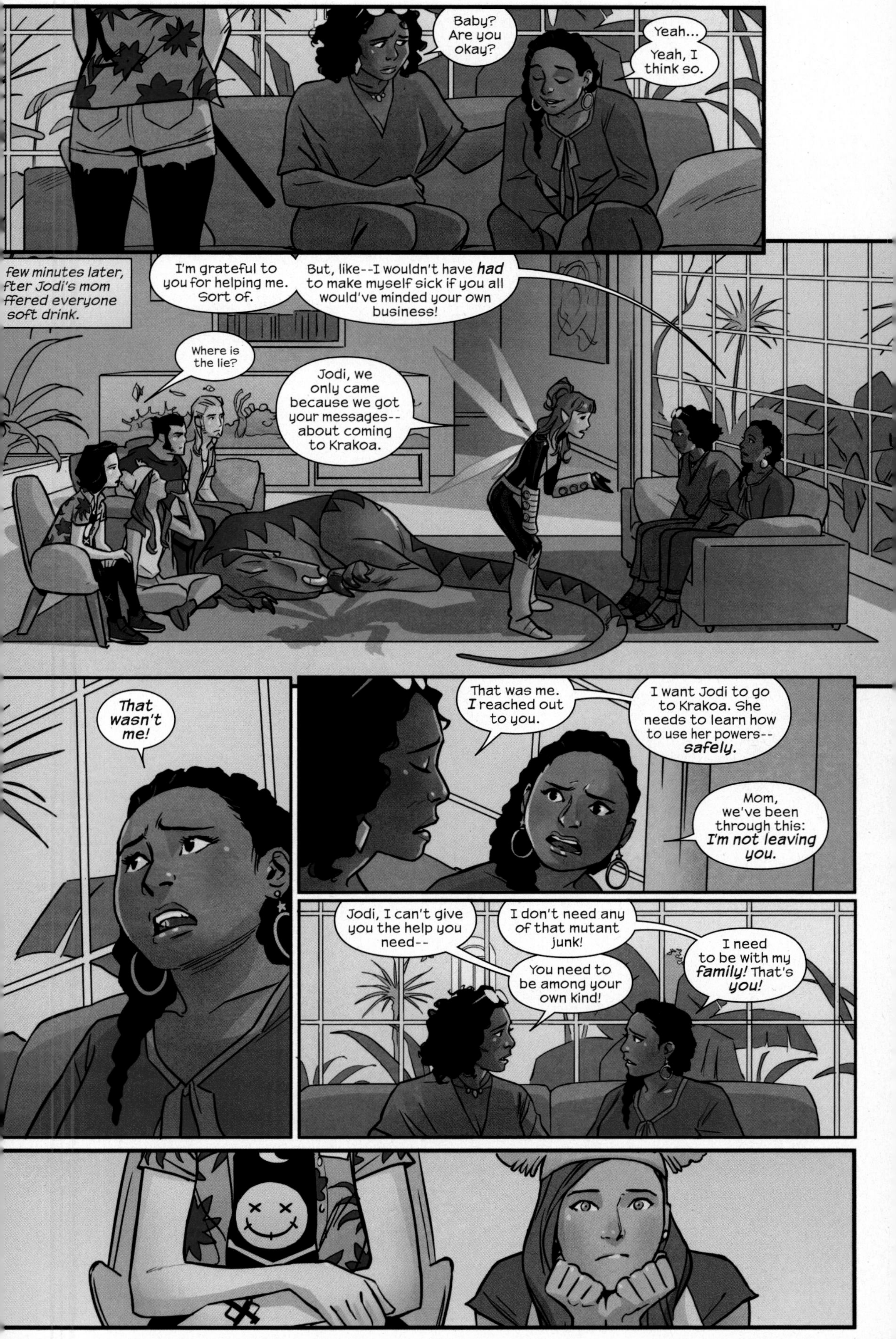
Baby? Are you okay?
Yeah...
Yeah, I think so.
few minutes later, fter Jodi's mom ffered everyone soft drink.
I'm grateful to you for helping me. Sort of.
But, like--I wouldn't have had to make myself sick if you all would've minded your own business!
Where is the lie?
Jodi, we only came because we got your messages--about coming to Krakoa.
That wasn't me!
That was me. I reached out to you.
I want Jodi to go to Krakoa. She needs to learn how to use her powers--safely.
Mom, we've been through this: I'm not leaving you.
Jodi, I can't give you the help you need--
I don't need any of that mutant junk!
You need to be among your own kind!
I need to be with my family! That's you!

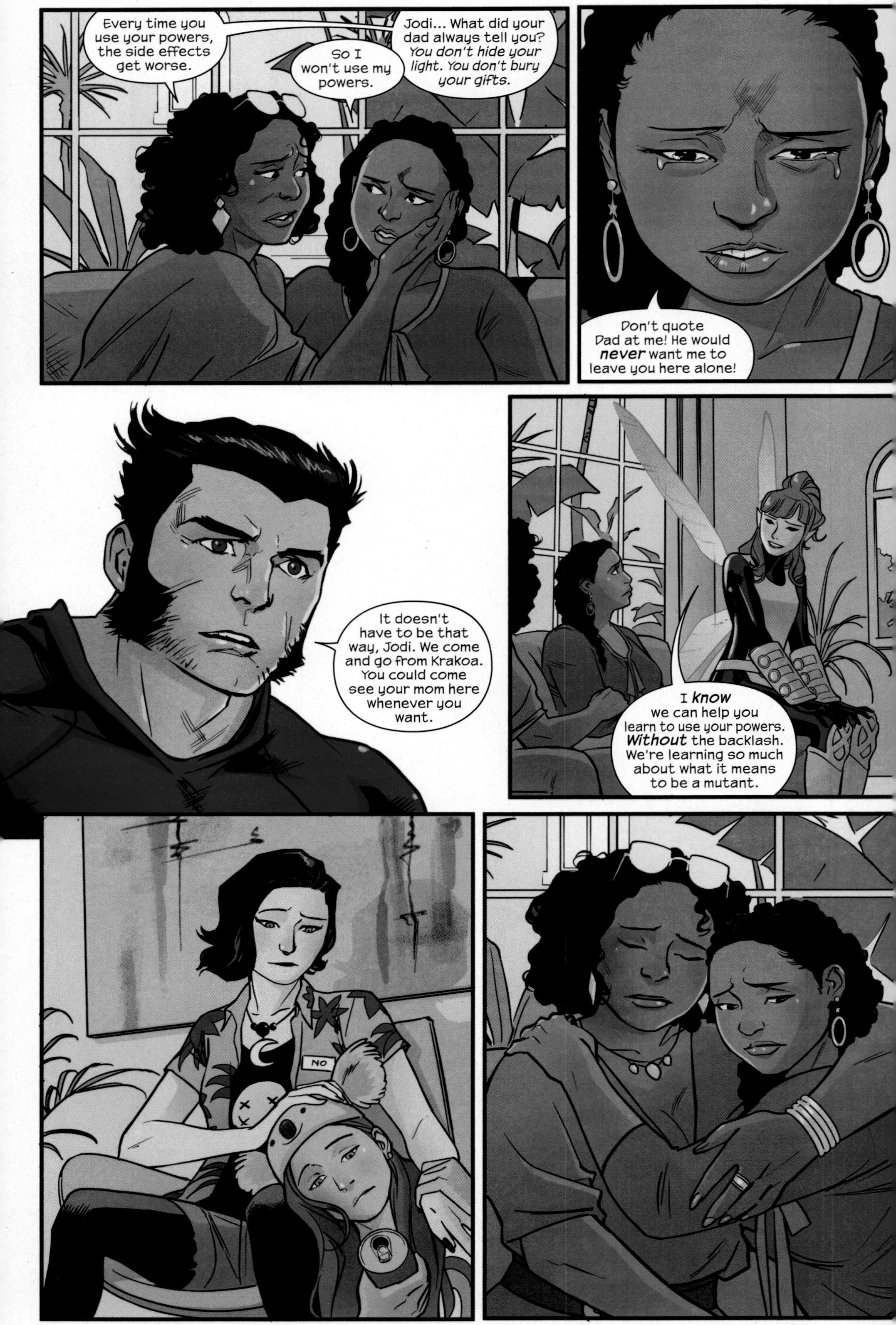
Every time you use your powers, the side effects get worse.
So I won't use my powers.
Jodi... What did your dad always tell you? *You don't hide your light. You don't bury your gifts.*
Don't quote Dad at me! He would ***never*** want me to leave you here alone!
It doesn't have to be that way, Jodi. We come and go from Krakoa. You could come see your mom here whenever you want.
I ***know*** we can help you learn to use your powers. ***Without*** the backlash. We're learning so much about what it means to be a mutant.
NO

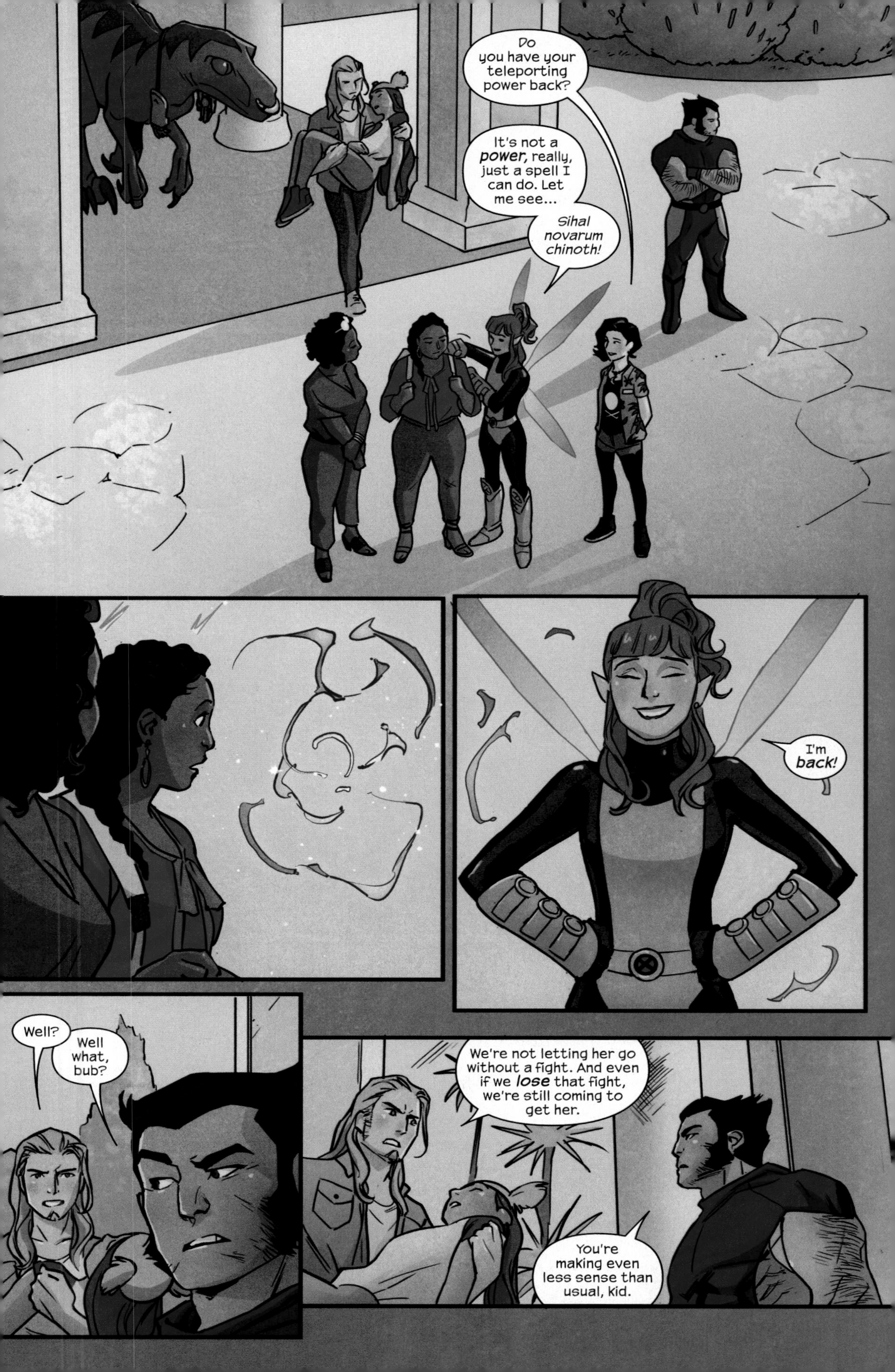
Do you have your teleporting power back?
It's not a *power,* really, just a spell I can do. Let me see...
Sihal novarum chinoth!
I'm *back!*
Well?
Well what, bub?
We're not letting her go without a fight. And even if we *lose* that fight, we're still coming to get her.
You're making even less sense than usual, kid.

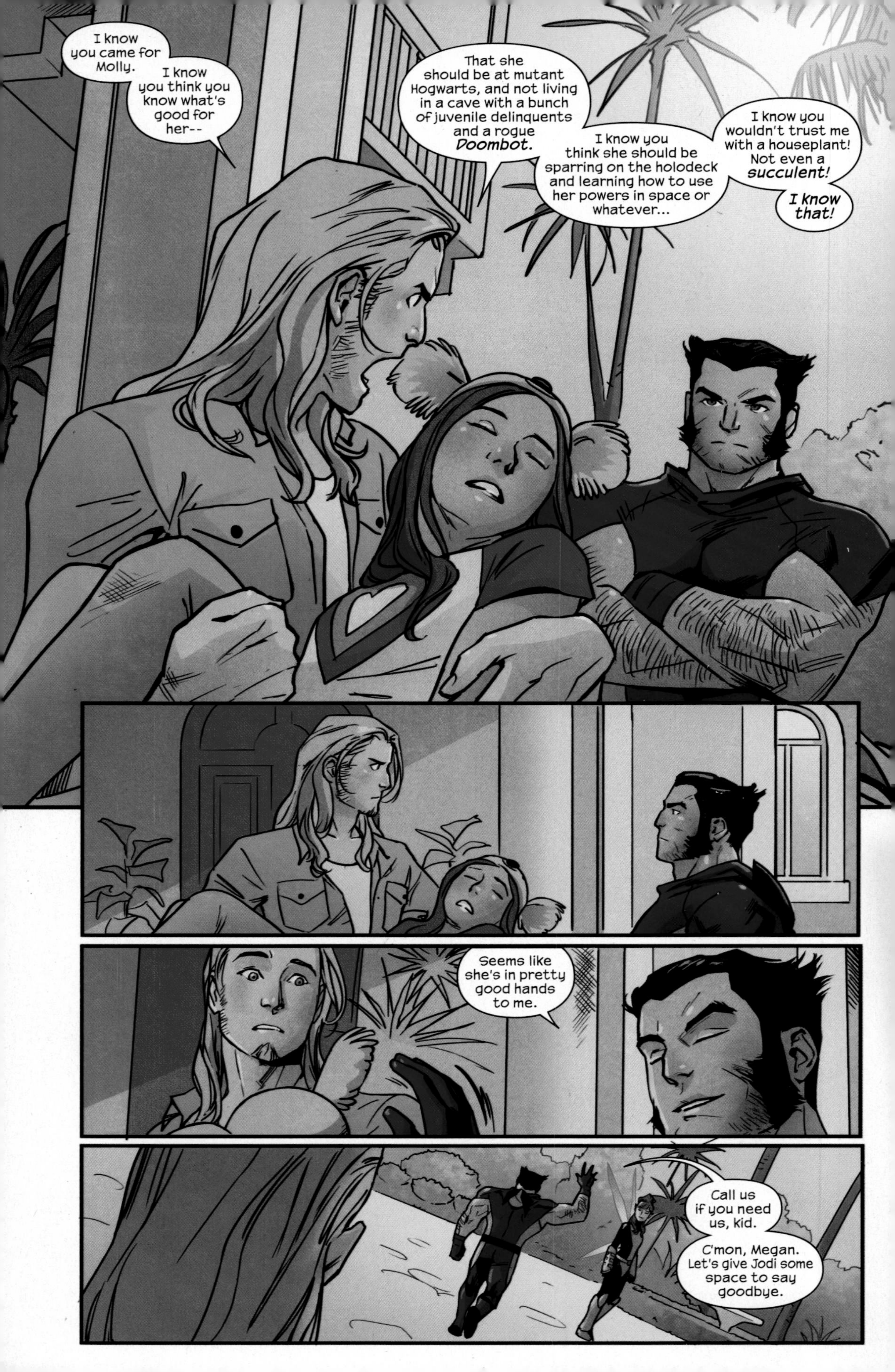

I know you came for Molly.
I know you think you know what's good for her--
That she should be at mutant Hogwarts, and not living in a cave with a bunch of juvenile delinquents and a rogue *Doombot.*
I know you think she should be sparring on the holodeck and learning how to use her powers in space or whatever...
I know you wouldn't trust me with a houseplant! Not even a *succulent!*
I know that!
Seems like she's in pretty good hands to me.
Call us if you need us, kid.
C'mon, Megan. Let's give Jodi some space to say goodbye.

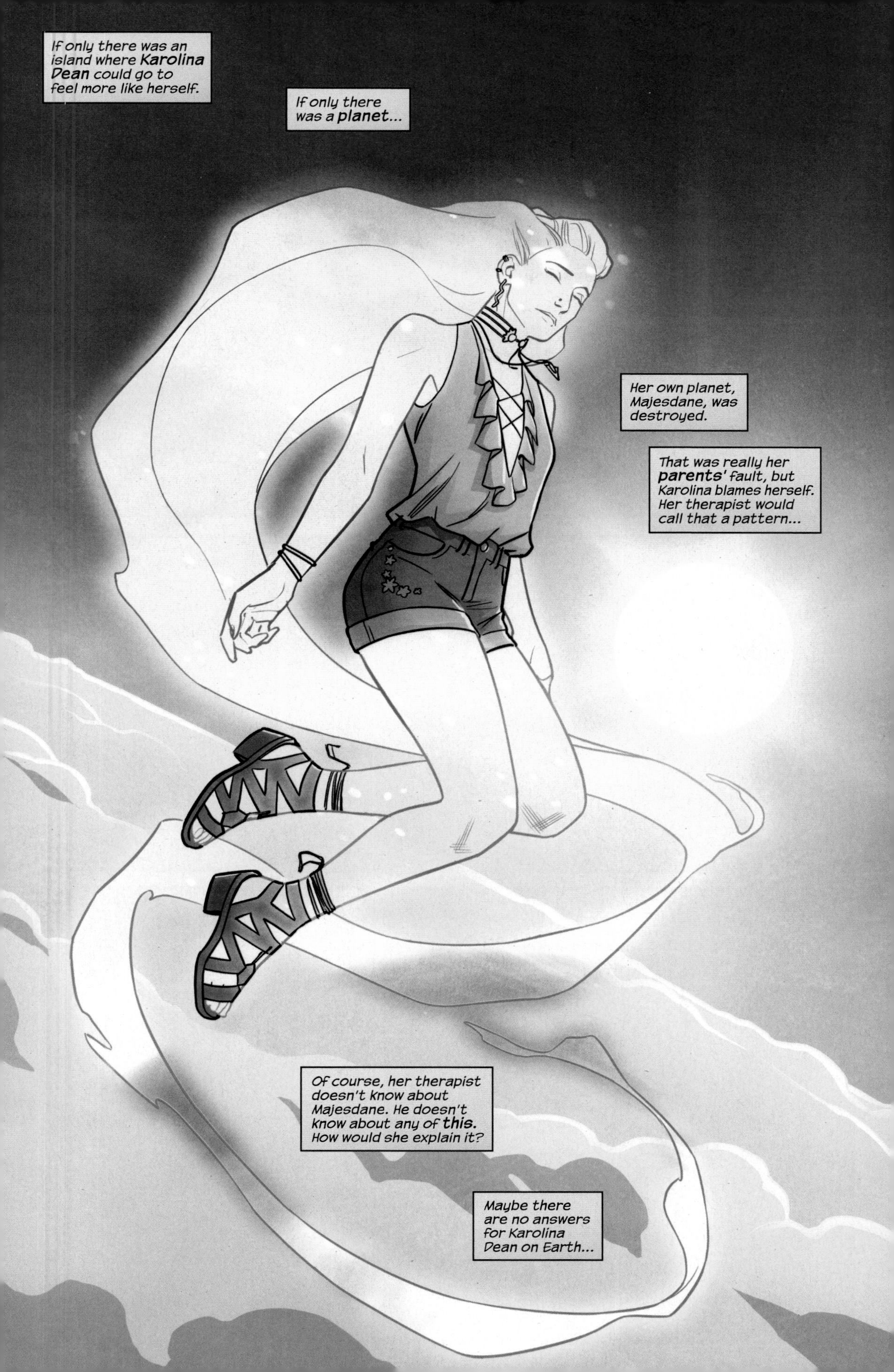
If only there was an island where Karolina Dean could go to feel more like herself.
If only there was a planet...
Her own planet, Majesdane, was destroyed.
That was really her parents' fault, but Karolina blames herself. Her therapist would call that a pattern...
Of course, her therapist doesn't know about Majesdane. He doesn't know about any of this. How would she explain it?
Maybe there are no answers for Karolina Dean on Earth...

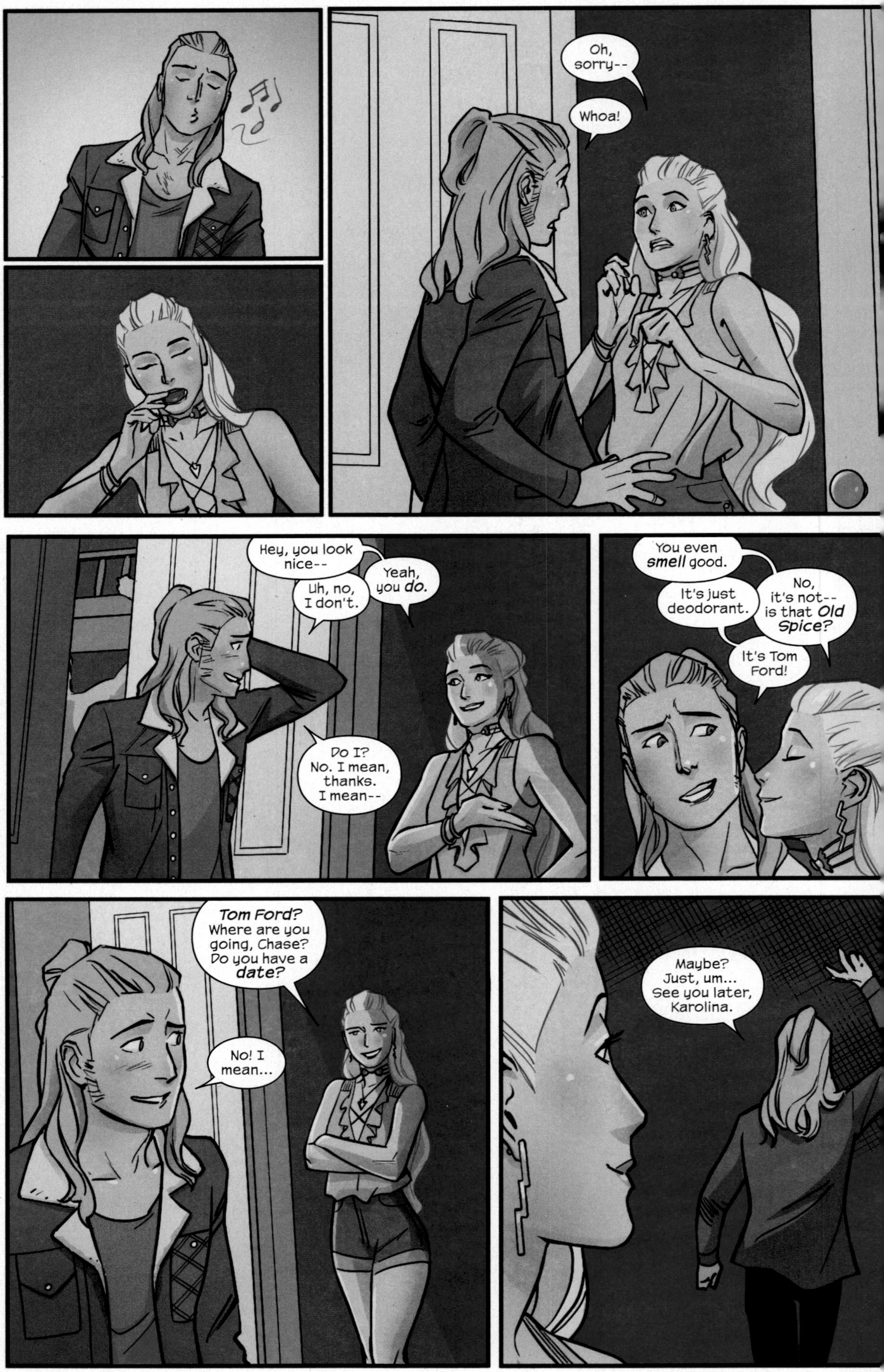
Oh, sorry--
Whoa!
Hey, you look nice--
Uh, no, I don't.
Yeah, you *do.*
Do I? No. I mean, thanks. I mean--
You even **smell** good.
It's just deodorant.
No, it's not-- is that *Old Spice?*
It's Tom Ford!
Tom Ford? Where are you going, Chase? Do you have a *date?*
No! I mean...
Maybe? Just, um... See you later, Karolina.

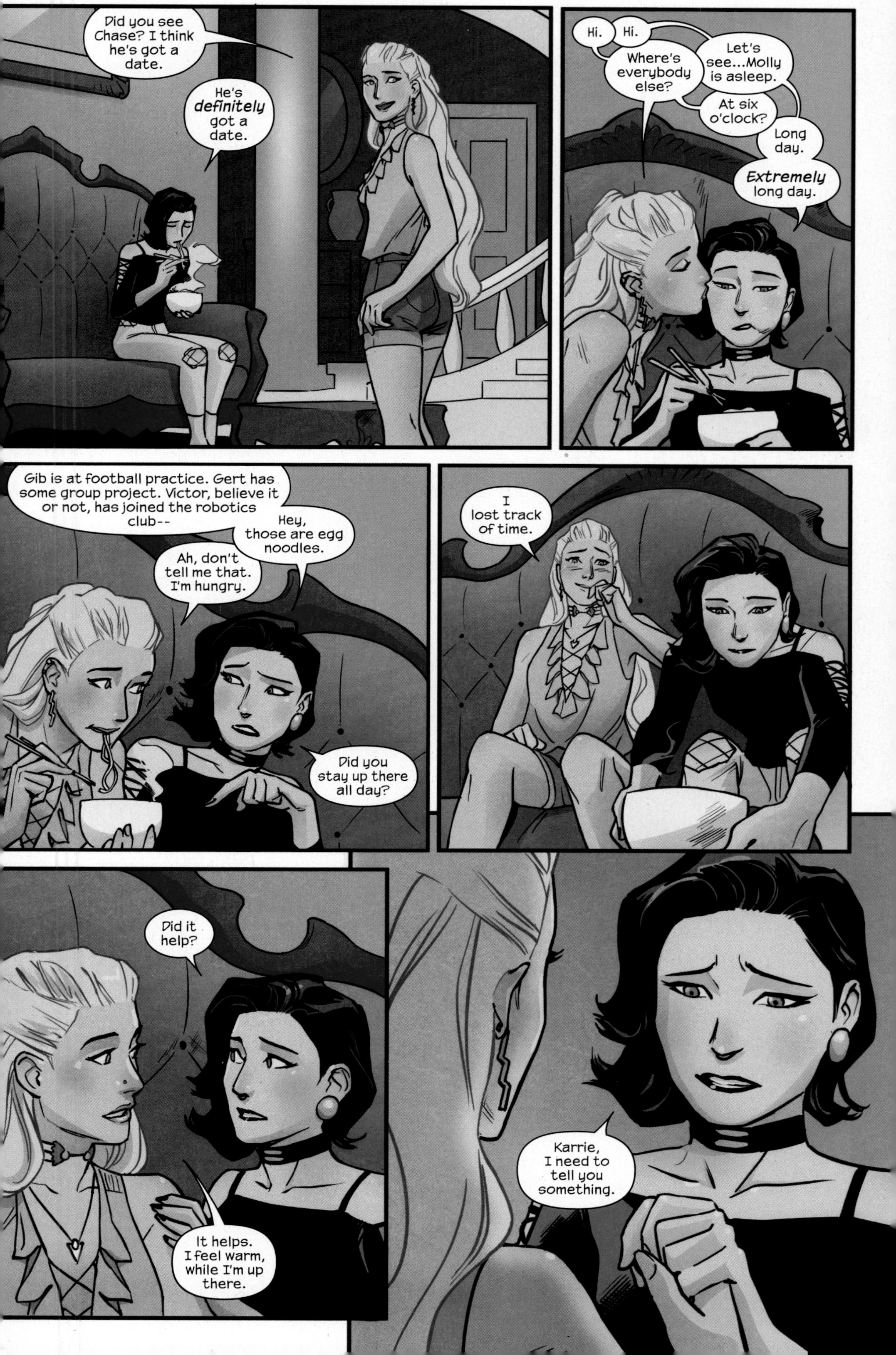

Did you see Chase? I think he's got a date.
He's *definitely* got a date.
Hi.
Hi.
Where's everybody else?
Let's see...Molly is asleep.
At six o'clock?
Long day.
Extremely long day.
Gib is at football practice. Gert has some group project. Victor, believe it or not, has joined the robotics club--
Hey, those are egg noodles.
Ah, don't tell me that. I'm hungry.
Did you stay up there all day?
I lost track of time.
Did it help?
It helps. I feel warm, while I'm up there.
Karrie, I need to tell you something.

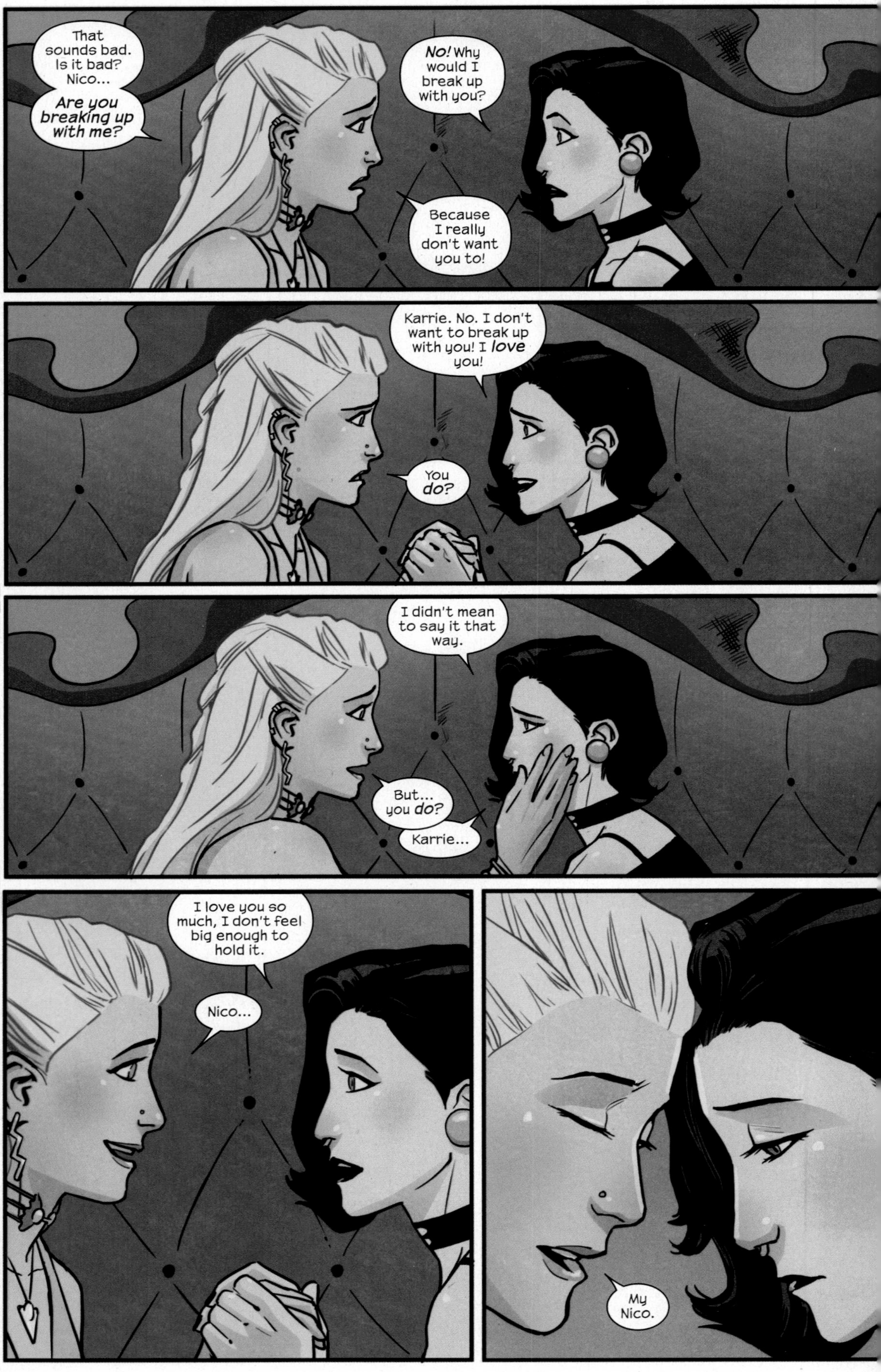
That sounds bad. Is it bad? Nico...
Are you breaking up with me?
No! Why would I break up with you?
Because I really don't want you to!
Karrie. No. I don't want to break up with you! I love you!
You do?
I didn't mean to say it that way.
But... you do?
Karrie...
I love you so much, I don't feel big enough to hold it.
Nico...
My Nico.

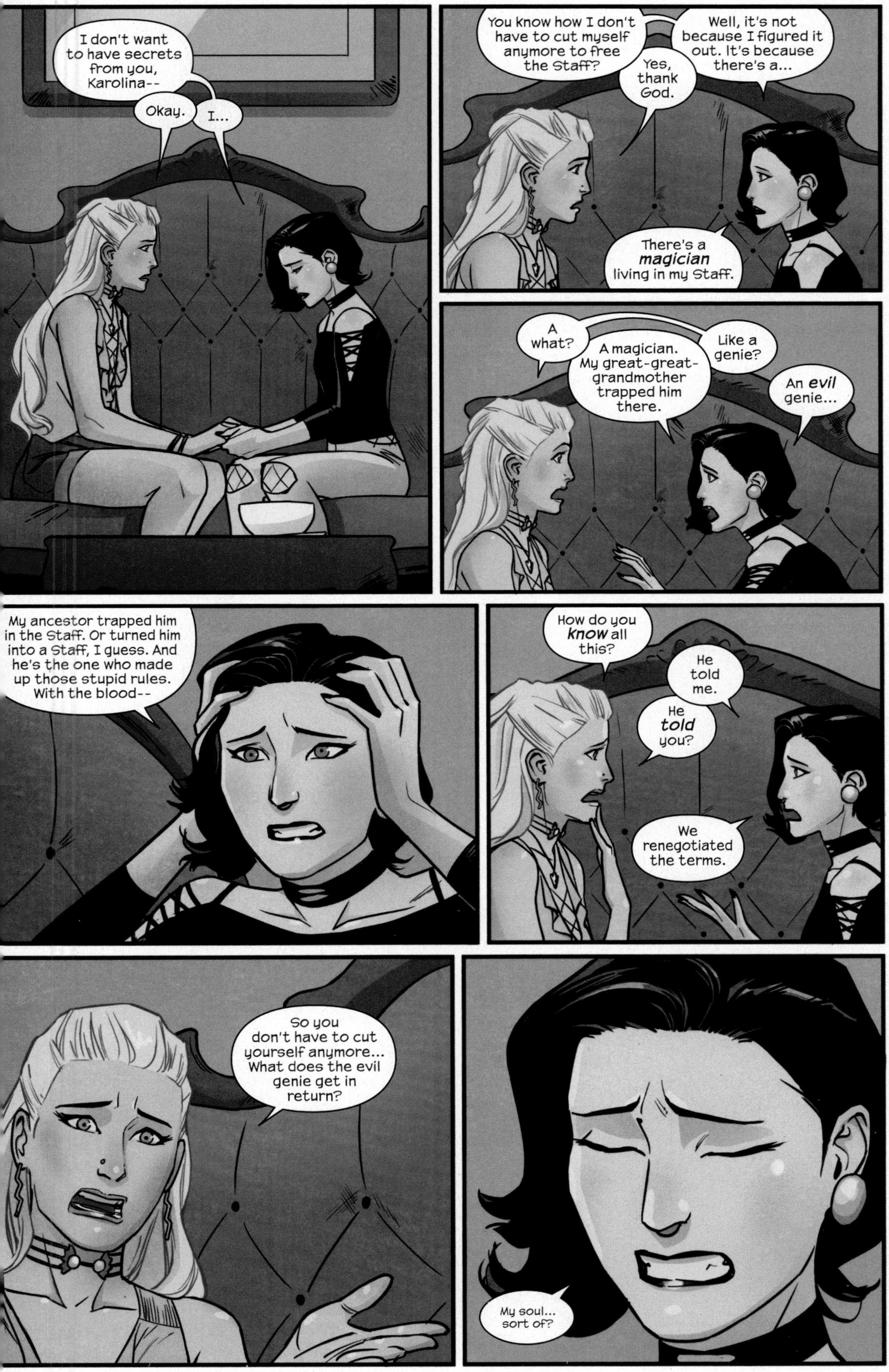

I don't want to have secrets from you, Karolina--
Okay.
I...
You know how I don't have to cut myself anymore to free the Staff?
Yes, thank God.
Well, it's not because I figured it out. It's because there's a...
There's a *magician* living in my Staff.
A what?
A magician. My great-great-grandmother trapped him there.
Like a genie?
An *evil* genie...
My ancestor trapped him in the Staff. Or turned him into a Staff, I guess. And he's the one who made up those stupid rules. With the blood--
How do you *know* all this?
He told me.
He *told* you?
We renegotiated the terms.
So you don't have to cut yourself anymore... What does the evil genie get in return?
My soul... sort of?

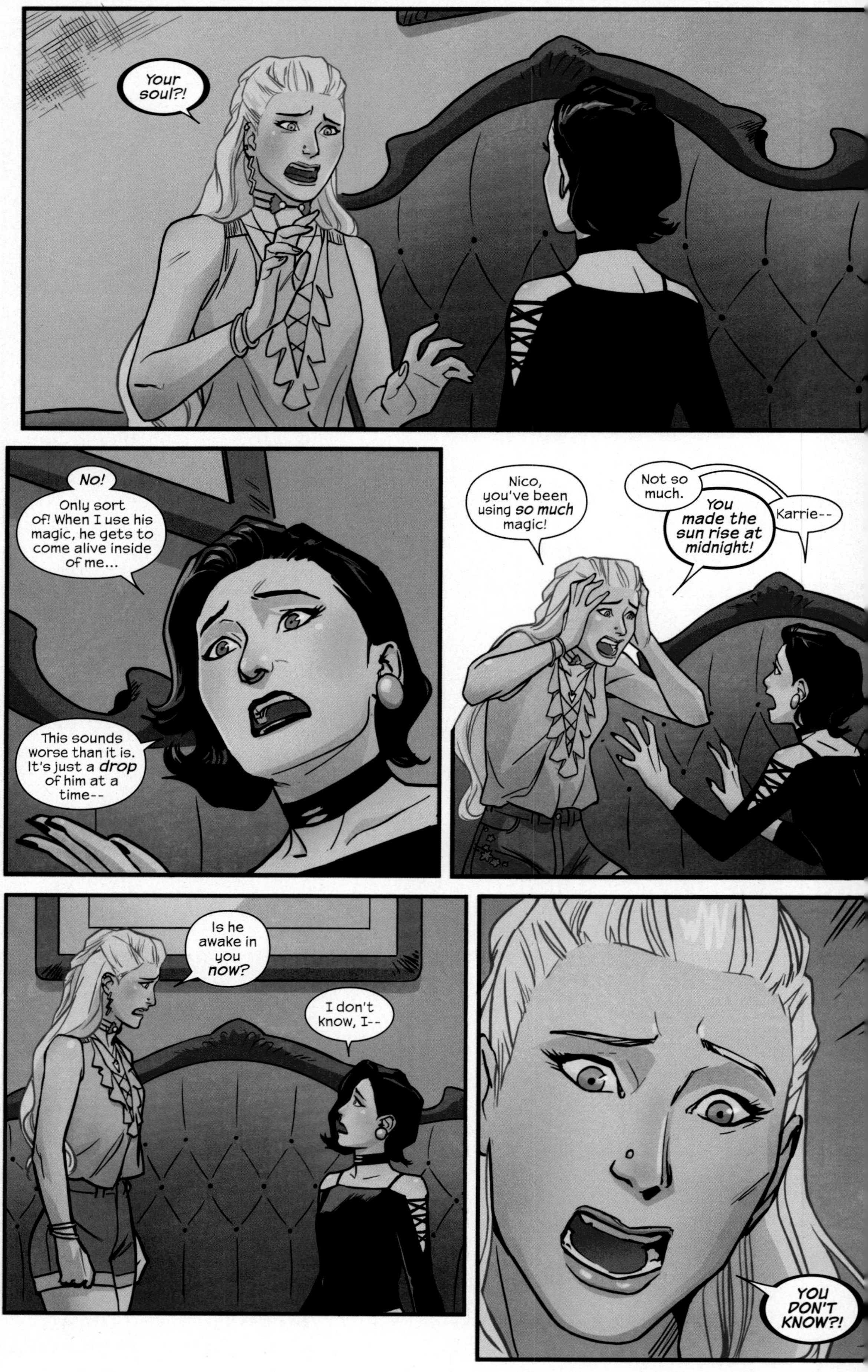

Your soul?!
No! Only sort of! When I use his magic, he gets to come alive inside of me...
This sounds worse than it is. It's just a drop of him at a time--
Nico, you've been using so much magic!
Not so much.
Karrie--
You made the sun rise at midnight!
Is he awake in you now?
I don't know, I--
YOU DON'T KNOW?!

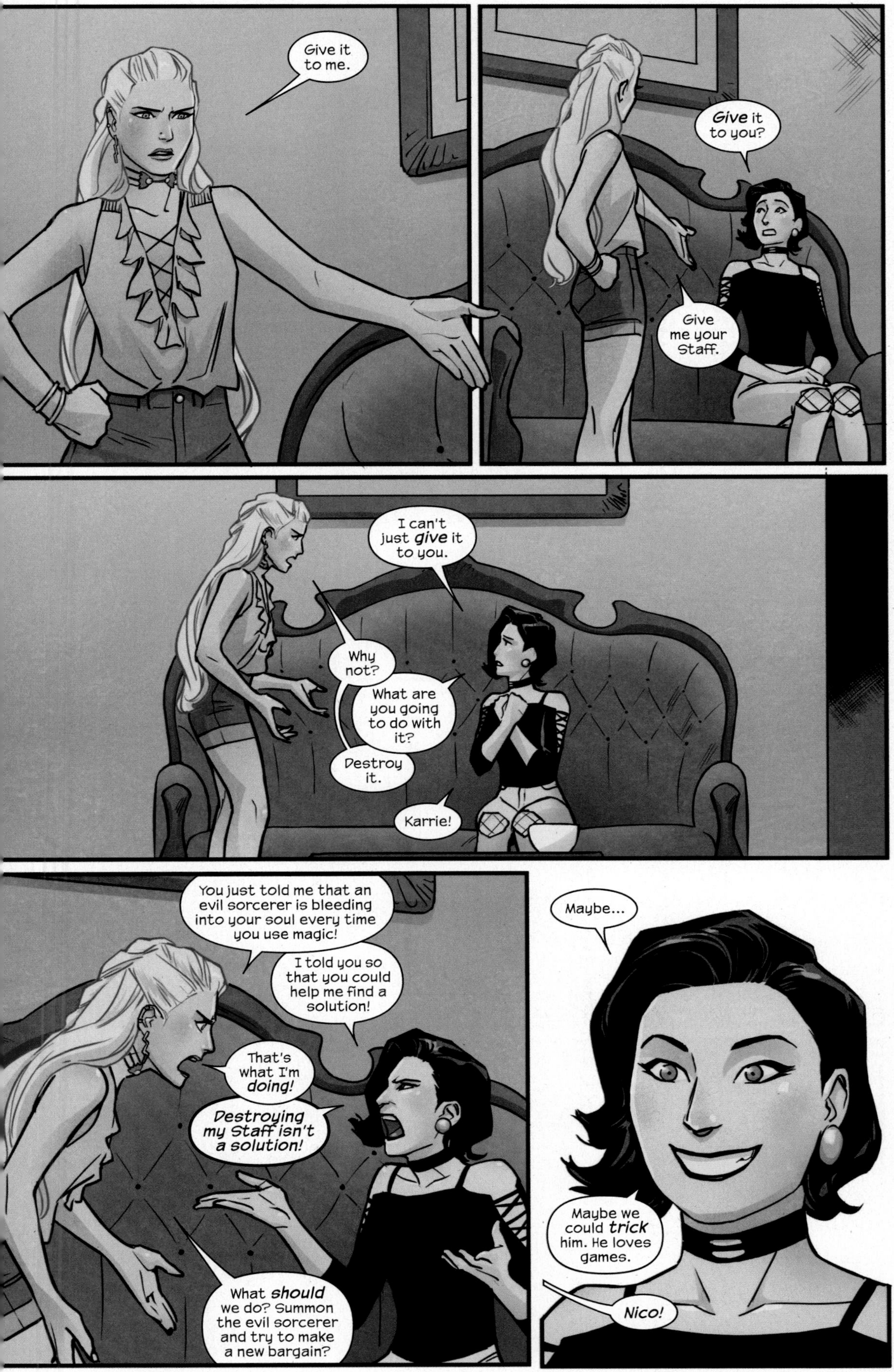
Give it to me.
Give it to you?
Give me your Staff.
I can't just *give* it to you.
Why not?
What are you going to do with it?
Destroy it.
Karrie!
You just told me that an evil sorcerer is bleeding into your soul every time you use magic!
I told you so that you could help me find a solution!
That's what I'm *doing!*
Destroying my Staff isn't a solution!
What *should* we do? Summon the evil sorcerer and try to make a new bargain?
Maybe...
Maybe we could *trick* him. He loves games.
Nico!

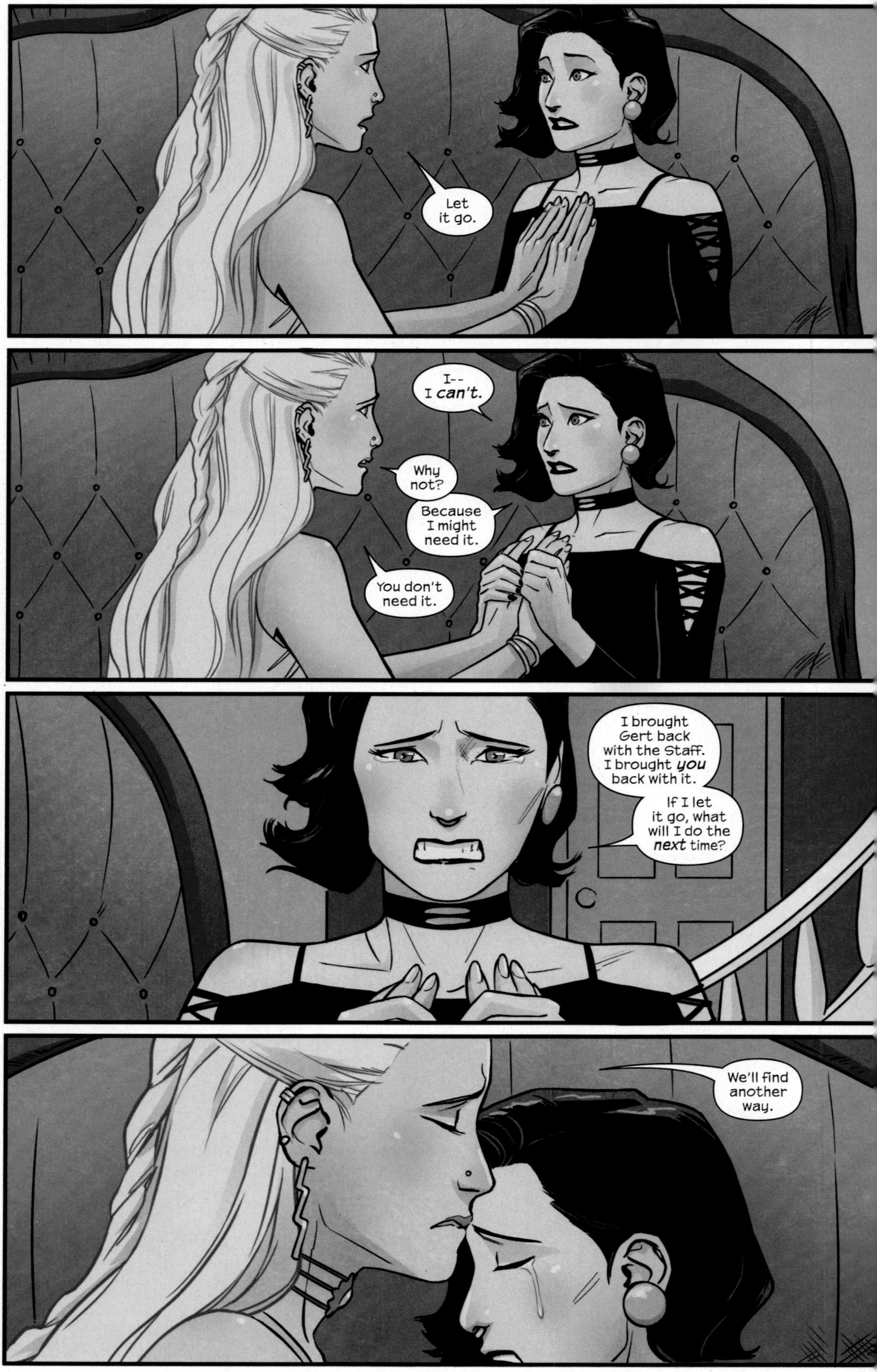
Let it go.
I-- I *can't.*
Why not?
Because I might need it.
You don't need it.
I brought Gert back with the Staff. I brought *you* back with it.
If I let it go, what will I do the *next* time?
We'll find another way.

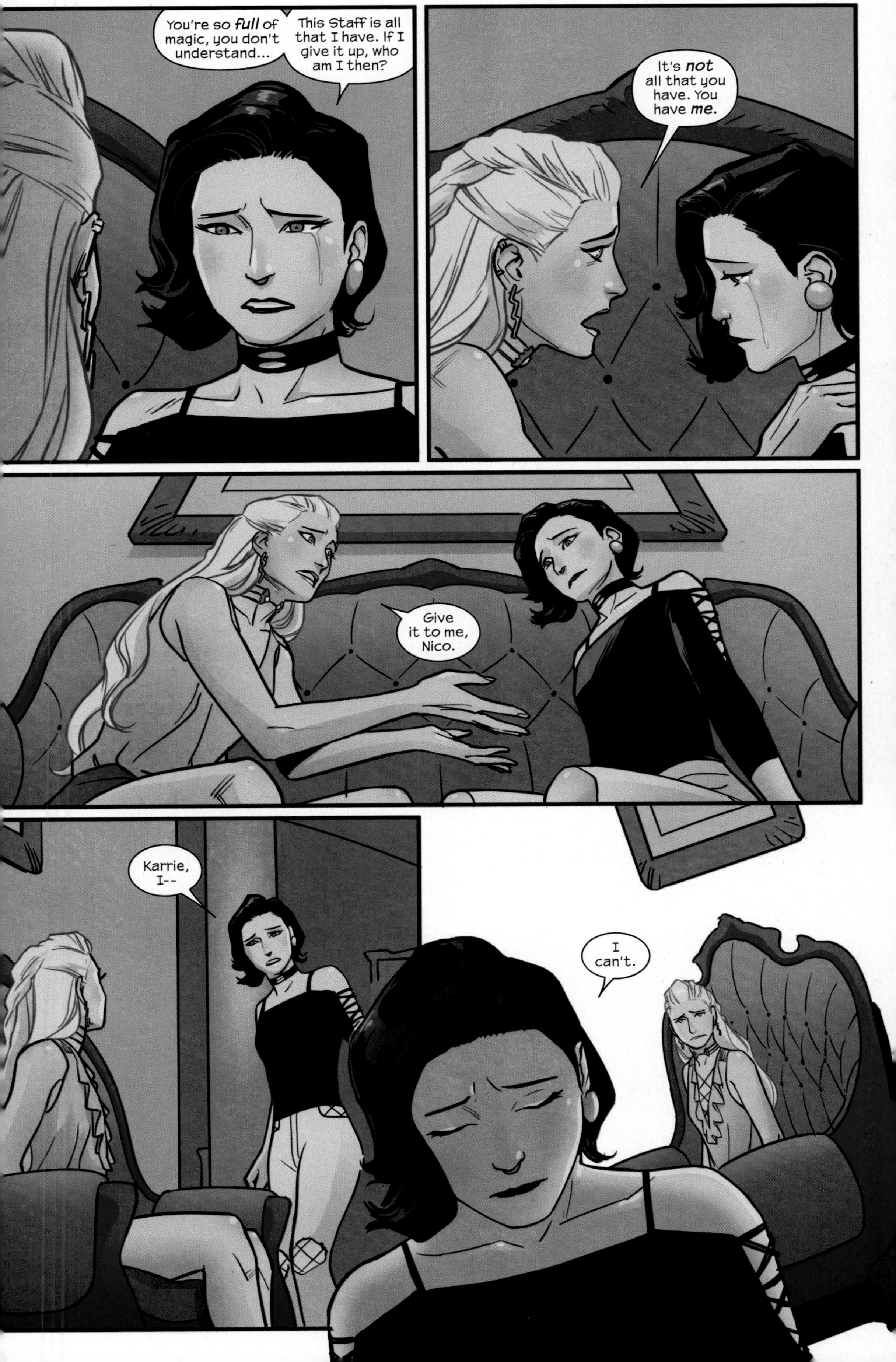
You're so *full* of magic, you don't understand...
This Staff is all that I have. If I give it up, who am I then?
It's *not* all that you have. You have *me.*
Give it to me, Nico.
Karrie, I--
I can't.

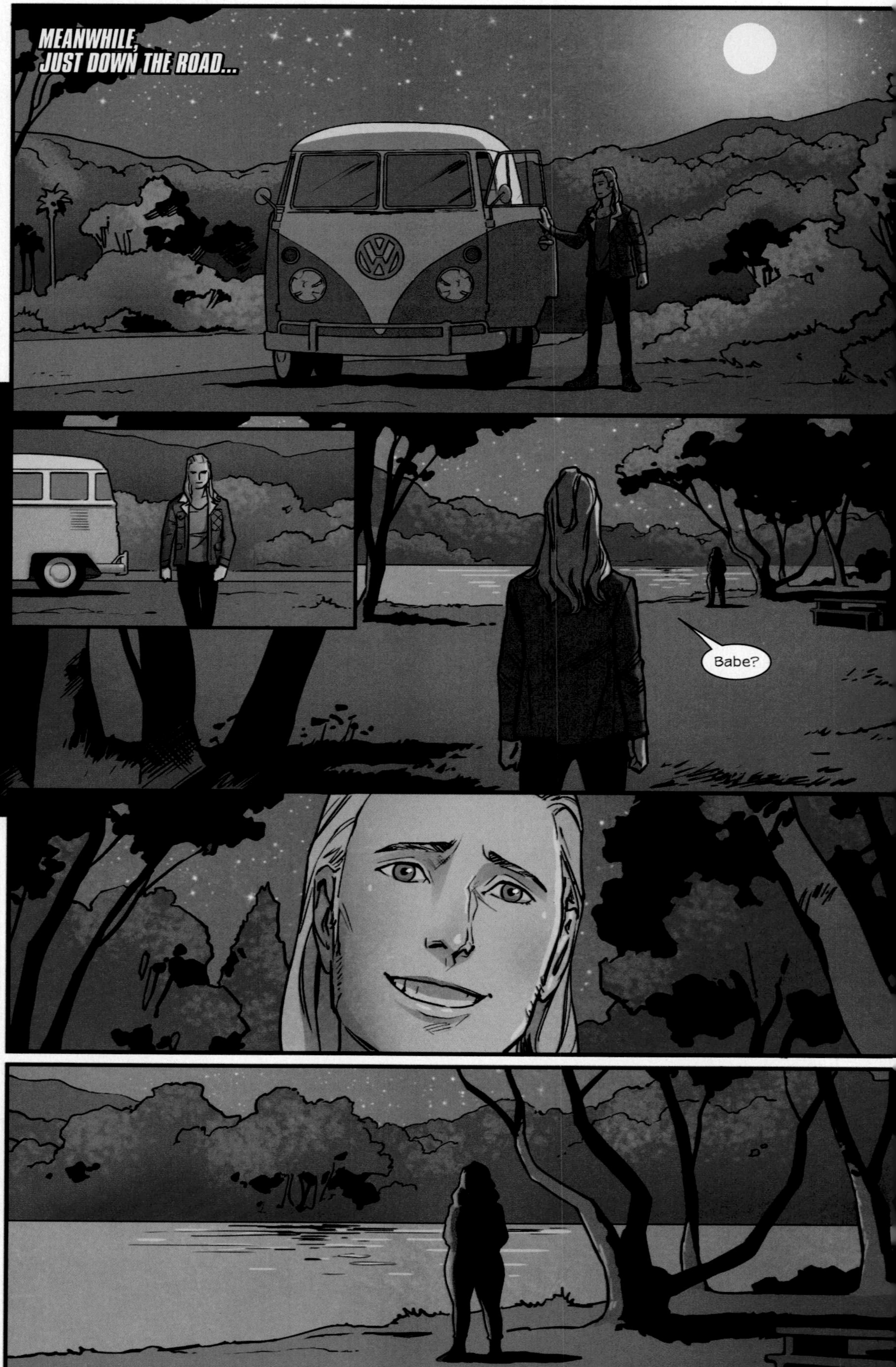
MEANWHILE, JUST DOWN THE ROAD...
Babe?

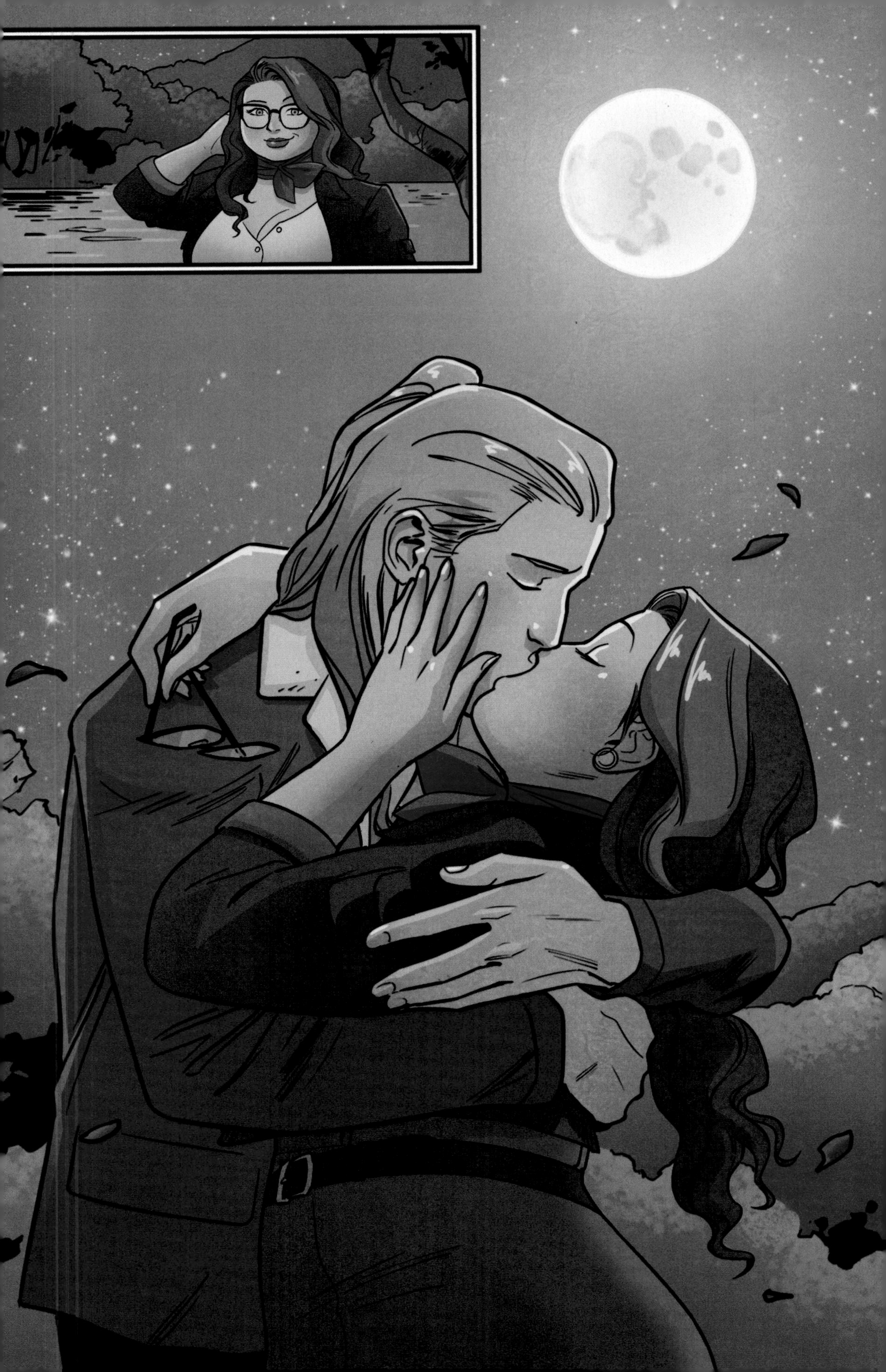

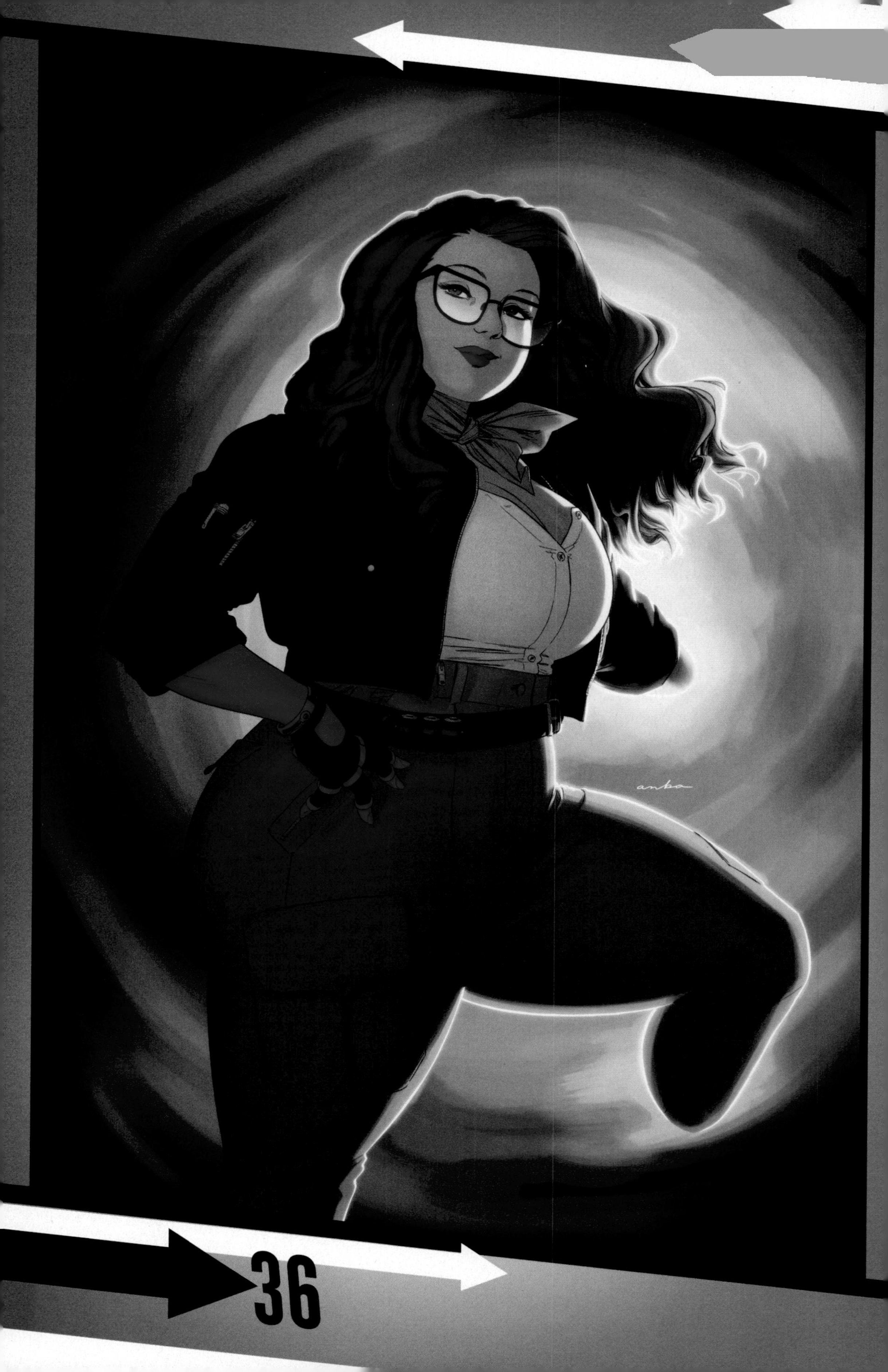
anba

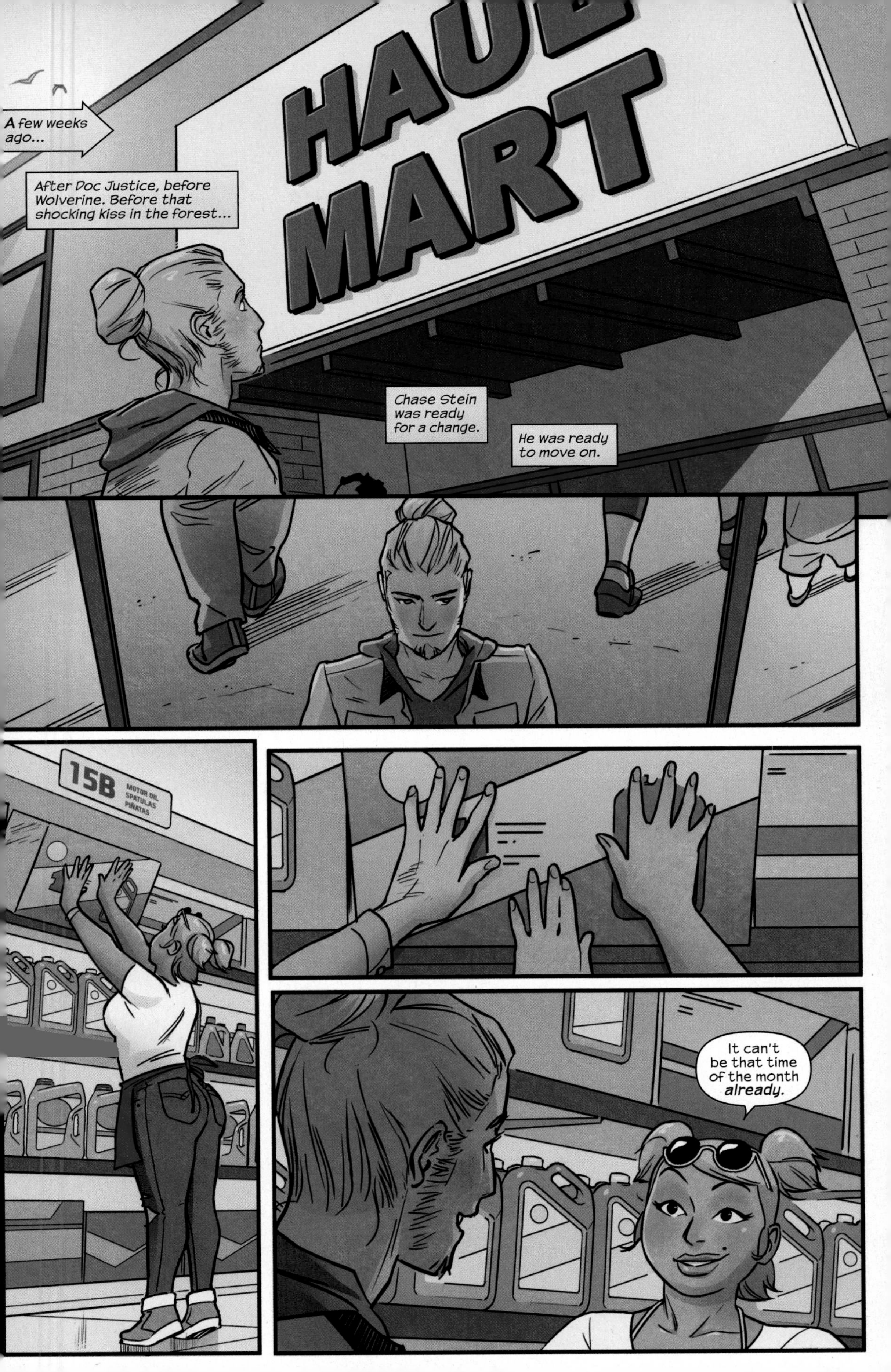
HAUL MART
A few weeks ago...
After Doc Justice, before Wolverine. Before that shocking kiss in the forest...
Chase Stein was ready for a change.
He was ready to move on.
15B MOTOR OIL SPATULAS PIÑATAS
It can't be that time of the month *already*.

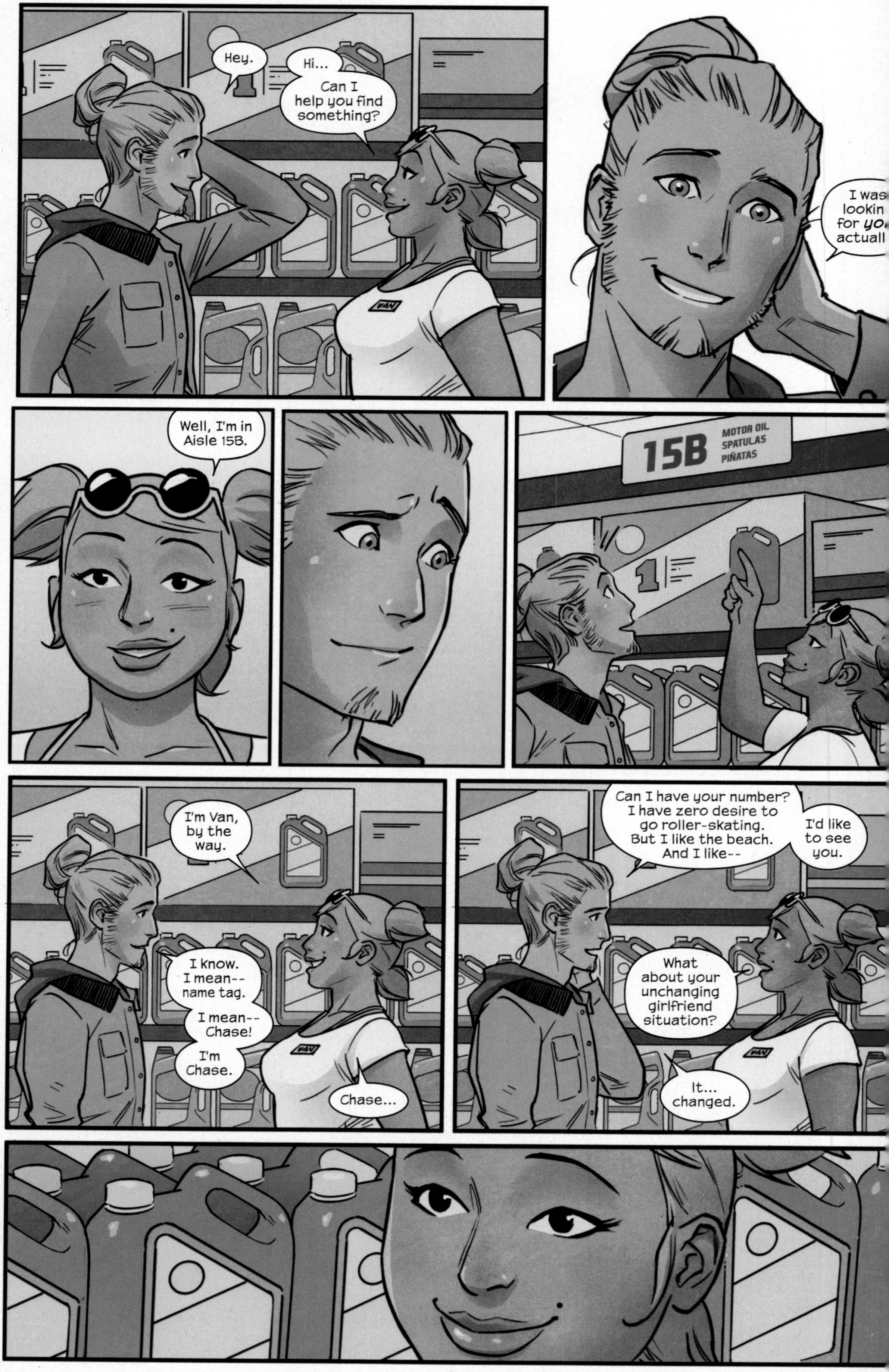
Hey.
Hi... Can I help you find something?
I was lookin for yo actuall
Well, I'm in Aisle 15B.
15B
MOTOR OIL
SPATULAS
PIÑATAS
I'm Van, by the way.
I know. I mean-- name tag.
I mean-- Chase!
I'm Chase.
Chase...
Can I have your number? I have zero desire to go roller-skating. But I like the beach. And I like--
I'd like to see you.
What about your unchanging girlfriend situation?
It... changed.

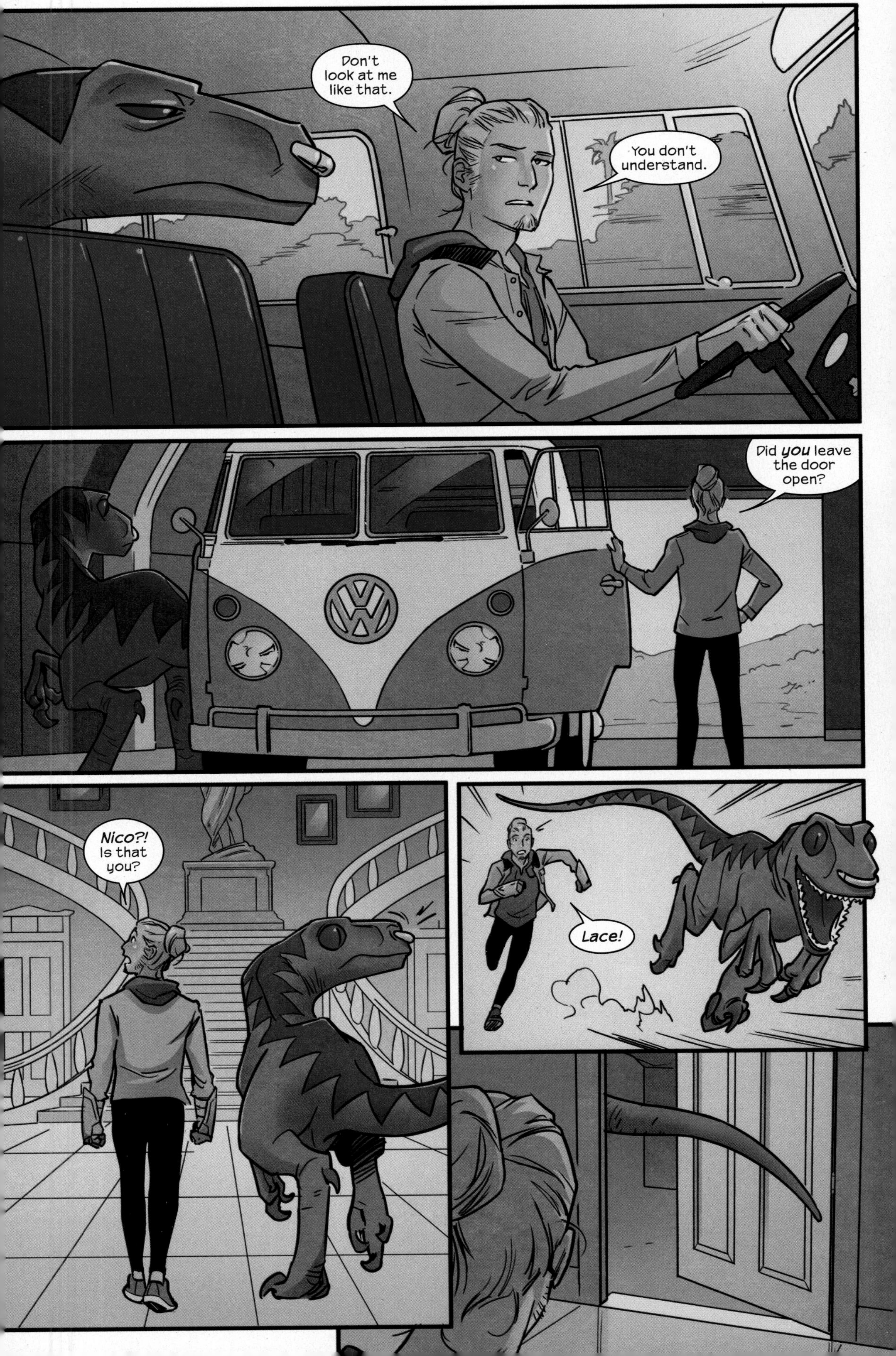
Don't look at me like that.
You don't understand.
Did *you* leave the door open?
Nico?! Is that you?
Lace!

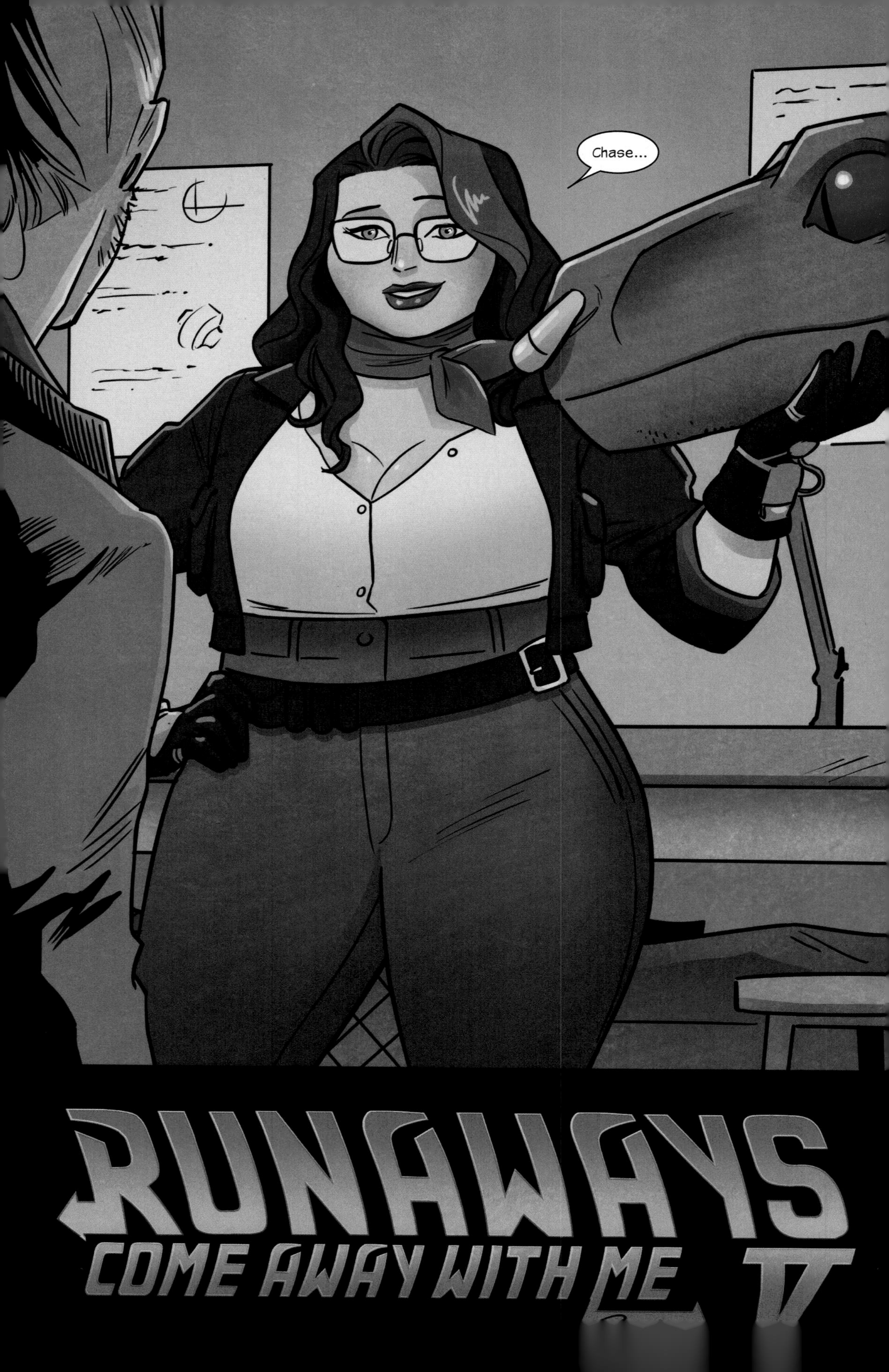
Chase...
RUNAWAYS
COME AWAY WITH ME

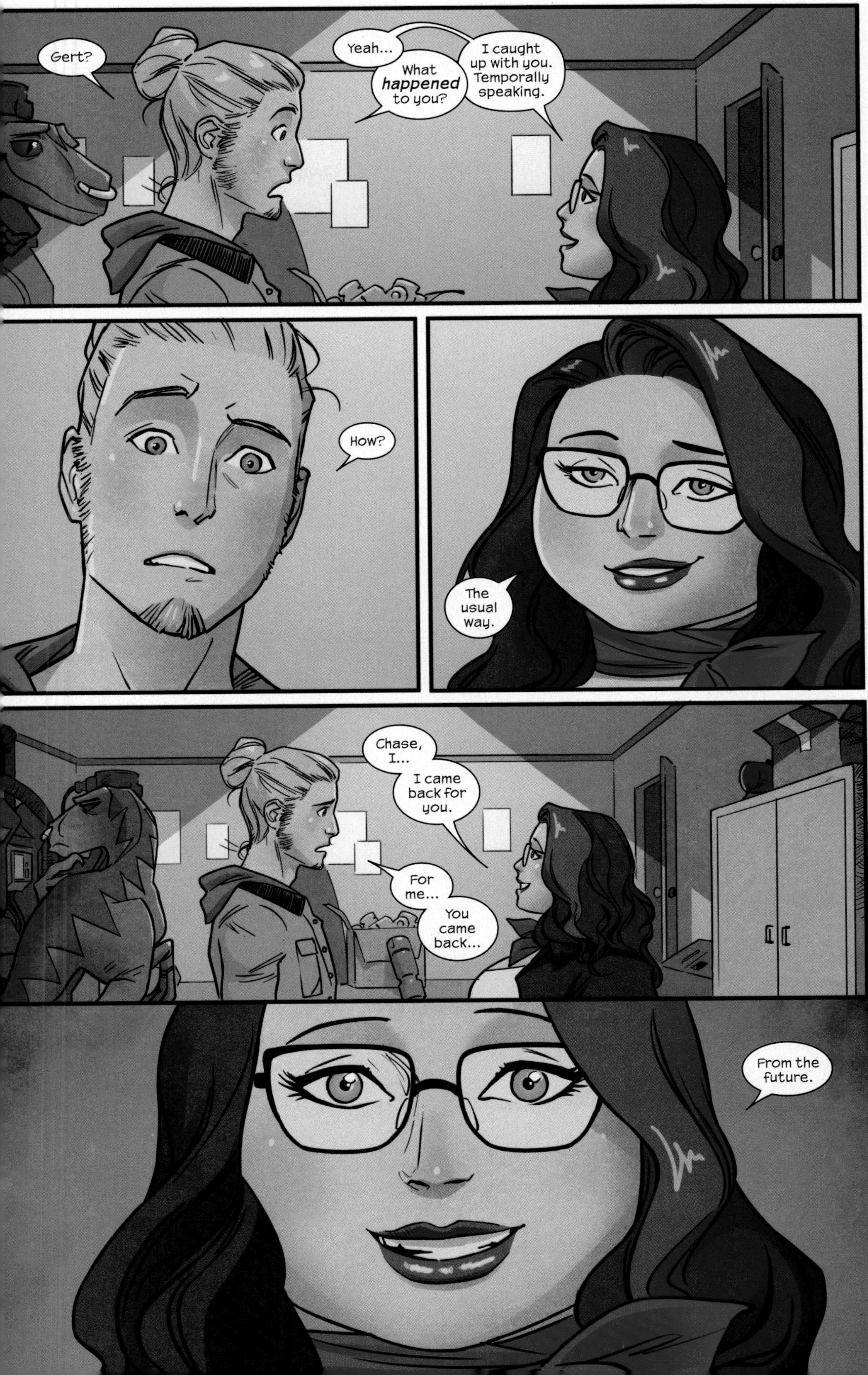

Gert?
Yeah...
What *happened* to you?
I caught up with you. Temporally speaking.
How?
The usual way.
Chase, I...
I came back for you.
For me...
You came back...
From the future.

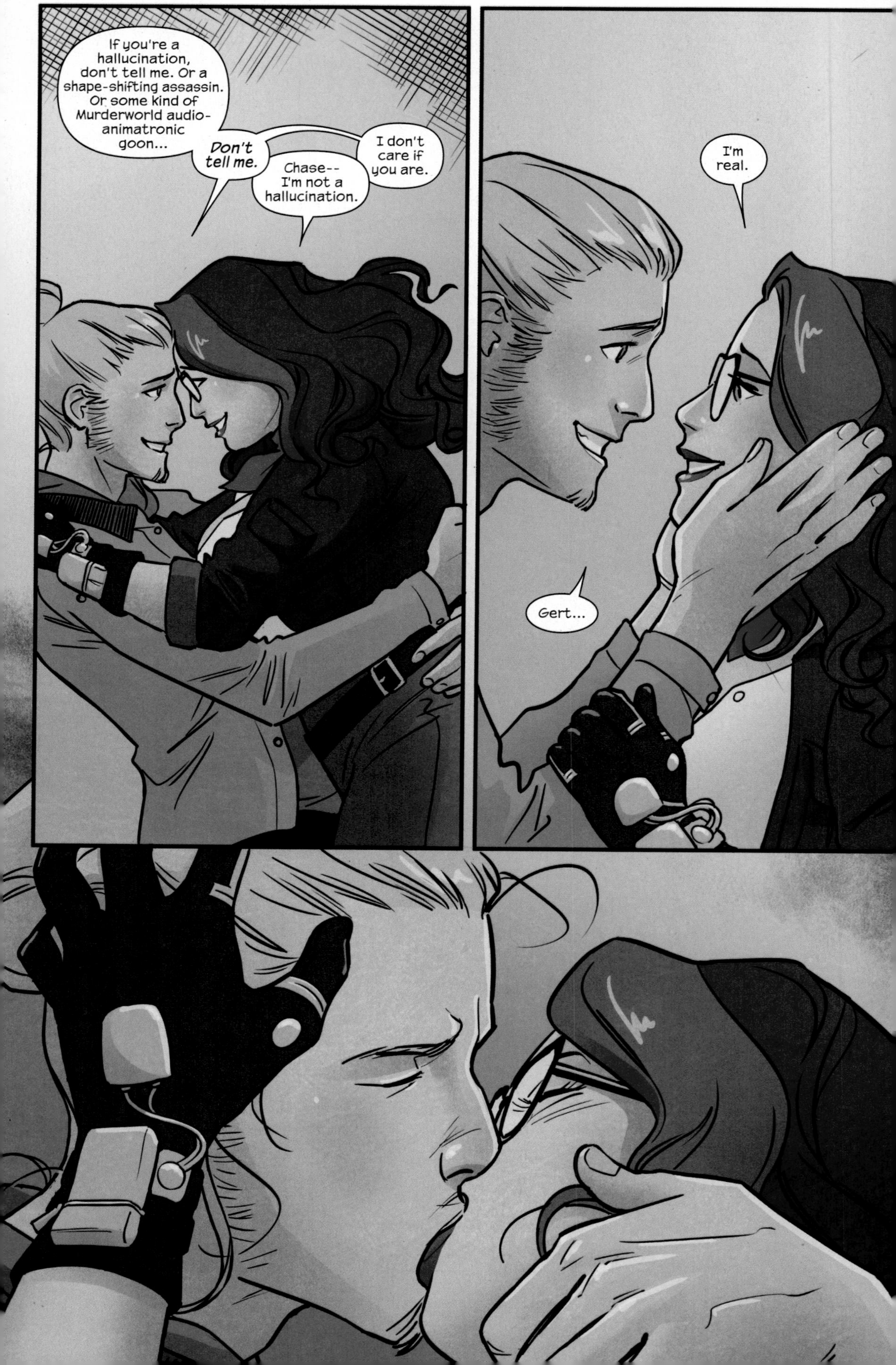
If you're a hallucination, don't tell me. Or a shape-shifting assassin. Or some kind of Murderworld audio-animatronic goon...
Don't tell me.
Chase-- I'm not a hallucination.
I don't care if you are.
I'm real.
Gert...

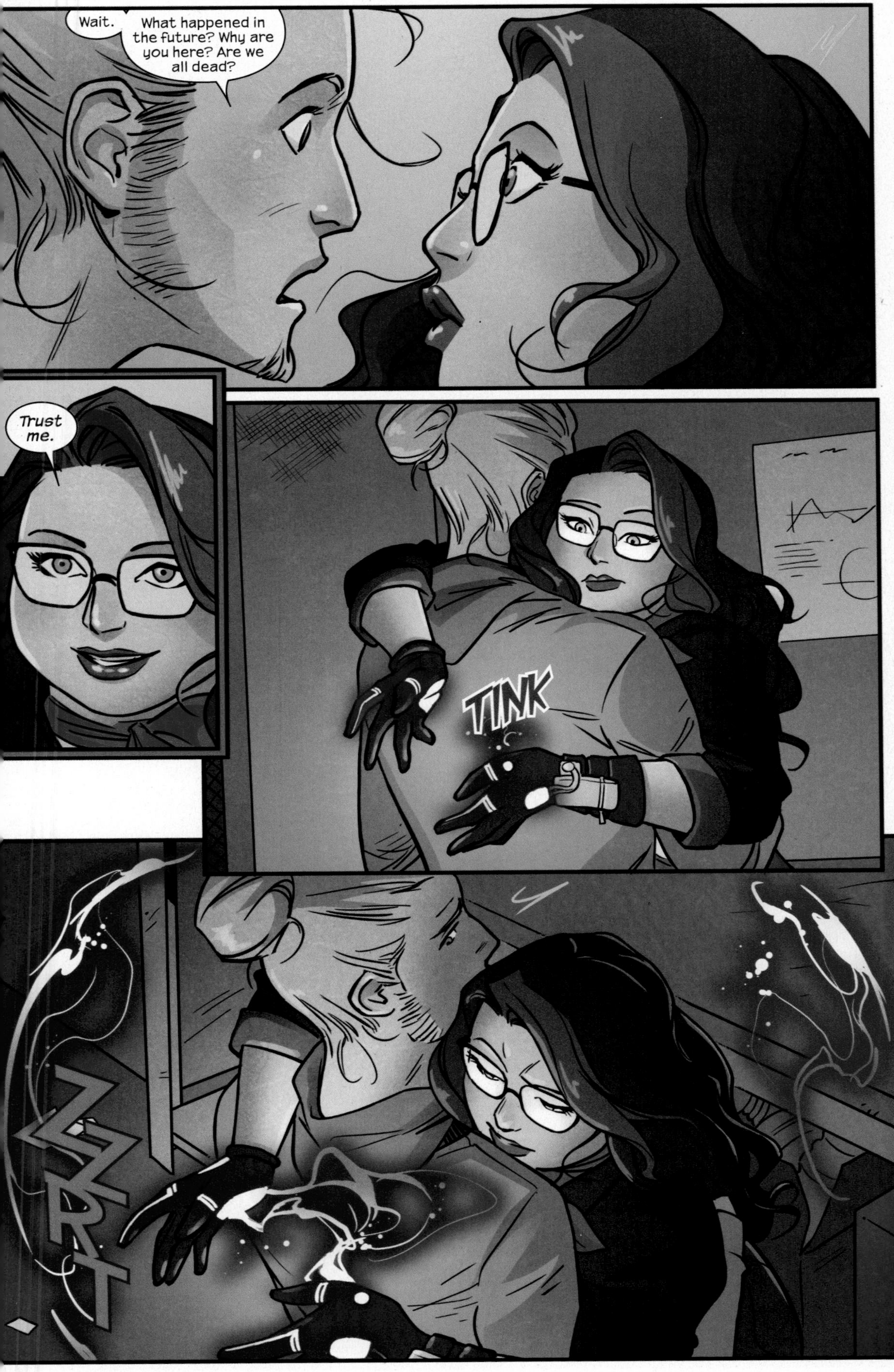

Wait.
What happened in the future? Why are you here? Are we all dead?
Trust me.
TINK
ZZRRT

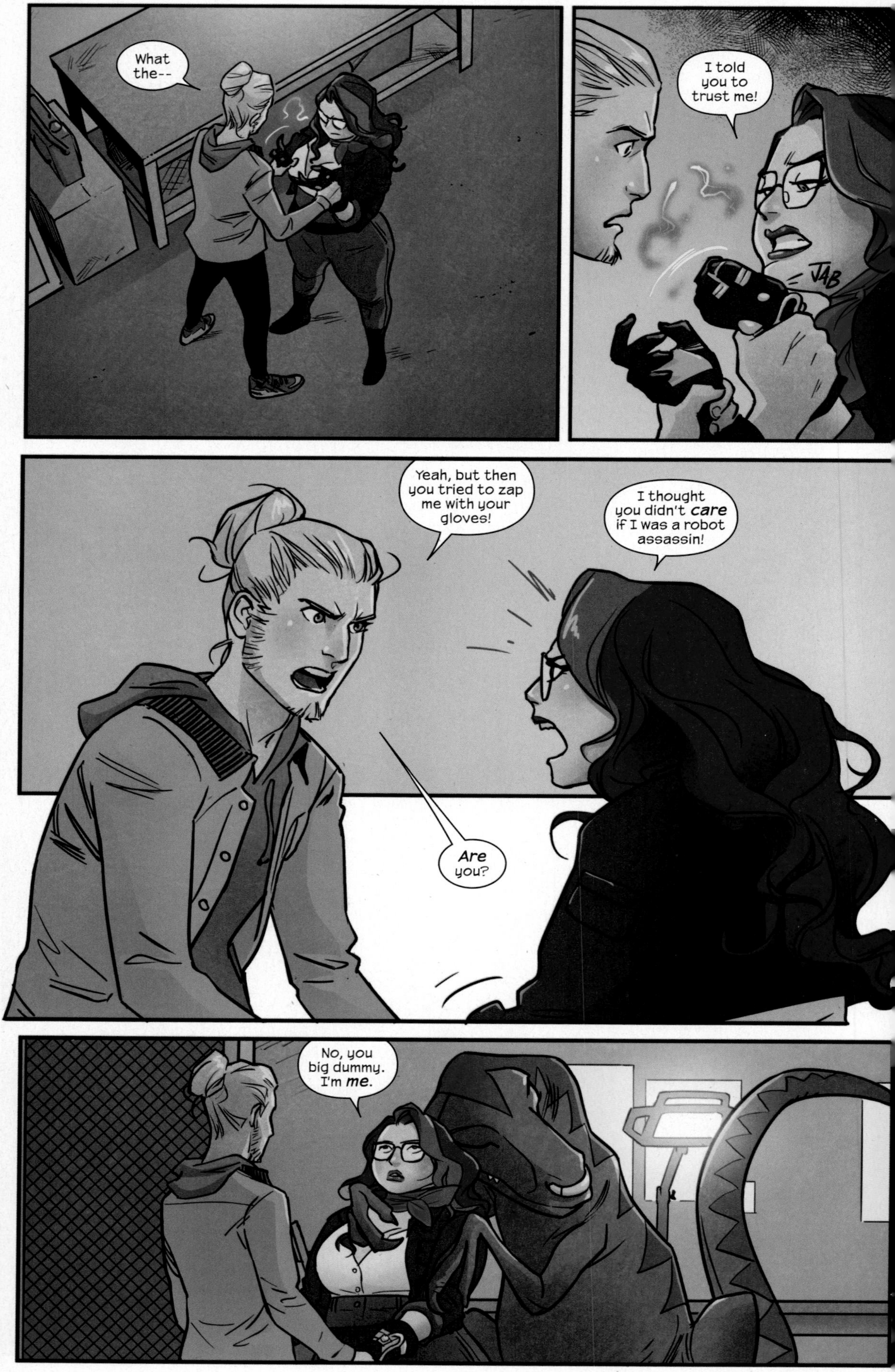

What the--
I told you to trust me!
JAB
Yeah, but then you tried to zap me with your gloves!
I thought you didn't *care* if I was a robot assassin!
Are you?
No, you big dummy. I'm *me*.

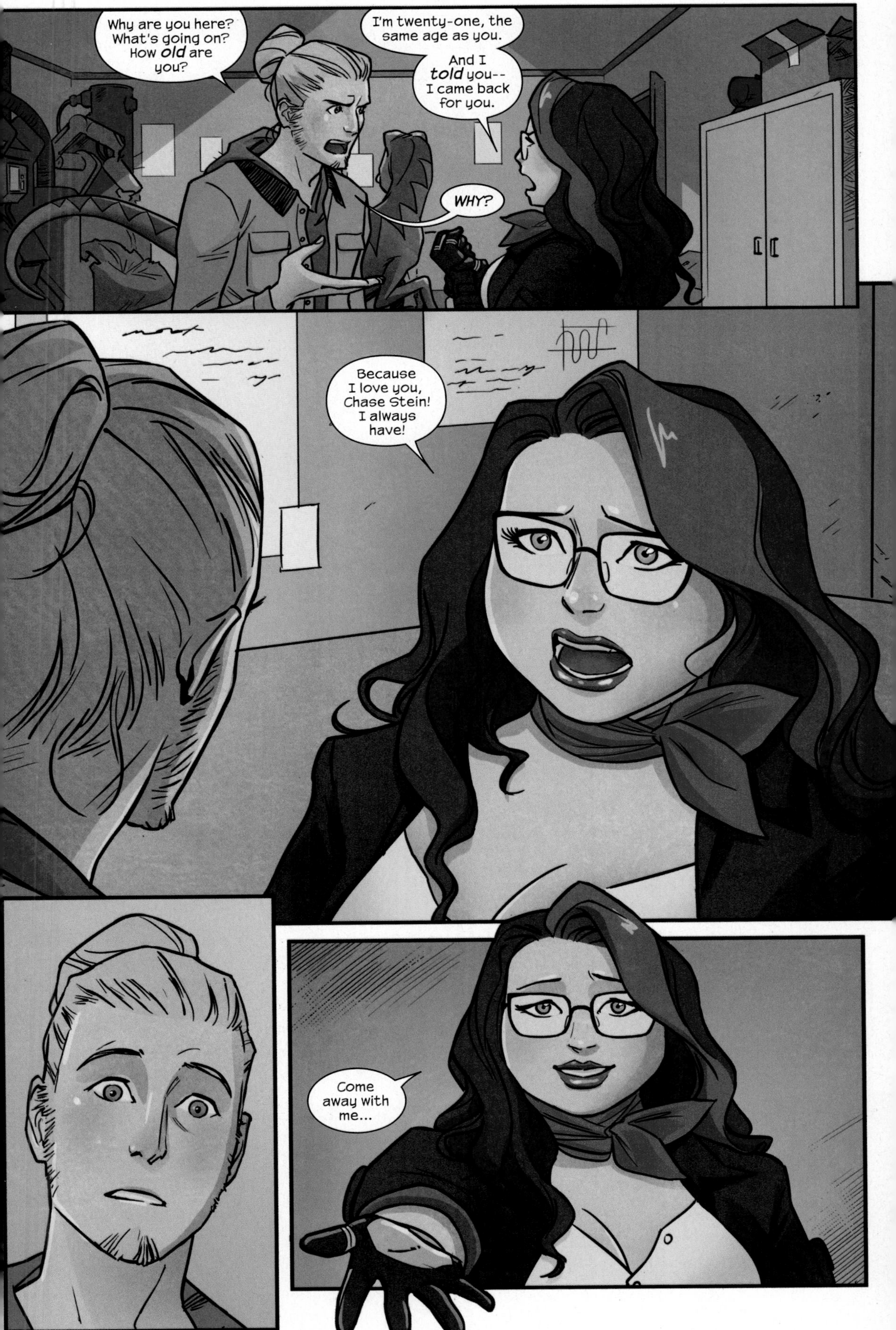
Why are you here? What's going on? How *old* are you?
I'm twenty-one, the same age as you.
And I *told* you-- I came back for you.
WHY?
Because I love you, Chase Stein! I always have!
Come away with me...

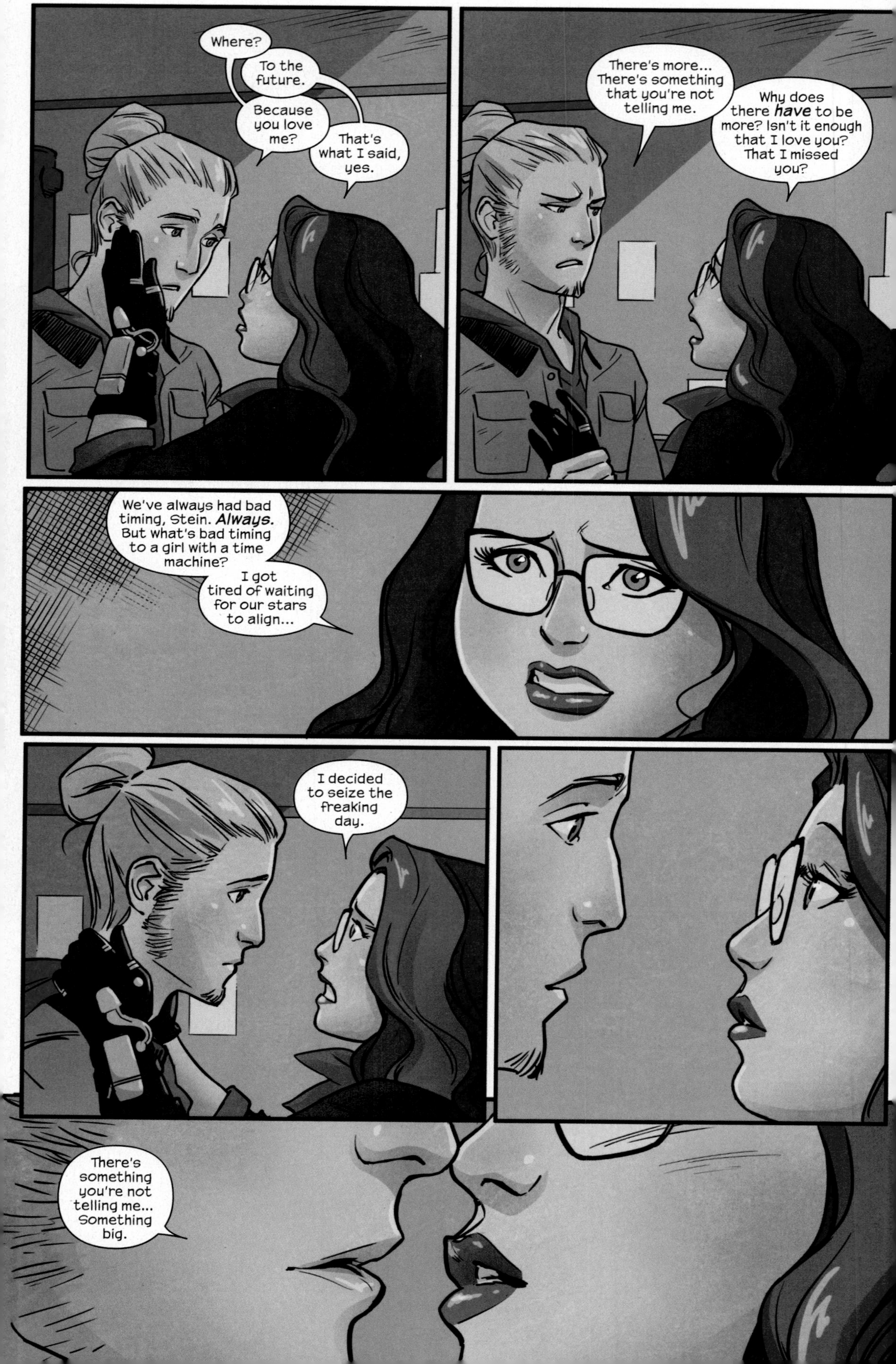
Where?
To the future.
Because you love me?
That's what I said, yes.
There's more... There's something that you're not telling me.
Why does there *have* to be more? Isn't it enough that I love you? That I missed you?
We've always had bad timing, Stein. *Always.* But what's bad timing to a girl with a time machine?
I got tired of waiting for our stars to align...
I decided to seize the freaking day.
There's something you're not telling me... Something big.

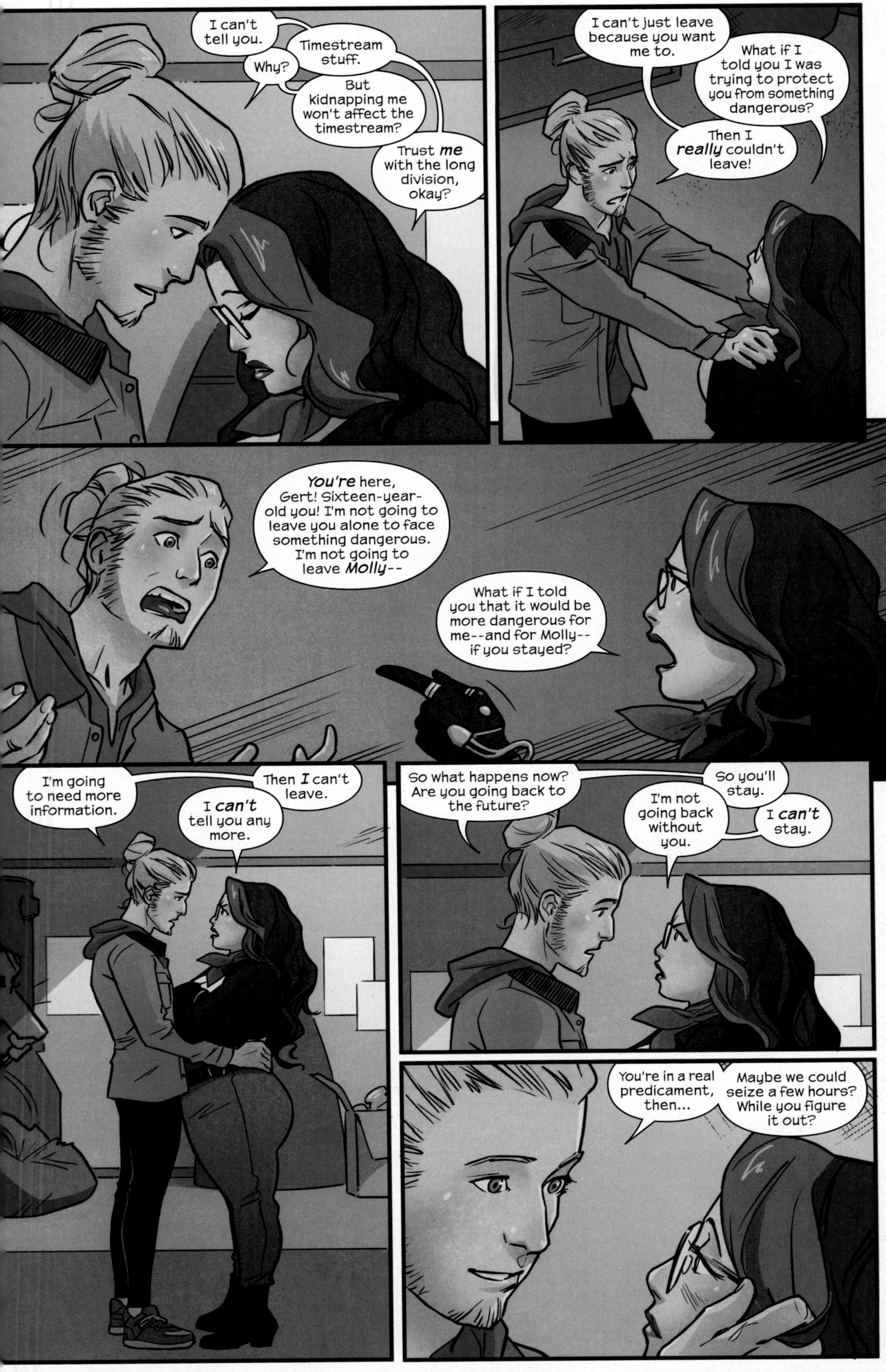
I can't tell you.
Why?
Timestream stuff.
But kidnapping me won't affect the timestream?
Trust *me* with the long division, okay?
I can't just leave because you want me to.
What if I told you I was trying to protect you from something dangerous?
Then I *really* couldn't leave!
You're here, Gert! Sixteen-year-old you! I'm not going to leave you alone to face something dangerous. I'm not going to leave *Molly*--
What if I told you that it would be more dangerous for me--and for Molly--if you stayed?
I'm going to need more information.
Then *I* can't leave.
I *can't* tell you any more.
So what happens now? Are you going back to the future?
So you'll stay.
I'm not going back without you.
I *can't* stay.
You're in a real predicament, then...
Maybe we could seize a few hours? While you figure it out?

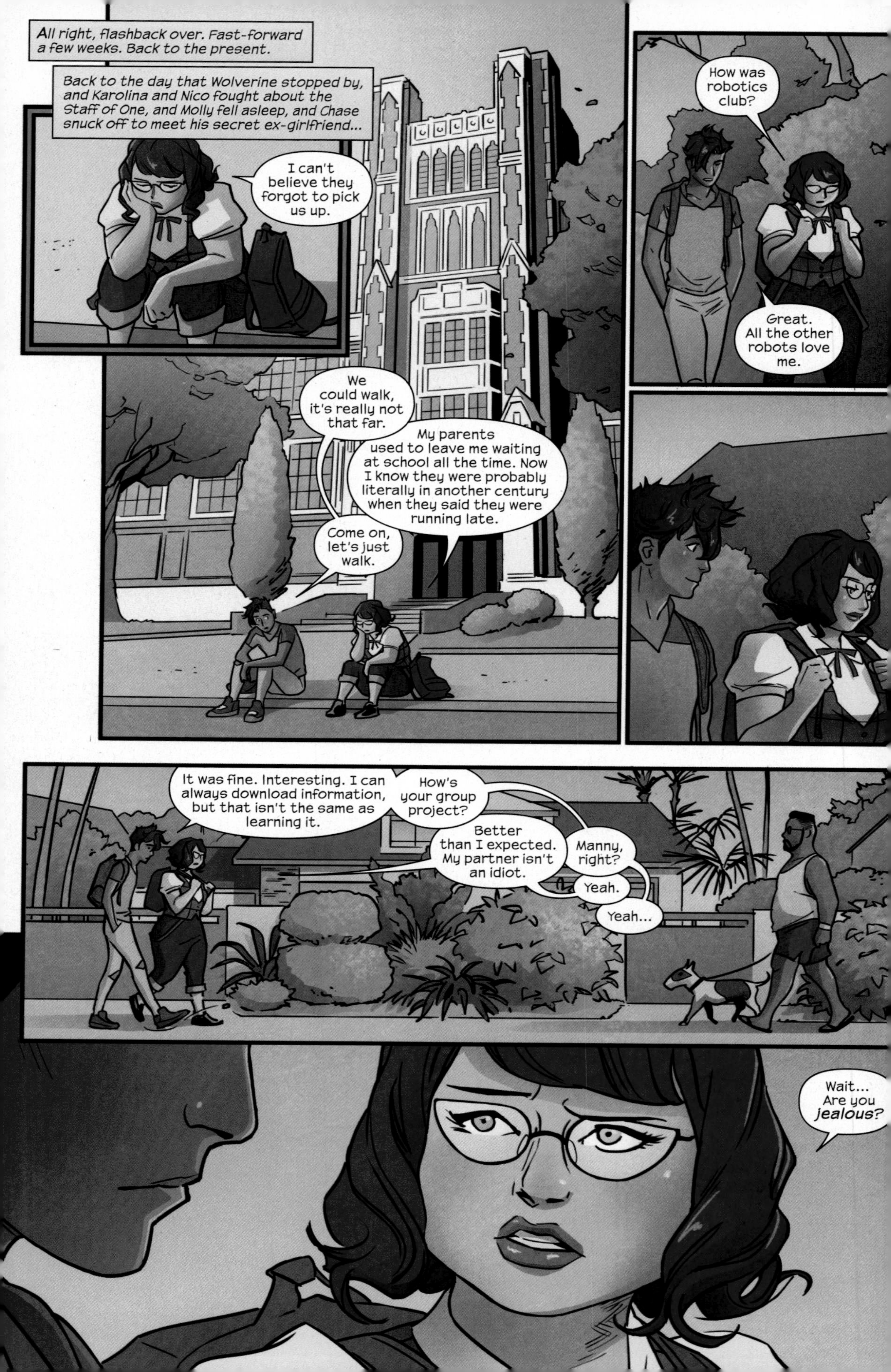
All right, flashback over. Fast-forward a few weeks. Back to the present.
Back to the day that Wolverine stopped by, and Karolina and Nico fought about the Staff of One, and Molly fell asleep, and Chase snuck off to meet his secret ex-girlfriend...
I can't believe they forgot to pick us up.
We could walk, it's really not that far.
My parents used to leave me waiting at school all the time. Now I know they were probably literally in another century when they said they were running late.
Come on, let's just walk.
How was robotics club?
Great. All the other robots love me.
It was fine. Interesting. I can always download information, but that isn't the same as learning it.
How's your group project?
Better than I expected. My partner isn't an idiot.
Manny, right?
Yeah.
Yeah...
Wait... Are you *jealous?*

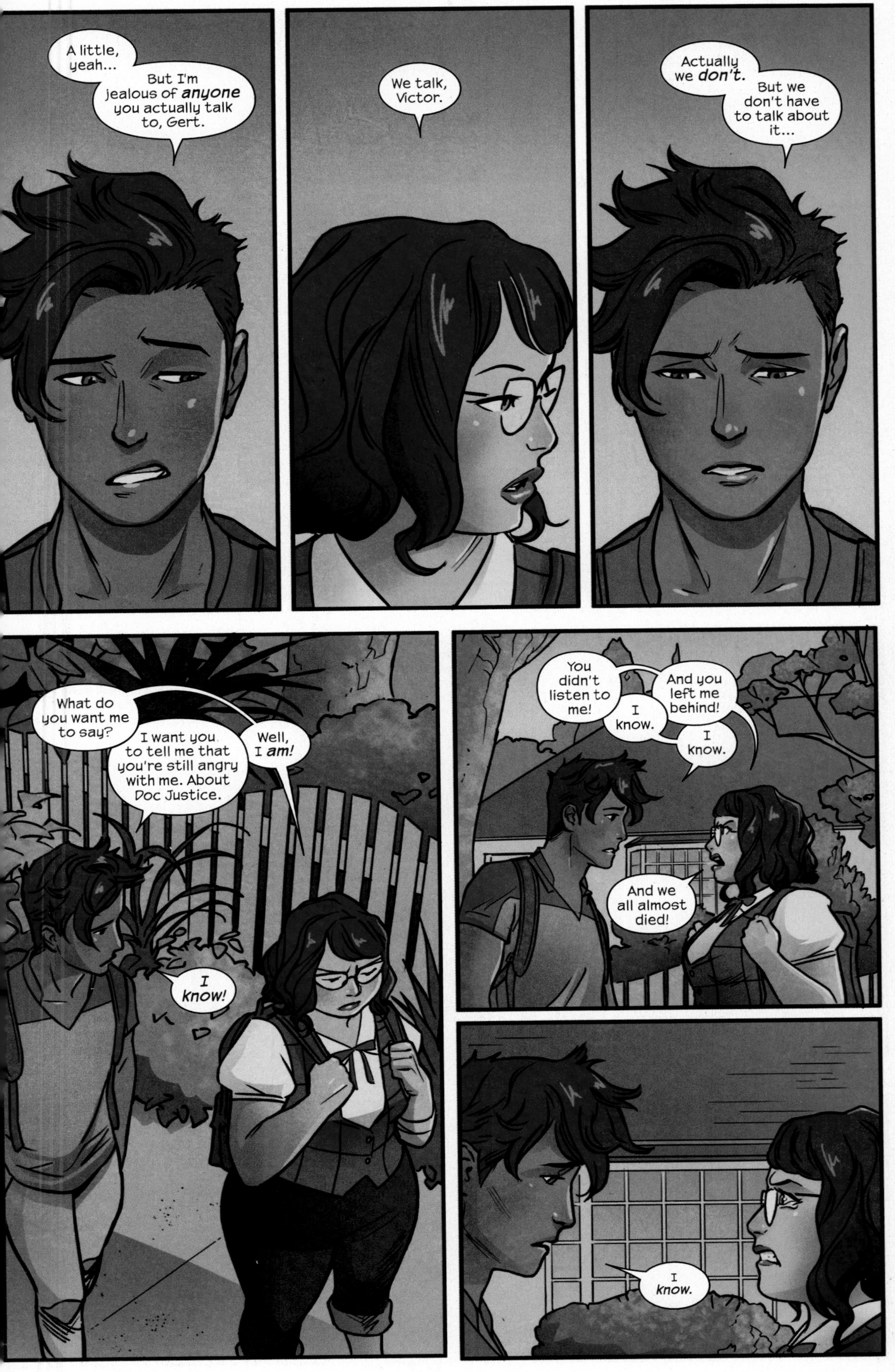

A little, yeah...
But I'm jealous of *anyone* you actually talk to, Gert.
We talk, Victor.
Actually we *don't.*
But we don't have to talk about it...
What do you want me to say?
I want you to tell me that you're still angry with me. About Doc Justice.
Well, I *am!*
I know!
You didn't listen to me!
I know.
And you left me behind!
I know.
And we all almost died!
I *know.*

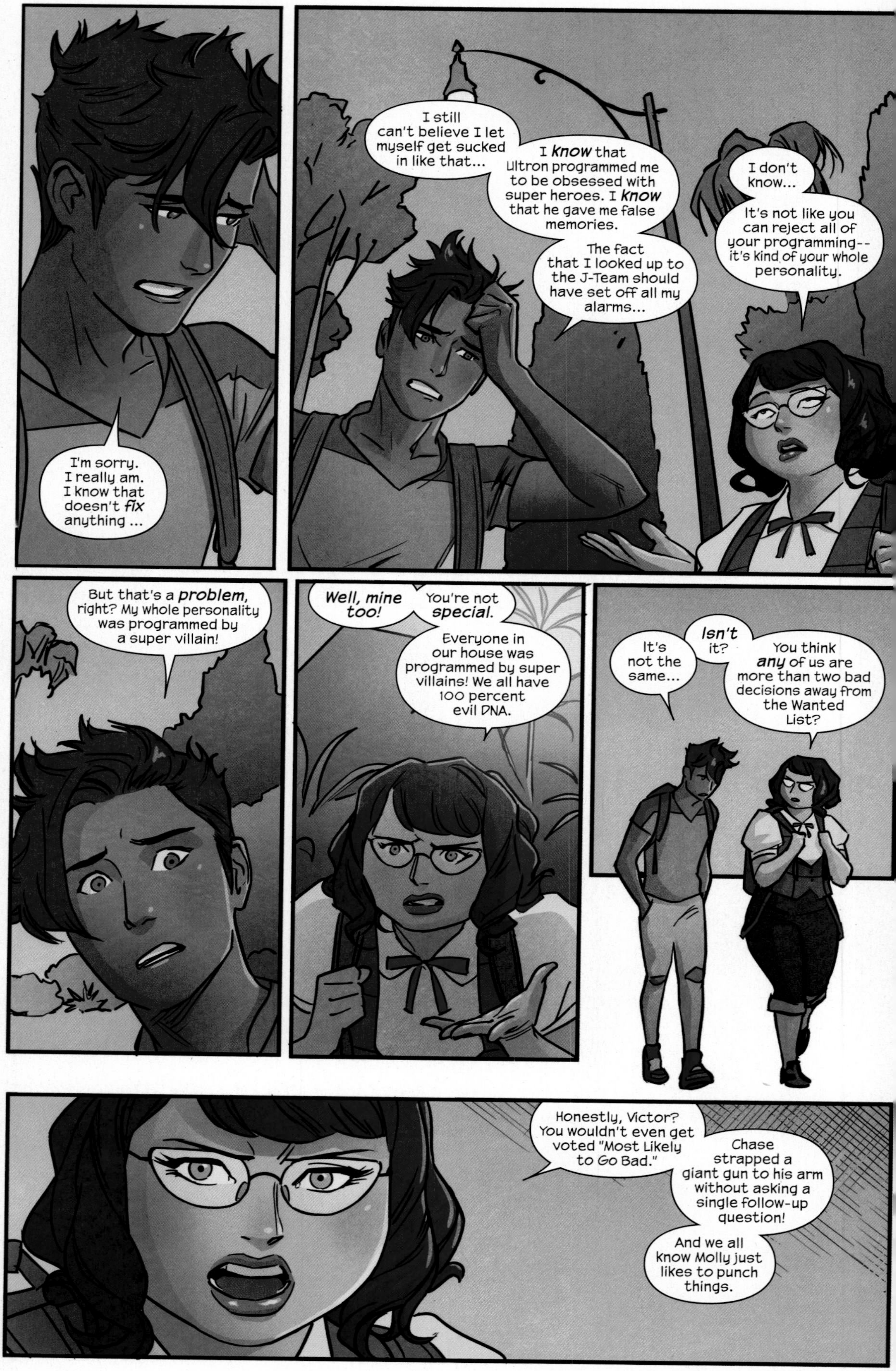
I'm sorry. I really am. I know that doesn't *fix* anything ...
I still can't believe I let myself get sucked in like that...
I *KNOW* that Ultron programmed me to be obsessed with super heroes. I *KNOW* that he gave me false memories.
The fact that I looked up to the J-Team should have set off all my alarms...
I don't know...
It's not like you can reject all of your programming-- it's kind of your whole personality.
But that's a *problem*, right? My whole personality was programmed by a super villain!
Well, mine too!
You're not *special*.
Everyone in our house was programmed by super villains! We all have 100 percent evil DNA.
It's not the same...
Isn't it?
You think *any* of us are more than two bad decisions away from the Wanted List?
Honestly, Victor? You wouldn't even get voted "Most Likely to Go Bad."
Chase strapped a giant gun to his arm without asking a single follow-up question!
And we all know Molly just likes to punch things.

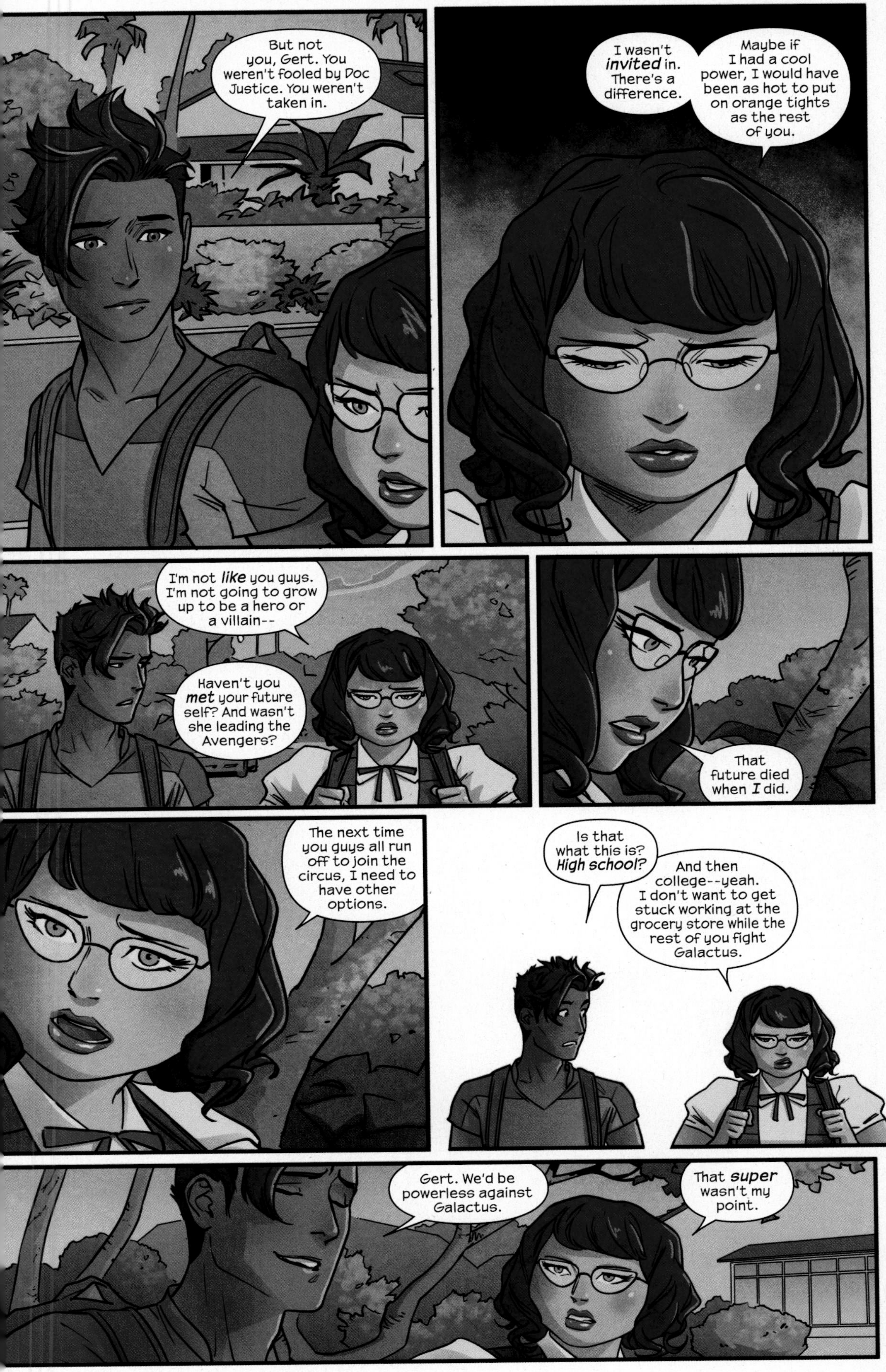

But not you, Gert. You weren't fooled by Doc Justice. You weren't taken in.
I wasn't *invited* in. There's a difference.
Maybe if I had a cool power, I would have been as hot to put on orange tights as the rest of you.
I'm not *like* you guys. I'm not going to grow up to be a hero or a villain--
Haven't you *met* your future self? And wasn't she leading the Avengers?
That future died when *I* did.
The next time you guys all run off to join the circus, I need to have other options.
Is that what this is? *High school?*
And then college--yeah. I don't want to get stuck working at the grocery store while the rest of you fight Galactus.
Gert. We'd be powerless against Galactus.
That *super* wasn't my point.

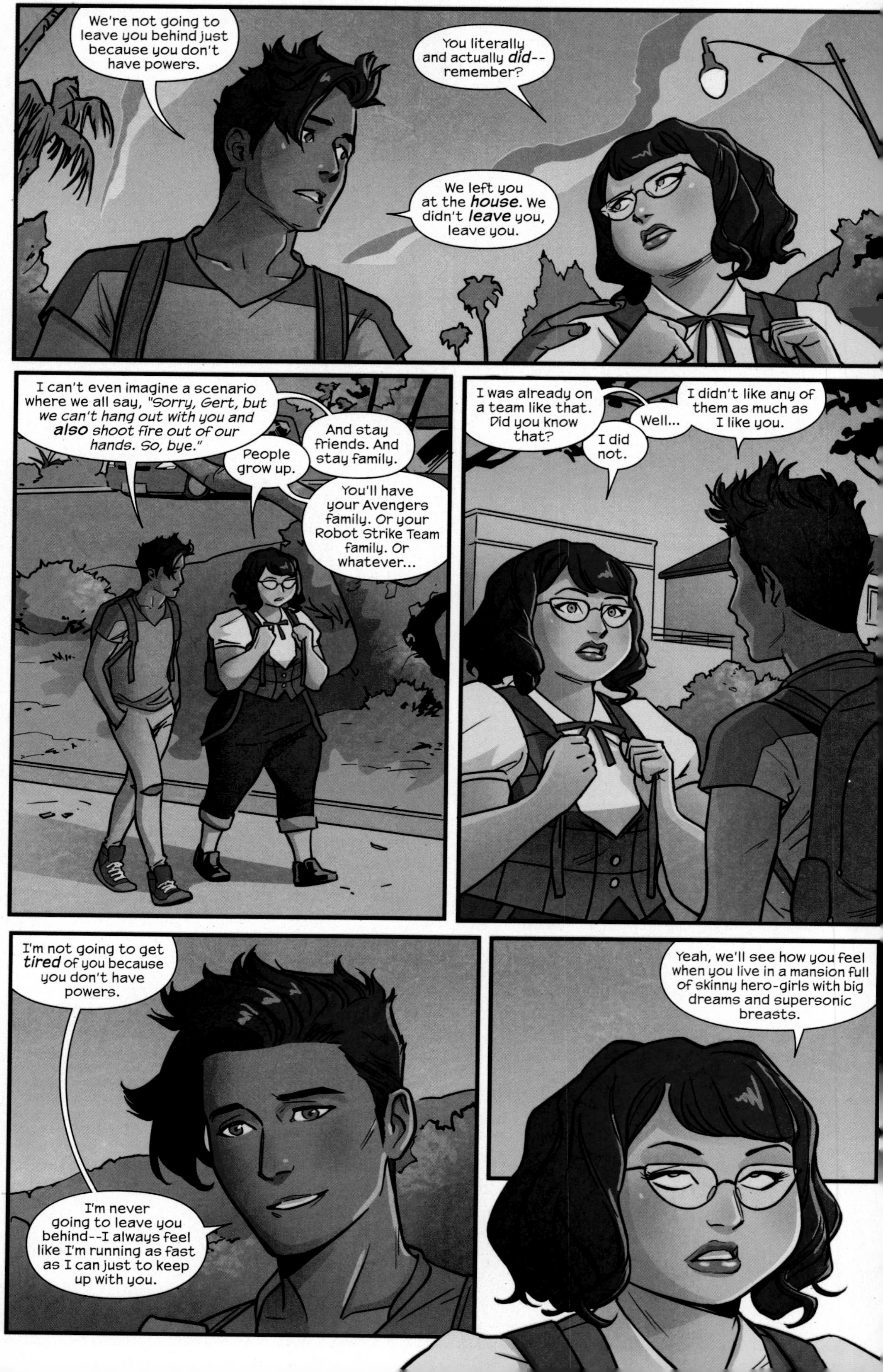
We're not going to leave you behind just because you don't have powers.
You literally and actually *did*-- remember?
We left you at the ***house***. We didn't ***leave*** you, leave you.
I can't even imagine a scenario where we all say, *"Sorry, Gert, but we can't hang out with you and **also** shoot fire out of our hands. So, bye."*
And stay friends. And stay family.
People grow up.
You'll have your Avengers family. Or your Robot Strike Team family. Or whatever...
I was already on a team like that. Did you know that?
I did not.
Well...
I didn't like any of them as much as I like you.
I'm not going to get ***tired*** of you because you don't have powers.
I'm never going to leave you behind--I always feel like I'm running as fast as I can just to keep up with you.
Yeah, we'll see how you feel when you live in a mansion full of skinny hero-girls with big dreams and supersonic breasts.

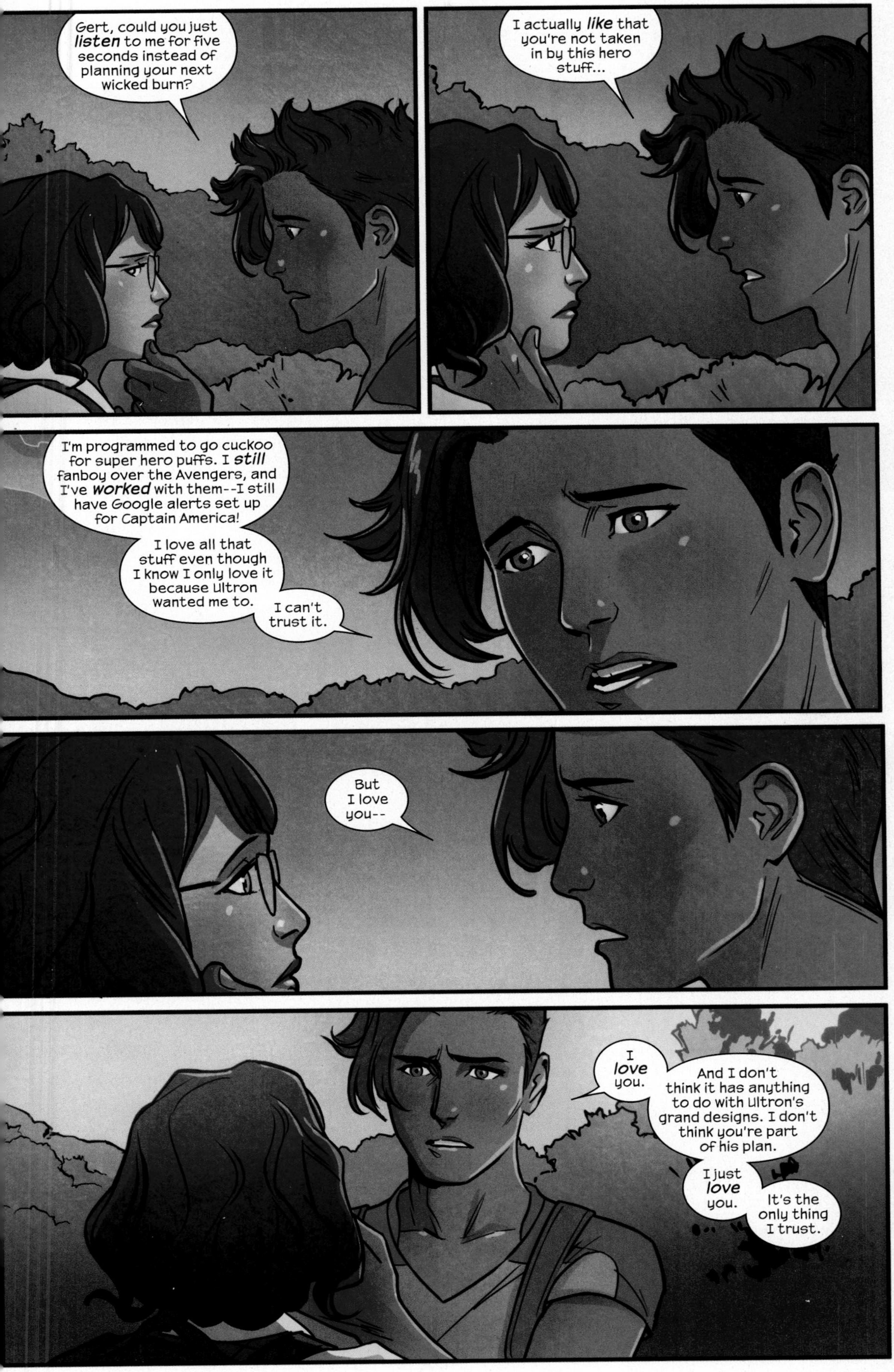
Gert, could you just *listen* to me for five seconds instead of planning your next wicked burn?
I actually *like* that you're not taken in by this hero stuff...
I'm programmed to go cuckoo for super hero puffs. I *still* fanboy over the Avengers, and I've *worked* with them--I still have Google alerts set up for Captain America!
I love all that stuff even though I know I only love it because Ultron wanted me to.
I can't trust it.
But I love you--
I *love* you.
And I don't think it has anything to do with Ultron's grand designs. I don't think you're part of his plan.
I just *love* you.
It's the only thing I trust.

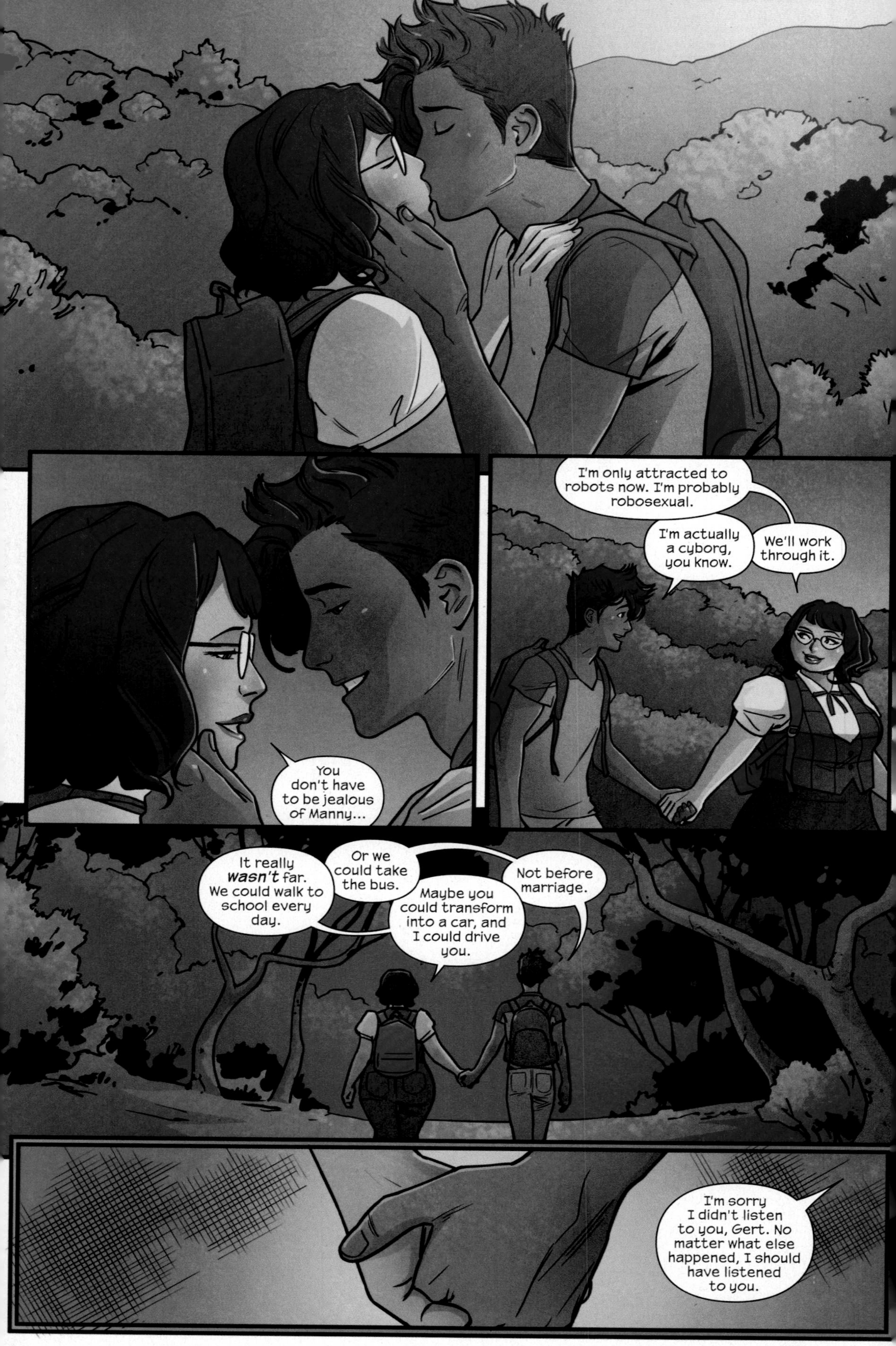
You don't have to be jealous of Manny...
I'm only attracted to robots now. I'm probably robosexual.
I'm actually a cyborg, you know.
We'll work through it.
It really wasn't far. We could walk to school every day.
Or we could take the bus.
Maybe you could transform into a car, and I could drive you.
Not before marriage.
I'm sorry I didn't listen to you, Gert. No matter what else happened, I should have listened to you.

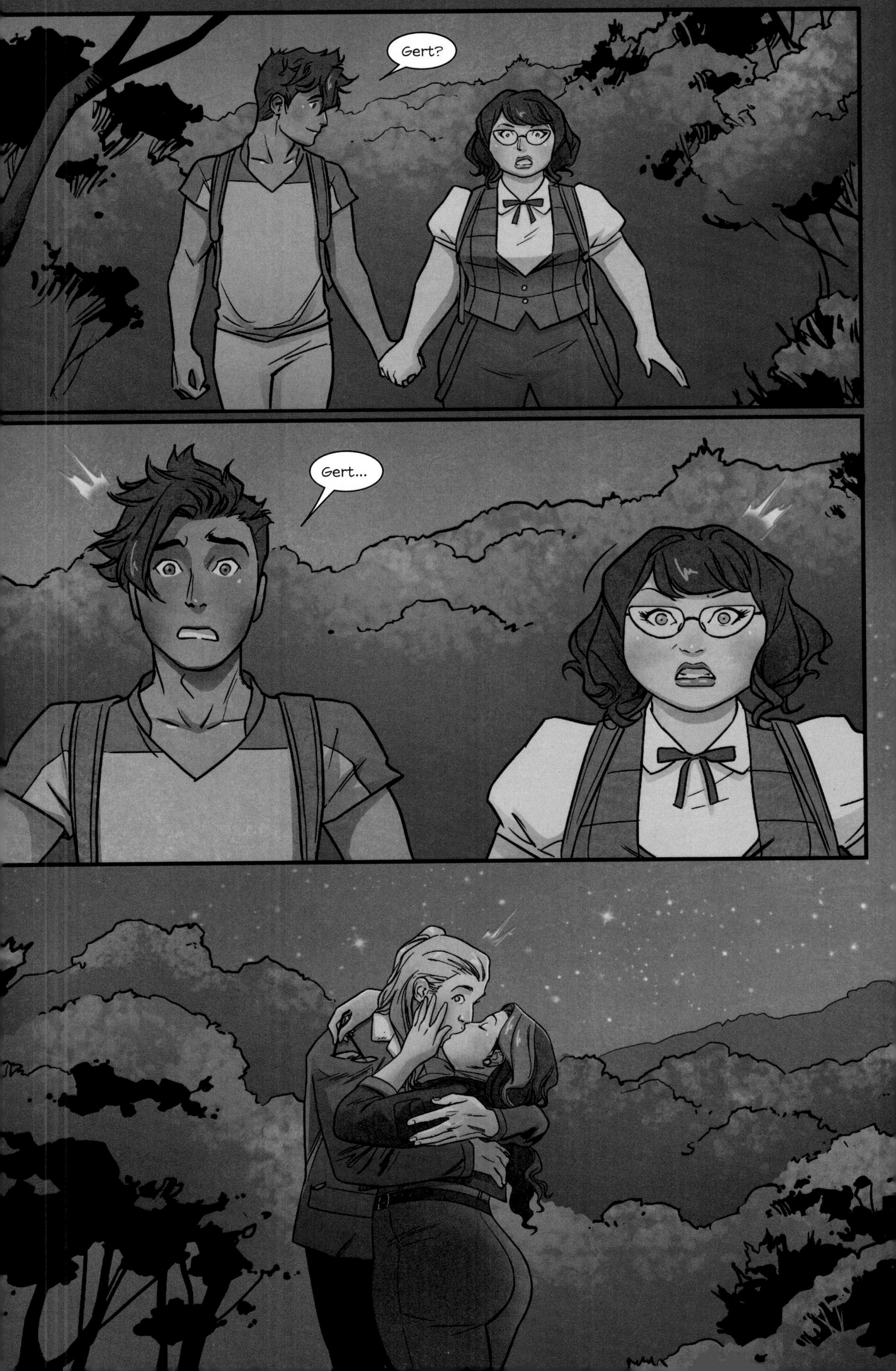
Gert?
Gert...

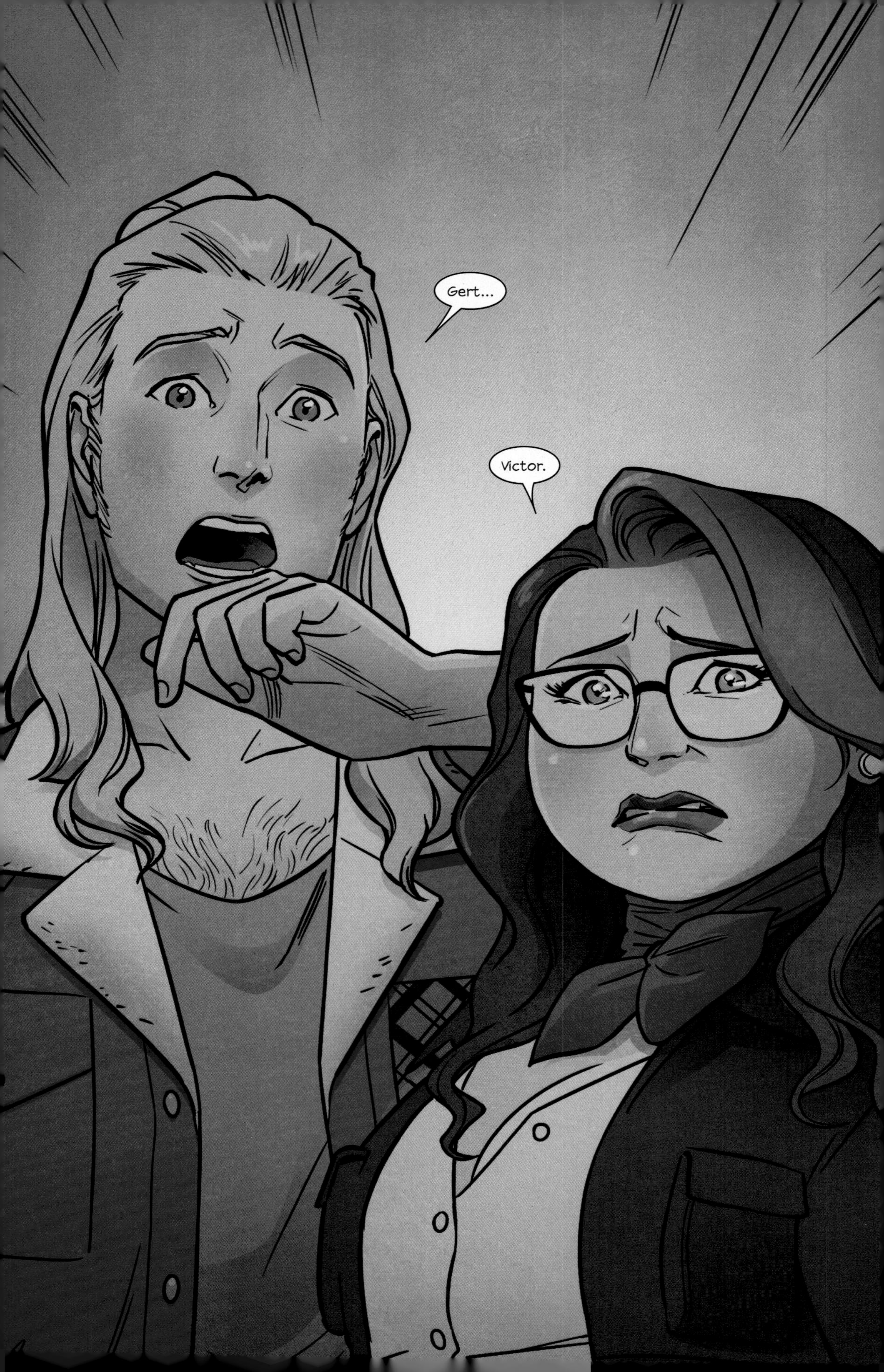
Gert...
Victor.

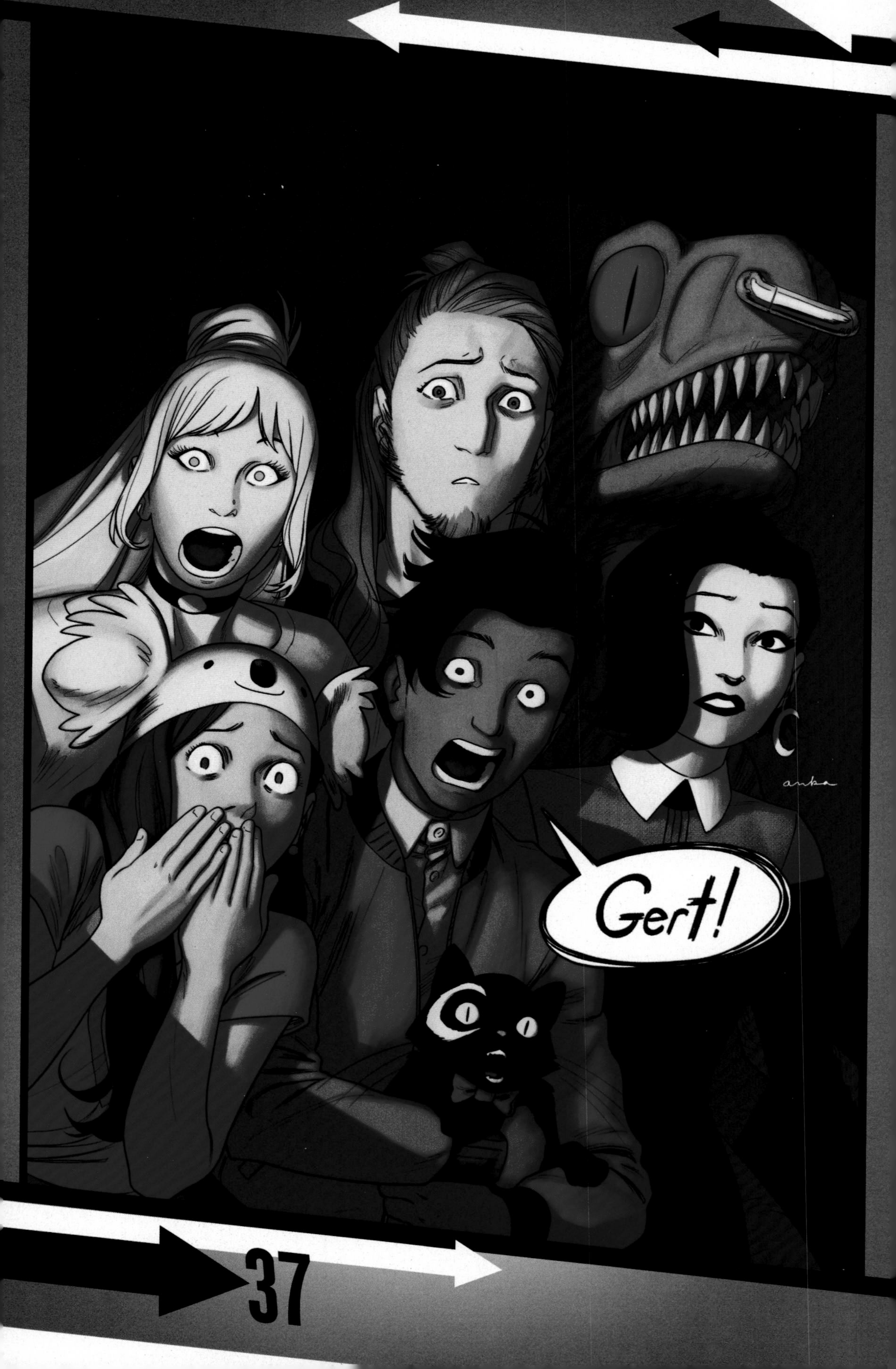
Gert!

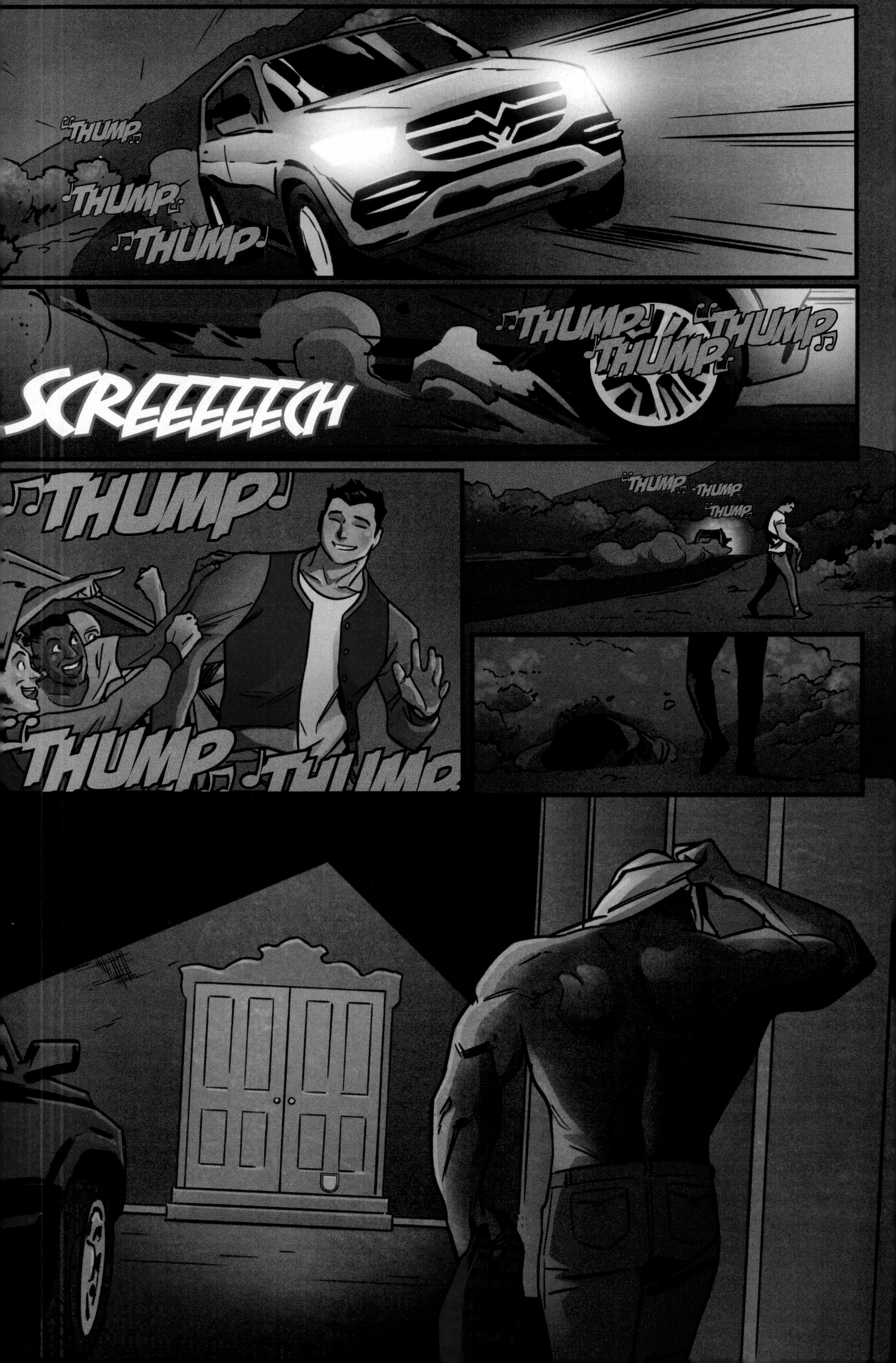
THUMP
THUMP
THUMP
SCREEEEEECH
THUMP
THUMP
THUMP
THUMP
THUMP
THUMP
THUMP
THUMP
THUMP

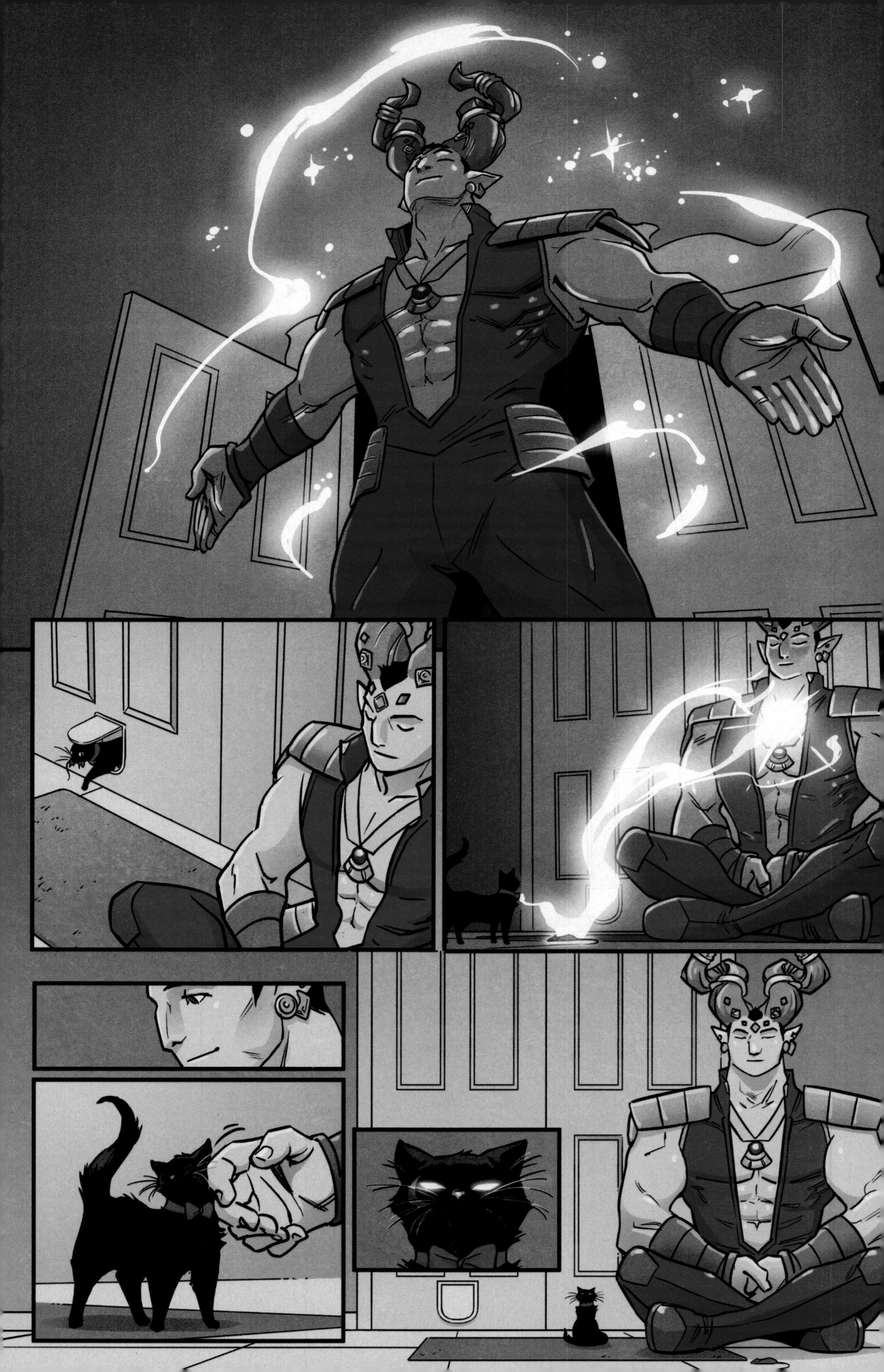

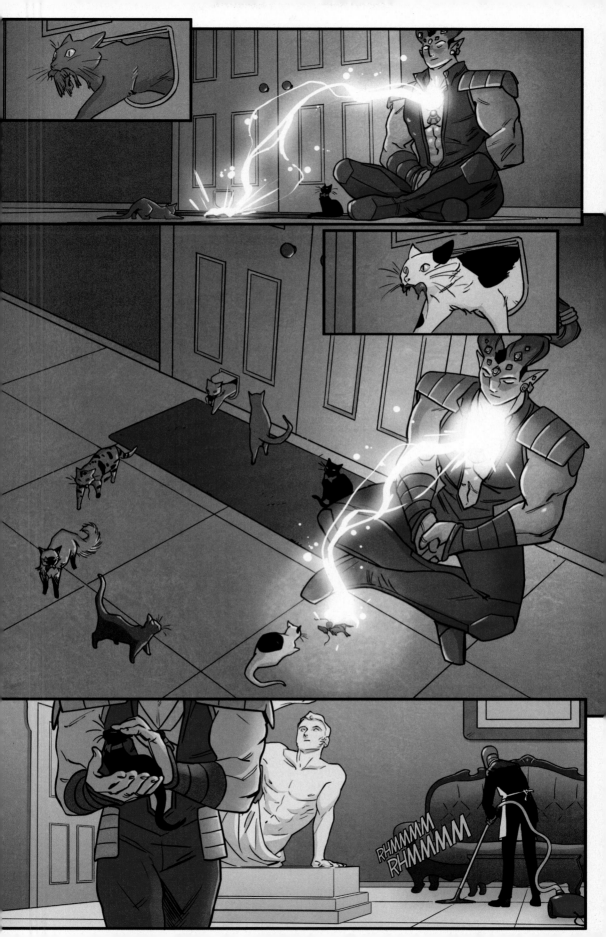

RHMMMM
RHMMMM

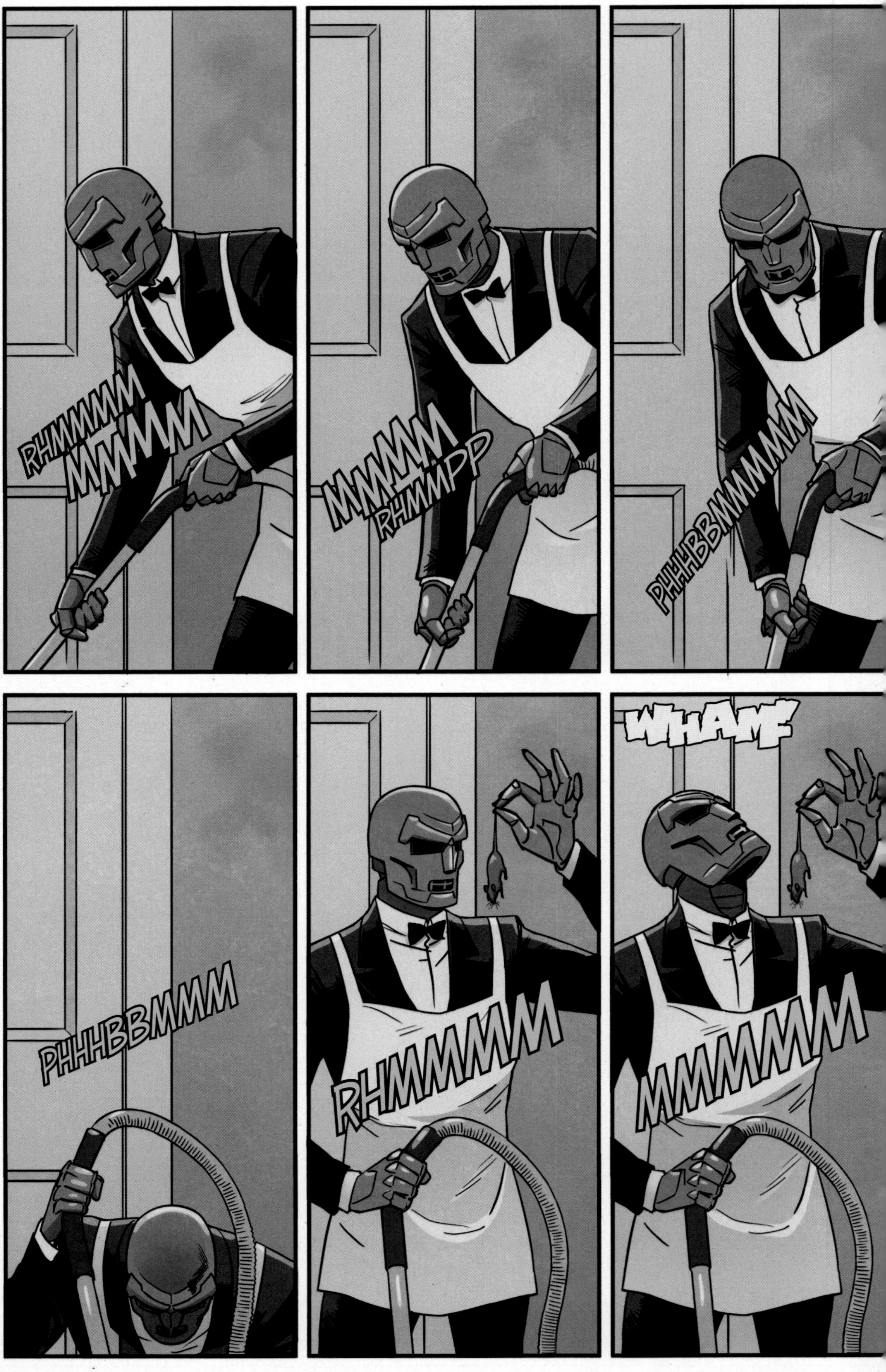
RHMMMM
MTMM
MMMM
RHMMPP
PHHBBMMMMM
PHHBBMMM
RHMMMM
WHAM
MMMMMM

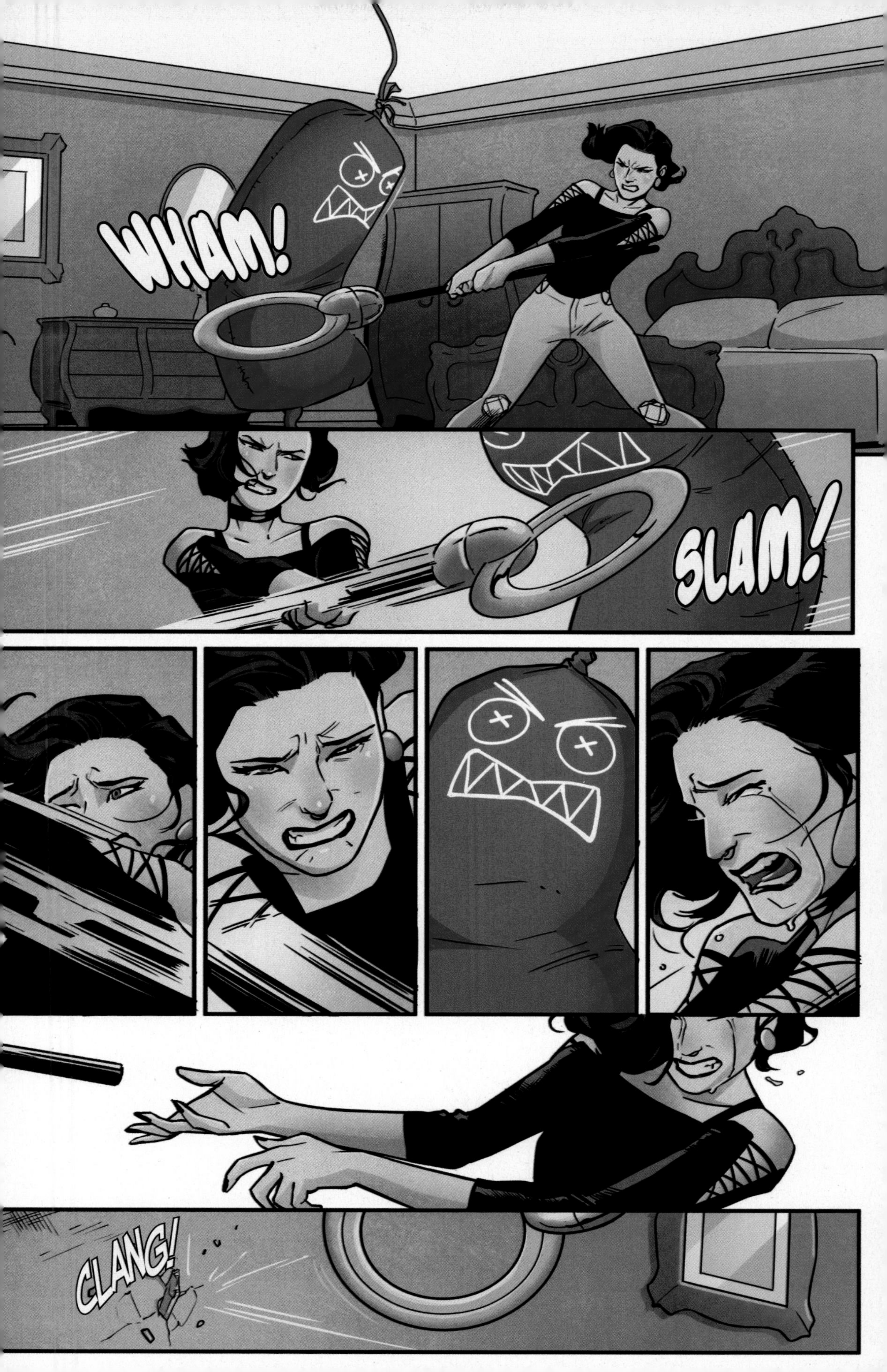
WHAM!
SLAM!
CLANG!

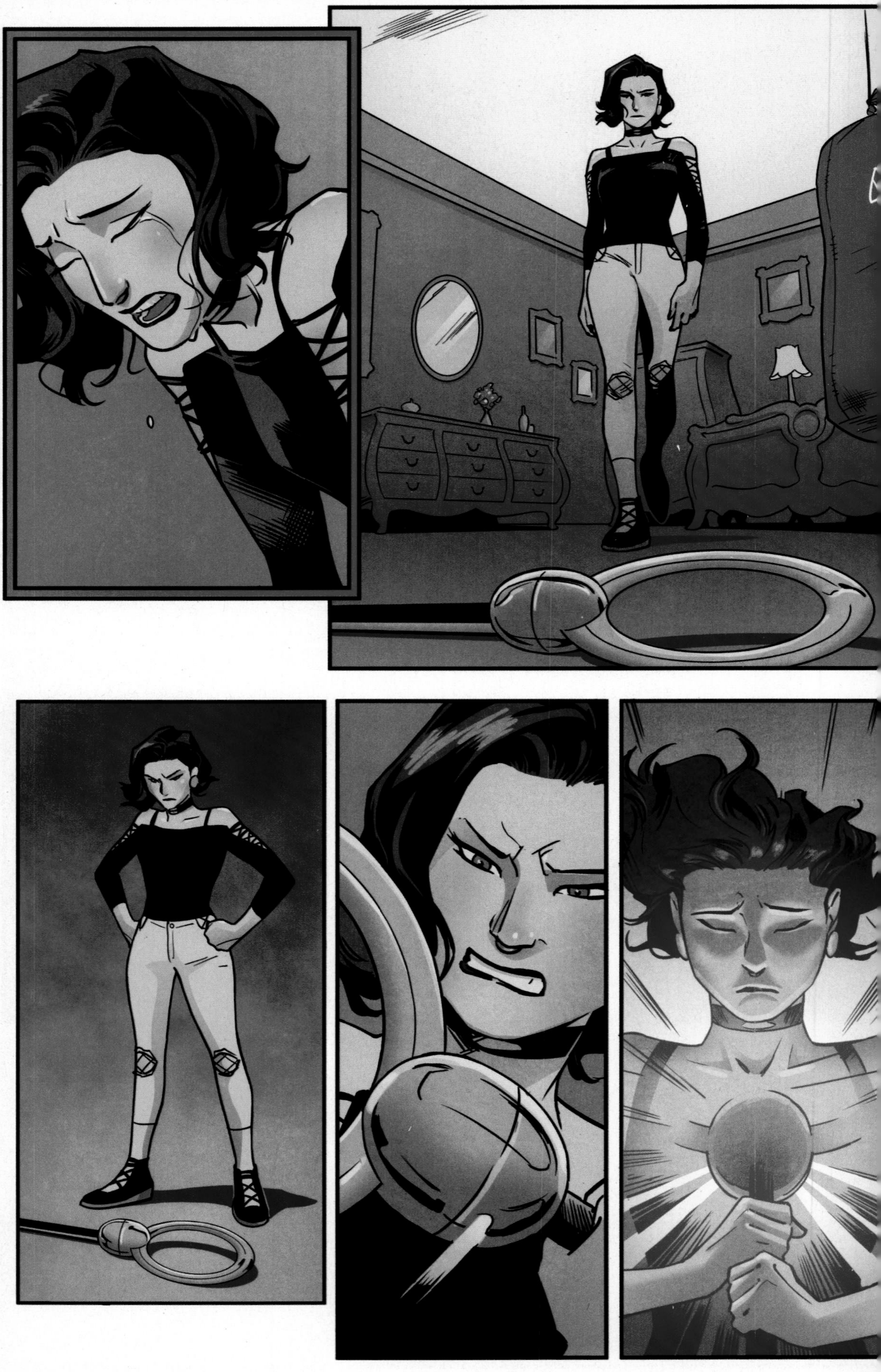

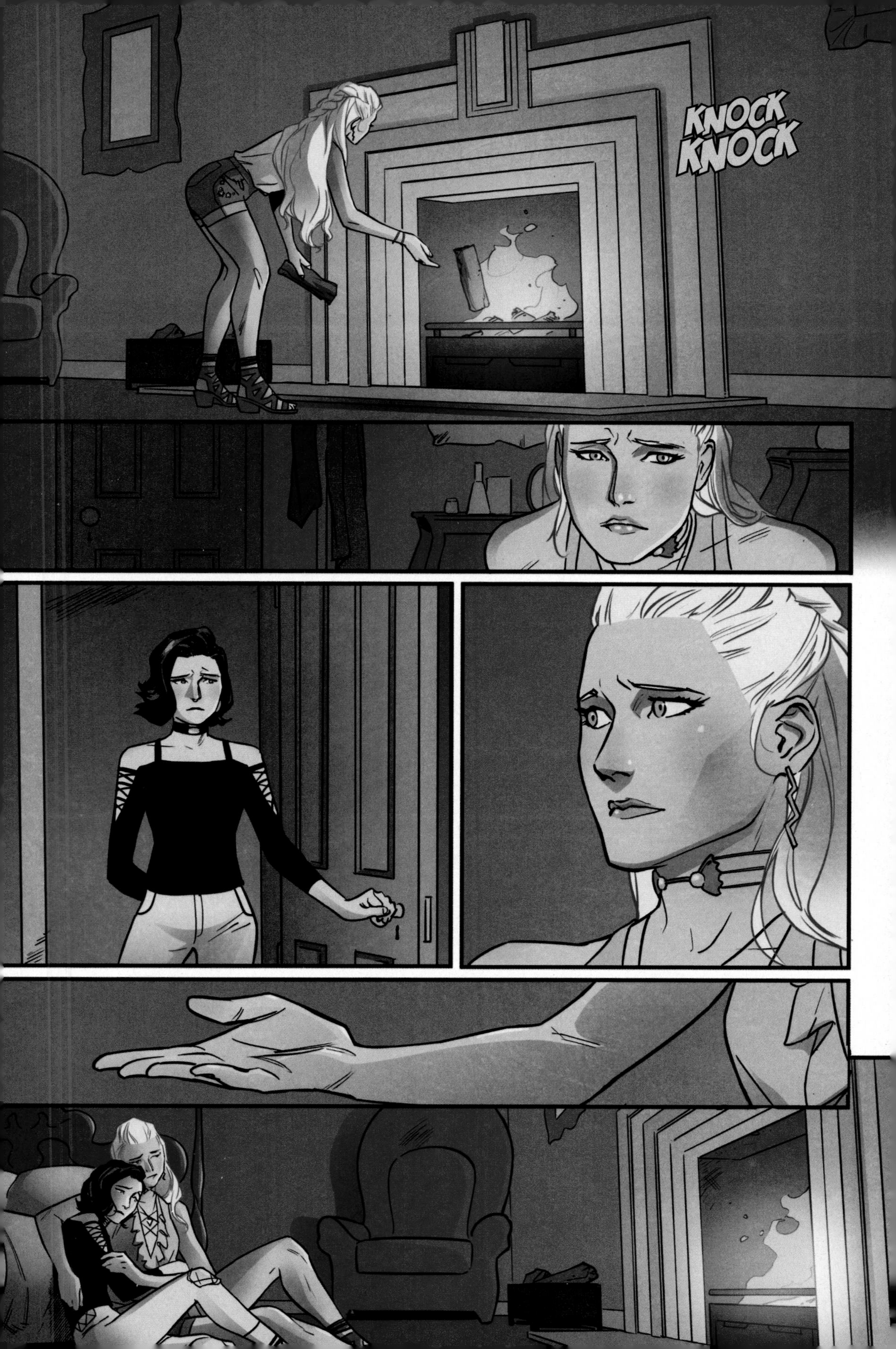
KNOCK
KNOCK

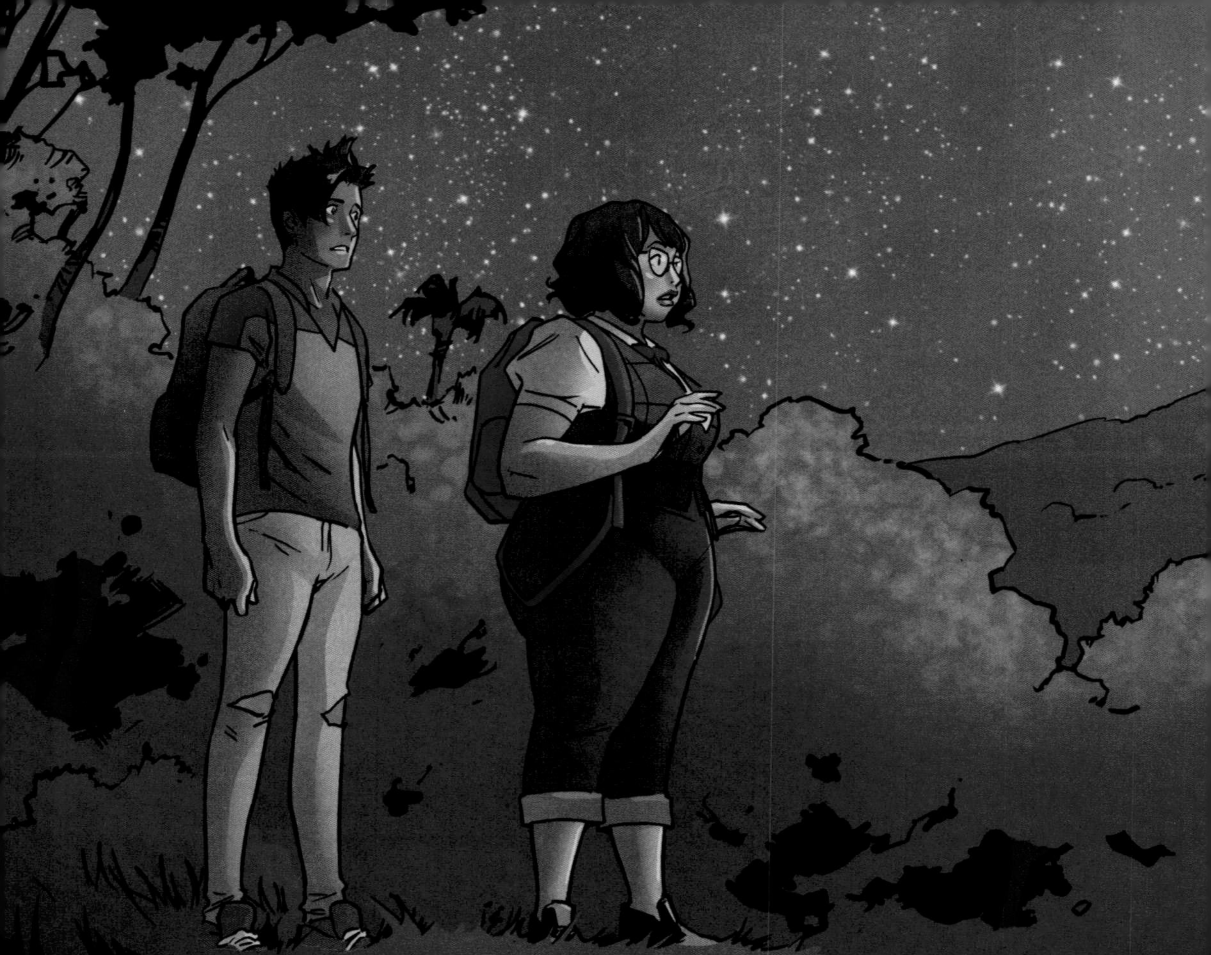
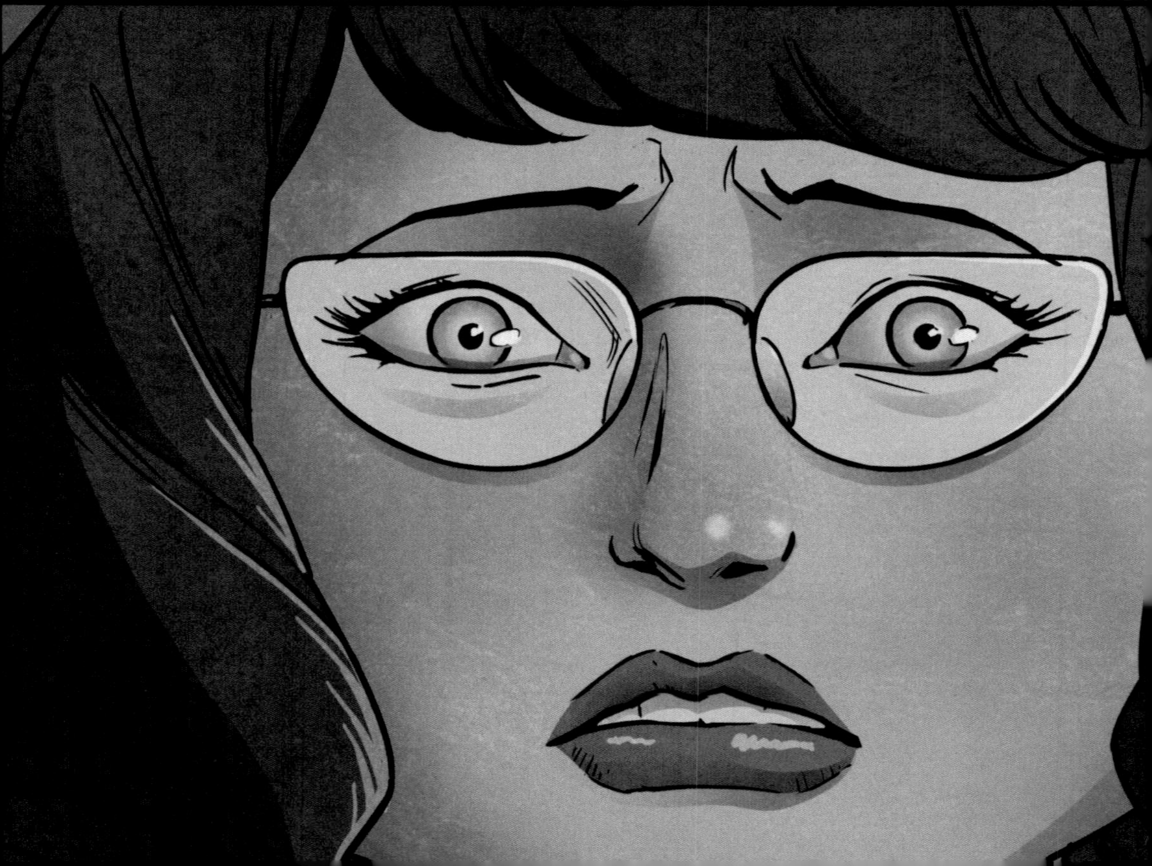

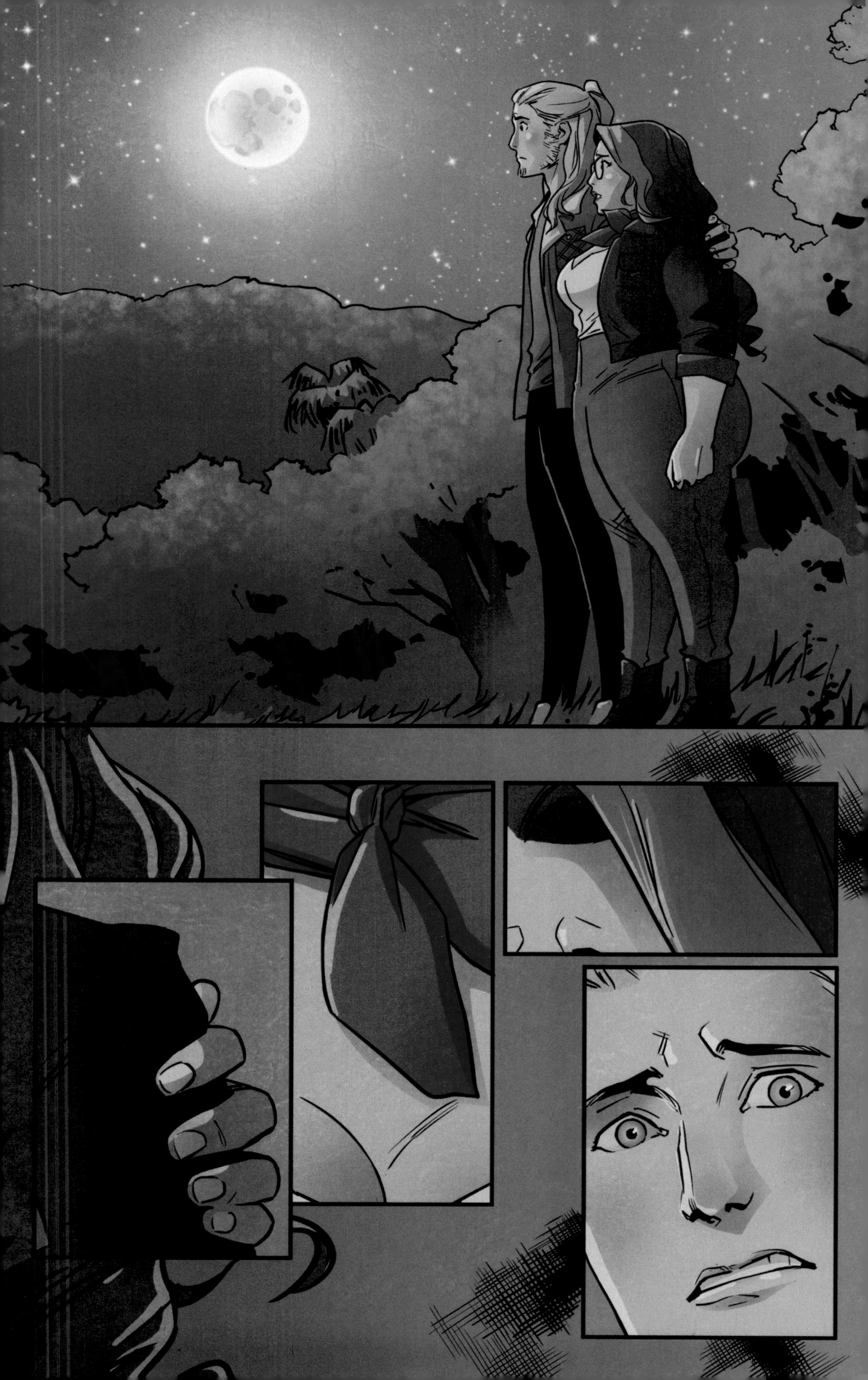

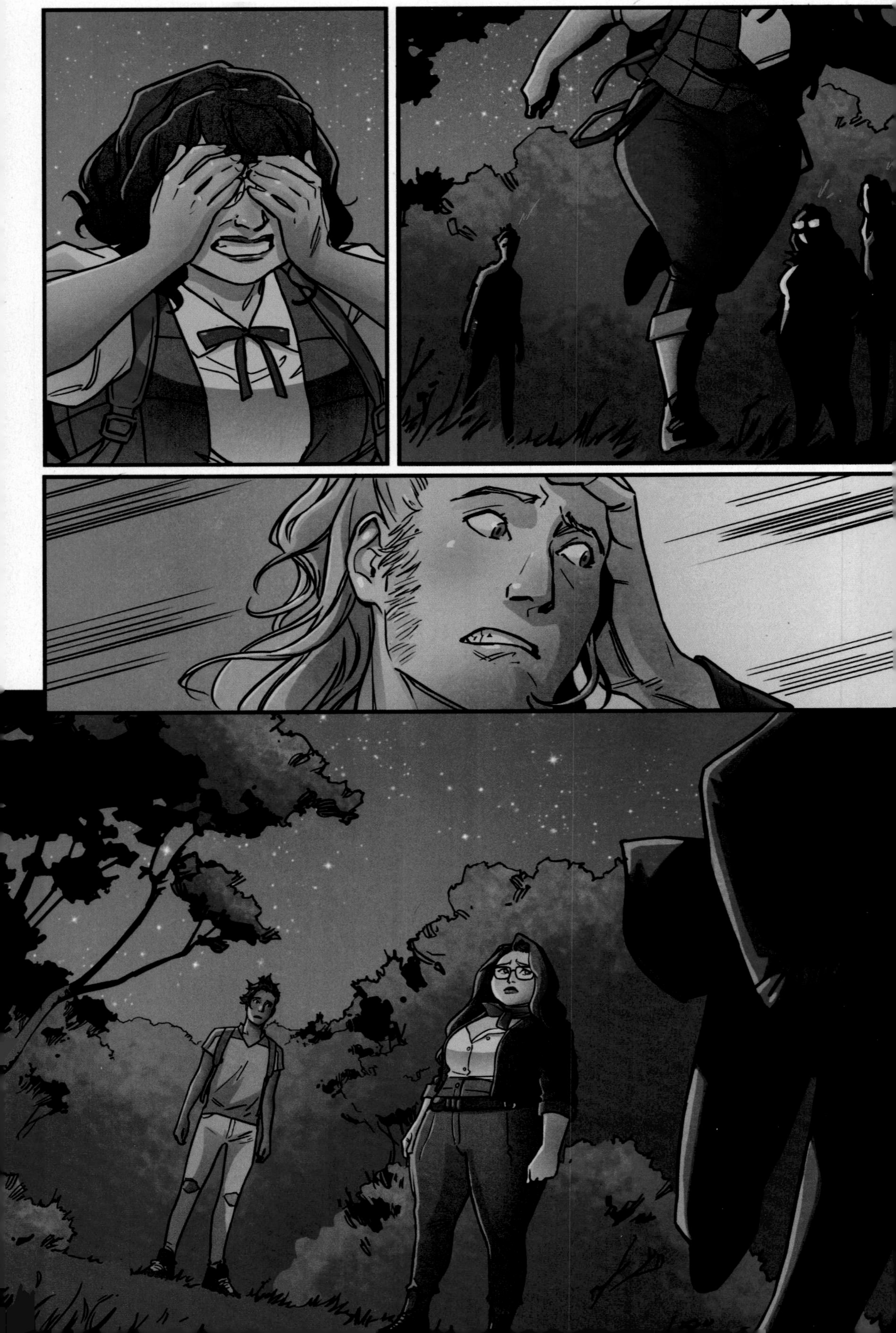

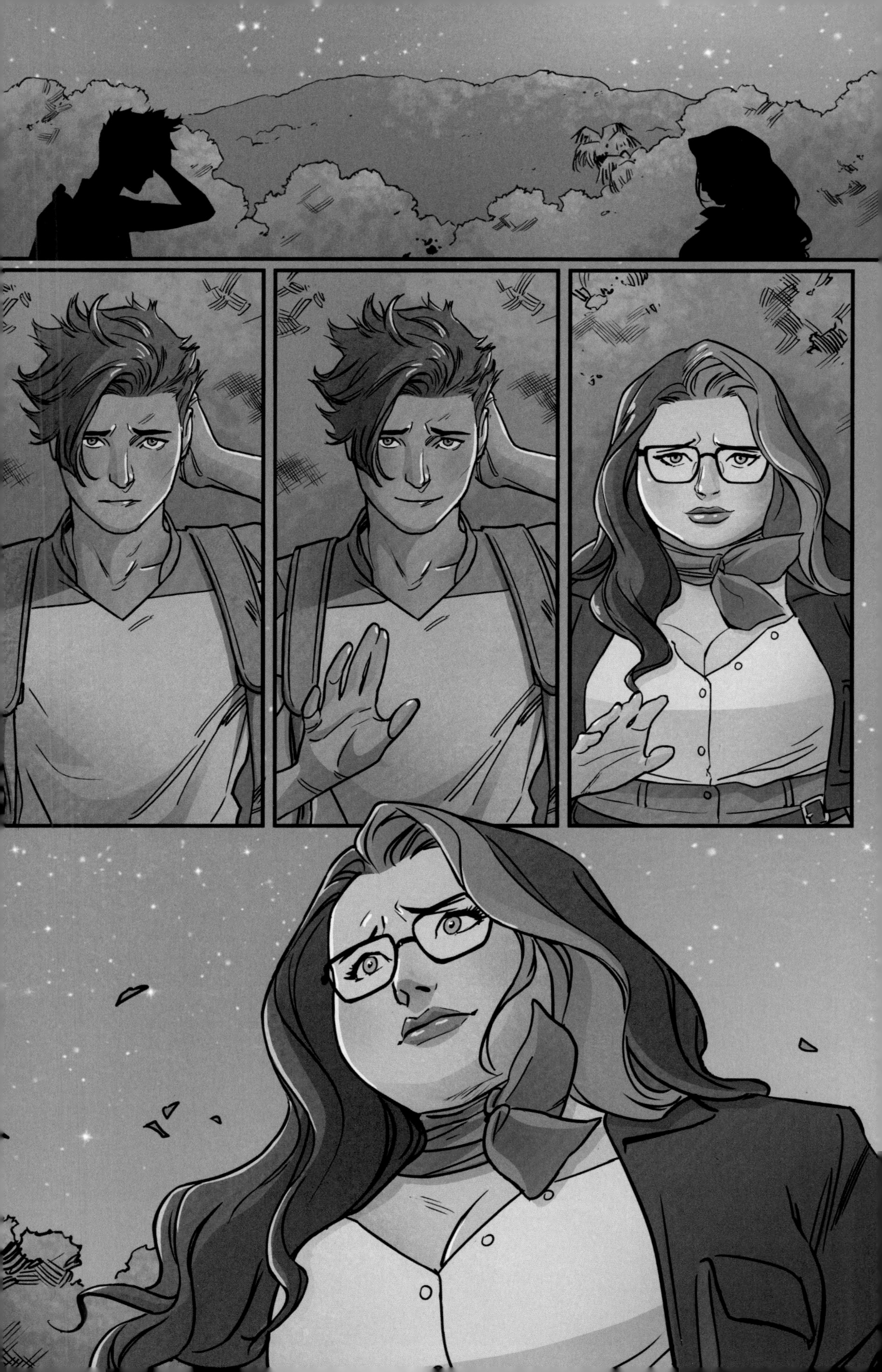

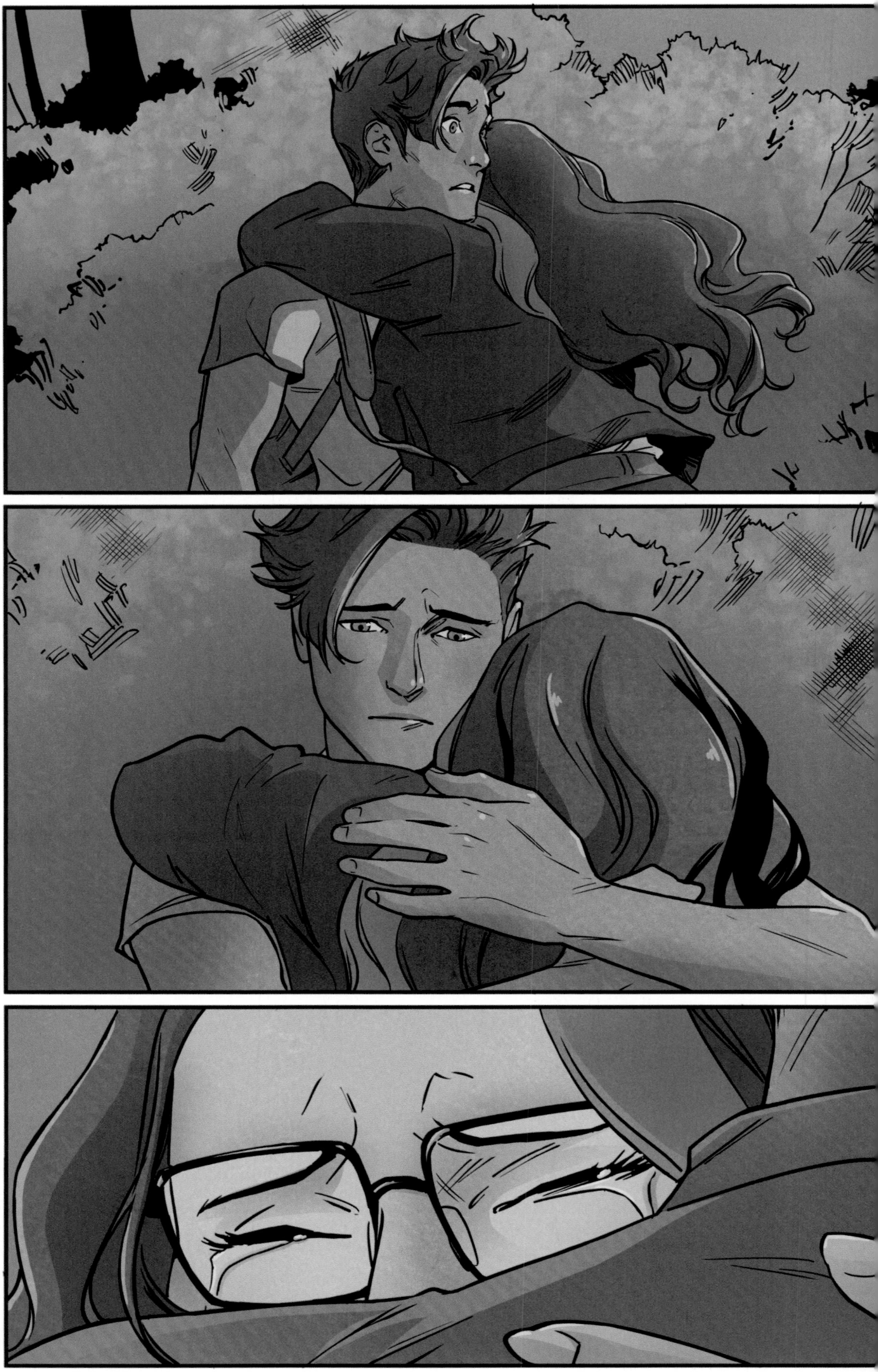

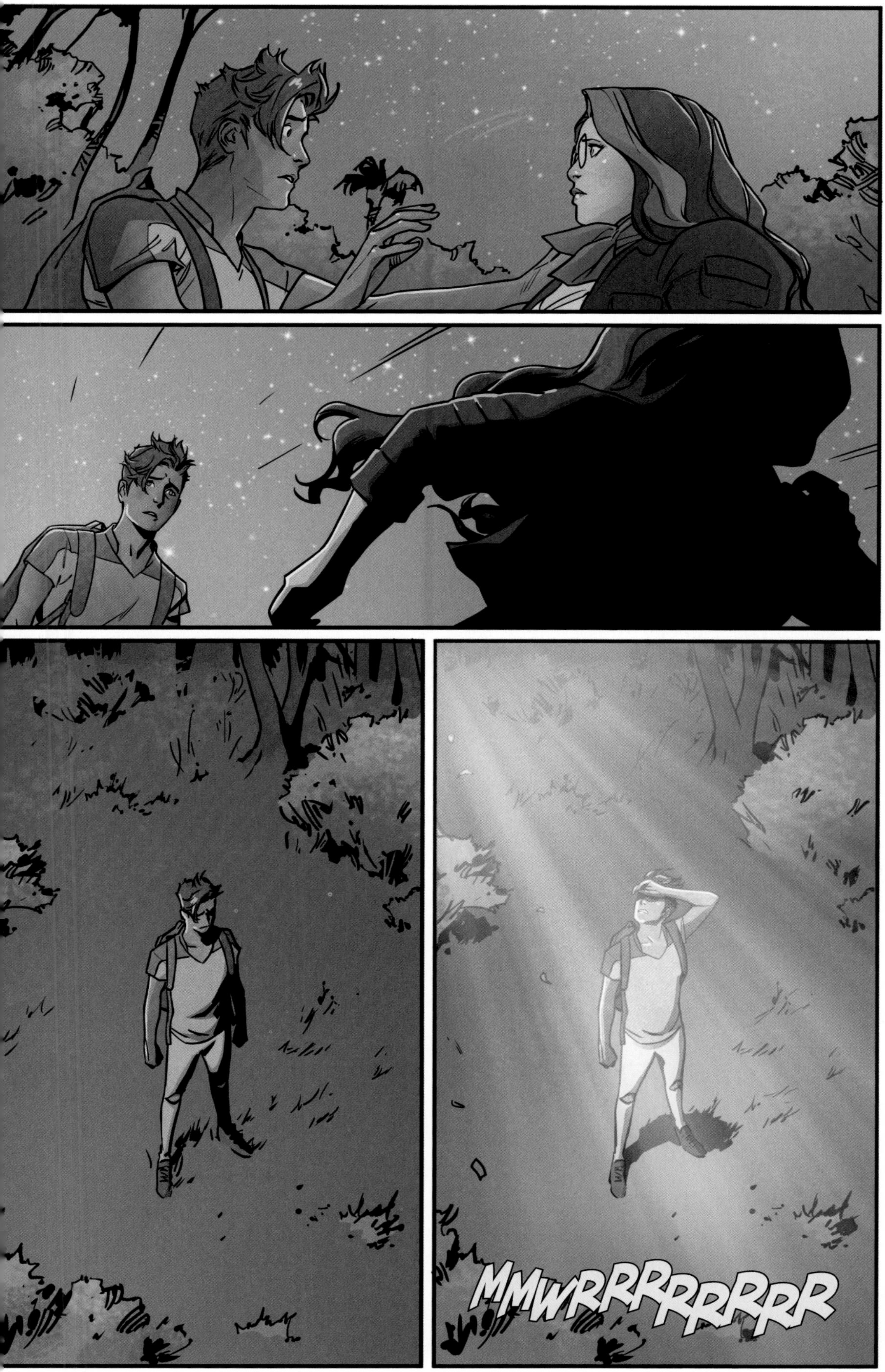
MMWRRRRRRRRR

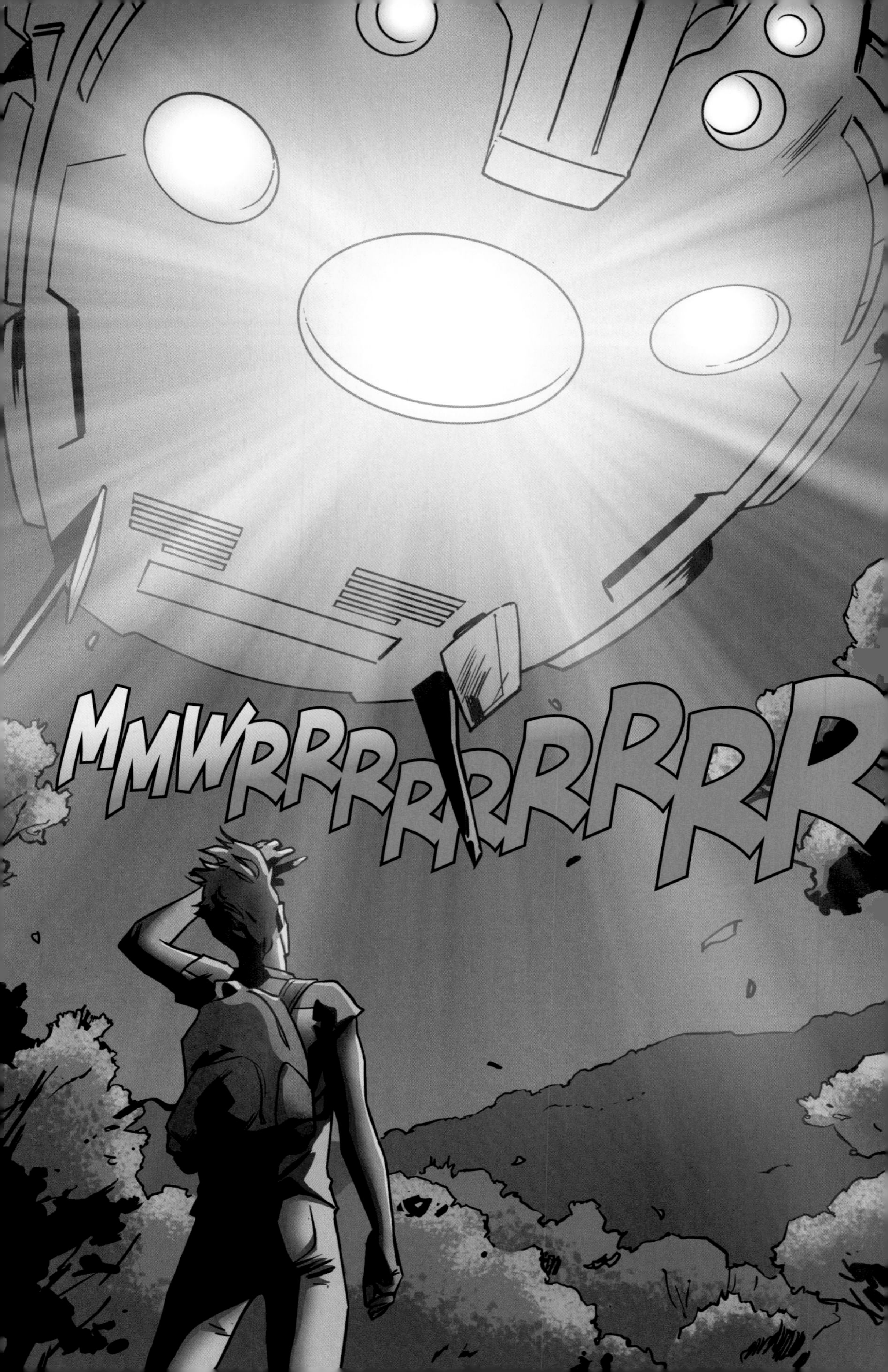
MMWRRRRRRRRR

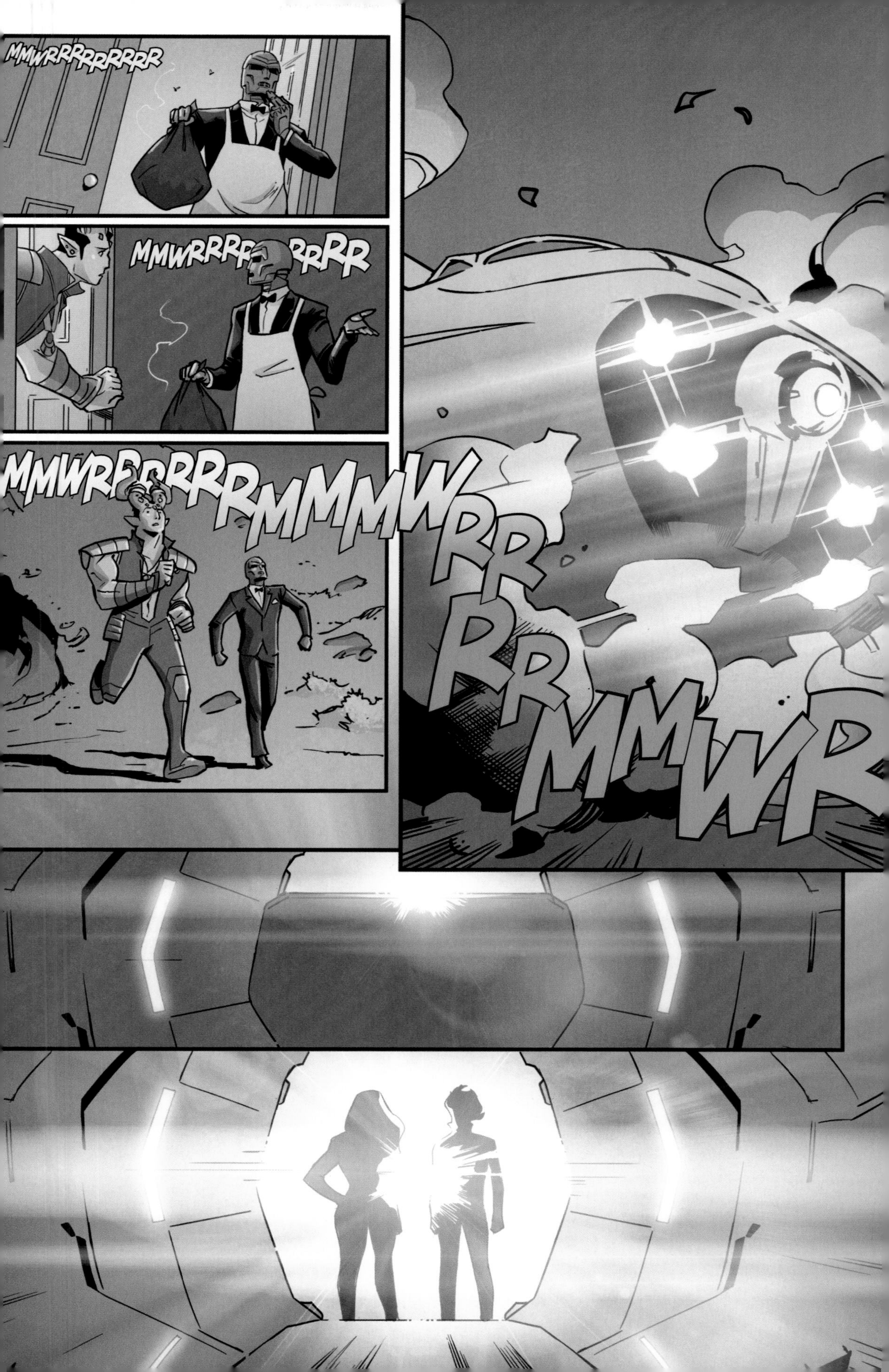
MMWRRRRRRRR
MMWRRRRRRRR
MMWRRRRRRMMMMWRRRRMMMWR

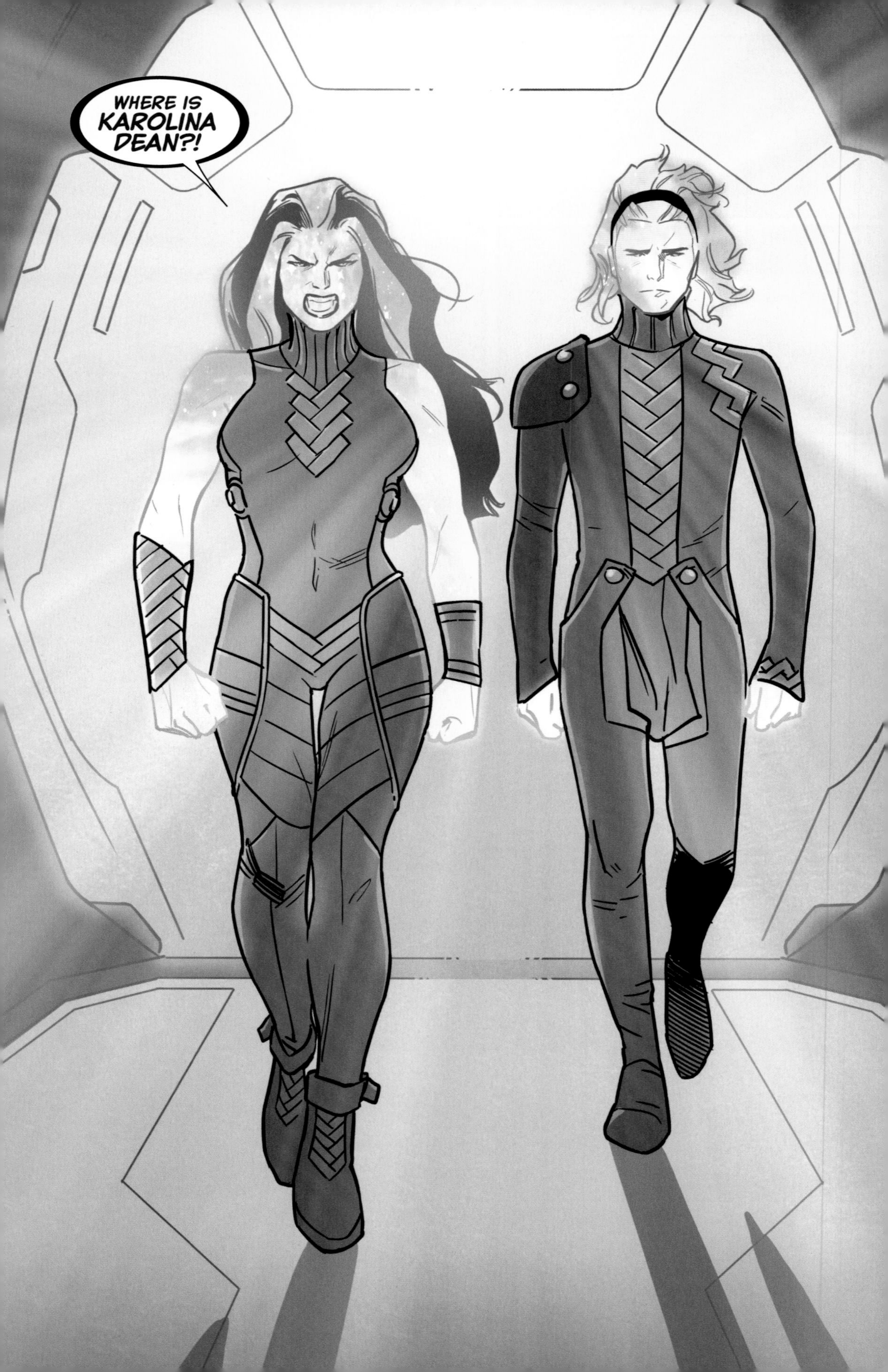
WHERE IS KAROLINA DEAN?!

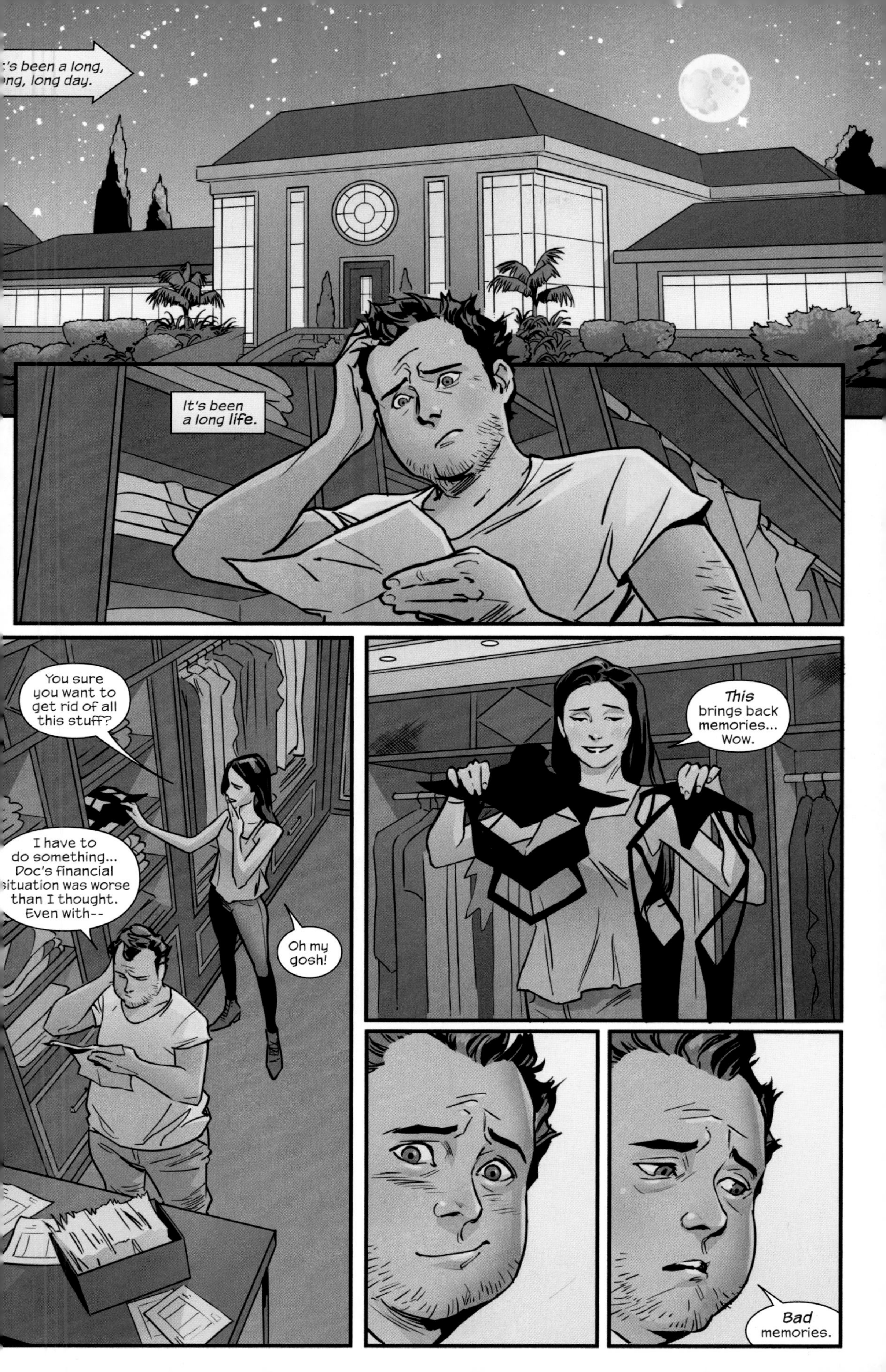

:'s been a long,
ong, long day.
It's been a long life.
You sure you want to get rid of all this stuff?
I have to do something... Doc's financial situation was worse than I thought. Even with--
Oh my gosh!
This brings back memories... Wow.
Bad memories.

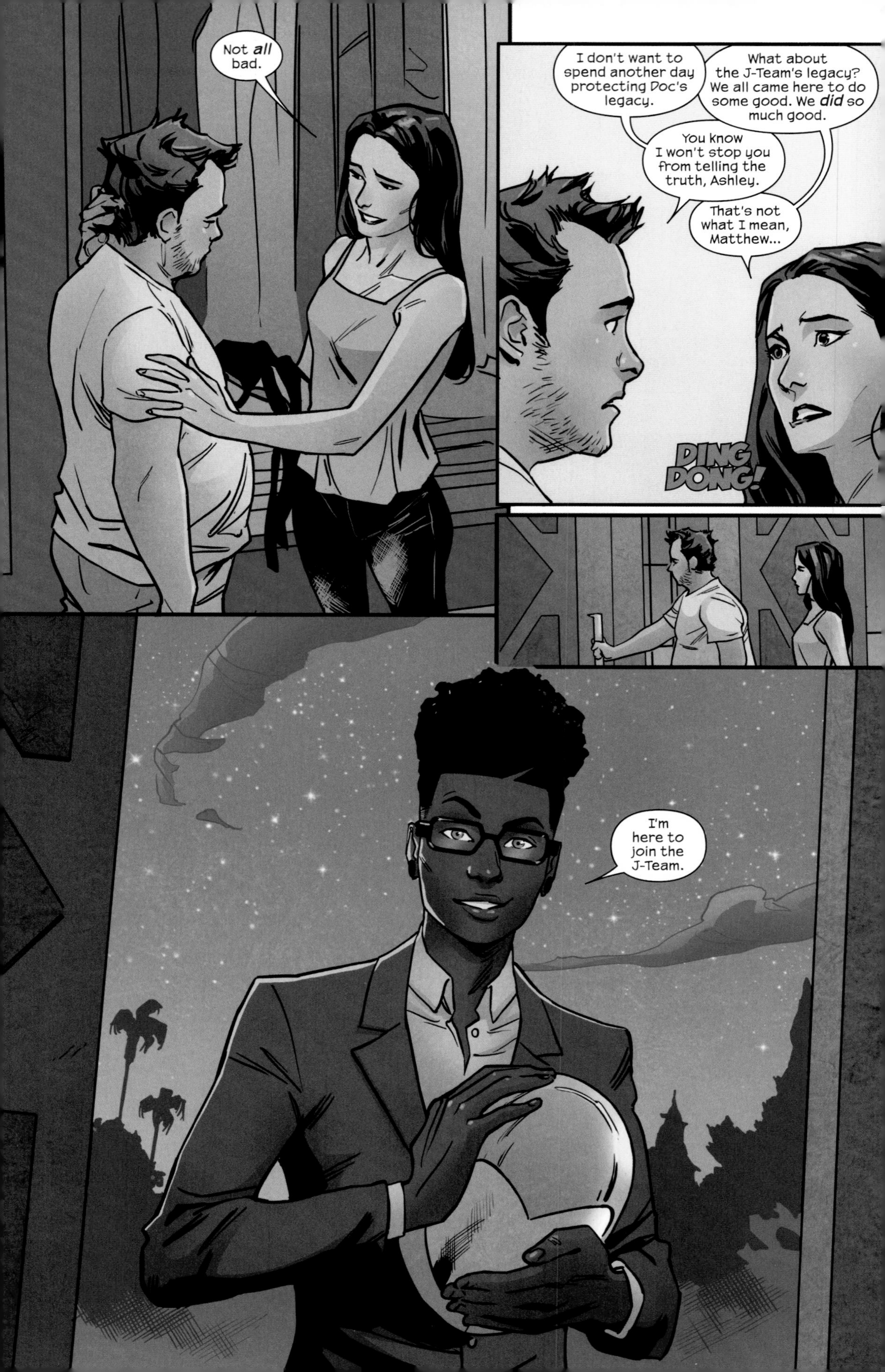
Not *all* bad.
I don't want to spend another day protecting Doc's legacy.
What about the J-Team's legacy? We all came here to do some good. We *did* so much good.
You know I won't stop you from telling the truth, Ashley.
That's not what I mean, Matthew...
DING DONG!
I'm here to join the J-Team.

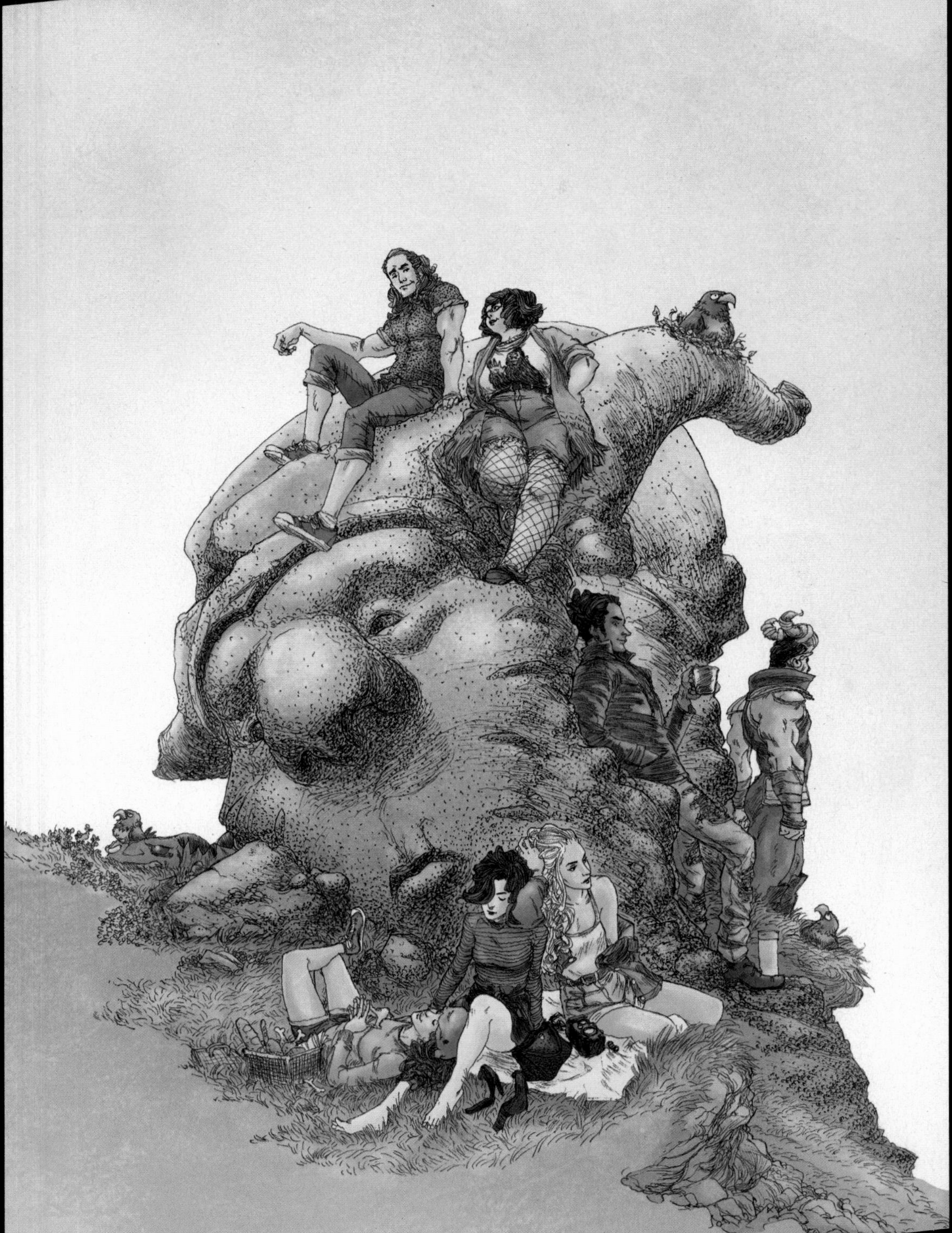

#38 VARIANT BY
ADRIAN ALPHONA & DEE CUNNIFFE

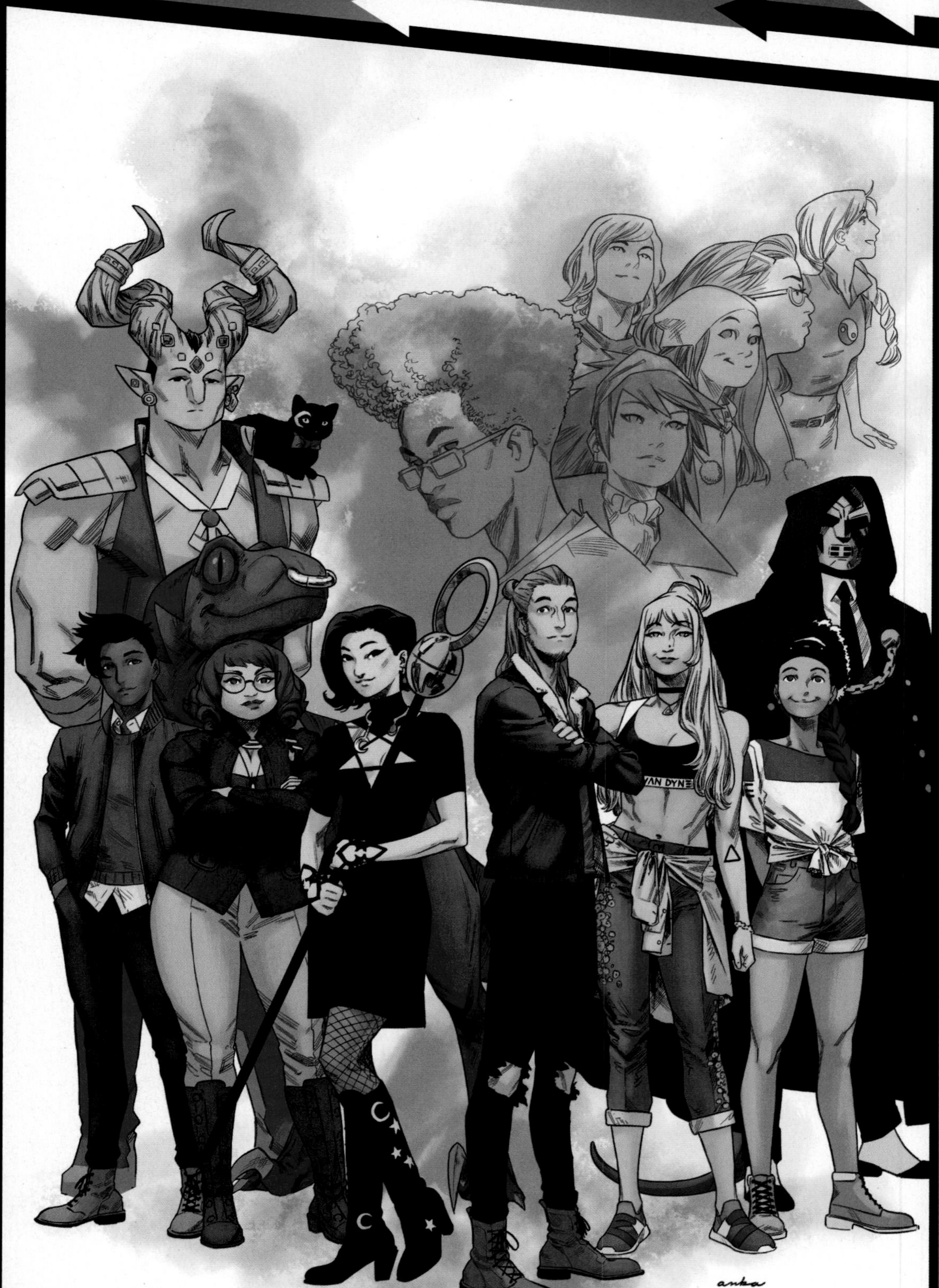
anka

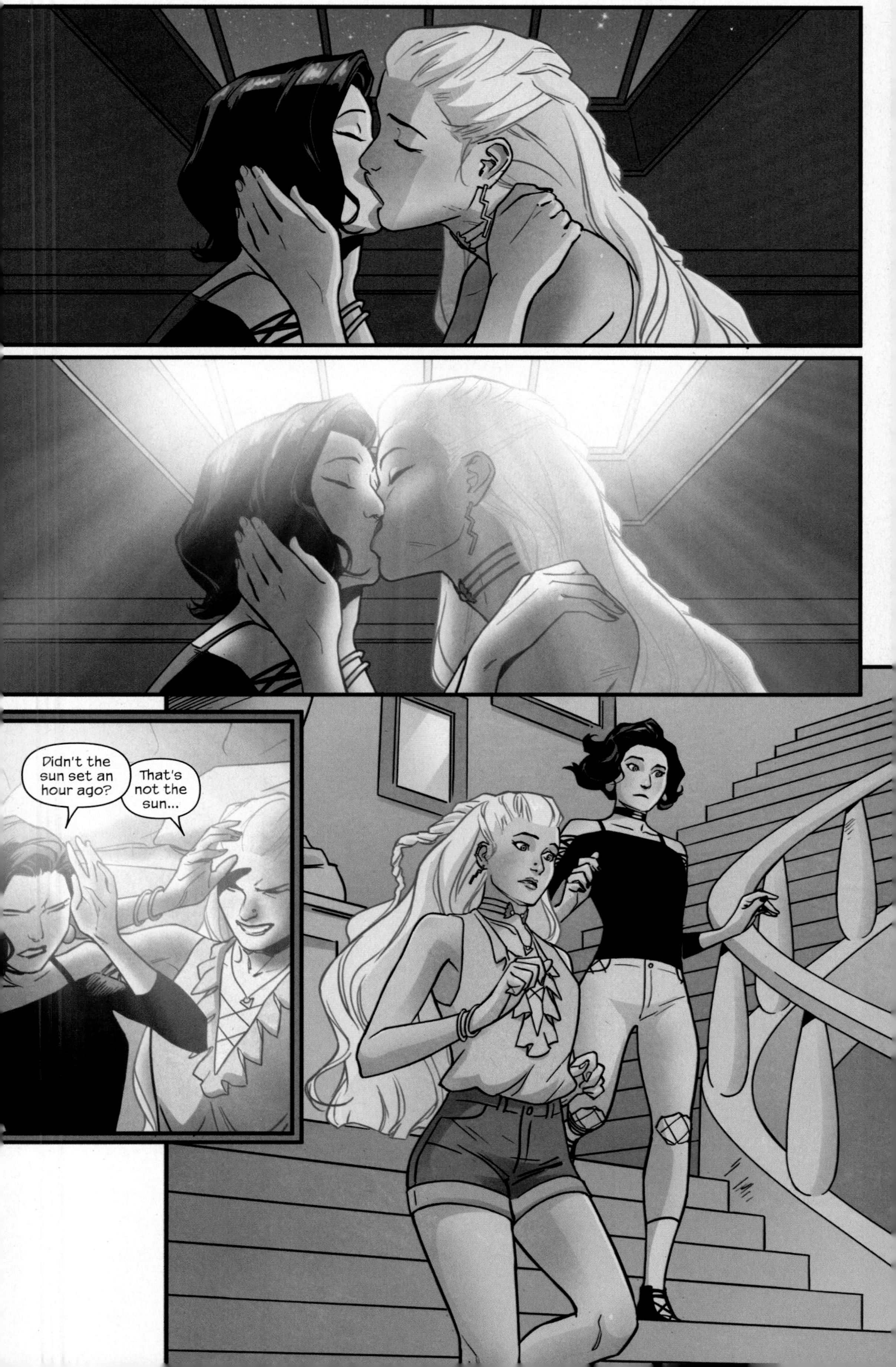
Didn't the sun set an hour ago?
That's not the sun...

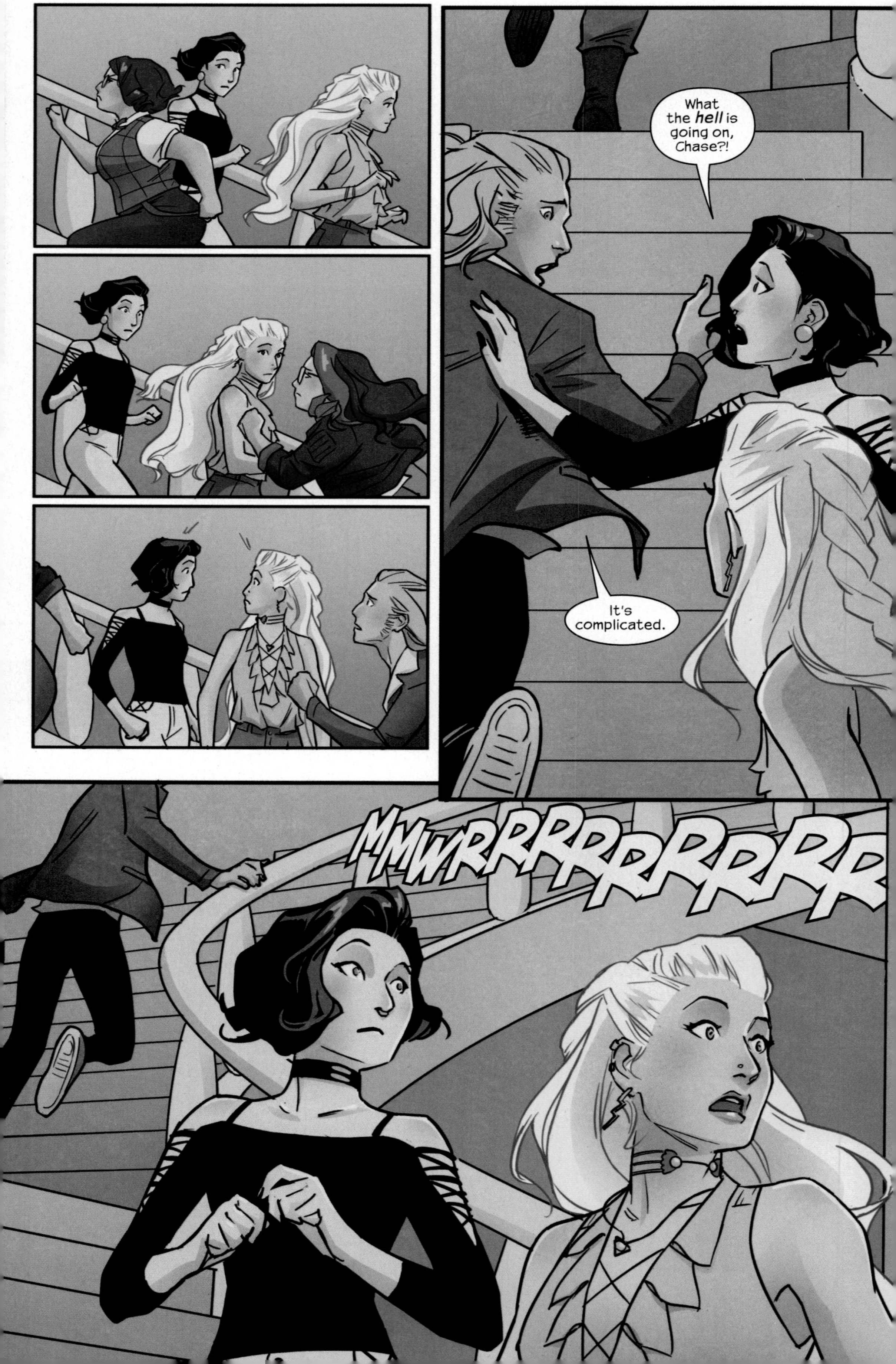
What the *hell* is going on, Chase?!
It's complicated.
MMWRRRRRRRRRR

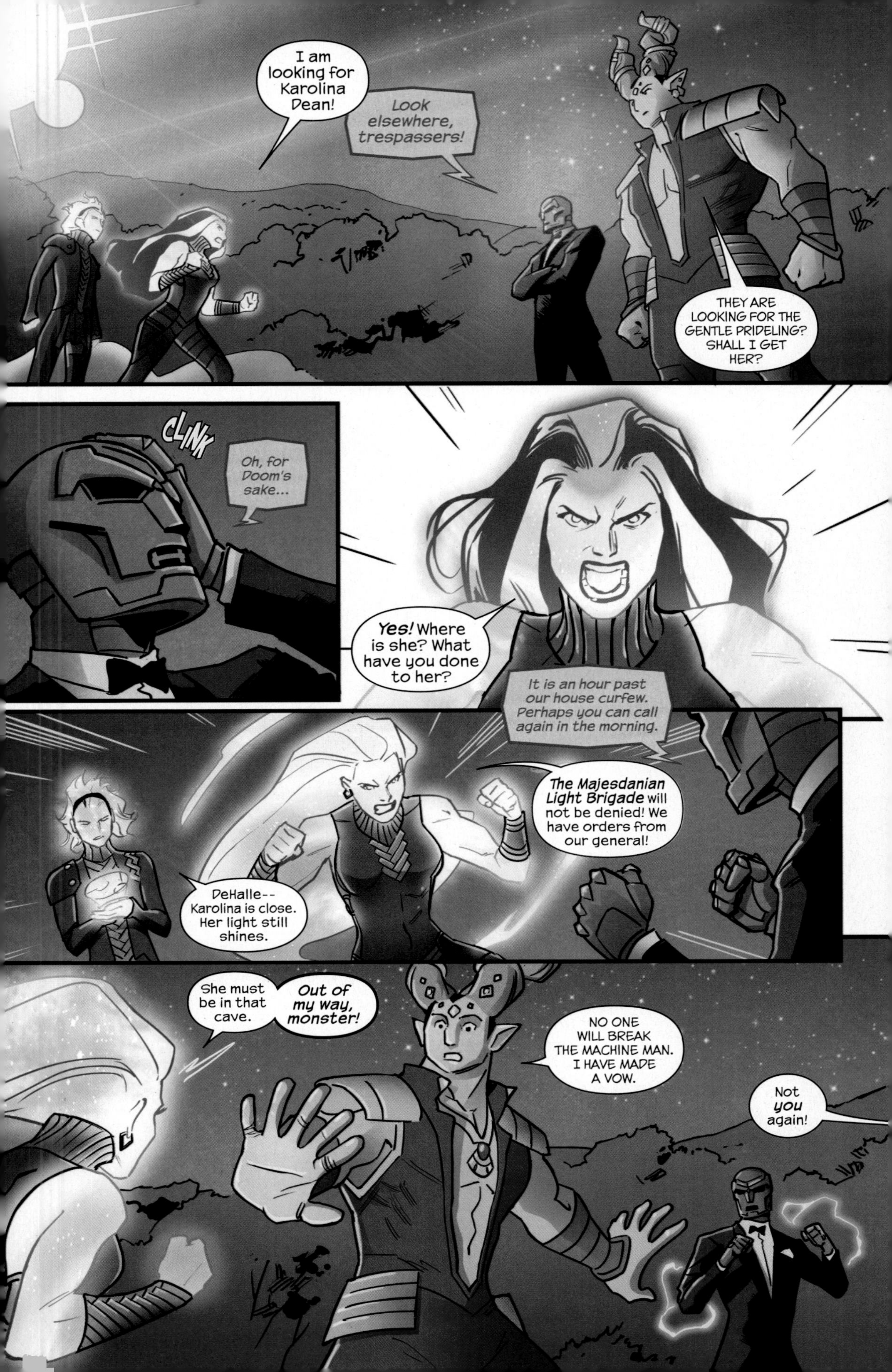
I am looking for Karolina Dean!
Look elsewhere, trespassers!
THEY ARE LOOKING FOR THE GENTLE PRIDELING? SHALL I GET HER?
CLINK
Oh, for Doom's sake...
Yes! Where is she? What have you done to her?
It is an hour past our house curfew. Perhaps you can call again in the morning.
The Majesdanian Light Brigade will not be denied! We have orders from our general!
DeHalle-- Karolina is close. Her light still shines.
She must be in that cave.
Out of my way, monster!
NO ONE WILL BREAK THE MACHINE MAN. I HAVE MADE A VOW.
Not you again!

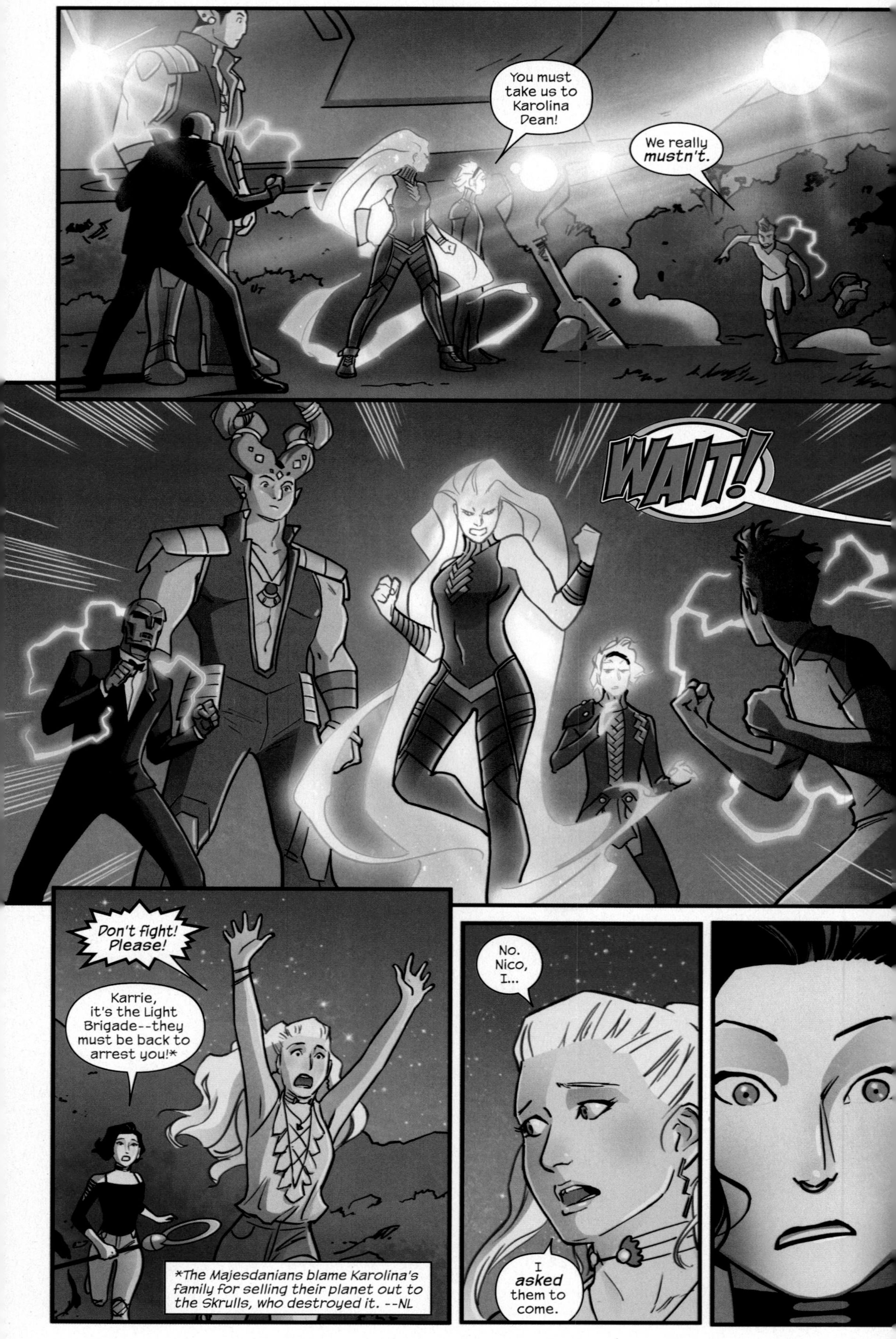

You must take us to Karolina Dean!
We really mustn't.
WAIT!
Don't fight! Please!
Karrie, it's the Light Brigade--they must be back to arrest you!*
*The Majesdanians blame Karolina's family for selling their planet out to the Skrulls, who destroyed it. --NL
No. Nico, I...
I asked them to come.

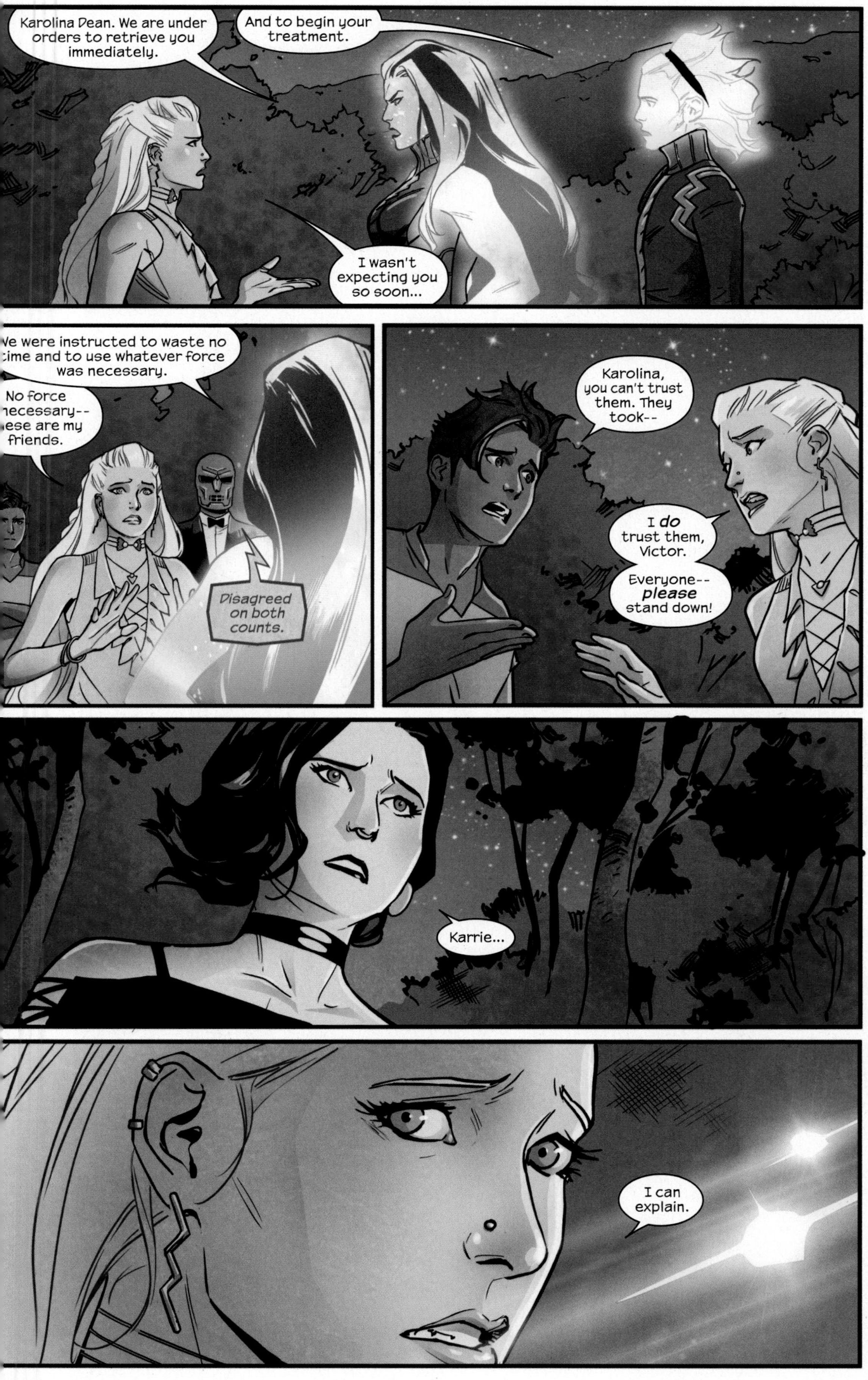

Karolina Dean. We are under orders to retrieve you immediately.
And to begin your treatment.
I wasn't expecting you so soon...
We were instructed to waste no time and to use whatever force was necessary.
No force necessary-- these are my friends.
Disagreed on both counts.
Karolina, you can't trust them. They took--
I *do* trust them, Victor.
Everyone-- ***please*** stand down!
Karrie...
I can explain.

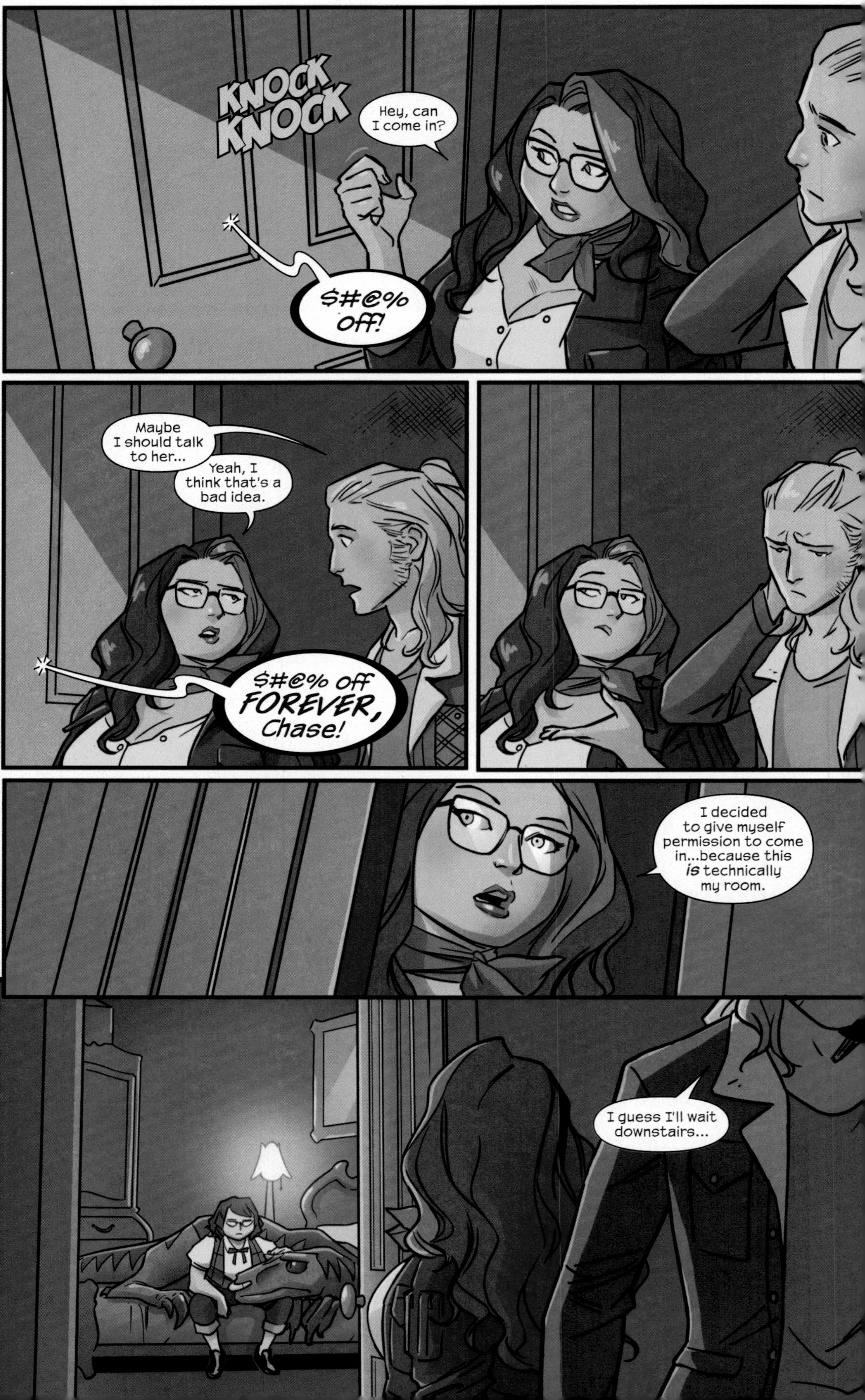
KNOCK KNOCK
Hey, can I come in?
$#@% off!
Maybe I should talk to her...
Yeah, I think that's a bad idea.
$#@% off FOREVER, Chase!
I decided to give myself permission to come in...because this *is* technically my room.
I guess I'll wait downstairs...

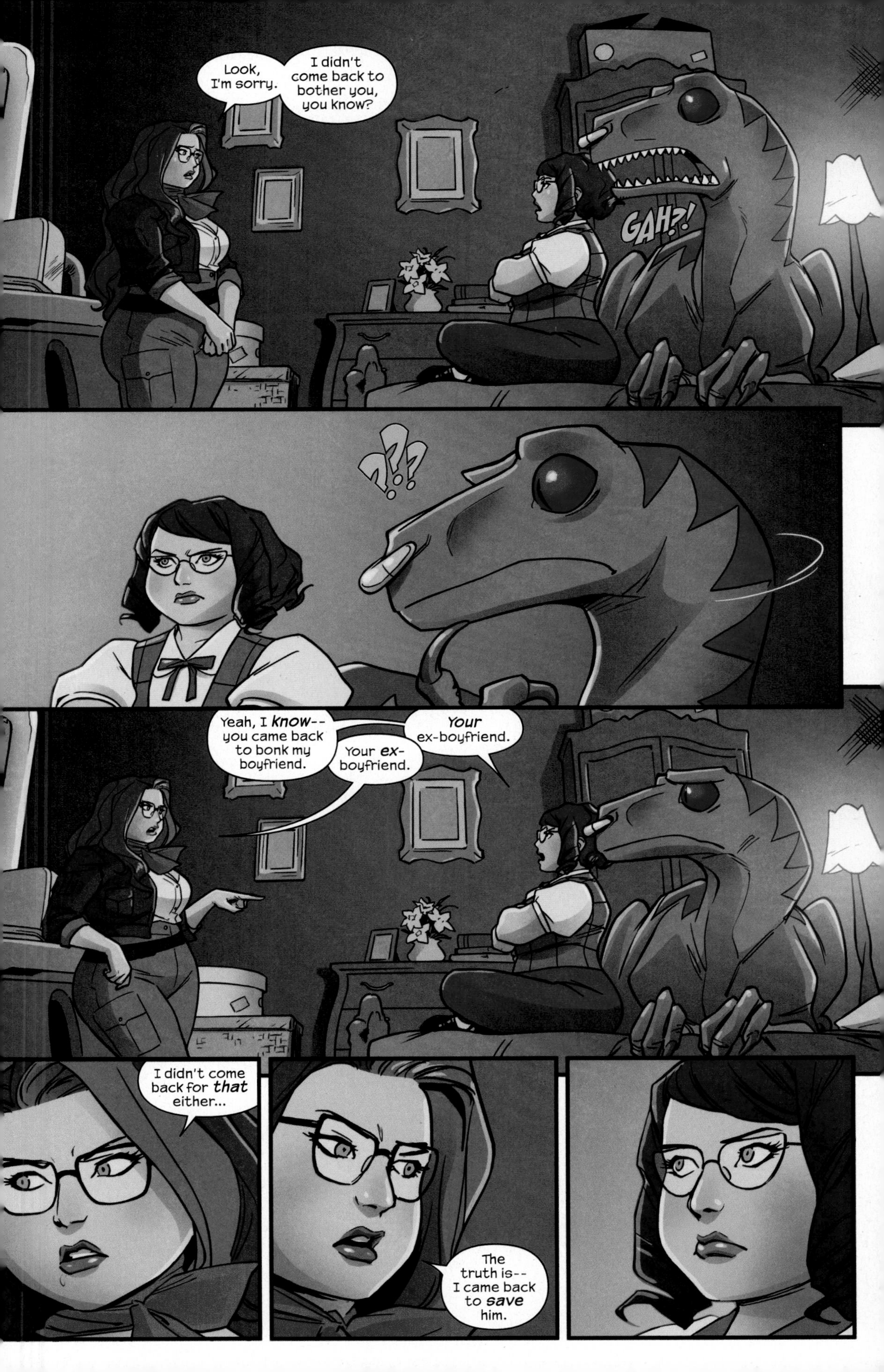
Look, I'm sorry.
I didn't come back to bother you, you know?
GAH?!
?!?!
Yeah, I *know*-- you came back to bonk my boyfriend.
Your ex-boyfriend.
Your *ex*-boyfriend.
I didn't come back for *that* either...
The truth is-- I came back to *save* him.

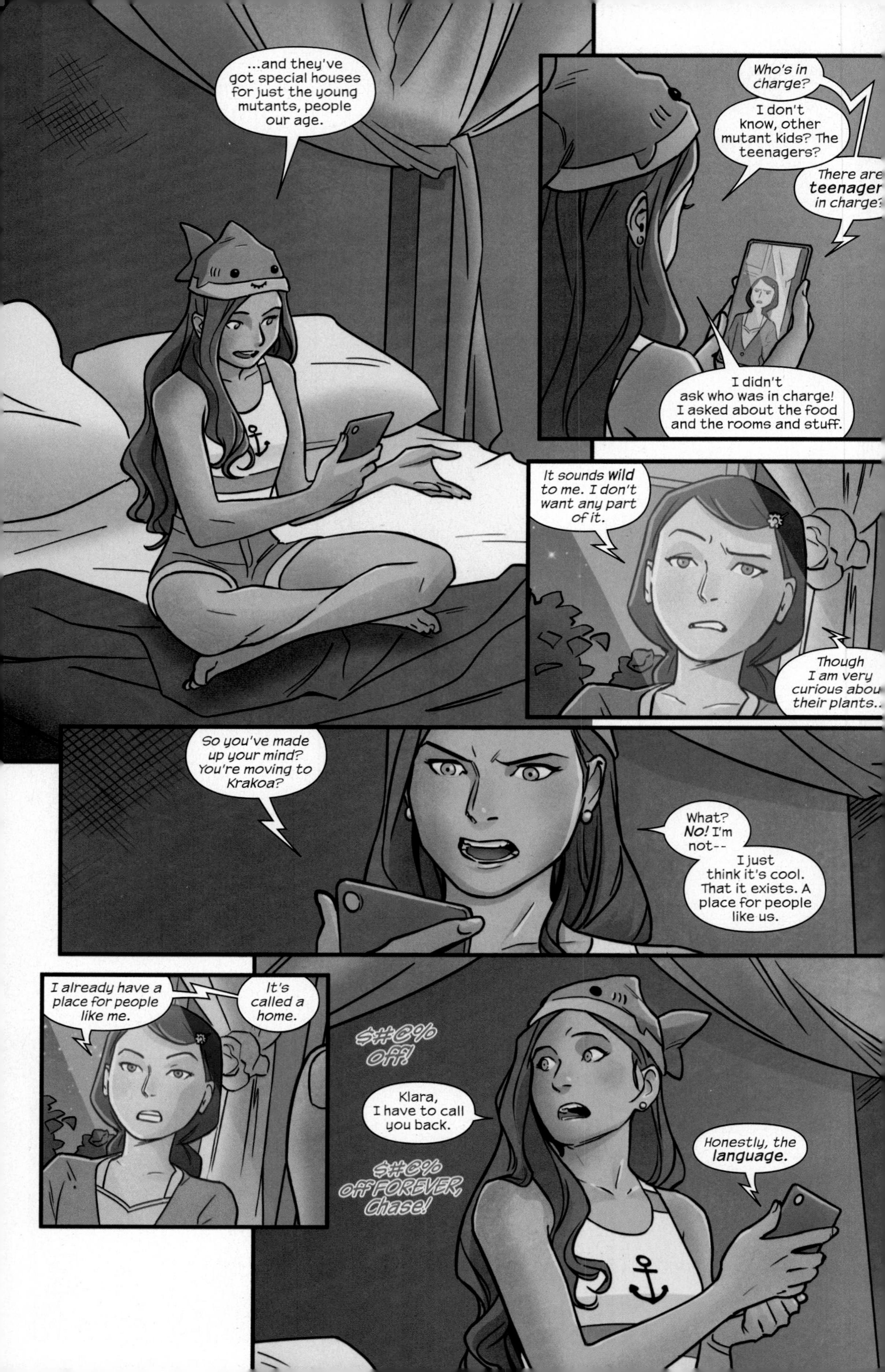
...and they've got special houses for just the young mutants, people our age.
Who's in charge?
I don't know, other mutant kids? The teenagers?
There are teenager in charge?
I didn't ask who was in charge! I asked about the food and the rooms and stuff.
It sounds wild to me. I don't want any part of it.
Though I am very curious abou their plants..
So you've made up your mind? You're moving to Krakoa?
What? No! I'm not--
I just think it's cool. That it exists. A place for people like us.
I already have a place for people like me.
It's called a home.
$#@% off!
Klara, I have to call you back.
$#@% off FOREVER, Chase!
Honestly, the language.

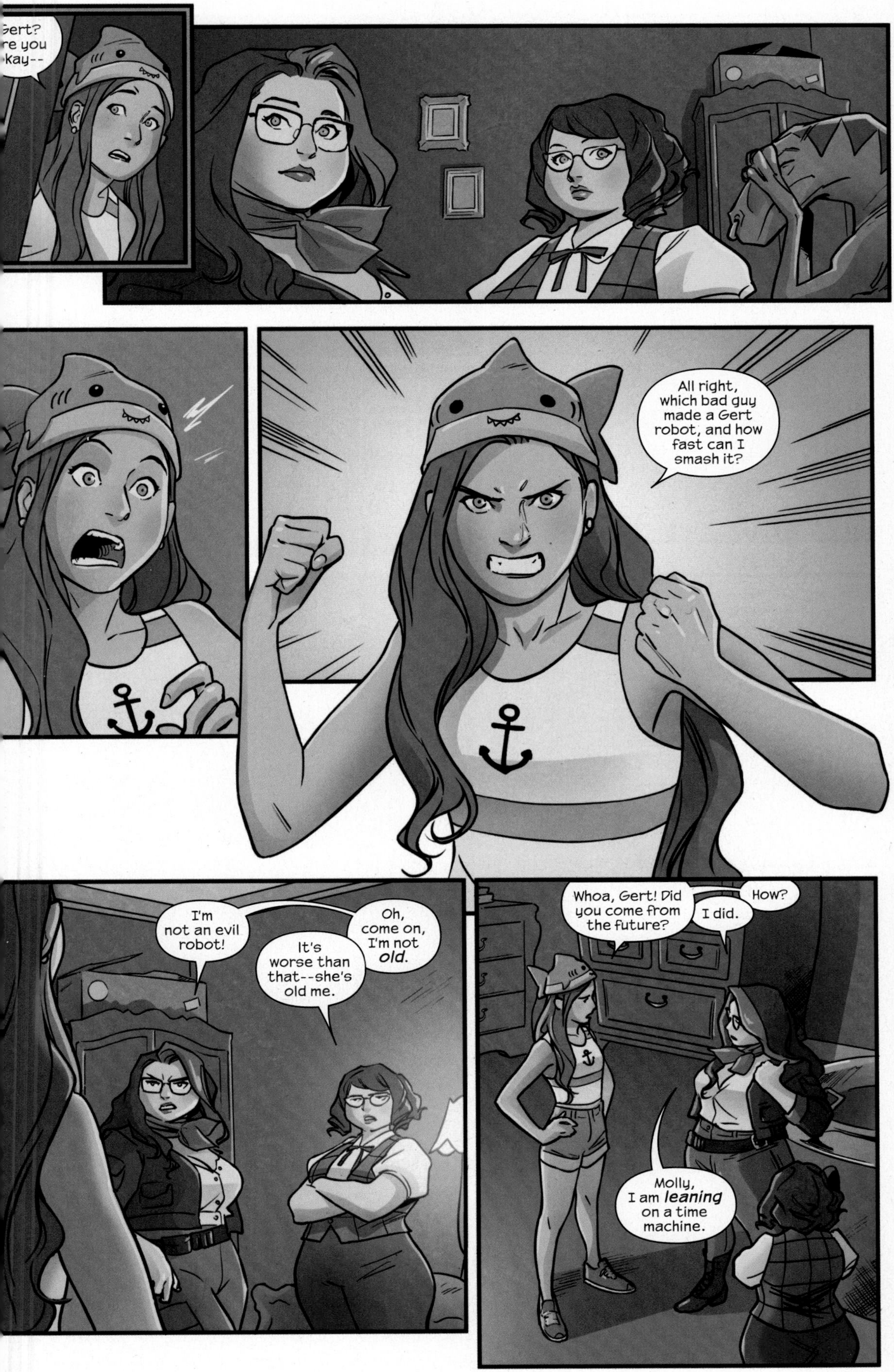
Gert? ...re you ...kay--
All right, which bad guy made a Gert robot, and how fast can I smash it?
I'm not an evil robot!
Oh, come on, I'm not *old*.
It's worse than that--she's old me.
Whoa, Gert! Did you come from the future?
How?
I did.
Molly, I am *leaning* on a time machine.

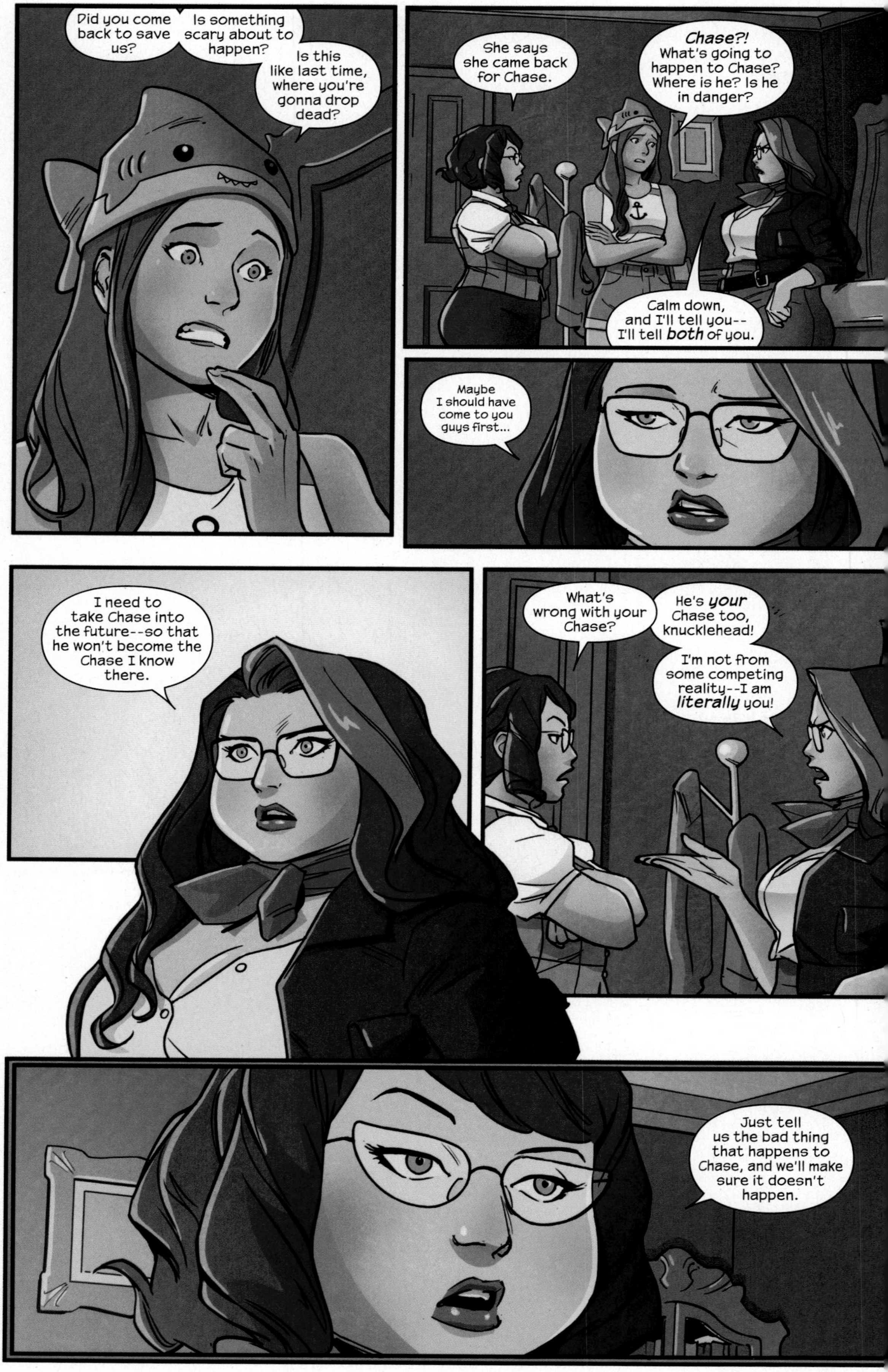
Did you come back to save us?
Is something scary about to happen?
Is this like last time, where you're gonna drop dead?
She says she came back for Chase.
Chase?! What's going to happen to Chase? Where is he? Is he in danger?
Calm down, and I'll tell you-- I'll tell ***both*** of you.
Maybe I should have come to you guys first...
I need to take Chase into the future--so that he won't become the Chase I know there.
What's wrong with your Chase?
He's ***your*** Chase too, knucklehead!
I'm not from some competing reality--I am ***literally*** you!
Just tell us the bad thing that happens to Chase, and we'll make sure it doesn't happen.

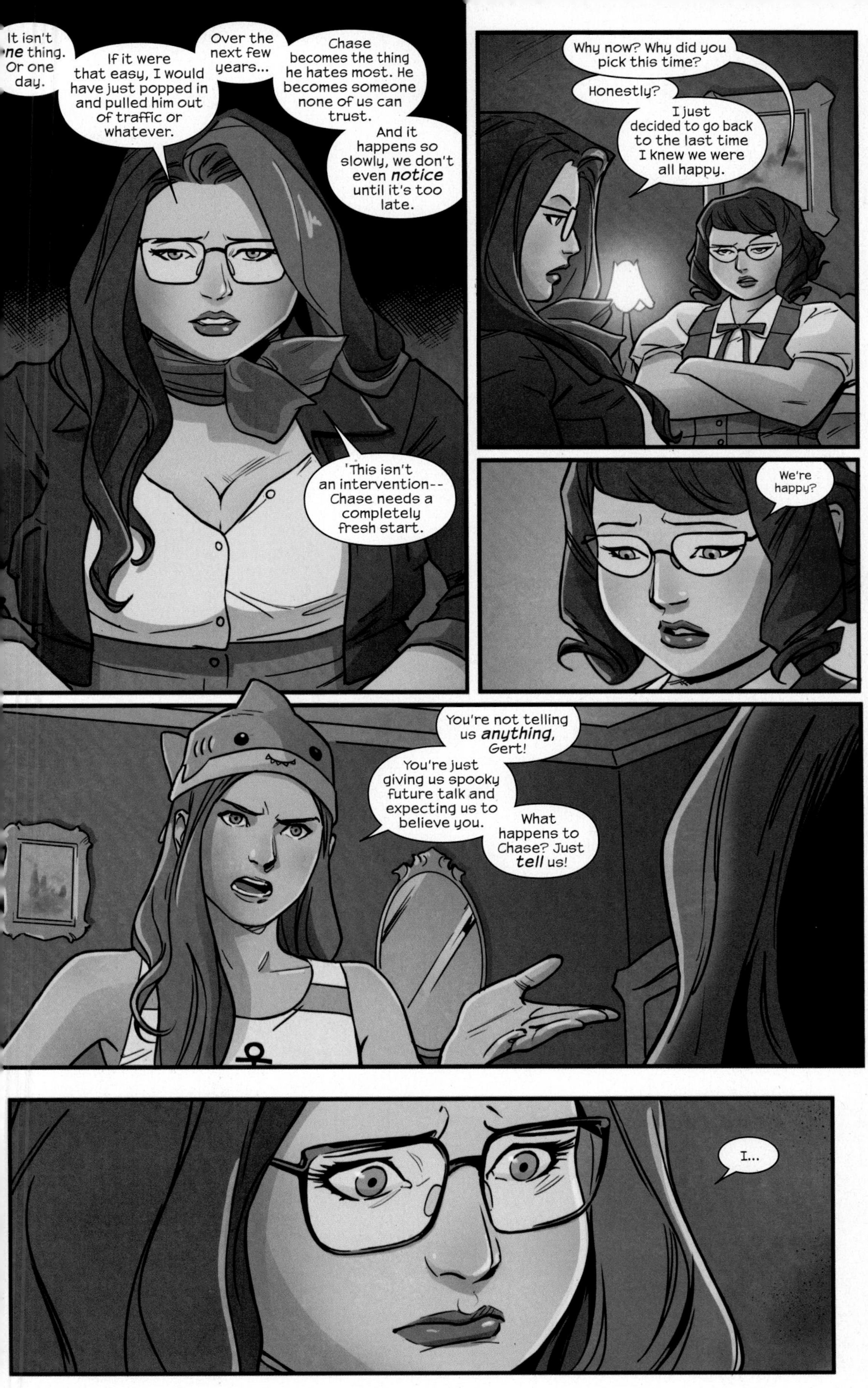
It isn't *ne* thing. Or one day.
If it were that easy, I would have just popped in and pulled him out of traffic or whatever.
Over the next few years...
Chase becomes the thing he hates most. He becomes someone none of us can trust.
And it happens so slowly, we don't even *notice* until it's too late.
'This isn't an intervention-- Chase needs a completely fresh start.
Why now? Why did you pick this time?
Honestly?
I just decided to go back to the last time I knew we were all happy.
We're happy?
You're not telling us *anything*, Gert!
You're just giving us spooky future talk and expecting us to believe you.
What happens to Chase? Just *tell* us!
I...

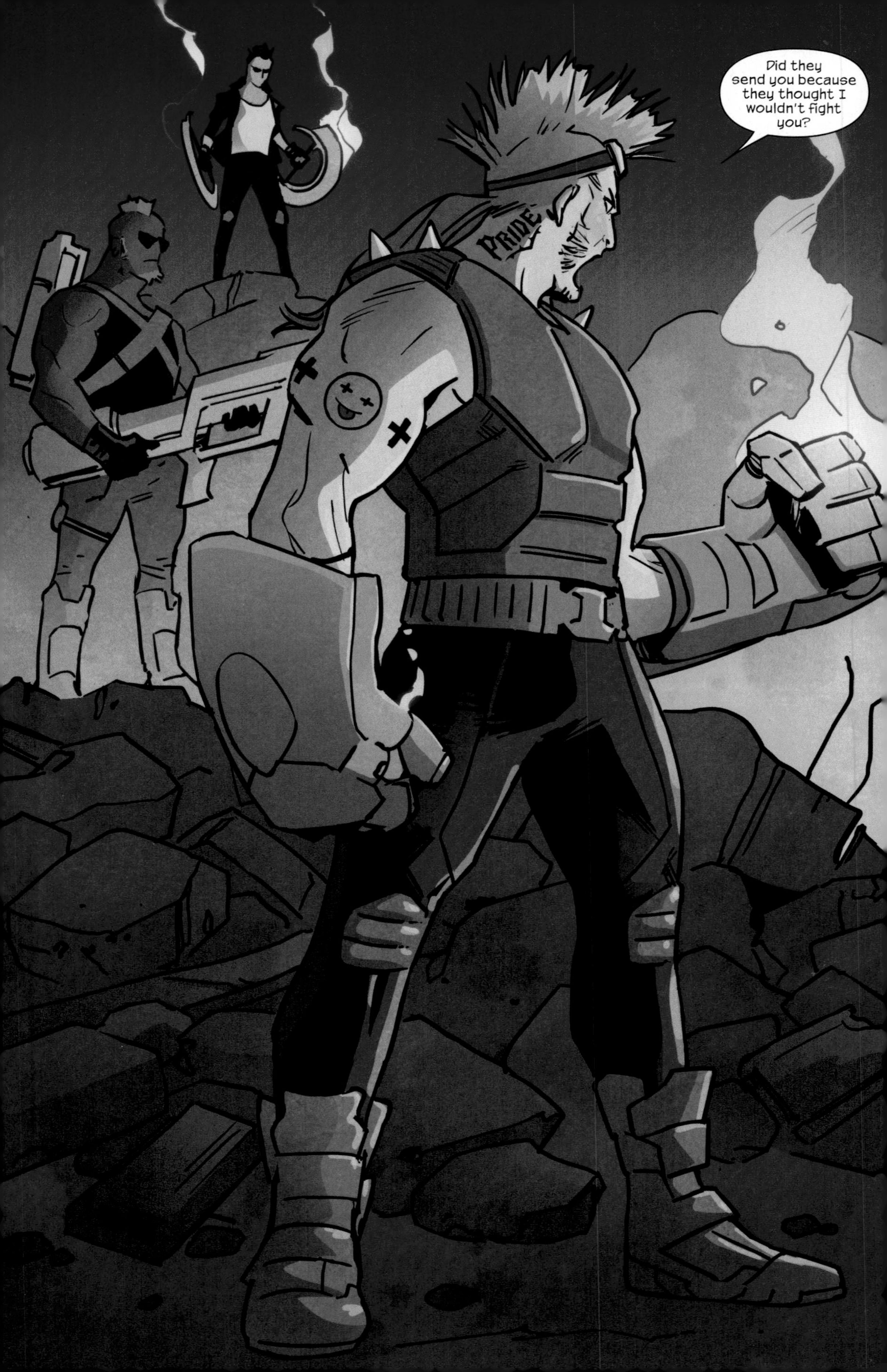
Did they send you because they thought I wouldn't fight you?
PRIDE

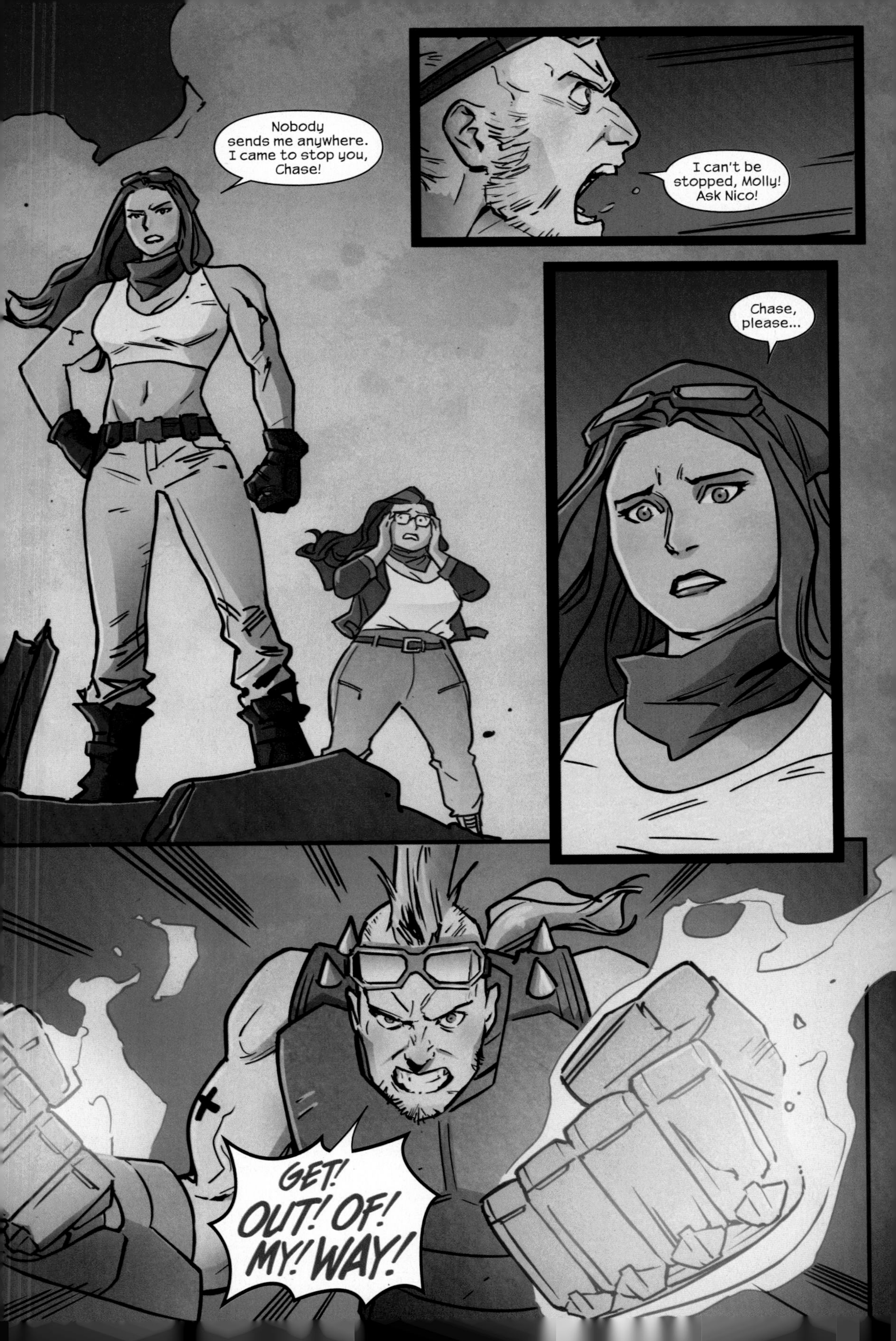
Nobody sends me anywhere. I came to stop you, Chase!
I can't be stopped, Molly! Ask Nico!
Chase, please...
GET! OUT! OF! MY! WAY!

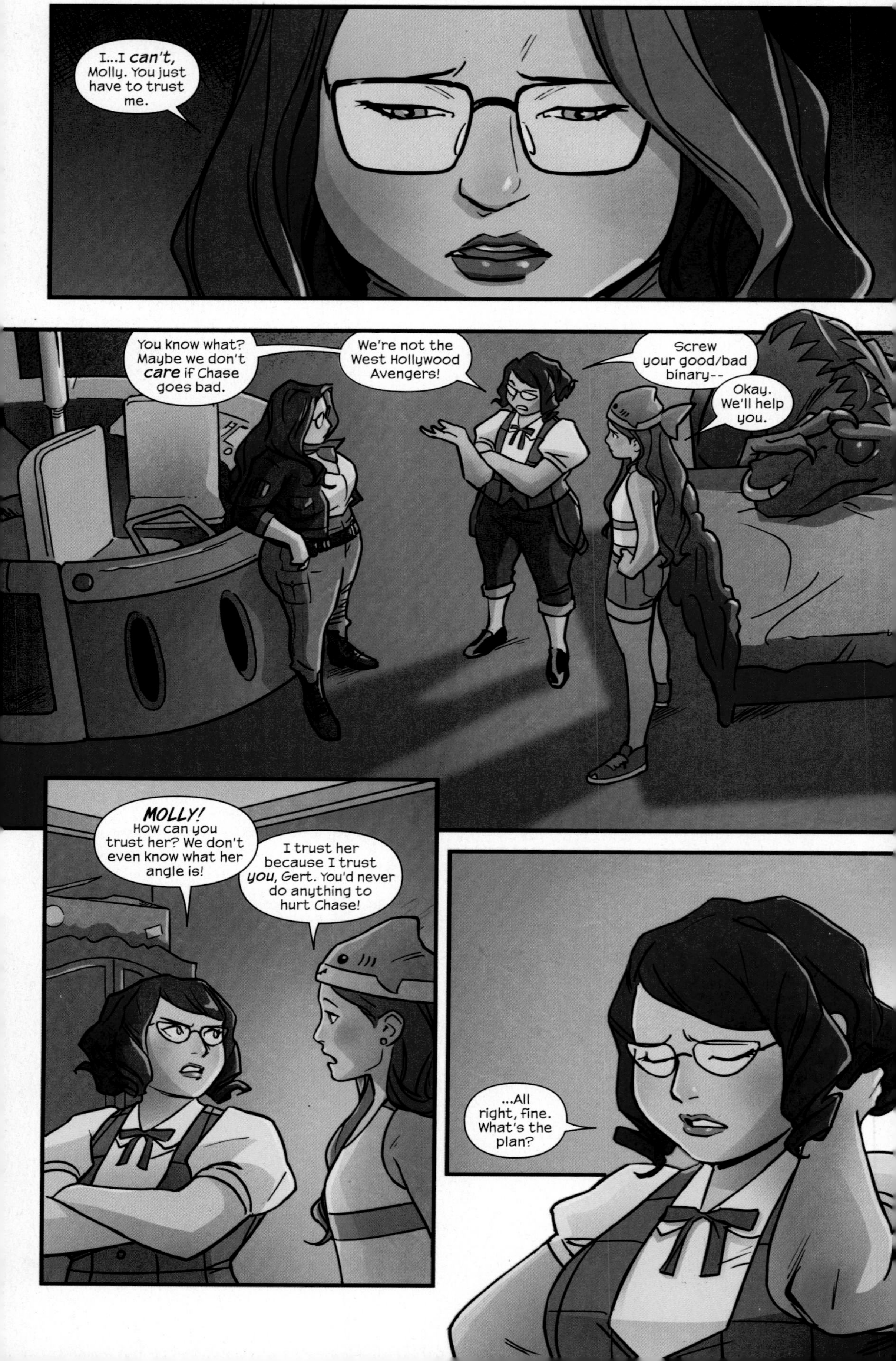
I...I can't, Molly. You just have to trust me.
You know what? Maybe we don't care if Chase goes bad.
We're not the West Hollywood Avengers!
Screw your good/bad binary--
Okay. We'll help you.
MOLLY! How can you trust her? We don't even know what her angle is!
I trust her because I trust you, Gert. You'd never do anything to hurt Chase!
...All right, fine. What's the plan?

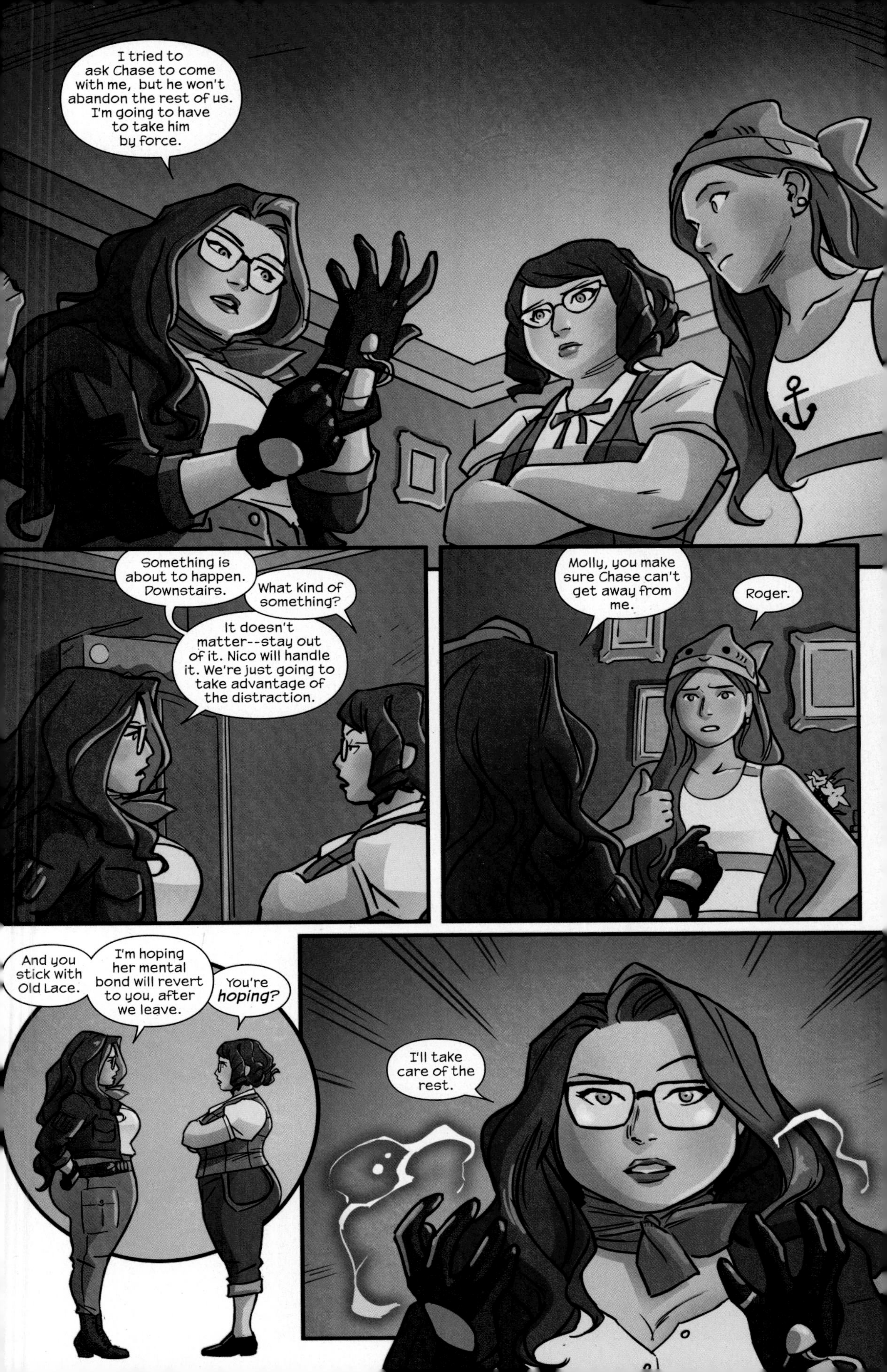
I tried to ask Chase to come with me, but he won't abandon the rest of us. I'm going to have to take him by force.
Something is about to happen. Downstairs.
What kind of something?
It doesn't matter--stay out of it. Nico will handle it. We're just going to take advantage of the distraction.
Molly, you make sure Chase can't get away from me.
Roger.
And you stick with Old Lace.
I'm hoping her mental bond will revert to you, after we leave.
You're *hoping*?
I'll take care of the rest.

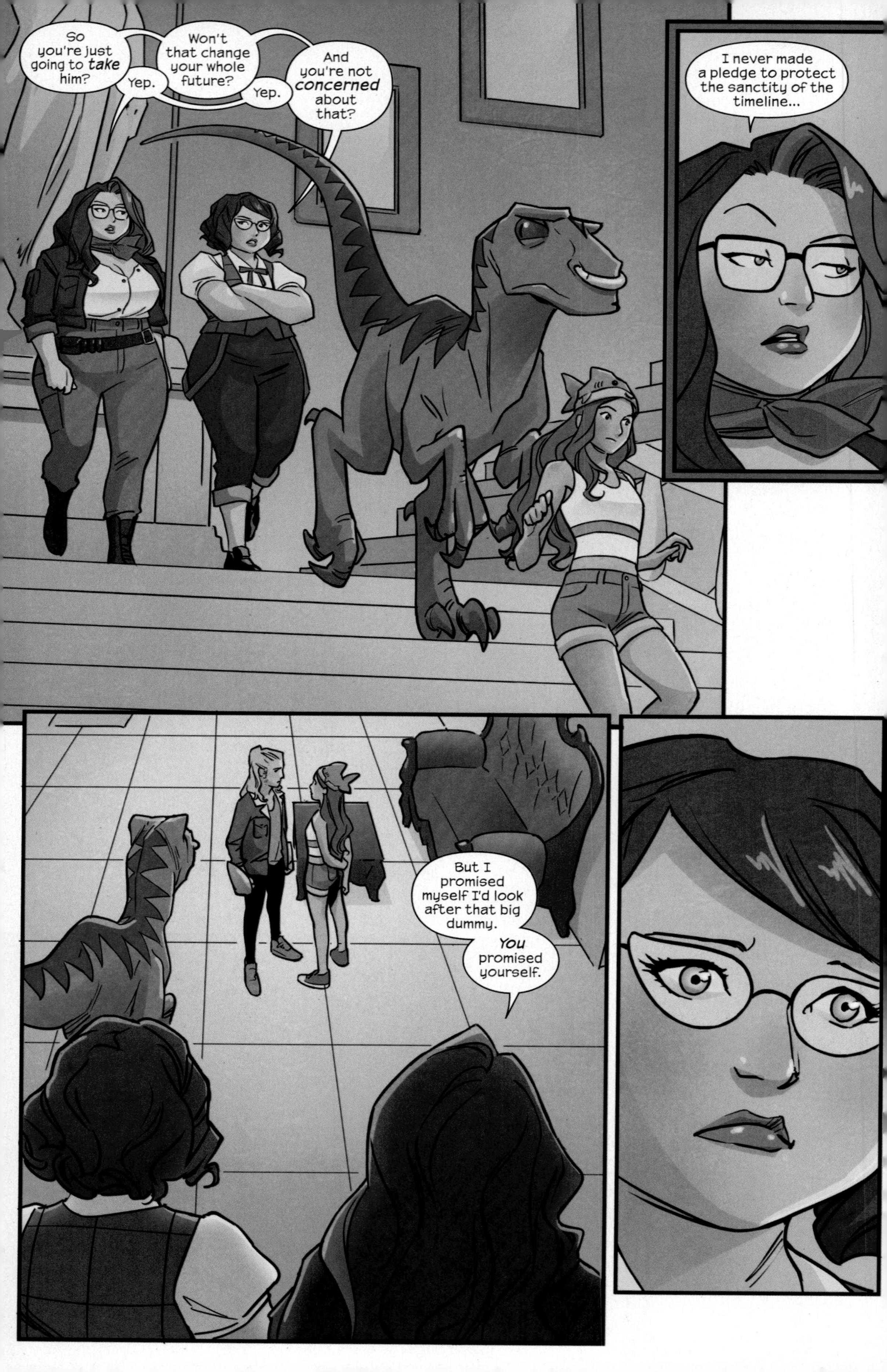
So you're just going to *take* him?
Yep.
Won't that change your whole future?
Yep.
And you're not *concerned* about that?
I never made a pledge to protect the sanctity of the timeline...
But I promised myself I'd look after that big dummy.
You promised yourself.

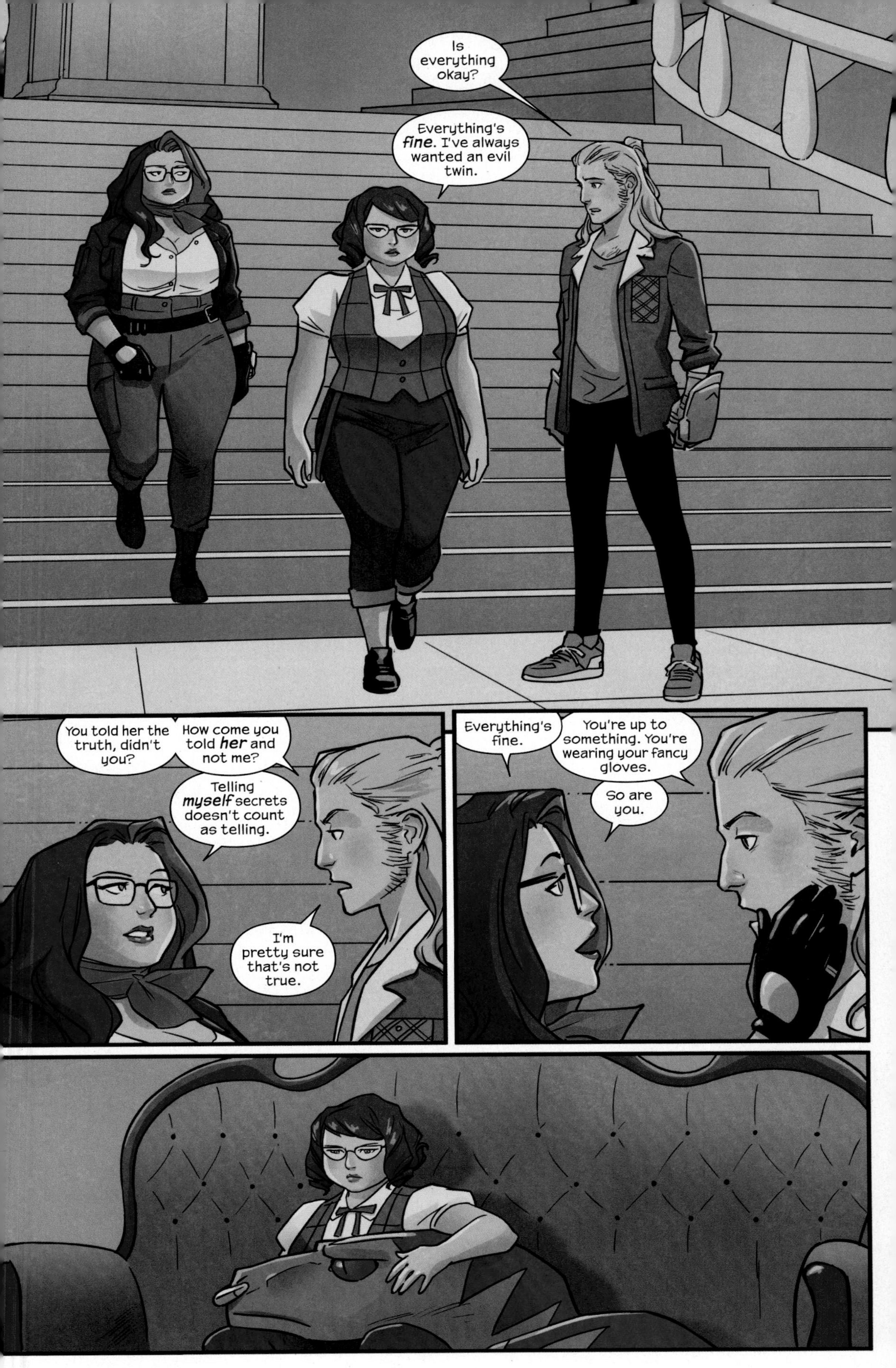
Is everything okay?
Everything's *fine*. I've always wanted an evil twin.
You told her the truth, didn't you?
How come you told *her* and not me?
Telling *myself* secrets doesn't count as telling.
I'm pretty sure that's not true.
Everything's fine.
You're up to something. You're wearing your fancy gloves.
So are you.

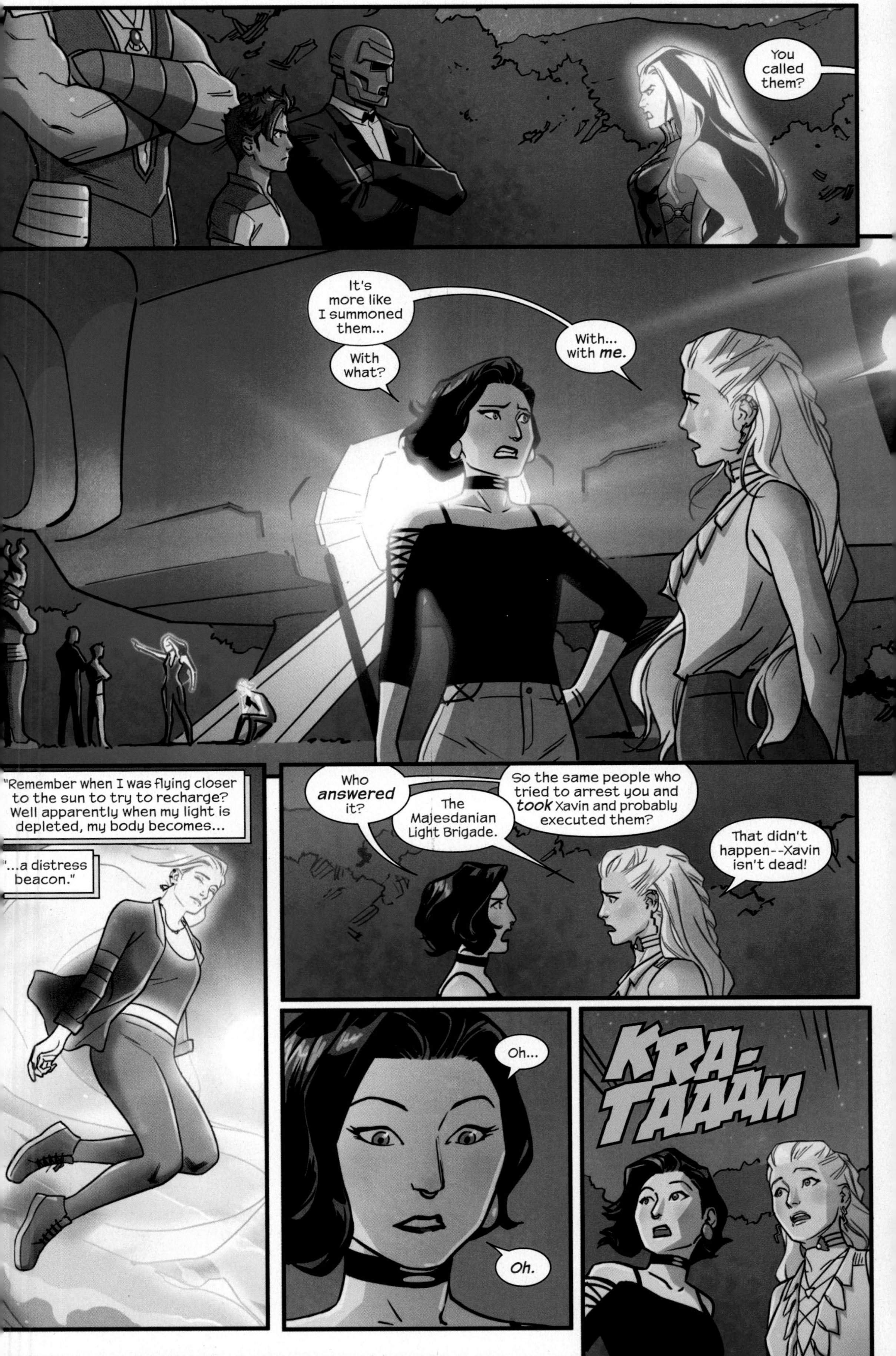
You called them?
It's more like I summoned them...
With what?
With... with *me.*
"Remember when I was flying closer to the sun to try to recharge? Well apparently when my light is depleted, my body becomes...
"...a distress beacon."
Who *answered* it?
The Majesdanian Light Brigade.
So the same people who tried to arrest you and *took* Xavin and probably executed them?
That didn't happen--Xavin isn't dead!
Oh...
Oh.
KRA-TAAAM

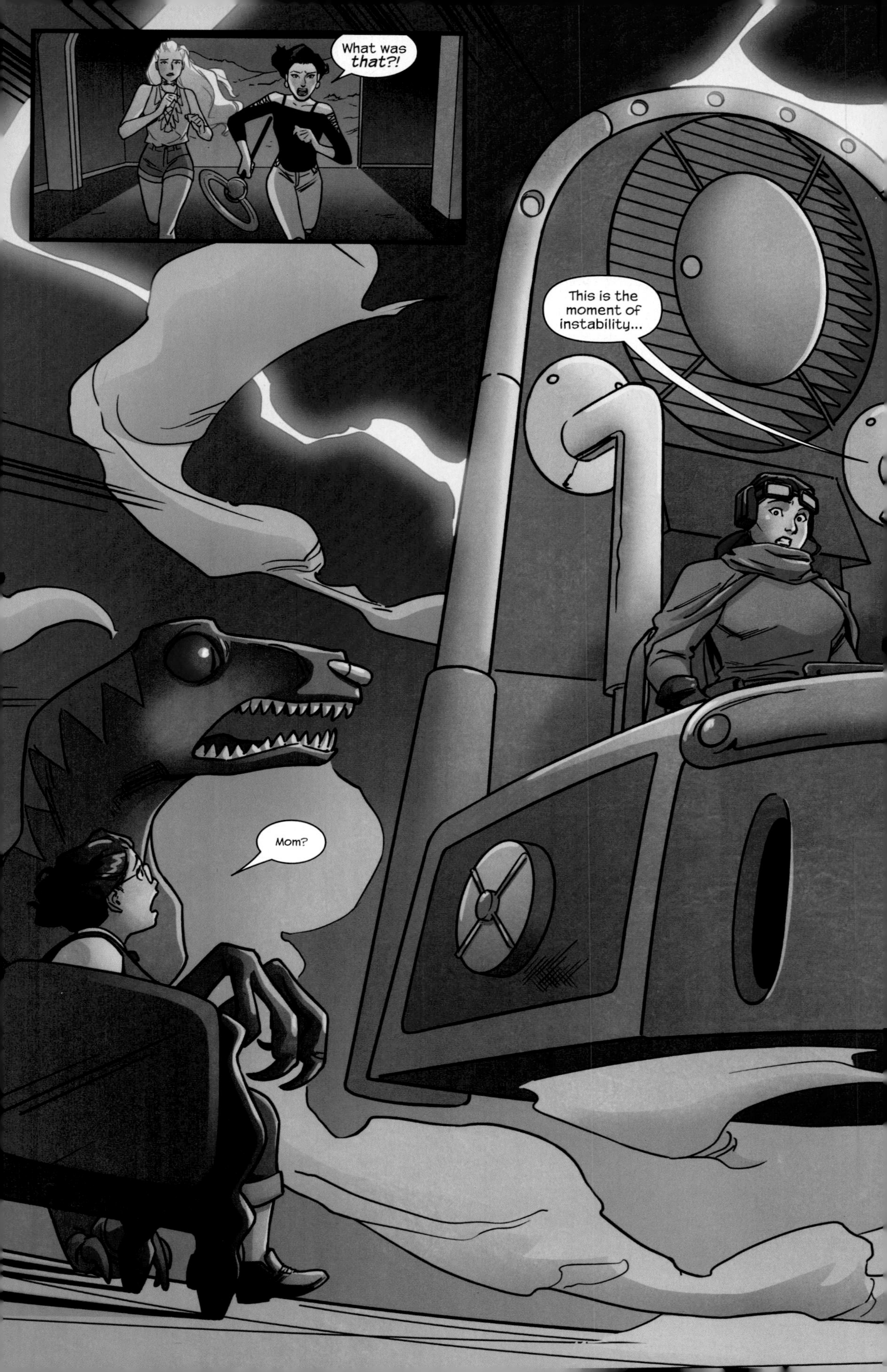
What was that?!
This is the moment of instability...
Mom?

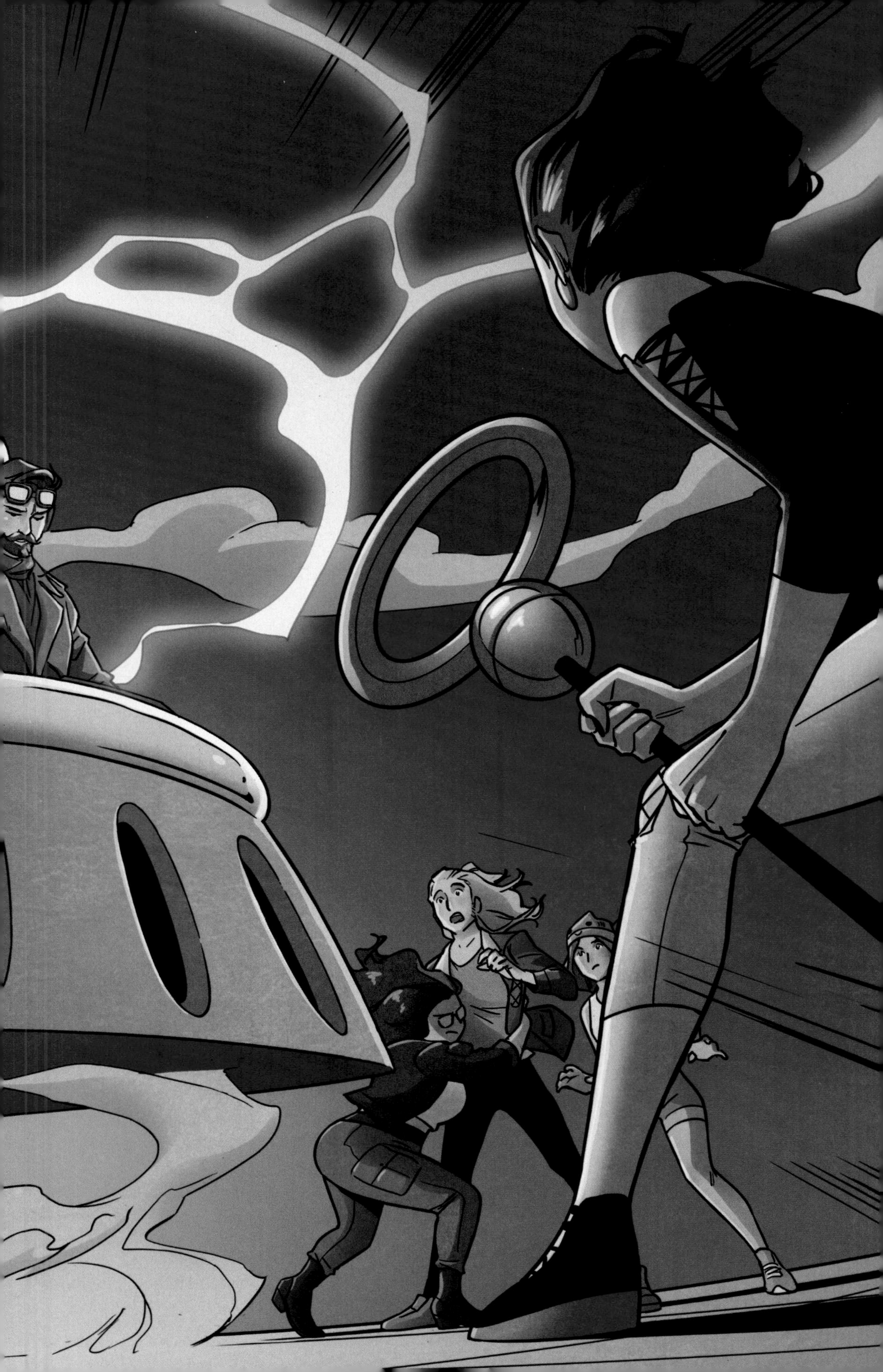

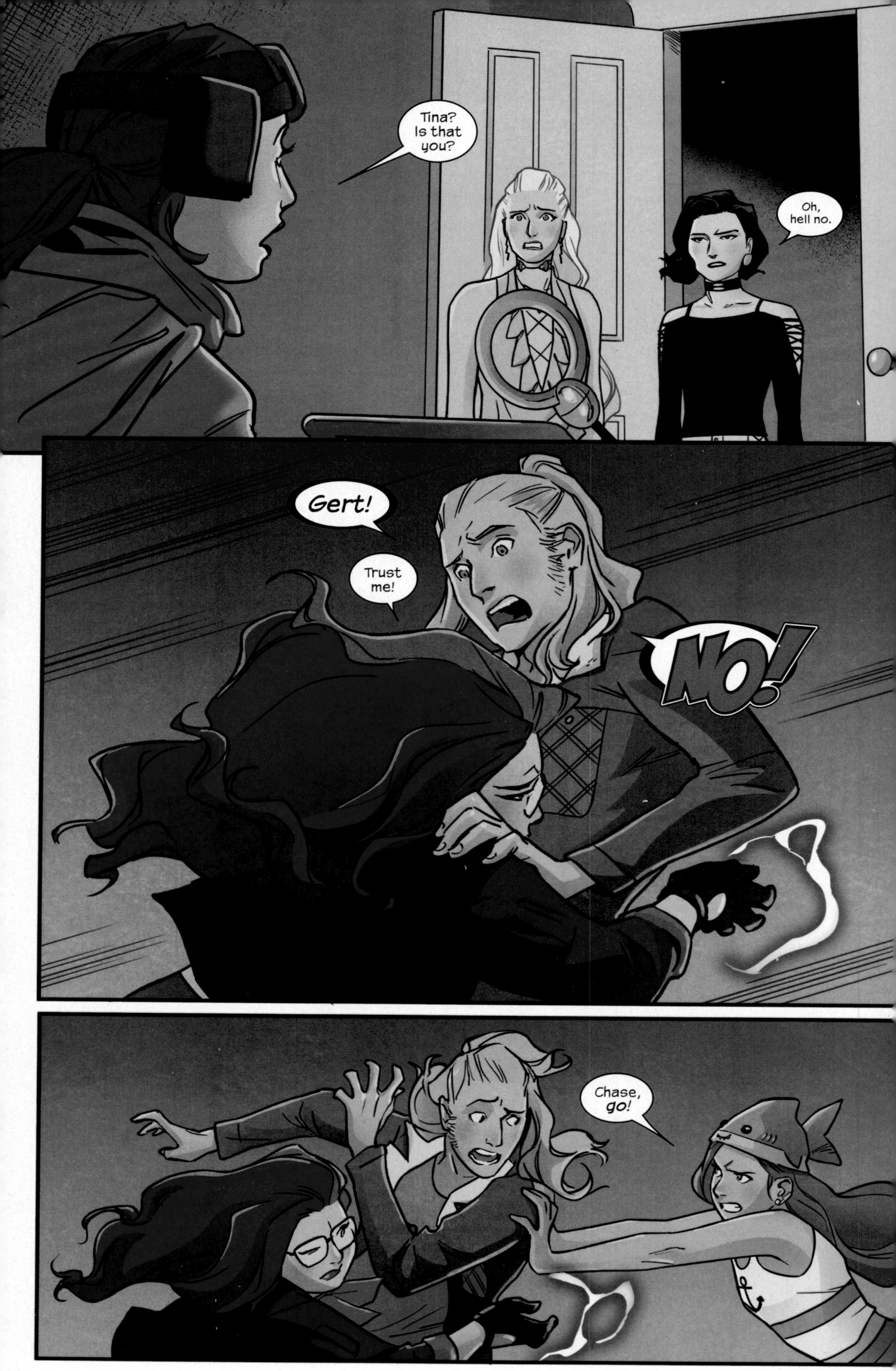
Tina? Is that you?
Oh, hell no.
Gert!
Trust me!
NO!
Chase, go!

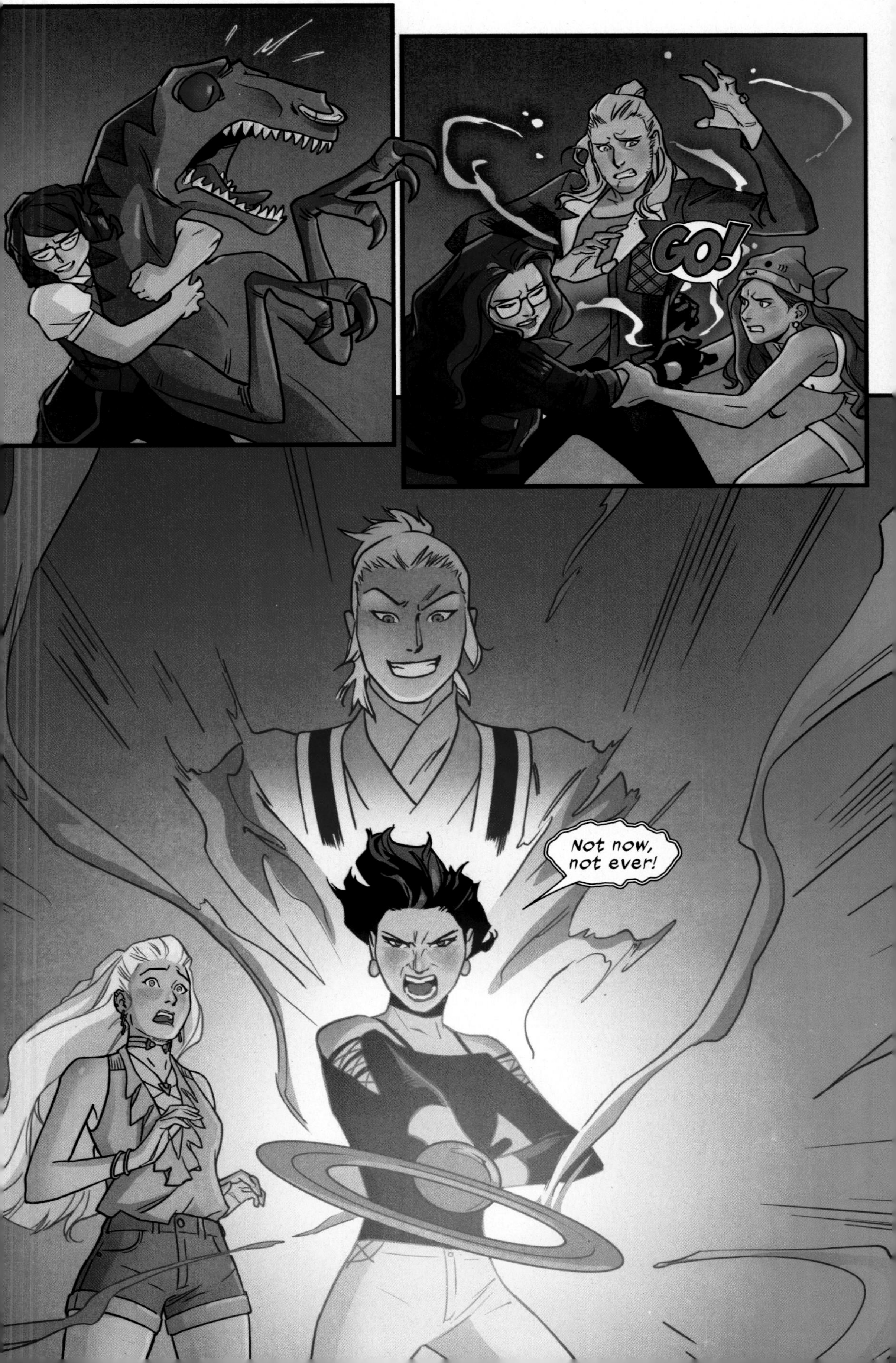
GO!
Not now, not ever!

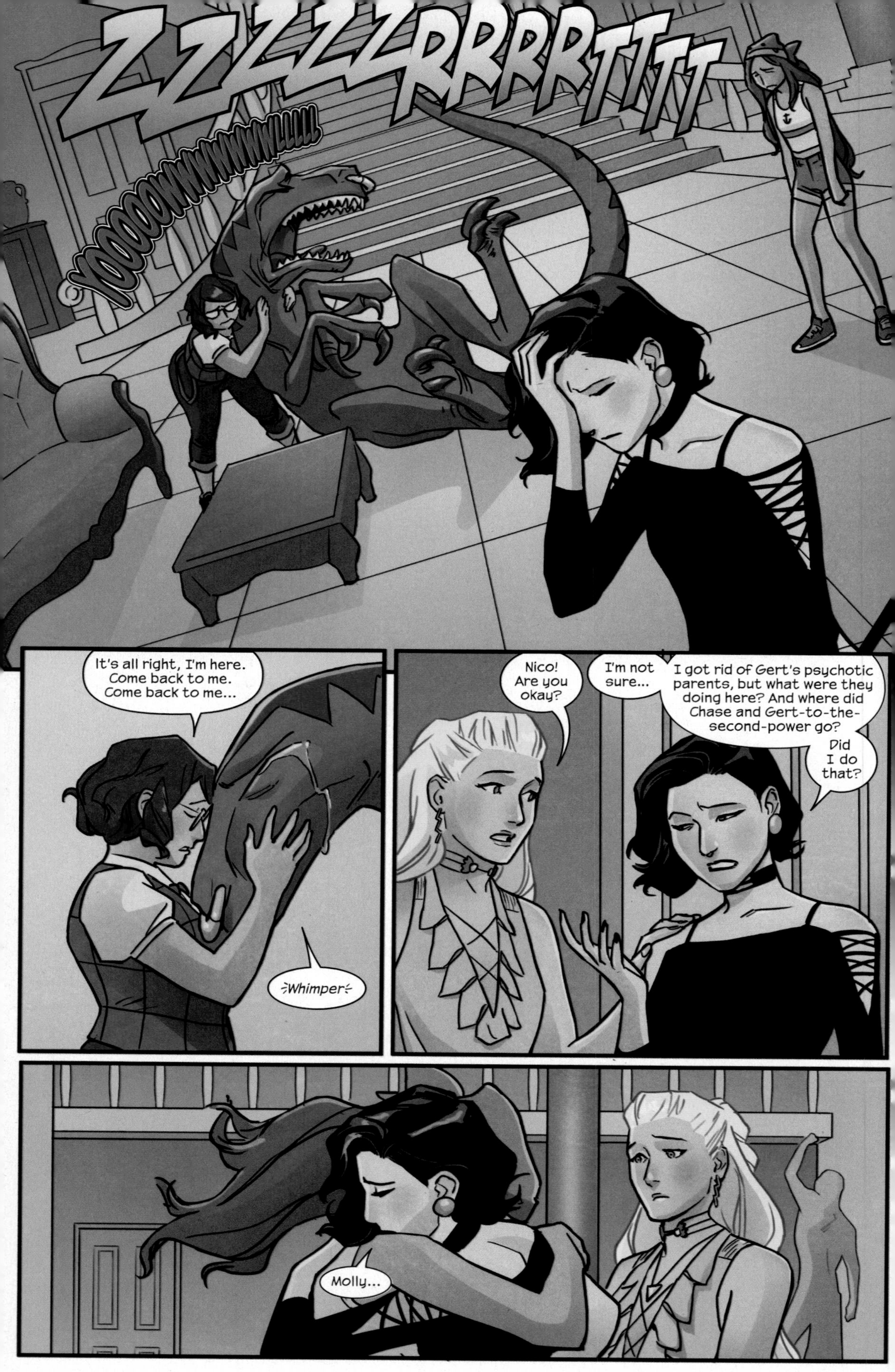
ZZZZZRRRRTTTT
YOOOOOWWWWWWWLLLLL
It's all right, I'm here. Come back to me. Come back to me...
Whimper
Nico! Are you okay?
I'm not sure...
I got rid of Gert's psychotic parents, but what were they doing here? And where did Chase and Gert-to-the-second-power go?
Did I do that?
Molly...

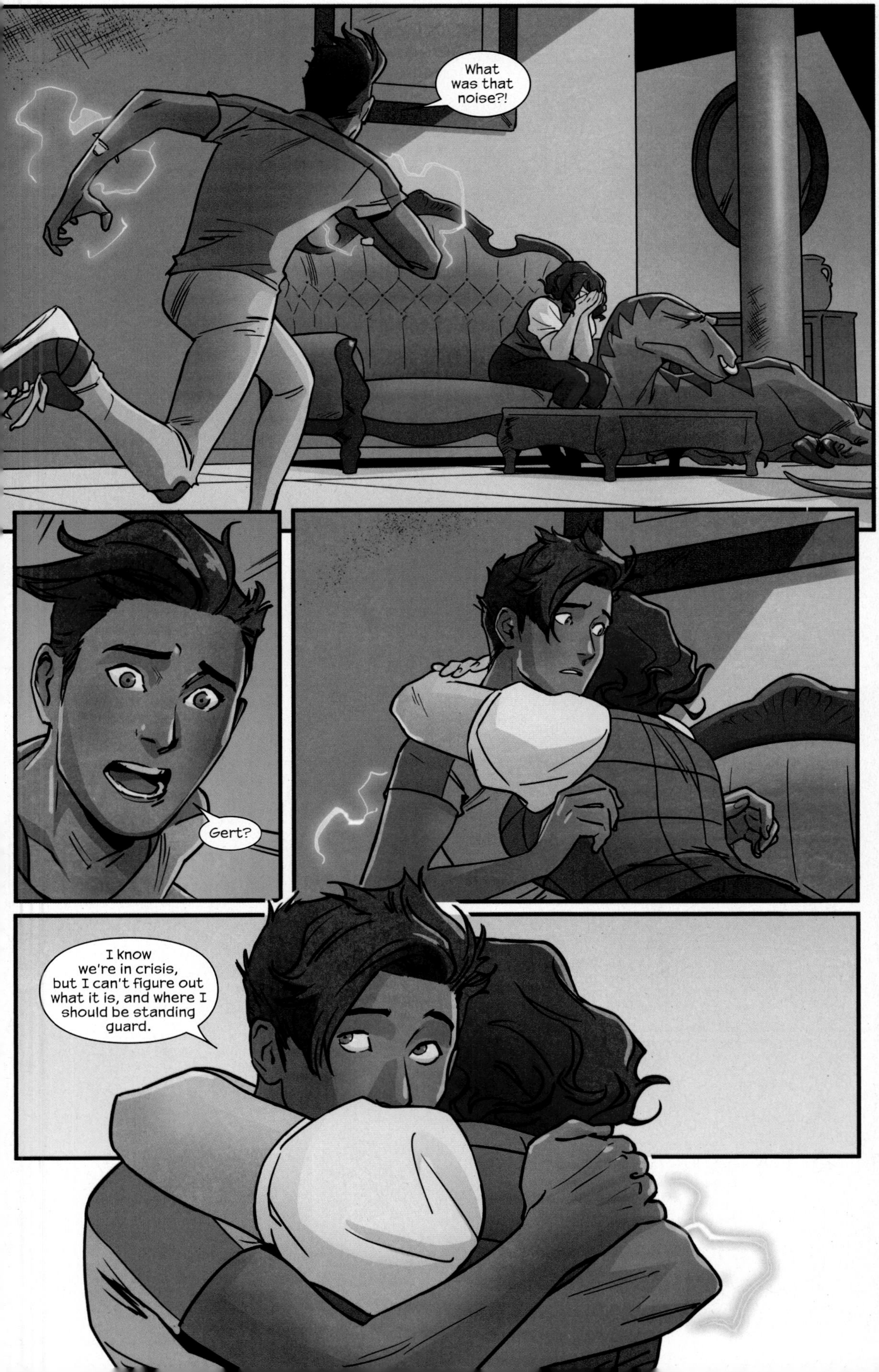
What was that noise?!
Gert?
I know we're in crisis, but I can't figure out what it is, and where I should be standing guard.

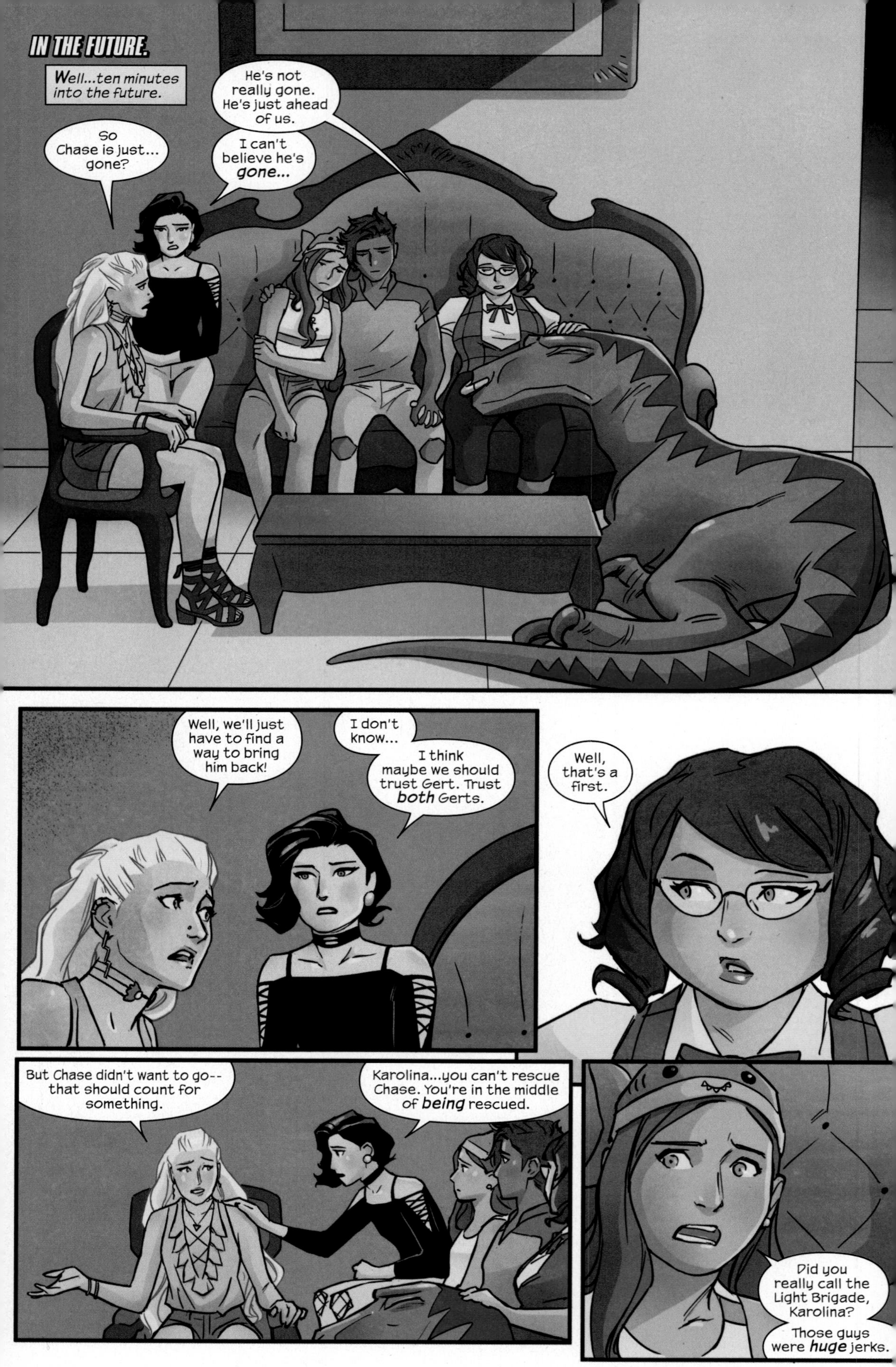
IN THE FUTURE.
Well...ten minutes into the future.
So Chase is just... gone?
I can't believe he's gone...
He's not really gone. He's just ahead of us.
Well, we'll just have to find a way to bring him back!
I don't know...
I think maybe we should trust Gert. Trust both Gerts.
Well, that's a first.
But Chase didn't want to go--that should count for something.
Karolina...you can't rescue Chase. You're in the middle of being rescued.
Did you really call the Light Brigade, Karolina?
Those guys were huge jerks.

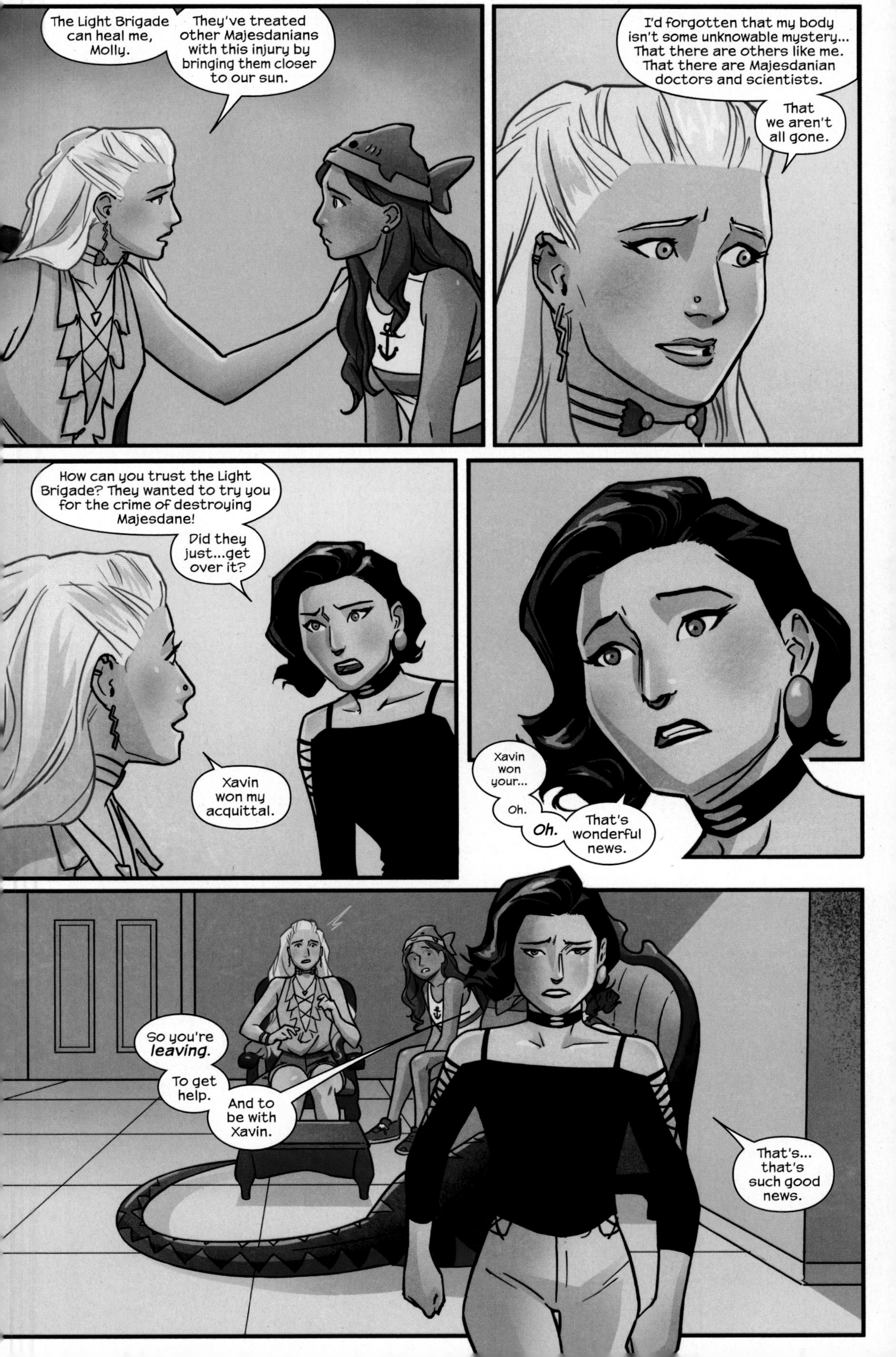
The Light Brigade can heal me, Molly.
They've treated other Majesdanians with this injury by bringing them closer to our sun.
I'd forgotten that my body isn't some unknowable mystery... That there are others like me. That there are Majesdanian doctors and scientists.
That we aren't all gone.
How can you trust the Light Brigade? They wanted to try you for the crime of destroying Majesdane!
Did they just...get over it?
Xavin won my acquittal.
Xavin won your...
Oh.
Oh.
That's wonderful news.
So you're *leaving*.
To get help.
And to be with Xavin.
That's... that's such good news.

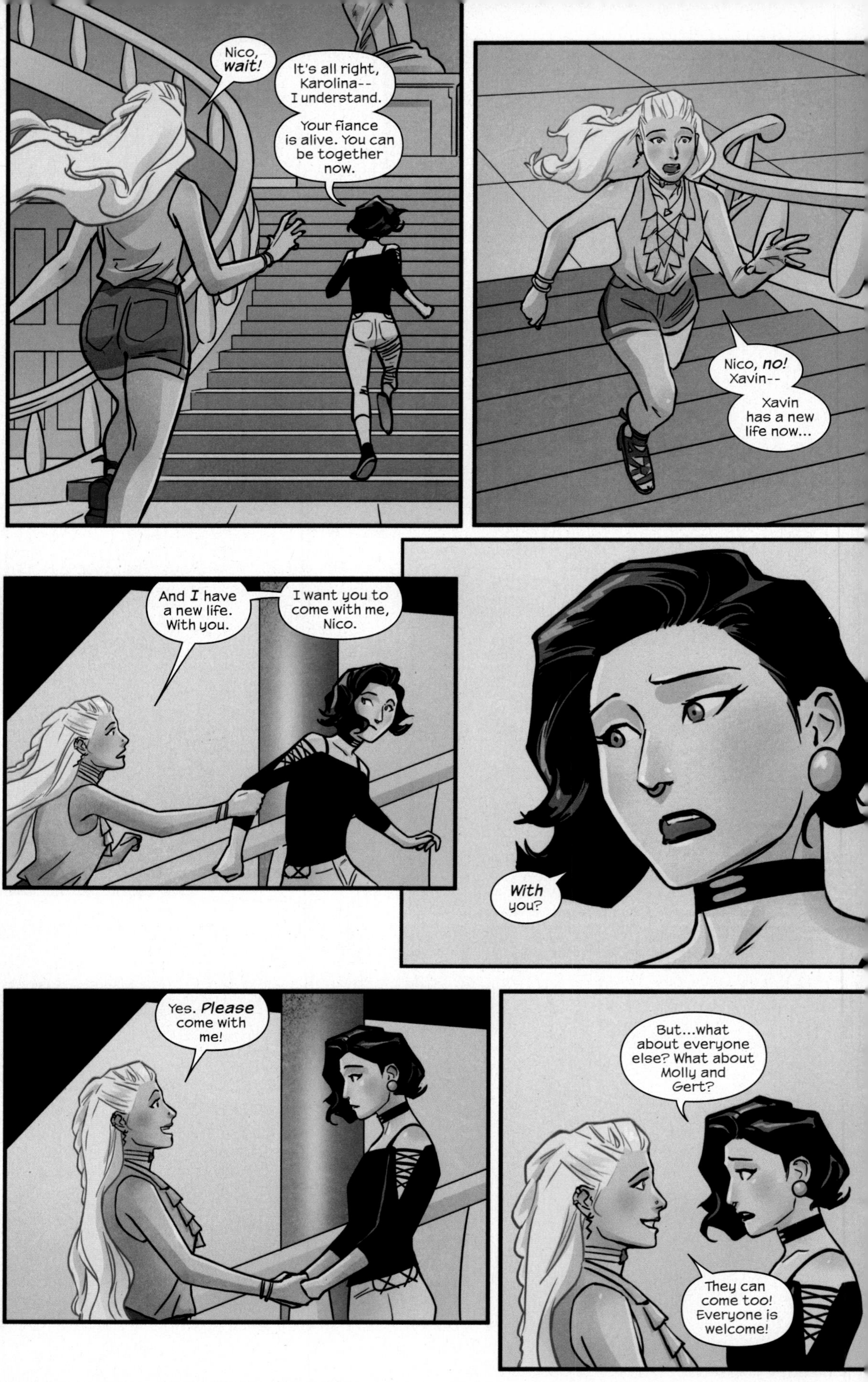
Nico, *wait!*
It's all right, Karolina-- I understand.
Your fiance is alive. You can be together now.
Nico, ***no!*** Xavin--
Xavin has a new life now...
And *I* have a new life. With you.
I want you to come with me, Nico.
With you?
Yes. *Please* come with me!
But...what about everyone else? What about Molly and Gert?
They can come too! Everyone is welcome!

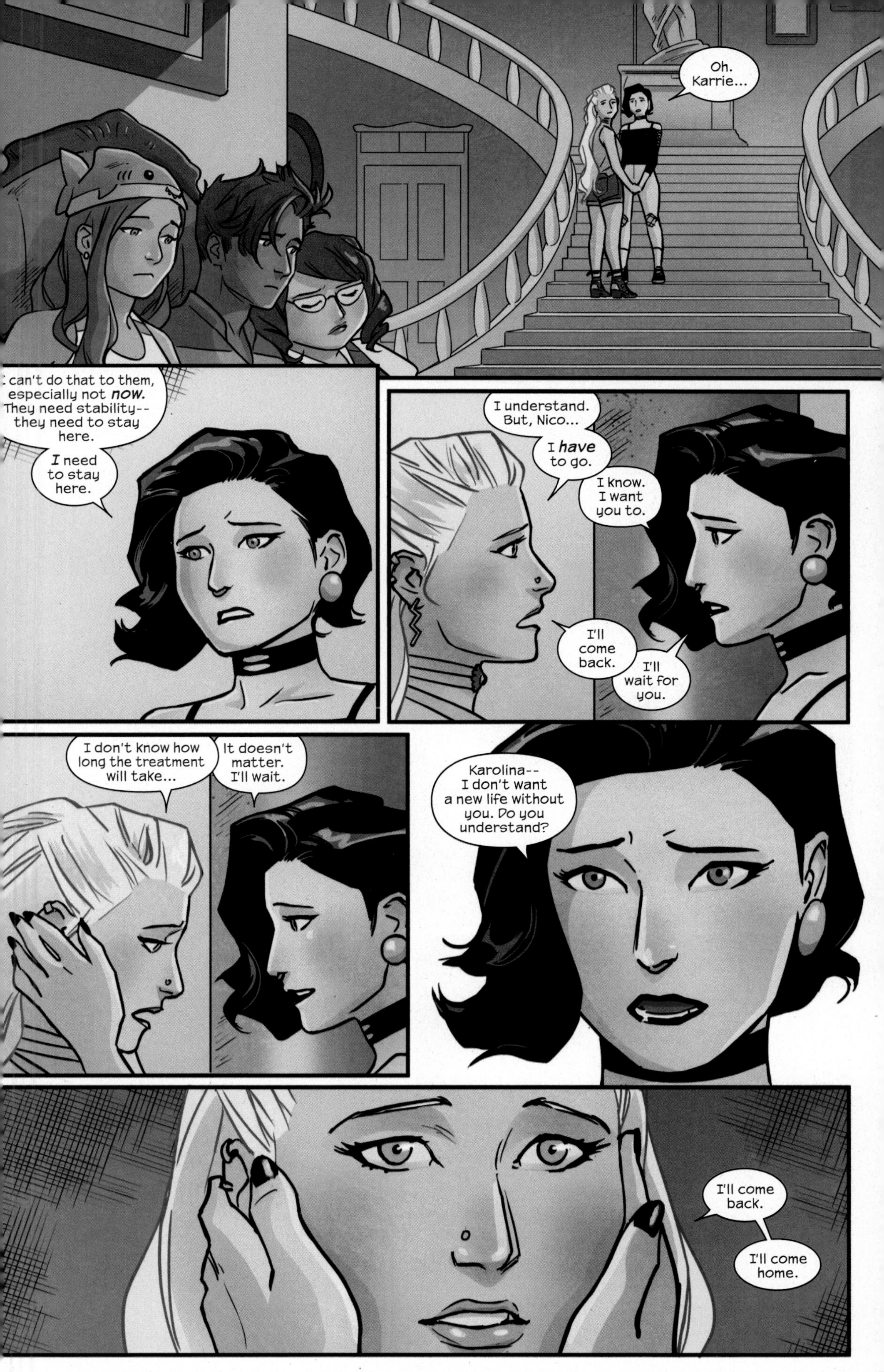
Oh. Karrie...
I can't do that to them, especially not *now.* They need stability-- they need to stay here.
I need to stay here.
I understand. But, Nico...
I *have* to go.
I know. I want you to.
I'll come back.
I'll wait for you.
I don't know how long the treatment will take...
It doesn't matter. I'll wait.
Karolina-- I don't want a new life without you. Do you understand?
I'll come back.
I'll come home.

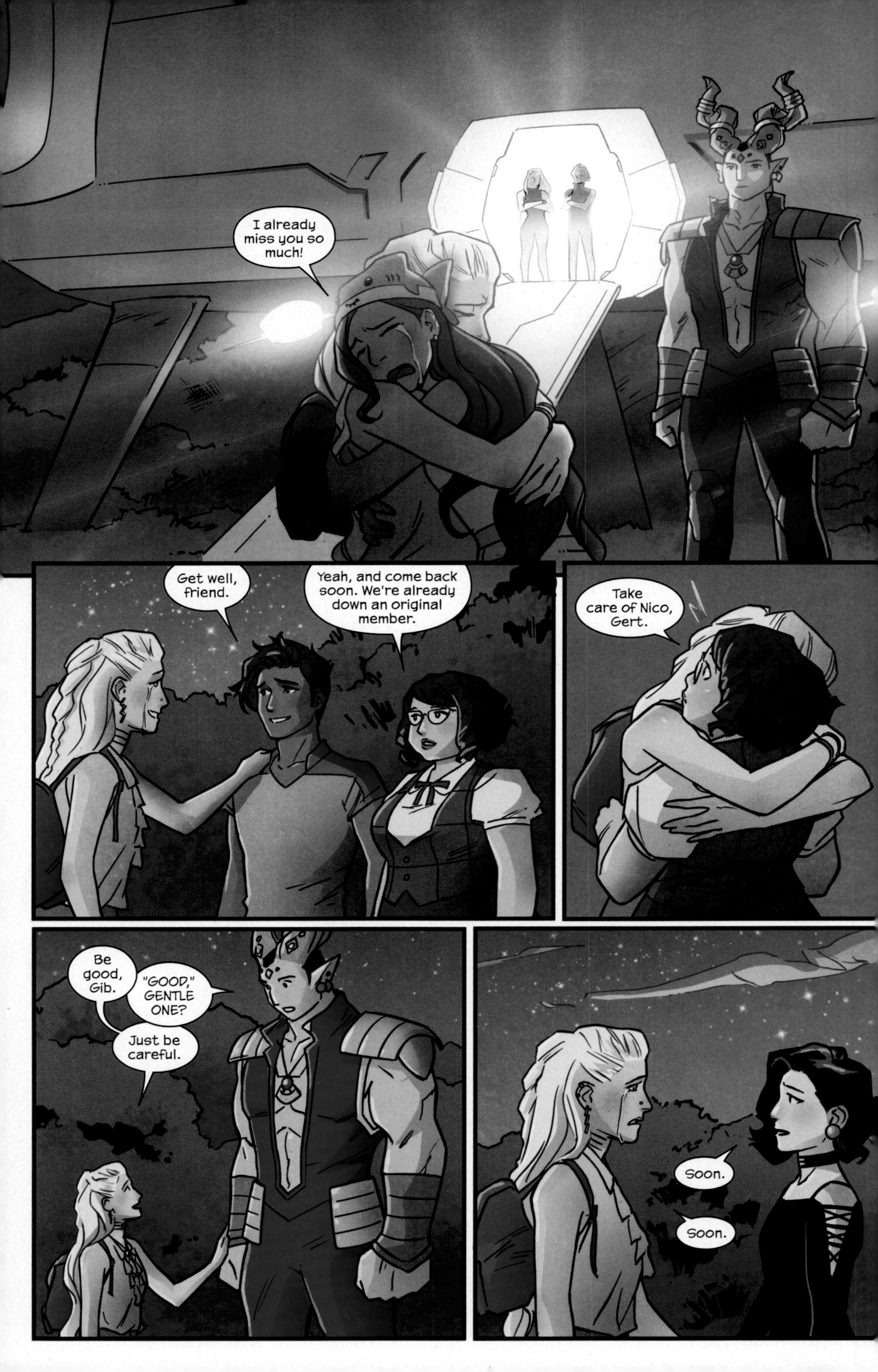
I already miss you so much!
Get well, friend.
Yeah, and come back soon. We're already down an original member.
Take care of Nico, Gert.
Be good, Gib.
"GOOD," GENTLE ONE?
Just be careful.
Soon.
Soon.

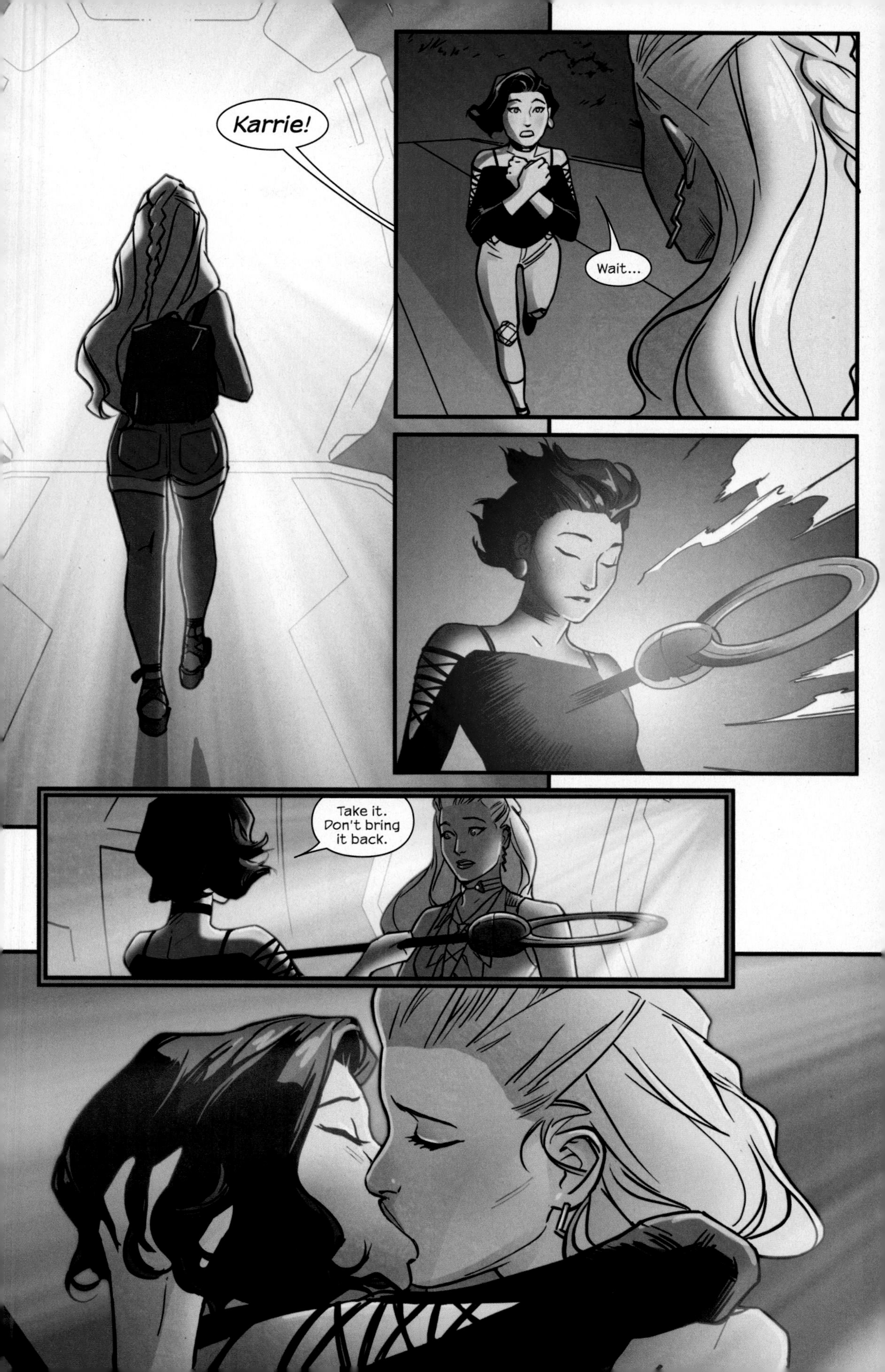
Karrie!
Wait...
Take it. Don't bring it back.

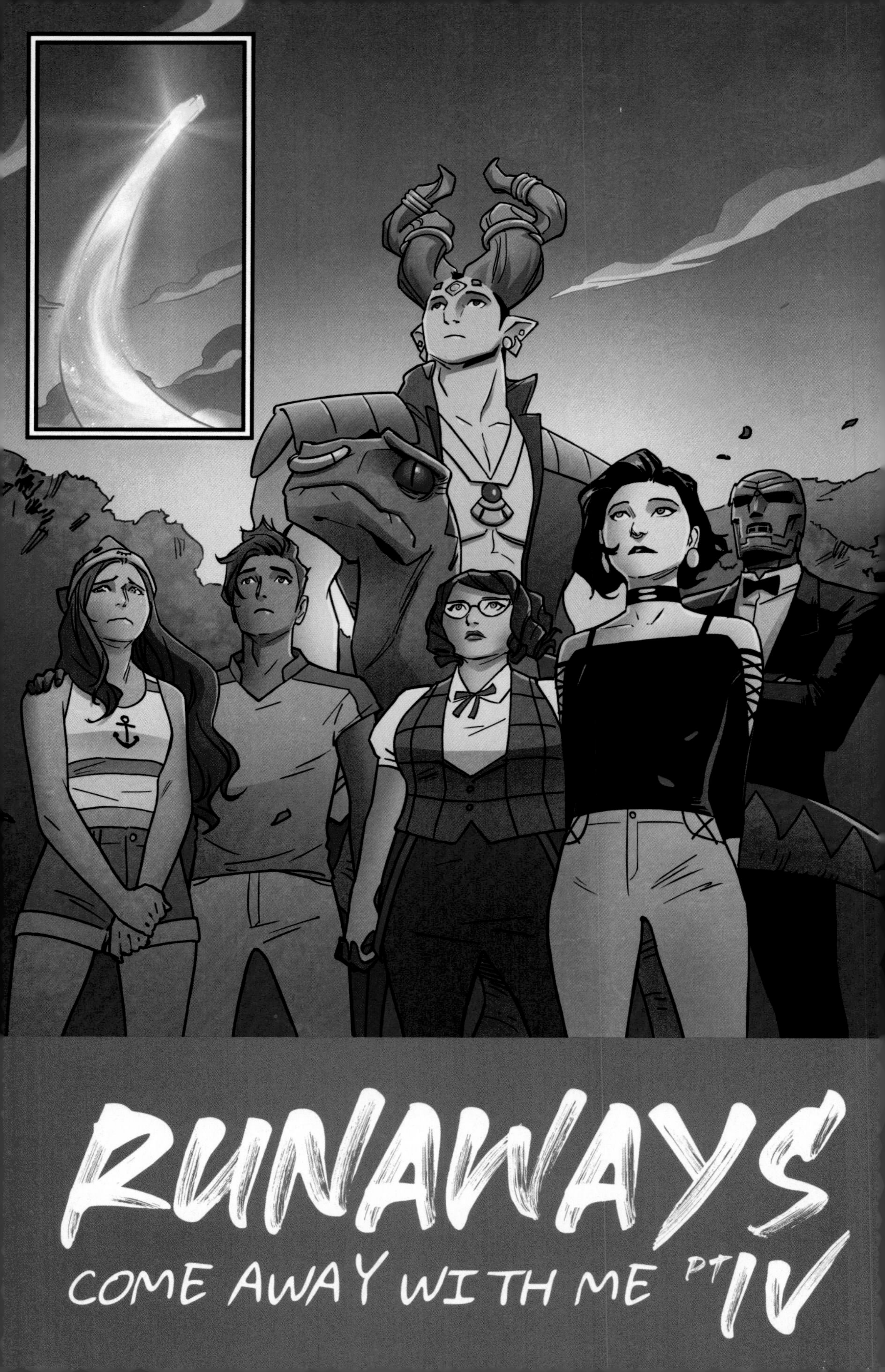

RUNAWAYS

COME AWAY WITH ME PT IV

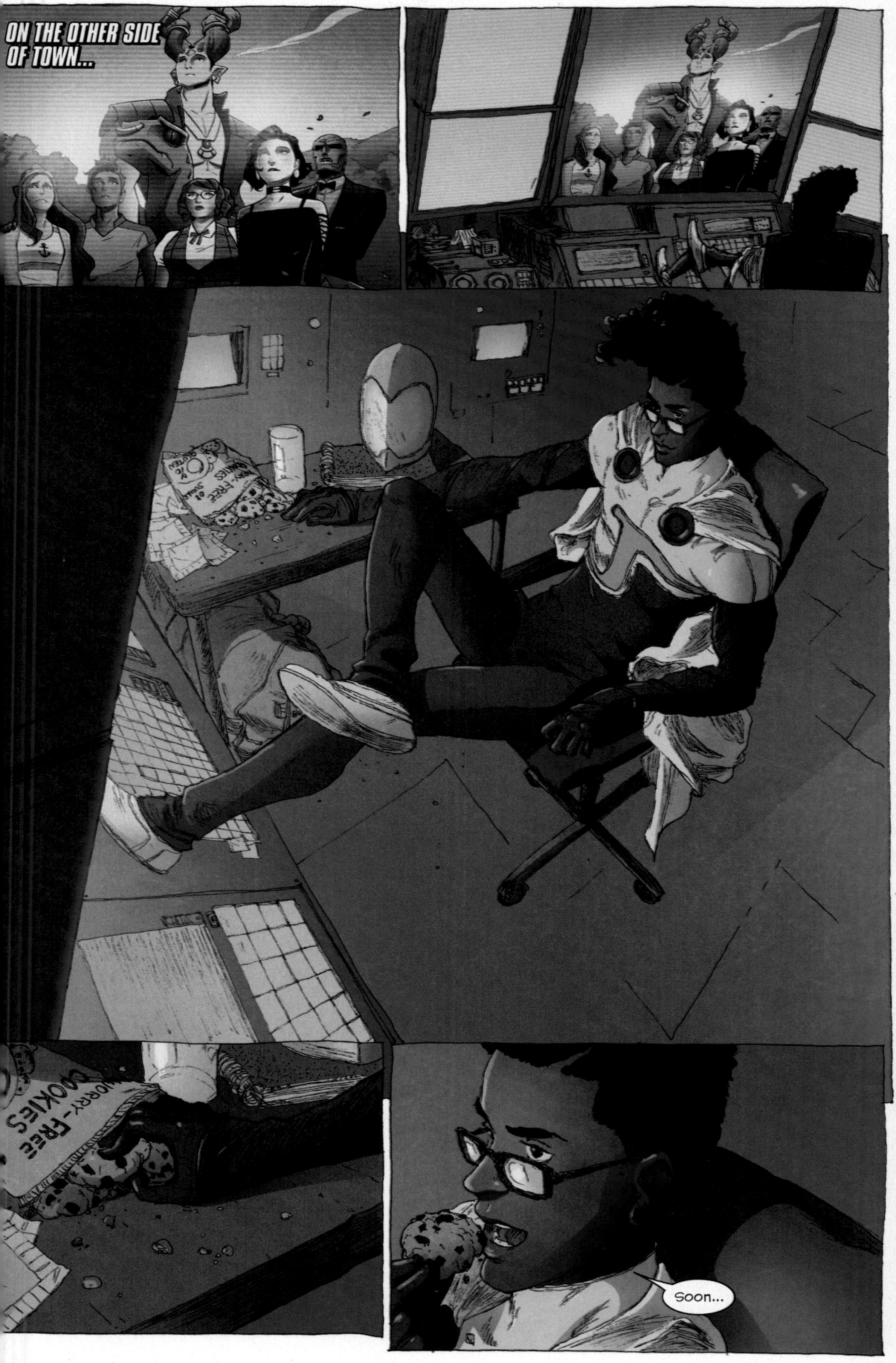
ON THE OTHER SIDE OF TOWN...
WORRY-FREE COOKIES
Soon...

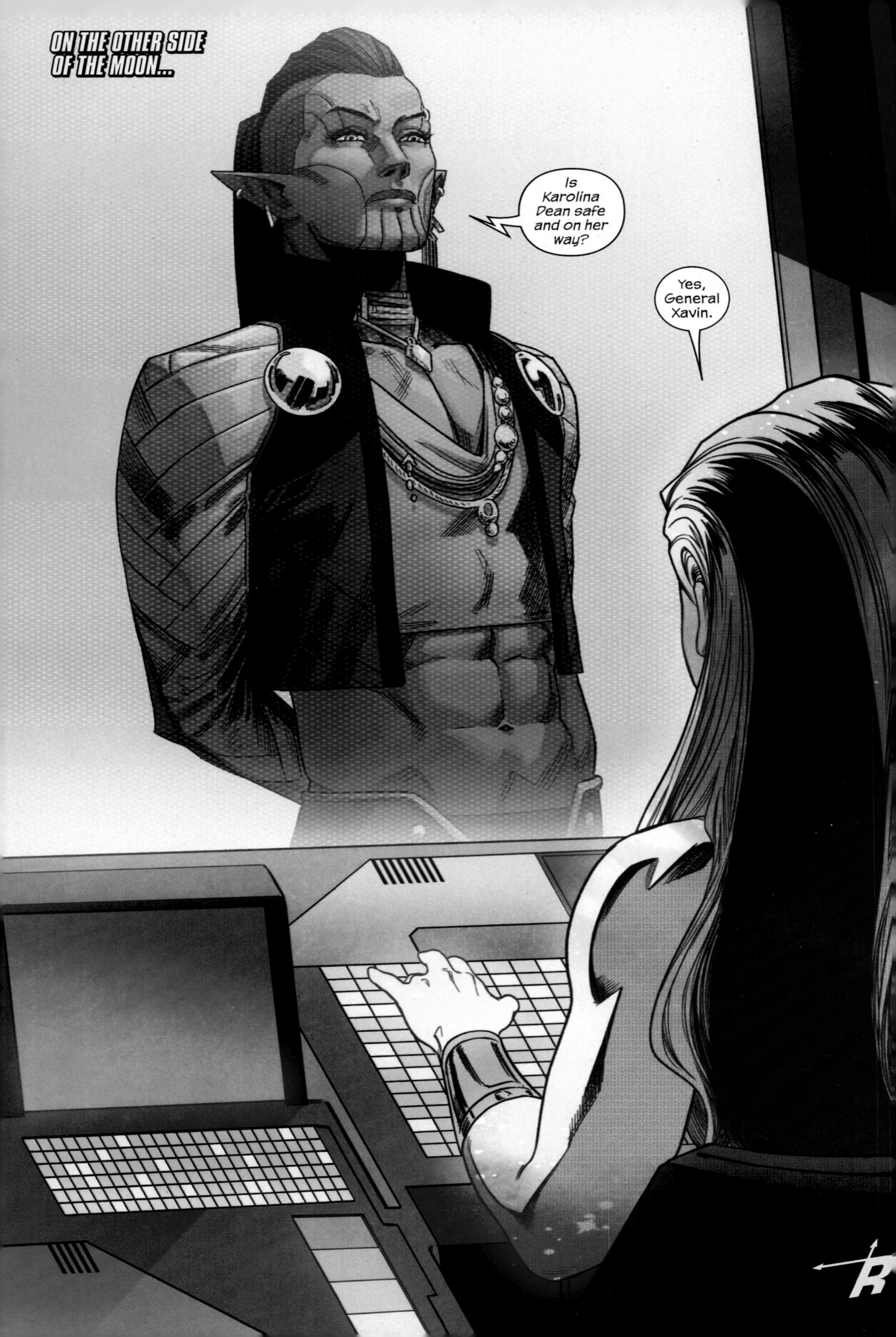
ON THE OTHER SIDE OF THE MOON...
Is Karolina Dean safe and on her way?
Yes, General Xavin.

RUNAWAYS #100 COVER GALLERY

Counting the original eighteen-issue volume, the second thirty-issue volume and the third fourteen-issue volume, issue #38 of this current volume is the one-hundredth issue of Runaways!

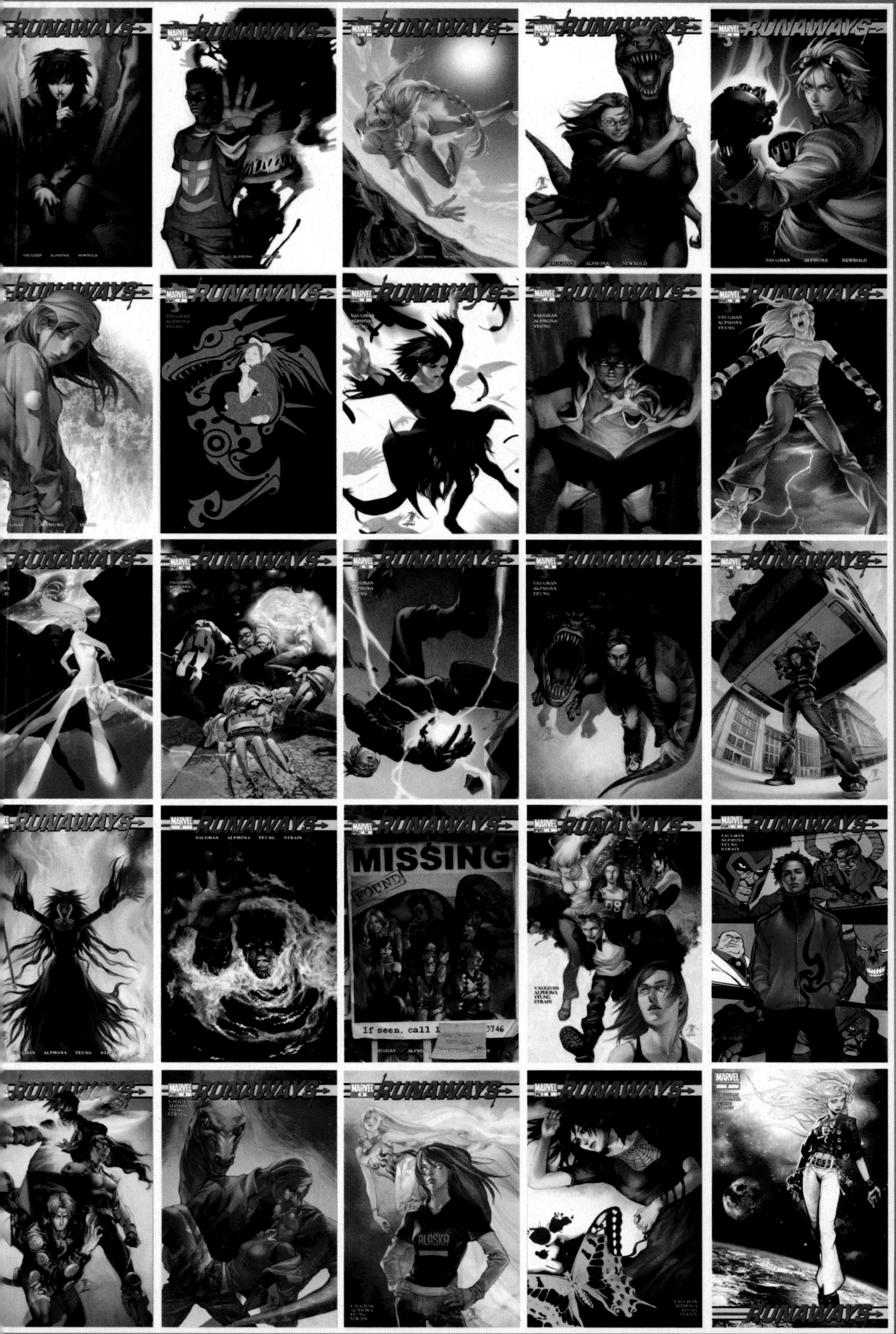

RUNAWAYS
VAUGHAN ALPHONA NEWBOLD
VAUGHAN ALPHONA YEUNG
VAUGHAN ALPHONA YEUNG STRAIN
MISSING
FOUND
If seen, call
ALASKA

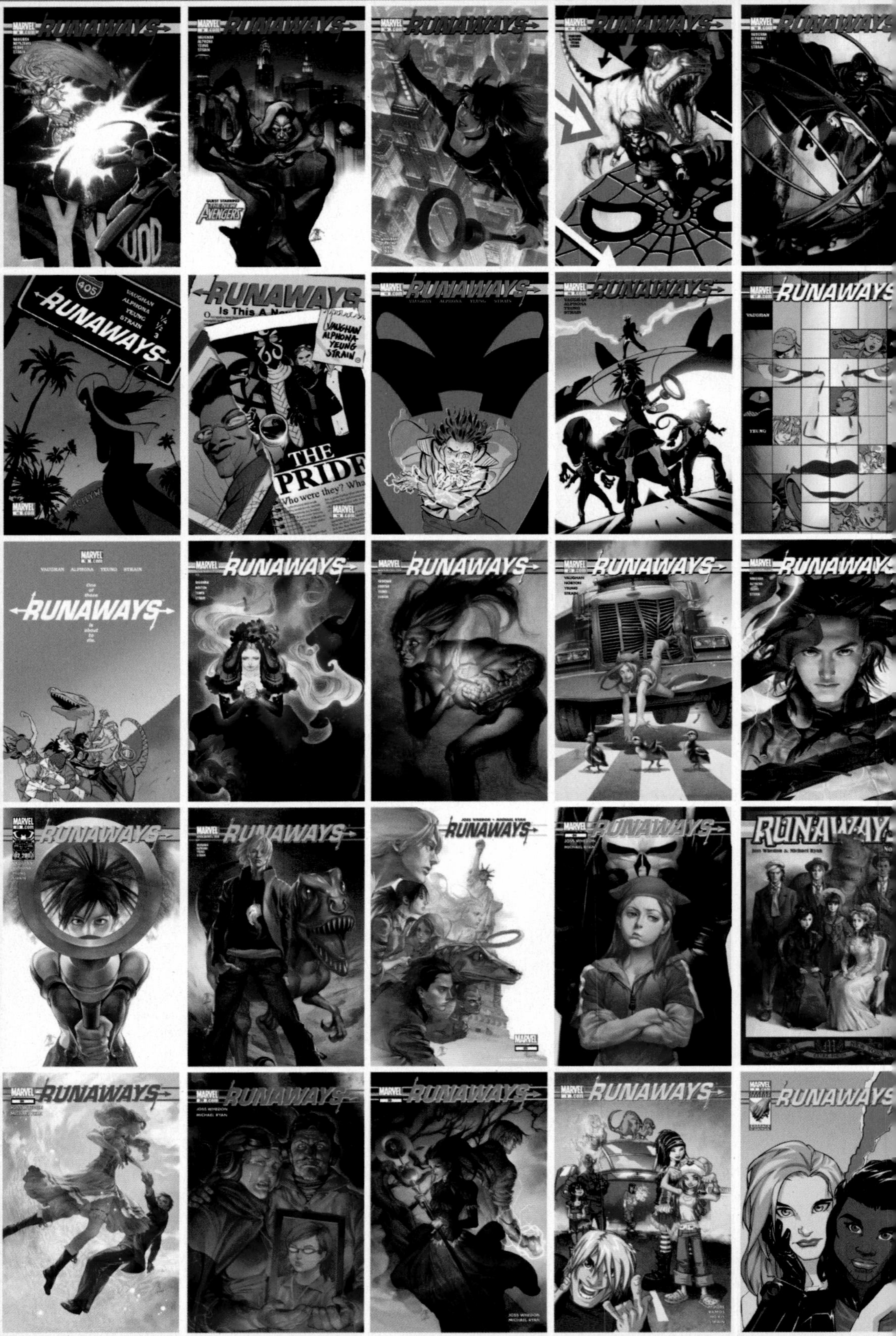

RUNAWAYS
405
VAUGHAN 1
ALPHONA ½
YEUNG ½
STRAIN 3
Is This A New
VAUGHAN
ALPHONA
YEUNG
STRAIN
THE PRIDE
Who were they? Wha
VAUGHAN ALPHONA YEUNG STRAIN
One of these RUNAWAYS is about to die.
JOSS WHEDON • MICHAEL RYAN
JOSS WHEDON
MICHAEL RYAN

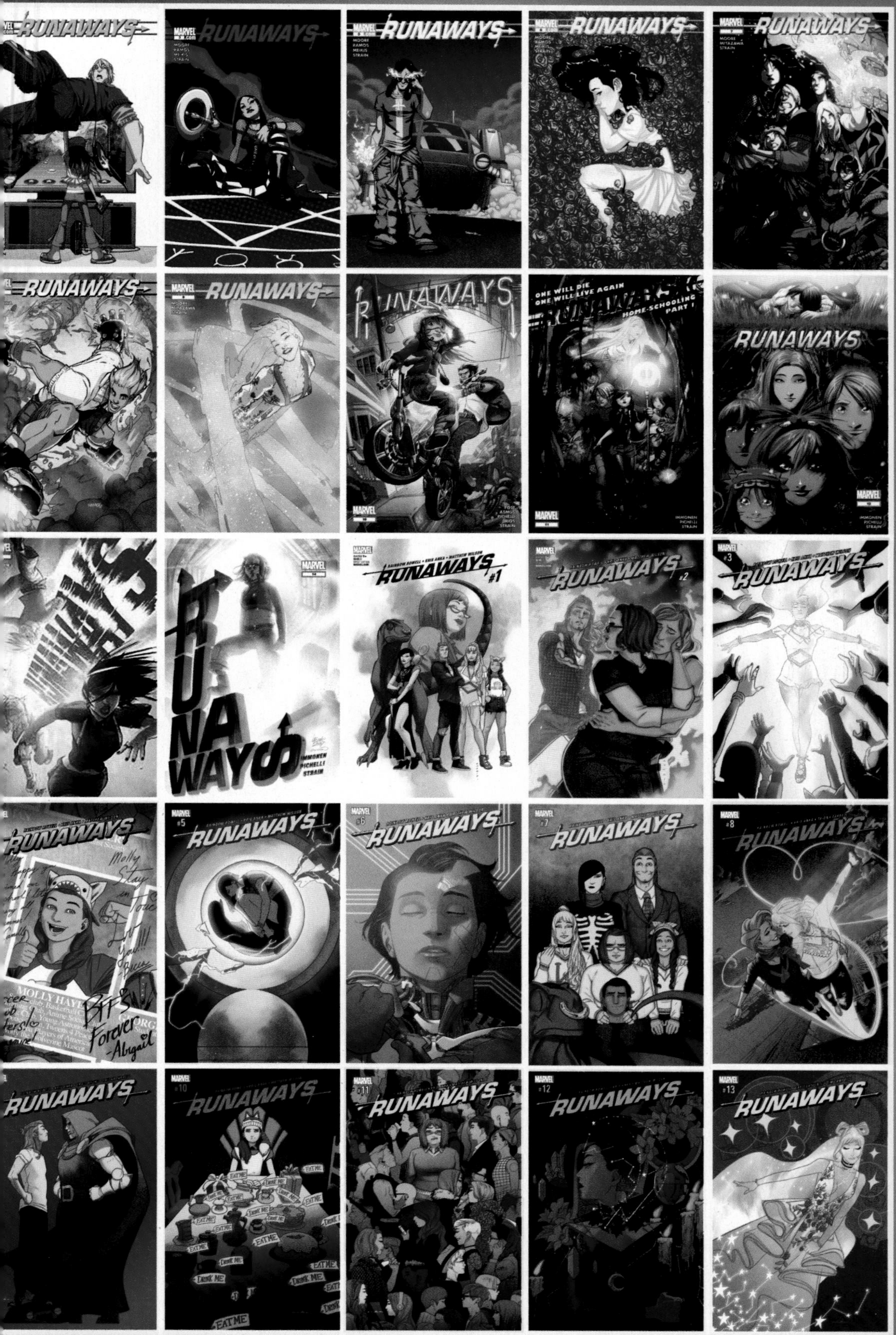

RUNAWAYS
MOORE
RAMOS
MEIKIS
STRAIN
MOORE
MIYAZAWA
STRAIN
ONE WILL DIE
ONE WILL LIVE AGAIN
HOME-SCHOOLING PART 1
IMMONEN
PICHELLI
STRAIN
#1
#2
#3
MOLLY HAYES
BFFS
Forever
-Abigail
#5
#6
#7
#8
#10
EAT ME
DRINK ME
#11
#12
#13

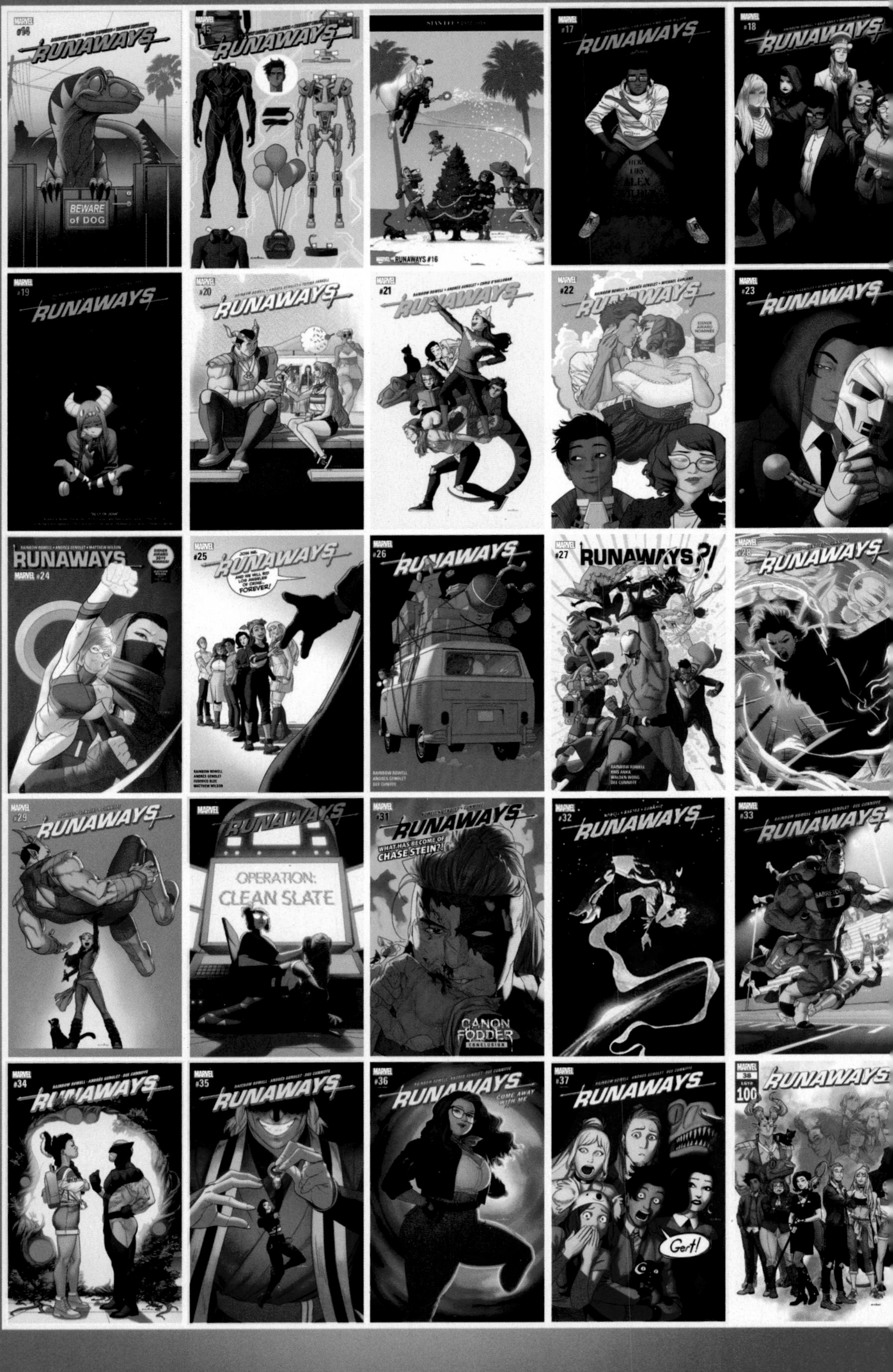
MARVEL #14
RUNAWAYS
BEWARE of DOG
MARVEL #15
RUNAWAYS
MARVEL RUNAWAYS #16
MARVEL #17
RUNAWAYS
MARVEL #18
RUNAWAYS
MARVEL #19
RUNAWAYS
MARVEL #20
RUNAWAYS
MARVEL #21
RUNAWAYS
MARVEL #22
RUNAWAYS
EISNER AWARD NOMINEE
MARVEL #23
RUNAWAYS
RAINBOW ROWELL • ANDRES GENOLET • MATTHEW WILSON
RUNAWAYS
EISNER AWARD NOMINEE
MARVEL #24
MARVEL #25
JOIN ME, RUNAWAYS AND WE WILL RID LOS ANGELES OF CRIME... FOREVER!
RAINBOW ROWELL
ANDRES GENOLET
FEDERICO BLEE
MATTHEW WILSON
MARVEL #26
RUNAWAYS
RAINBOW ROWELL
ANDRES GENOLET
DEE CUNNIFFE
MARVEL #27
RUNAWAYS?!
RAINBOW ROWELL
KRIS ANKA
WALDEN WONG
DEE CUNNIFFE
MARVEL #28
RUNAWAYS
MARVEL #29
RUNAWAYS
MARVEL
RUNAWAYS
OPERATION: CLEAN SLATE
MARVEL #31
RUNAWAYS
WHAT HAS BECOME OF CHASE STEIN?!
CANON FODDER CONCLUSION
MARVEL #32
RUNAWAYS
MARVEL #33
RAINBOW ROWELL • ANDRES GENOLET • DEE CUNNIFFE
RUNAWAYS
SABRETOOTHS
MARVEL #34
RAINBOW ROWELL • ANDRES GENOLET • DEE CUNNIFFE
RUNAWAYS
MARVEL #35
RAINBOW ROWELL • ANDRES GENOLET • DEE CUNNIFFE
RUNAWAYS
MARVEL #36
RUNAWAYS
COME AWAY WITH ME
MARVEL #37
RUNAWAYS
Gert!
MARVEL 38 LGY# 100
RUNAWAYS